CCNA Routing & Switching

Lab Workbook

200-120

CertificationKits CCNA Routing & Switching Lab Workbook 200-120

Printed in the United States of America

Fourth Revision, First Printing October 2014

Library of Congress Cataloging-in-Publication Number:

ISBN: 978-0-578-12584-8

Warning and Disclaimer
This book is designed to provide self-study labs to help you prepare for your Cisco CCNA certification exam. Every effort has been made to make this book as complete and accurate as possible, but no warranty or fitness is implied.

The information is provided on an "as is" basis. The author, CertificationKits LLC, and publisher shall have neither liability nor responsibility to any persons or entity with respect to any loss or damages arising from the information contained in this book for from the use of the discs or programs that may accompany it.

Trademark Acknowledgements
All terms mentioned in this book that are known to be trademarks or service marks have been appropriately capitalized. The publisher, author or CertificationKits LLC cannot attest to the accuracy of this information. Use of a term in this book should not be regarded as affecting the validity of any trademark or service mark.

Contents

Introduction

We would like to thank-you for purchasing your **CertificationKits.com CCNA Routing & Switching Lab Workbook 200-120**.

You may ask why we have not included a full blown Cisco CCNA study guide in our lab workbook? Well the answer is very simple. We have found that every person has their own preference on what author or publisher they prefer. So we will leave it up to you to decide if you like the Sybex CCNA Study Guide, the Bryant Advantage CCNA Study Guide or the Cisco Press CCNA Study Guide. So as I am quite sure you will come to realize, our products compliment their study guides and vice versa.

Another helpful source of Cisco CCNA certification information is at our website in our CCNA Study Center which you can access via the left hand navigation pane by clicking the CCNA Study Center link. In this section you will find our Getting Started section which covers many helpful hints and common mistakes students make that could drive you crazy for hours. So please take a look at it. Also in this section, you will find our CCNA Videos section which assists in getting you up to speed in your lab. So please make it a point to take a peek at the videos too.

You may also find it beneficial to visit and share our Facebook page at www.facebook.com/CertificationKits.

Finally, feel free to check our website at www.CertificationKits.com as we are always adding new content to assist in your Cisco studies.

How to Use This Book

The CertificationoKits.com CCNA Routing & Switching Lab Workbook 200-120 was designed to guide you through hands-on exercises on Cisco routers and switches. To be successful on the exam and achieve your CCNA certification, you should do everything you can to arm yourself with a variety of tools and training materials to support your learning efforts. Used to its fullest extent, the CertificationKits.com Self Study Lab Workbook can help solidify the various test topics in your mind by actually "seeing" it in action.

As mentioned before, a set of routers and switches and this lab workbook will compliment your other study resources. We highly suggest you round out our CCNA study resources with a one of the many Cisco CCNA Study Guides that are available on the market and a CCNA practice exam simulator such as the one we include with our kits. We have found that the combination of these three resources will greatly increase your odds of not only passing the exam, but also then having a firm understanding of the Cisco concepts which you can then bring into the "real world" as you would not have simply memorized or brain dumped the answers.

As you start to progress through the lab workbook, you may find that you do not have enough routers or switches to complete the entire lab. Don't worry. In that case, configure your equipment to simulate the lab as closely as you can as in a majority of the cases 90% of the concepts will still work just not on as grand of a scheme. For example if you only have two routers and you stumble upon a three router lab, simply configure just R1 and R2 and you more than likely will just not have as complicated of a lab scenario.

Another possibily is that you will not have the same exact router types that are detailed in the equipment requirements. Don't sweat it. A majority of the labs will still work with a few tweaks. So let me cover a few quick scenarios. Let's say the lab calls for an 1841 and you have a 2620 router. From a FastEthernet interface perspective, the syntax and commands are the same. So no problem there. But from a Serial interface perspective the syntax is a little different. The 2620 will designate a serial port as S0/0 and an 1841 might be S0/0/0. Now let's look at it if you have a 2501 or a 2610 10mb router. 95% of the labs will still work just fine. But the 2501 or 2610 routers only have a 10mb Etherent interface and some things don't work on 10mb interfaces that do work on 100mb interfaces. Additionally the syntax for identifying a 10mb Ethernet interface on a 2501 or a 2610 is *e0* whereas on a 1841 router the syntax for identifying a 100mb Ethernet interface is *fa0/0*. So when/if the router responds that the syntax is incorrect, you will be able to use the help command by typing a question mark to see a list of available commands supported along with the syntax. Just think of those situations as a challenge. It will make you look up what the correct syntax is and I don't know about you, but I know I tend to remember things better when I had a problem that I had to fix. I also do understand that you want to purchase a kit that is exactly like the book. But the reality at the end of the day most people want an economical kit. If we did not adapt the models and modules included to help you get a reasonably priced kit, you probably would not buy it. Anyway do you really think all of the routers and switches that you will see in the real world will only be the models you are familiar with? Absolutely not! Especially if you work for a large service firm like Cisco or IBM. Finally, we also give you the option to "cheat" by providing you a chart which illustrates most of the possible variations in Appendix A.

All of the labs require that you have a PC and a console cable to console into the routers and switches. Thus we will list those as requirements on the first few labs and not on subsequent labs as it simply is a waste of space. Now we also mention it multiple times on our website but I will mention it here too. If your computer does not have a 9 pin serial port in it, you will need either to install one or get a USB to 9 pin serial adapter to covert the console cable to something your computer can work with. Please don't get mad at us. This is how Cisco sends them out and when we tried including USB to Serial adapters in the kits too many people complained they did not want them.

As you flip through the book, you may be asking yourself why do some of the topology diagrams have lighting bolts in them and others just have a straight line? The lighting bolt is the symbol for a DTE/DCE back to back serial cable. The straight line is for a Cat5 cable. The Cat 5 cable can either be straight through or crossover cables. So make sure you read the lab requirements and understand when you will use each as it is an exam concept.

As you progress through the book, you may wonder why on some labs we simply mention using a crossover Cat 5 cable to connect two routers together and then on others we provide the option of using a crossover Cat 5 cable or a switch and two straight through cables? Simply to try to reinforce either way will work and so you know when to use a crossover cable and when not to as again that is an exam concept.

Here are some sample symbols.

The round circle with two arrows in and two arrows out represents a router.

The square with the four arrows pointing out represents a switch.

As mentioned before, this is a serial link.

_____ A straight line is a normal Ethernet patch cable.

If you purchased a kit from us, this legend below will help you identify the different cables by color that could have come with the kit. Keep in mind, it is possible they could have changed, but for the most part they usually stay the same.

Etherent Patch Cable – Blue
Ethernet Crossover Patch Cable - Red

WIC-1DSU-T1 Crossover Cable - White
Access Rollover Cables – Grey or Light Blue

Very Important WIC-1DSU-T1 Serial Port Based Kits
These kits are a little different than our kits that use 2500 series routers, WIC-1T, WIC-2T, WIC-2A/S or NM-4A/S modules. When you are using any of the above modules, you need to set the *clock rate* command as specified in the lab to set the clock rate source and designate the DCE side of the WAN link. So you simply follow the labs verbatim and you are good to go.

However, if you have a kit that comes with **WIC-1DSU-T1** modules, you need to ignore the *clock rate* part of the lab and follow the instructions below.

Since there is no DCE side per se, you do not need to configure the clock rate command. So you may be asking how is the clocking done? Well, what you will do is for the router in the lab that has the clock rate command, you will configure it with the the ***service-module T1 clock source internal*** command instead. Then on the other router you should configure an extra command which is the ***service-module T1 clock source line*** command. This way they will sync up. That said, a majority of the time if you don't configure either of those commands it will still work.

We will remind you of this for the first few labs that use serial links and then you should be able to remember it on your own thereafter.

Please read the <u>entire</u> book through. Why? We explain how to read the different lab formats we use the first time each is used. Thus, if you skip sections, you may not understand the lab setup properly and get confused.

Routers & Switches Required

You may ask, what is the suggested equipment to compliment this lab workbook? Keep in mind this is a suggestion and you can complete many of the labs with more or less equipment. I will provide you some basic guidelines and if you have any additional questions, please feel free to contact us at sales@CertificationKits.com

The book was last updated using the following devices:

- Three 1841 dual FastEthernet routers with one serial port in two units and one with two serial ports (please be aware we do move the serial port from one router to another in some labs). If you do not have dual Ethernet ports on all three routers, the labs will still work but not be as complex. Simply strip off the extra segments to the PCs in the topology.
- For two of the four Frame-Relay labs, we included a forth router with three or more serial interfaces and then added one additional serial interface to an existing router. If you do not have a forth router, you can simply do the labs configuring only two of the three spokes off the Frame-Relay router and simply follow the logic of the lab.
- Three 3550 Switches running EMI IOS. But one 3550 and two 2950 switches running EI(or better) will work fine. If you only have 2950 switches running SI, a few Enhanced QoS, MISTP, 802.1w RSTP and Layer 3 commands will not work that we cover.

Generally we would like to see three routers or more in your lab. That is not to say that you will not see value in only having two routers as many people are limited to a smaller lab due to their budget. Two routers will give you the ability to see the routes and information propagate. Three routers will give us some extra flexibility in creating some more complex scenarios such as Frame-Relay labs and Multiple Path labs. If at all possible, try to have at lease one router with a 100mb Ethernet port. This will give you the ability to inter-vlan routing which can't be done on a 10mb Ethernet interface (at least according to Cisco and without jumping through tons of hoops).

We would also like to see multiple switches in your lab environment. Very similar to the router theory behind three routers, three switches will give you the ability to actually see concepts in actual action. Some examples are how STP works, VTP Domain information propagation and trunking across multiple switches. In regard to specific models, we suggest you purchase at the very minimum 2950 switches or better. The 1900, 2912, 2916, 2924, 3512 and 3524 switches are total paper weights. We also suggest you include at least one 2950C, 2950G or 2950T in your lab as they run an enhanced version of the IOS as the standard version does not and supports a few more commands that are on the exam. Finally a nice to have as prices are coming down is a 3550 or 3560 switch as those are Layer 3 switches which can also do routing!

Identifying Router Components and Accessories

We will begin by introduing some of the common componets you will find in most labs.

Due to their low cost the Cisco 2500 Series router is very popular in home labs. It is an older fixed port router that you cannot upgrade except for the DRAM, flash and boot roms. Let's take a look at the exterior of a 2501 as shown in Figure 1-1.

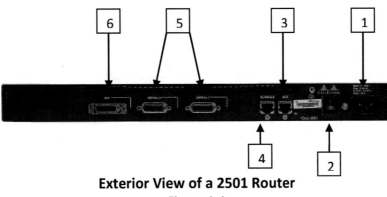

Exterior View of a 2501 Router
Figure 1-1

1 – Power Cord Connection

2 – Power Switch

3 – AUX port. This allows out-of-bandwidth configuration of a router. Generally you will see a modem connected to this port so an administrator can dial-in and make configuration changes.

4 – Console port. This is where you will connect your console cable so you can configure the router locally. You will find a picture of a console kit below in Figure 1-2.

5 – Serial ports. Two synchronous serial ports. Generally in a production environment you will usually connect your CSU/DSU to one of these ports via a serial cable. In our lab environment, this is where you will connect your back to back cable which simulates a WAN connection. You will find a picture of a DB60 to DB 60 back to back cable below in Figure 1-3.

6 – AUI port. This 15 pin port is your 10mb Ethernet connection. You will connect your transceiver shown in Figure 1-4 to convert the 15 pin port to an RJ-45 style Ethernet port.

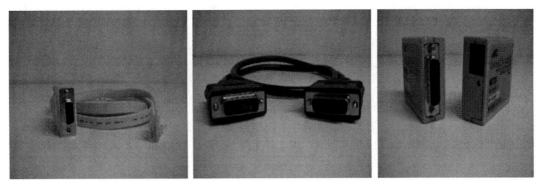

| Figure 1-2 | Figure 1-3 | Figure 1-4 |

Another popular series of routers in home labs are the Cisco 2600 series. We have selected to show you a Cisco 2610XM router as this is a great low cost router too. The 2600 series is a modular router with generally one built-in LAN port. The modularity of this series router makes it very popular as you can just purchase the functionality you need and pop it in one of the various expansion slots. Let's examine the exterior of a 2610XM below as shown in Figure 1-5.

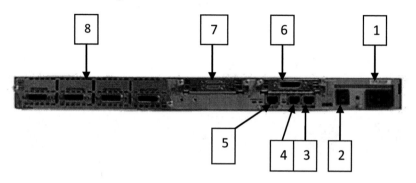

Exterior View of a 2600 Router
Figure 1-5

1 – Power Cord Connection

2 – Power Switch

3 – AUX port. This allows out-of-bandwidth configuration of a router. Generally you will see a modem connected to this port so an administrator can dial-in and make configuration changes.

4 – Console port. This is where you will connect your console cable so you can configure the router locally.

5 – 100mb Ethernet LAN port.

6 – WIC-1T module. This is a wan module slot. This module has a single DB60 synchronous serial port. Generally in a production environment you will usually connect your CSU/DSU to this port via a serial cable. In our lab environment, this is where you will connect your back to back cable which simulates a WAN connection. You can see a close-up picture of a WIC-1T module on the right in Figure 1-6.

7 – WIC-2T module. This is a wan module slot. This module has two smart synchronous serial ports and give you a higher density of ports per card. Generally in a production environment you will usually connect your CSU/DSU to this port via a serial cable. You can see a close-up picture of a WIC-2T module on the left in Figure 1-6.

In our lab environment, this is where you will connect your back to back cable which simulates a WAN connection. You will find a picture of a Smart Serial to DB60 back to back cable below in Figure 1-7. This illustrates that you can connect a Smart Serial port to a DB60 serial port.

8 – NM-4A/S module. This is a network module slot. Shown is a 4 port serial module. There are various other modules that can be inserted in this slot. Examples would include an NM-1FE-TX which will provide you an extra 100mb Ethernet port or a NM-32A which allows you to add 32 asynchronous connections.

9 – WIC-1DSU-T1 module. This is an RJ-45 style serial module used in some of our kits as shown in Figure 1-8.

| Figure 1-6 | Figure 1-7 | Figure 1-8 |

Next let's open a unit up and take a look inside. After all, after you get certified you will be paid to open these things up and do all sorts of things to them. So no time like the present!

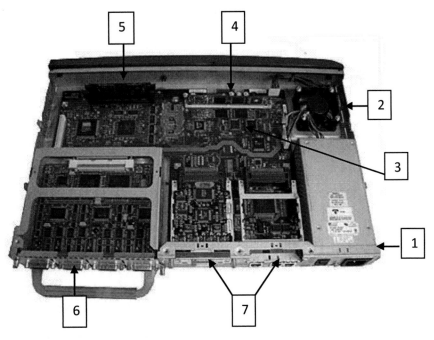

Interior View of a 2600 Router

Figure 1-8

1 – AC power supply
2 – Cooling fan.
3 – Boot ROMs
4 – Flash memory. This is where the router stores the IOS.
5 – DRAM. This is volatile memory.
6 – NM slot. This is your network module slot.
7 – WIC slots. These are two wan interface card slots.

Next let's look at a Cisco 1841 router. This is a very popular router for CCNA home labs since it is an ISR (Integrated Services Router) device and can run IOS 15. We will not cover every module or cable as we already covered the main ones you will see in your lab above.

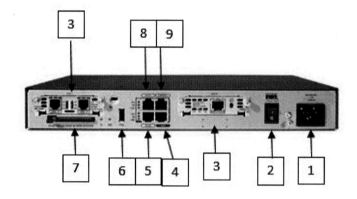

1 – Power Cord Connection

2 – Power Switch

3 – WIC Slot. These slots are technically HWIC slots that accept WIC, VWIC(data only), or HWIC modules. This is where you will install your WAN interface cards such as a WIC-1T, WIC-2T, WIC 2A/S or WIC-1DSU-T1 modules to simulate your WAN connections in your CCNA lab. Notice we have two of these slots on the router. Slot 1 is on the left and Slot 0 is on the right. The syntax is S0/0/0 for Slot 0 and S0/1/0 for Slot 1 if there is only one port on the module. Now let's say we have a WIC-2T module in each unit. A WIC-2T has two ports on it. Then the card in Slot 0 would be referenced as S0/0/0 and S0/0/1. The card in Slot 1 would then be referenced as S0/1/0 and S0/1/1. You will get some hands on with this as you start your labs and it will make much more sense. But in a nutshell it is a slot/sub slot/port schema where the slot will always be 0 for now. Then you look at the slot number on the 1841 to see the second number and then look on the card if there are multiple ports to specify the number of each.

4 – AUX port. This allows out-of-bandwidth configuration of a router. Generally you will see a modem connected to this port so an administrator can dial-in and make configuration changes.

5 – 100mb FastEthernet LAN port FA0/0.

6 – USB port. Configurable with an optional USB token for secure configuration distribution and off-platform storage of VPN credentials.

7 – Compact Flash. This is where you will install and save your IOS files to for the router to run from. Previous versions of Cisco routers such as the 2500 and 2600 series has proprietary flash modules. This is much more convenient and easy to swap out.

8 – 100mb FastEthernet LAN port FA0/1.

9 – Console port. This is where you will connect your console cable so you can configure the router locally.

Let's now look at a 2801. Again this is becoming a very popular router in CCNA labs as the prices have come down on this unit because it can support IOS 15 and can support Voice features, VWICs and PVDMs that the 1841 cannot. It also is a bit more expandable than the 1841 as we see that we have four slots compared to the two on the 1841. So let's look at them in a little bit more detail.

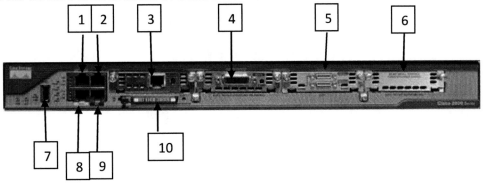

1 – FastEthernet 0/1

2 – Console Port. This is where you will connect your console cable so you can configure the router locally.

3 – WIC Slot 3. This is referenced as S0/3/0 and it has a WIC-1DSU-T1 serial module installed into it.

4 – WIC Slot 2. This is referenced as S0/2/0 and has a WIC-1T serial module installed into it.

5 – WIC Slot 1. This is referenced as S0/0/0 and S0/0/1 for ports 0 and 1 on it respectively since the serial module has two ports on it.

6 – WIC Slot 0. This is for Voice modules only.

7 – USB port. Configurable with an optional USB token for secure configuration distribution and off-platform storage of VPN credentials.

8 – FastEthernet 0/0

9 – AUX port. This allows out-of-bandwidth configuration of a router. Generally you will see a modem connected to this port so an administrator can dial-in and make configuration changes.

10 - Compact Flash. This is where you will install and save your IOS files to for the router to run from. Previous versions of Cisco routers such as the 2500 and 2600 series has proprietary flash modules. This is much more convenient and easy to swap out.

Router Connectivity

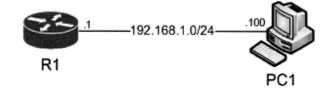

The purpose of this lab is to have you log into a router for the first time. Then we will explore the various prompts and configure connectivity between PC1 and the router.

Hardware & Configuration Required for this Lab

- One Cisco router with one Ethernet or FastEthernet port
- One crossover Cat 5 cable for a direct PC to router connection or connect the PC and router to a switch via two straight through Cat 5 cables
- One PC to console into the router
- One console cable

Commands Used in this Lab

enable - Used to move from unprivileged mode to privileged mode
show ip interface brief - Displays a brief summary of the interfaces on the router, what IPs they have configured, and their status
configure terminal - Moves into configure mode, most configuration is done in this mode
interface - Moves into the interface configuration mode, this is where you would configure anything to do with the actual interfaces on a router
ip address - Configures an IP address on an interface
no shutdown - Enables deactived configuration, this is used in a number of places but mostly for enabling interfaces
do - Allows you to run privileged level commands in configuration modes
ping - A very useful dianostic tool that lets you know if an IP address is reachable
copy running-config startup-config - Saves a copy of a the running configuration to NVRAM so it can survive a reboot
copy startup-config running-config - Merges the saved configuration in NVRAM with the running configuration
write - A shorter command to save the running config to NVRAM

show running-config - View the running config
show startup-config - View the saved config in NVRAM

Welcome to the world of Cisco! Now you may be wondering how do I actually connect to the router? In your kit you should have a light blue or white console kit. This is a cable that on one end has a 9 pin serial port and on the other end has an RJ-45 connector. You will take the 9 pin side and connect it into the 9 pin serial port on your computer and put the other end into the console port on the router. But what happens if your computer does not have a 9 pin serial port? You can purchase a USB to 9 pin serial port converter to ultilize your USB port. We have these available on our website or you can also find them at Staples; although they charge more for them.

Choosing a terminal emulator client - Over the course of your career you will probably end up using every terminal emulation client known to man. While they all get the job done, some have better features then others.

This lab will go over how to log into router via the console cable with the following terminal emulator clients:
Hyperterminal - One of the most popular terminal clients because it is installed on all Windows systems by default (it was removed in Vista and above)
PuTTY - One of the most beloved lightweight terminal clients. Every engineer should have PuTTY handy.

Let's start off with Hyperterminal. As mentioned above, Hyperterminal is popular for the sole reason that it is readily available on most PCs (if you want to install it on Vista or above, you can download a trial version at: (http://www.hilgraeve.com)

To connect to a console connection with Hyperterminal do the following:
1. When you open Hyperterminal you will need to enter a name for the connection. This can be any name you choose.

2. On the next page you'll have to change **Connect using** to the com/serial port you are using on your computer (this can be a somewhat random port if you are using a USB to serial converter).

3. On the Com Port Settings page you will need to enter the connection settings the router uses. By default Cisco devices will use the following:
Bits per second: **9600**
Data bits: **8**
Parity: **None**
Stop bits: **1**
Flow control: **None** (very important, do not leave as Hardware)

Using PuTTY to connect to a console is much quicker. Simply set the **Connection Type** to Serial(your appropriate serial port number), set the speed to 9600 and change the Flow Control to None.

Now that you have a client to connect to the router, it's time to...connect to the router! When you first connect to a new router it won't have any configuration so the first thing it will do is ask if you want to use a setup wizard.

% Please answer 'yes' or 'no'.
    Would you like to enter the initial configuration dialog? [yes/no]:

Generally speaking, nobody uses the initial setup but we'll go through it here.

% Please answer 'yes' or 'no'.
 Would you like to enter the initial configuration dialog? [yes/no]: **yes**
At any point you may enter a question mark '?' for help.
    Use ctrl-c to abort configuration dialog at any prompt.
    Default settings are in square brackets '[]'.
Basic management setup configures only enough connectivity
    for management of the system, extended setup will ask you
    to configure each interface on the system
Would you like to enter basic management setup? [yes/no]: **yes**
    Configuring global parameters:
 Enter host name [Router]: **R1**
 The enable secret is a password used to protect access to
    privileged EXEC and configuration modes. This password, after
    entered, becomes encrypted in the configuration.
    Enter enable secret: **certificationkits**
 The enable password is used when you do not specify an
    enable secret password, with some older software versions, and
    some boot images.
    Enter enable password: **cisco**
 The virtual terminal password is used to protect
    access to the router over a network interface.
    Enter virtual terminal password: **certificationkits**
    Configure SNMP Network Management? [no]:
Current interface summary

Interface   IP-Address   OK? Method Status   Protocol
    FastEthernet0/0   unassigned   YES unset administratively down down
Enter interface name used to connect to the
    management network from the above interface summary: FastEthernet0/0
Configuring interface FastEthernet0/0:
    Use the 100 Base-TX (RJ-45) connector? [yes]: **yes**
    Operate in full-duplex mode? [no]: **yes**
    Configure IP on this interface? [no]: **yes**
    IP address for this interface: **192.168.1.1**
    Subnet mask for this interface [255.255.255.0] :
    Class C network is 192.168.1.0, 24 subnet bits; mask is /24
The following configuration command script was created:
hostname R1

```
  enable secret 5 $1$PjIE$nHao8mx37DU2119i07lst/
  enable password cisco
  line vty 0 4
  password certificationkits
  no snmp-server
  !
  no ip routing
!
  interface FastEthernet0/0
  no shutdown
  media-type 100BaseX
  full-duplex
  ip address 192.168.1.1 255.255.255.0
  no mop enabled
  !
  end
[0] Go to the IOS command prompt without saving this config.
  [1] Return back to the setup without saving this config.
 [2] Save this configuration to nvram and exit.
Enter your selection [2]: 0
  % You can enter the setup, by typing setup at IOS command prompt
```

The main problem with the initial setup is that it simply takes too long and doesn't configure enough for it to be useful.

Let's take a look at the router without the initial setup.

```
Router con0 is now available
Press RETURN to get started.
Router>
```

When you log into the router you will start out in **unprivileged mode** which is shown with a **>** prompt. This mode doesn't allow much and for the most part is only used for basic troubleshooting. Next we'll need to move into privileged mode by typing the **enable** command.

Router>**enable**

Privileged mode is where you find all the information you'll need on the router, you can view configuration, routing tables, interface statistics, and much more. Privileged mode is shown with the # prompt. For example we can see a summary of the interfaces on the router with: **show ip interface brief**

Router#**show ip interface brief**

```
Interface          IP-Address   OK? Method Status        Protocol
FastEthernet0/0        unassigned    YES unset  administratively down down
```

The final main mode is **configure terminal** which is where all the configuration on the router goes.

Router#**configure terminal**
Enter configuration commands, one per line. End with CNTL/Z.

In all modes you can use the question mark **?** to view available commands with a brief description. Below shows some of the many options available in configure mode.

Router(config)#**?**
Configure commands:
```
  aaa                  Authentication, Authorization and Accounting.
  aal2-profile         Configure AAL2 profile
  access-list          Add an access list entry
  alarm-interface      Configure a specific Alarm Interface Card
  alias                Create command alias
  alps                 Configure Airline Protocol Support
  appletalk            Appletalk global configuration commands
  application          Define application
  arap                 Appletalk Remote Access Protocol
  archive              Archive the configuration
  arp                  Set a static ARP entry
  async-bootp          Modify system bootp parameters
  atm                  Enable ATM SLM Statistics
  backhaul-session-manager   Configure Backhaul Session Manager
  banner               Define a login banner
  bba-group            Configure BBA Group
  boot                 Modify system boot parameters
  bridge               Bridge Group.
```

Cisco devices use a hierarchical command structure which means that all interface settings would be under the interface sub-config mode.

Router(config)#**interface ?**
```
  Async           Async interface
  BVI             Bridge-Group Virtual Interface
  CDMA-Ix         CDMA Ix interface
  CTunnel         CTunnel interface
  Dialer          Dialer interface
  FastEthernet    FastEthernet IEEE 802.3
  Group-Async     Async Group interface
  Lex             Lex interface
  Loopback        Loopback interface
  MFR             Multilink Frame Relay bundle interface
```

Multilink   Multilink-group interface
Null   Null interface
Port-channel   Ethernet Channel of interfaces
Tunnel   Tunnel interface
Vif   PGM Multicast Host interface
Virtual-PPP   Virtual PPP interface
Virtual-Template   Virtual Template interface
Virtual-TokenRing Virtual TokenRing
range   interface range command

Since we need to need to configure an IP address on the Fa0/0 interface we'll examine the Fa0/0 options. Notice that the prompt changes to (config-if)# when we enter fa0/0.

Router(config)#**interface fa0/0**
Router(config-if)#**?**
Interface configuration commands:
access-expression   Build a bridge boolean access expression
appletalk   Appletalk interface subcommands
arp   Set arp type (arpa, probe, snap) or timeout
auto   Configure Automation
backup   Modify backup parameters
bandwidth   Set bandwidth informational parameter
bgp-policy   Apply policy propagated by bgp community string
bridge-group   Transparent bridging interface parameters
carrier-delay   Specify delay for interface transitions
cdp   CDP interface subcommands

Now we will set an IP address and enable the interface. Most commands have context sensative help by using the **?** in the command.

Router(config-if)#**ip address ?**
A.B.C.D IP address
dhcp   IP Address negotiated via DHCP
pool   IP Address autoconfigured from a local DHCP pool
Router(config-if)#**ip address 192.168.1.1 ?**
A.B.C.D IP subnet mask
Router(config-if)#**ip address 192.168.1.1 255.255.255.0**
Router(config-if)#**no shutdown**
%LINK-3-UPDOWN: Interface FastEthernet0/0, changed state to up
%LINEPROTO-5-UPDOWN: Line protocol on Interface FastEthernet0/0, changed state to up

In newer IOS versions (12.2(8) or higher), you can use the **do** command to run privilege level commands from configure mode. It's a valuable time saver. Here we will verify the Fa0/0 IP address.

Router(config-if)#**do show ip interface brief**
Interface   IP-Address   OK? Method Status   Protocol

FastEthernet0/0   192.168.1.1   YES manual up   up

The next step to get connectivity going would be to setup a host (your PC) with an IP in the 192.168.1.0/24 subnet.

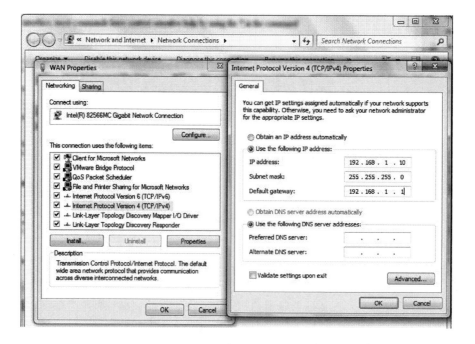

After we have set the IP on the host we should be able to ping the router.

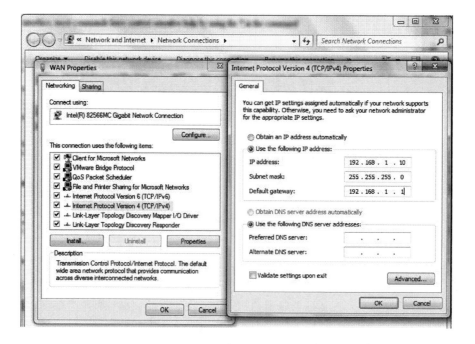

We can also ping the host from the router to confirm connectivity.

R1#**ping 192.168.1.10**
Type escape sequence to abort.
   Sending 5, 100-byte ICMP Echos to 192.168.1.10, timeout is 2 seconds:
   .!!!!

Success rate is 80 percent (4/5), round-trip min/avg/max = 1/32/64 ms

Important Note - Please make sure you turn off Windows Firewall or any other Firewall program on your computer. By default they will prevent the computer from responding to pings and this portion of the lab may fail.

Now that we have confirmed the configuration is working, it is important to save your changes often to avoid any lost configuration if the router reboots for any reason. You can do this with **copy running-config startup-config**.

R1#**copy run start**
  Destination filename [startup-config]?
  Building configuration...
  [OK]

copy running-config startup-config is the new method for saving the current config to nvram. The older command is **write memory** and this is still popular with Network Engineers because it can be shorted to just **wr** which makes it quick and easy to save.

  R1#**wr**
  Building configuration...
  [OK]

It's always a good idea to review the current configuration before making any changes if you aren't familiar with the device or before saving to ensure there are no errors in the config. To check the config you can use the **show running-config** command.

R1#**show run**
 Building configuration...
Current configuration : 492 bytes
  version 12.4
  service timestamps debug datetime msec
  service timestamps log datetime msec
  no service password-encryption
  hostname R1
  boot-start-marker
  boot-end-marker
  memory-size iomem 5
  ip cef
  interface FastEthernet0/0
  ip address 192.168.1.1 255.255.255.0
  duplex auto
  speed auto
  ip http server
  no ip http secure-server
  control-plane

```
line con 0
line aux 0
line vty 0 4
end
```

You can also review the saved nvram configuration by using the **show startup-config** command.

R1#show start
```
  Using 492 out of 129016 bytes
  version 12.4
  service timestamps debug datetime msec
  service timestamps log datetime msec
  no service password-encryption
  hostname R1
  boot-start-marker
  boot-end-marker
  memory-size iomem 5
  ip cef
  interface FastEthernet0/0
ip address 192.168.1.1 255.255.255.0
duplex auto
speed auto
ip http server
no ip http secure-server
control-plane
line con 0
line aux 0
```

Identifying Router and Switch IOS

In this lab we will use the Cisco Internetwork Operating Systems (IOS) Command Line Interface (CLI) to identify the version, capabilities, location within the flash storage, and filename of the IOS image file which is running the router or switch. Thus we will learn to recognize the image version and feature set.

Hardware & Configuration Required for this Lab
- One Cisco router or switch
- One PC to console into the router or switch
- One console cable
- There are no required configurations. Only that the Cisco device has booted an IOS image. Make a terminal connection to manage the router using the console port.

Cisco devices operate by executing the programming code contained in software image files. Just like how a computer has an operating system, Cisco networking devices have an operating system which consists of a single file. Without the operating system image file, a Cisco device cannot function any more than a computer can operate without an operating system like Windows, MacOS, or Linux. By replacing operating system images with different versions or with versions with different capabilities, a Cisco network device can be upgraded, patched, or can accommodate features as long as they are within hardware RAM and flash capabilities.

Image File Name and Meaning (new method)
Although each software image is specific to the device and model, an image will be generically referenced here as an "IOS image". An IOS (Internetwork Operating System) image is specific to the model of the device. A Cisco 3845 router, from the 3800 series of routers, will be not able to use an IOS image from a Cisco 2811 router, any other model of router, or any switch or firewall or other device. However, a Cisco device can replace its image with another image, specific to the model of the hardware, and gain update code or additional features.

The IOS image also has a major version number, minor version number, and a revision number, like 12.3.26d. The IOS image, specifically for routers and switches, also has an included name.

Example:	c2800nm-adventerprisek9-mz.124-25c.bin		
	Device Model	Feature Set	Major.Minor.Revision
	2800 Router	Advanced Enterprise	12.4.25c

The above example shows the IOS image for a Cisco 2800 series router with an Advanced Enterprise feature set, revision 12.4.25c.

At the time of this writing in 2012, most every image on a Cisco router will be 12.x.x or higher or 15.x.x. or higher, mostly in the 12.3.x, 12.4.x, and 15.x.x ranges. An IOS image version 12.3.26 would be older than a newer 12.4.25c while an image version of 11.1.15 or a 9.1.4 would be inconceivably old and outdated. Independent of the revision, an IP Base feature set would be more basic than an Advanced Enterprise feature set, described later.

Image File Name and Meaning (old method)

Previous to the names like "IPBASE" and "ADVENTERPRISE", IOS feature sets were identified by letters. Here is a quick chart and example for IOS images prior to 12.4 that used the older format which are more likely to be seen on 2500 and early 2600 series routers:

i = Base IP Routing   j = Enterprise (everything)
is = IP Plus   k9 = with Encryption
p = Service Provider   y = IP Routing, no high-end protocols like
BGP

Example: **c2500-ik8os-l.122-29b.bin**
                 Device Model   Feature Set
Major.Minor.Revision
                 2500 Router   IP & Firewall + Encryption   12.2.29b

The above example shows the IOS image for a Cisco 2500 series router with an feature set supporting IP routing, firewall, and base level encryption.

This is an example of some of the other letters identifying IOS feature sets:

Y   IP on 170 Series Routers
S   IP Plus
S6   IP Plus – No ATM
S7   IP Plus – No Voice
J   Enterprise
O   IOS Firewall/Intrusion Detection
K   Cryptography / IPSEC /SSH
K8   56bit Encryption
K9   Triple DES / AES Encryption (strong cryptography)

This is not an inclusive list and not every router model will have every feature set available. Voice (VoIP) capable routers may not have firewall IOS feature sets available and perhaps some larger model routers may not have the variety of IP Plus feature set varieties.

The newer classifications of "IP Base", "Advanced IP Services", "Advanced Security", "Advanced Enterprise", and so on, are to simply the feature sets and standardize the previous assortments.

Cisco Switches

Cisco switch IOS versions do not directly match router IOS versions. A Cisco switch IOS might be current with a 12.1.x IOS while a connected Cisco router might be current with a 12.4.x IOS. Switch images have different features since switches are different devices. However they can include routing features if the switch is a layer 3 (L3) switch which is capable of routing between the switchports. If the switch is L3, then it has routing features and protocols as well in addition to the switching capabilities.

Cisco Firewalls and Other Devices

Cisco PIX firewalls and ASA (Adaptive Security Appliance a.k.a. firewall) image versions follow a different series. 8.0.x through 8.4.x version are common at this time. A Cisco PIX with version 6.3.5 or 7.x.x might be unable to support modern features and a 5.5.4 version would be inconceivably outdated. Like the old method of router names, most all of the firewall images will include "k9" in the filename to indicate that the firewall image has encryption capabilities. Unlike routers and switches, firewalls have features enabled by entering an activation key to unlock features. The same up-to-date image is still used, but the activation key specifically keyed to the device serial number, once entered, it allows more capabilities after the next reboot.

Other Cisco appliances, like the Cisco wireless controllers and Cisco VoIP phones follow different OS image and IOS versions. So the versions are consistent only within the categories or types of devices. A Cisco wireless controller with an image version of 7.0 will not mean that it is outdated compared to a router with image version 12.1.

What you need to know is that each category of equipment follows its own version path. While Cisco routers and switches will have similar feature sets and close version numbers, it is more important to research the version within the product type than to compare the numeric version of a router image to the numeric version of a firewall image.

Lab Exercise

Identify the Image

The "show version" command will provide information about the current IOS image.

> Router> **show version**

This command is common within all routers, switches, firewalls, and other devices and can be executed from an unprivileged (exec mode) or privileged (level 15) non-config prompt.

Cisco IOS Software, C2600 Software (**C2600-ADVENTERPRISEK9_SNA-M**), **Version 12.4(25d),** RELEASE SOFTWARE (fc1)
Technical Support: http://www.cisco.com/techsupport
Copyright (c) 1986-2010 by Cisco Systems, Inc.
Compiled Wed 18-Aug-10 04:49 by prod_rel_team

ROM: System Bootstrap, Version 12.2(7r) [cmong 7r], RELEASE SOFTWARE (fc1)

Router uptime is 3 weeks, 1 day, 21 hours, 52 minutes
System returned to ROM by power-on
System image file is **"flash:c2600-adventerprisek9_sna-mz.124-25d.bin"**

This product contains cryptographic features and is subject to United
States and local country laws governing import, export, transfer and
use. Delivery of Cisco cryptographic products does not imply
third-party authority to import, export, distribute or use encryption.
Importers, exporters, distributors and users are responsible for
compliance with U.S. and local country laws. By using this product you
agree to comply with applicable laws and regulations. If you are unable
to comply with U.S. and local laws, return this product immediately.

A summary of U.S. laws governing Cisco cryptographic products may be found at:
http://www.cisco.com/wwl/export/crypto/tool/stqrg.html

If you require further assistance please contact us by sending email to
export@cisco.com.

Cisco 2611XM (MPC860P) processor (revision 1.0) with **127308K/3764K bytes of memory.**   (*Add the two values together to get the actual amount of RAM.*)
Processor board ID JAXO00000ACE
M860 processor: part number 5, mask 2
2 FastEthernet interfaces
2 Serial interfaces
32K bytes of NVRAM.
49152K bytes of processor board System flash (Read/Write)

Configuration register is 0x2102

From this output, you should be able to determine the following:

- The IOS image file is named "c2600-adventerprisek9_sna-mz.124-25d.bin".
- The IOS image file is on the storage media called "flash:".
- The IOS image version is 12.4.25d.
- The IOS image has the "Advanced Enterprise with SNA" feature set.

- The router was powered on (not a 'reload' or software/hardware crash) and has been running for 3 weeks, 1 day, 21 hours, and 52 minutes since the last start-up.

Additionally, this command shows system hostname, the hardware and physical interfaces recognized by the Cisco device and IOS, and the configuration register. Other than "power-on", there could have been a scheduled reload or a crash, in which crashes have crash files.

Identify the File Storage Locations

The "show file systems" command will show what file storage devices exist in the router's flash storage media. Commonly all devices will either have "flash:" or "bootflash:".

```
Router# show file systems
File Systems:

      Size(b)    Free(b)    Type Flags Prefixes
          -          -    opaque   rw  archive:
          -          -    opaque   rw  system:
      29688      26721     nvram   rw  nvram:
          -          -    opaque   rw  null:
          -          -    network  rw  tftp:
          -          -    opaque   ro  xmodem:
          -          -    opaque   ro  ymodem:
  *  49807356   18594520    flash   rw  flash:
          -          -    opaque   wo  syslog:
          -          -    network  rw  rcp:
          -          -    network  rw  pram:
          -          -    network  rw  ftp:
          -          -    network  rw  http:
          -          -    network  rw  scp:
          -          -    network  rw  https:
          -          -    opaque   ro  cns:
```

Identify the IOS Image File

The Cisco CLI (command line interface) follows classic DOS or Linux directory commands. The "CD" (change directory) command can switch between available file systems and directories within the file systems if the file system supports directories and sub-directories. It can also show the current directory with the "PWD" command. All of these are available in enabled / privileged / privileged level 15 mode.

Example:
Router# **cd flash:**

Router# **pwd**
flash:
Router# **dir**

Example:
Router# **dir flash:**

Example:
Router# **dir flash:/html**
Router# **dir**
Directory of flash:/
1 -rw-   30643812   <no date> c2600-adventerprisek9_sna-mz.124-25d.bin
49807356 bytes total (19163480 bytes free)

In this particular example, there is one file in the "flash:" file system. There is only one filename ending with .bin, and that is the image file. The router, in this case, will load the first .bin file in the flash as the IOS image, unless otherwise specified. Specific images are specified with a "system boot image" command in the saved configuration. This might be required by a few remaining devices, like the Cisco 4500 series chassis based switches, but is otherwise not required (and perhaps not recommended) if only one IOS image is in the primary flash file system.

If a router or switch had crashed, a crashlog file would be in the file system and would be available for download via FTP or TFTP for analysis. Other files might include HTML files if the device can provide basic status messages over a web interface. For voice over IP (VoIP) capable routers, phone image files, music on hold, and other files might be present, depending on the device's IOS features and needs. Perhaps an image file for another router might be stored in the flash of a nearby router for easy transfer. It could happen!

Other file location examples might include "bootflash:" when the device has internal flash storage other than external flash drive card slots that might be named "slot0:" or "disk0:". There may even be the capability to copy files from USB flash drives on device "usb:". Usually, the default name "flash:" relates to the primary flash file system.

Features
IOS images will contain various features. Routers with limited RAM and flash file systems unable to carry the larger IOS image files may need to run limited feature set images. By purchasing the license to download and run the enhanced feature sets, if the device is capable, the IOS images can perform more features within the device.
Examples: (not a complete listing)

- IP Base   Basic routing, routing protocols, enough to operate
- IP Voice   IP Base + features for VoIP and telephony services
- Service Provider Services   IP Voice + service provider features like MPLS
- Advanced Security   IP Base + security features like firewall, SSH, VPN
- Advanced IP Services   IP Base + Advanced Security + Service Provider
- Advanced Enterprise Services   Full Cisco IOS Software Feature Set

There are other feature sets not listed here, and the legacy IOS images followed a naming convention which used numbers and letters to represent the features of the IOS image.

Example:

> c2600-ik9o3s3-mz.122-15.T9.bin
> Cisco 2600 series routers, IP features, Enterprise Feature Set, 12.2.15-T9 revision

All of the conventions of the legacy IOS image features are not covered here.

Connect to a router, then later a switch, and use the show ver command to determine the following fields of information for each:

1. What is the device model?   _____

2. What is the IOS version?   _____

3. What is the IOS feature set?   _____
   This may not be applicable to all switches, but at least find out where to look.

4. How long has the device been running? _____

5. By what method did the device start?   _____

6. What is the device serial number?   _____

Cisco 1700/1800/2500/2600 Series Router
Password Types & Password Recovery

In this lab we will enter ROMMON mode and bypass the startup-configuration to reset console, VTY (telnet and SSH access), and enable mode passwords. We will then save the configuration with the new passwords.

Hardware & Configuration Required for this Lab
- One Cisco router
- One PC to console into the router
- One console cable

Sometimes the password or login for managing a router or switch becomes lost or unknown. Password recovery, involving direct access to the device via console, allows Cisco devices to become accessible again. This might be needed when acquiring used equipment or recycling devices within a networked environment with undocumented configurations and passwords.

Passwords for logging into a Cisco device for management, as well as the entire configuration, can be bypassed by entering ROMMON mode on a Cisco device, changing the configuration register value, booting or rebooting the device, then possibly loading the saved configuration once logged in (that was a mouthful which you may have to reread a few times). This will result in gaining enabled mode (privilege level 15) access prior to loading the configuration with the password settings, but with the ability to enter configuration mode. This would allow the configuration to be saved with the new login information.

ROMMON
An opportunity exists within the first few seconds of a Cisco device's boot process to enter ROMMON mode. On routers, use of the BREAK key in the terminal emulator on the console will enter ROMMON at boot time. On some switches, where the router method fails, hold in the Mode button on the front of the switch when applying power and continue holding until the ROMMON prompt appears on the terminal.

- A direct console connection is required; not remote access via telnet or SSH.
- ROMMON can only be accessed as the Cisco device is initially booting.

- When operating in this mode, the Cisco network device is not operating or performing its function. The IOS and configuration are not loaded, so no features function.
- Within the first seconds of booting, repeatedly press the BREAK key. Some terminal emulators have a feature to send a BREAK code in place of using the keyboard.

ROMMON primarily allows two functions since you are running actually a mini-IOS.

- File Copy – On some models, a file or IOS image can be copied to the device flash over the console connection by use of the XMODEM protocol. This is very slow, but could be a last resort to fixing a corrupted or missing IOS image file.
- Configuration Register Change – This may not seem like much in words, but this feature changes a hexadecimal value which the router interprets to bypass saved configurations and ultimately will allow password recovery.

        Rommon 1>

The numeric digit in the prompt will increment as each command line is entered.

Think of ROMMON on a Cisco device as the BIOS Setup on a PC and the configuration register on a Cisco device as the boot sequence in the BIOS Setup on a PC. ROMMON can be accessed on a Cisco device even if an IOS image is not present. Just as the BIOS Setup on a PC is available even if the operating system, like Windows, is corrupt or not present. Changing the configuration register value on a Cisco device changes how the Cisco device boots, just like how the BIOS Setup on a PC changes the order of drives which a PC attempt to use to boot.

Configuration Register

The configuration register's value is normally **0x2102**. This means that the router will boot normally and load the startup-configuration. If the IOS image cannot load, then the router will enter ROMMON. If the password recovery process is used, then the startup-configuration will not be erased. The console port will use 9600bps.

The configuration register, or confreg, can be changed within **configuration mode** on a Cisco device:

        Router> **enable** (*Later examples may not continue showing "enable".*)
        Router# **configure terminal** (***Later examples will abbreviate this as "config t".***)
        Router(config)# **config-register 0x2102**
        Router(config)# **end**

When working in **ROMMON**, after interrupting the boot sequence of a Cisco device you can change it as follows:

Rommon1# **confreg 0x2142** *(o/r 0x2142 is for 2500 series routers)*

Not all Cisco devices use hexadecimal values. Some use menus to change the settings; some firewalls require a file to be uploaded; some switches need a button pressed at boot time.

Sample Configuration Register Values

0x2102   Normal Setting – 9600bps console, boot the IOS and load startup-config

0x2142   Password Recovery – 9600bps console, boot the IOS and bypass startup-config

0x3922*   Fast Console – 11520bps console session, boot the IOS and load startup-config

* This varies from one model to the next.

Other configuration register values exist. The main purpose of introducing these three is to convey that normally you will see the configuration-register set to 0x2102 when the router is reading the contents of the configuration file at boot. Additionally, you can set the router to ignore the contents of the configuration file upon next boot by setting the configuration-register to 0x2142 when you need to do a password reset. Finally, primarily in a situation where you need to upload the IOS over an XMODEM console session (remember a console session is 9600bps by default) you can set the configuration-register so the console session will run at a much faster speed like 115200bps.

Note: If the console speed is changed through the configuration register, then the console connection is lost until the terminal emulator is configured to match. Cisco devices are expected to have a console port speed of 9600bps. Changing the console speed from 9600 to 115200 without conspicuous documentation or knowledge could cause confusion and be diagnosed as a device with a bad console port as the next time you console in you will see garbage characters on the screen. Simply reset the baud rate on the Cisco device to 9600 in that case.

Router Configuration

Start with a clean configuration on the router. This can be accomplished by executing "write erase" from enabled (privilege level 15) mode, then reloading the router.

```
Router> enable
Router# write erase
```

Erasing the nvram filesystem will remove all configuration files! Continue? [confirm]**y**
[OK]
Erase of nvram: complete
Router# **reload**
Proceed with reload? [confirm]**y**
Oct 22 06:57:17.251: %SYS-5-RELOAD: Reload requested by console.
(the router will reboot and reload at this point)

Lab Exercise
Set the login and enable passwords

Although this step is not necessary, it adds realism. These passwords can be replaced with anything since they will be circumvented by the password recovery process.

> Router> **enable**
> Router# **config t**
> Router(config)# **hostname Router1**
> Router1(config)# **enable secret ccna** (*Always use "enable secret" and never "enable password" as the "enable secret" command automatically encrypts the password using MD5 hash algorithm.*)
> Router1(config)# **no enable password**
> Router1(config)# ! (*Config files sometimes separate configuration commands with an exclamation point. Note that the CLI ignores input beginning with an "!".*)
> Router1(config)# **line con 0**
> Router1(config-line)# **password CertKits**
> Router1(config-line)# **login** *(activates the prompt for a password on the line)*
> Router1(config-line)# **line vty 0 15**
> Router1(config-line)# **password certkits**
> Router1(config-line)# **end**
> Router1#**copy run start**
> Destination filename [startup-config]? **hit enter**
> Building configuration...
> Router1#**exit**

After you type exit, you will be brought back to the initial router console prompt. Notice you are now being prompted for a password before you even ty to get into enable mode. Try logging in with the password of cisco three times. Notice you were denied, but not locked out. Now try the password we set above for line vty 0 15. No dice. Now try the enable secret password as that seems to be a pretty powerful password. Nope, that is for enable mode and we are simply trying to login to basic user mode. Now try the password for the console session of line con 0. Notice that this was the same password as the VTY lines except for the capitalization. So the password is case sensitive. Also note the name of the router as we will highlight this in a bit.

Boot and Enter ROMMON

Shut the router off and then make a console connection and then boot the router. Within seconds of starting the router, begin sending the BREAK sequence from the terminal until the ROMMON prompt appears.

Rommon 1>

Set the Configuration Register

Set the configuration register to 0x2142 to bypass loading the startup-configuration on the next boot. Then reload the router.

> Rommon 1> **confreg 0x2142** (o/r 0x2142 for the 2500 series only)
> Rommon 2> **reset** (The ROMMON command "reset" is the same as "reload" in the CLI. For the 2500 series, use simply an i to reset the router.)

Boot the Router

Allow the router to boot and notice the router seems to be set back to factory defaults. Skip the initial configuration, when prompted. Notice our router's name is no longer Router1. Now run a show version in user mode.

> Router> **show version**

Observe the current configuration register setting at the bottom of the "show version" output.

> Cisco Internetwork Operating System Software
> IOS (tm) C2600 Software (C2600-ADVSECURITYK9-M), Version 12.3(26), RELEASE SOFTWARE
> (content omitted for brevity)
> **Configuration register is 0x2142**

Load the Configuration and Set New Passwords

Enter enabled/privileged mode, load the startup-configuration, then enter configuration mode to enter new passwords. Once the passwords have been set, reset the configuration register to the normal setting of 0x2102. Save the running configuration to flash and reboot the router to test.

> Router> **enable**
> Router# **copy startup-config running-config**
> Destination filename [running-config]? (Just press enter for "running-config".)

Notice the router's name is now Router1 again as we can get in and reset all the passwords without losing the other configuration of the router.

> Router1# **config t** (Later examples may not continue showing "config t".)
> Router1(config)# **enable secret password123**
> Router1(config-line)# **line con 0**
> Router1(config-line)# **password cisco**
> Router1(config-line)# **line vty 0 15**
> Router1(config-line)# **password cisco**
> Router1(config-line)# **config-register 0x2102**

Router1(config)# **end**
Router1# **copy running-config startup-config**
Destination filename [startup-config]? (Just press enter for "startup-config".)
Router1# **show ver**

Look at the show ver output and note how the configuration register is set to 0x2142 but at reboot it will change to 0x2102 due to the configuration command we did above.

Router1# **reload**
Proceed with reload? [confirm] (Just press enter to continue with the reload)

Once the router has rebooted, login to enable mode with the password set above and observe the current configuration register utilizing the "show version" command as shown below.

Router1#**show version**

Cisco Internetwork Operating System Software
IOS (tm) C2600 Software (C2600-ADVSECURITYK9-M), Version 12.3(26), RELEASE
SOFTWARE
(content omitted for brevity)
Configuration register is 0x2102

Cisco Router Password Recovery Review

Questions

1. What CLI mode is used on a Cisco router for password recovery?

   _____

2. What method must be used to connect to the router to do password recovery?_____

3. What key in the terminal must be used to enter ROMMON at boot time?

   _____

4. What is the normal configuration register value on a Cisco router?

   _____

5. What configuration register value is used on a Cisco router for password recovery?

   _____

Answers

1. ROMMON
2. Console
3. BREAK
4. 0x2102
5. 0x2142

Configure Login, EXEC, and MOTD Banners

In this lab we will set a login banner, exec mode banner, and message of the day (MOTD) banner on a router.

Hardware & Configuraiton Required for this Lab
- One Cisco router
- One PC to console into the router
- One console cable

Banners are displayed at the time of login to present messages to users connecting to the CLI of Cisco devices for command line management. Login banners are often used to present warnings against unauthorized use, but they can also be used to identify devices and present notices to those people managing and administering the equipment. A typical login banner might warn unauthorized users that connections are logged while a message of the day (MOTD) banner will mention that this device is in production and to contact the Help Desk prior to enacting changes or rebooting the equipment.

Create Banners

Set messages to be displayed upon the next connection to the router. These will be entered line by line before the configuration entry ends, unlike any previous configuration command settings. The delimiting character is something that will mark the beginning and the end of the multi-line input. This should be a character that will not appear within the banner text, such as a symbol like $ or %. These banners can also be several lines in length.

Login banners appear above the console login and at the start of telnet and SSH connections. So let's go into config mode and configure each.

> Router1(config)# **banner login %**
> Enter TEXT message. End with the character '%'.
> **Do not attempt unauthorized access into this router.**
> **Connections will be logged. %**
> (Note: *The '%' marks both the beginning and end of the input.*)

MOTD banners appear on console, and VTY (telnet/SSH) connections after the login banner.

> R1(config)# **banner motd &**
> Enter TEXT message. End with the character '&'.

Maintenance planned for 9pm EST (GMT -5).   This router will be offline after that time.
% (Note: *The '&' marks both the beginning and end of the input.*)

Exec banners appear after a successful login before the exec prompt.

R1(config)# **banner exec #**
Enter TEXT message. End with the character '#'.
Reminder: Please backup your changes by copying the configuration to the TFTP server. # (Note: *The '#' marks both the beginning and end of the input.*)
R1(config)# **end**
R1#**exit**

Logout of the command line interface (CLI) on the console and press ENTER to login again.

Press RETURN to get started.

Maintenance planned for 9pm EST (GMT -5).   This router will be offline after that time.

Do not attempt unauthorized access into this router.
Connections will be logged.

Password: (*This will only appear if a line con0 password is set.*)

Reminder: Please backup your changes by copying the configuration to the TFTP server.

Configure Login, EXEC, and MOTD Banners Review

Questions

1. Which banner appears first? _____

2. Which banner appears last before the password prompt?_____

3. Which banner appears after login?_____

4. What is the purpose of a delimiting character in a banner configuration command?
   _____

5. Which of the following is a bad example of a delimiting character: e, $, #, %
   _____

6. What are some of the purposes of the login banner?
   _____

7. What is the default behavior of a Cisco router or switch if no banners are configured?
   _____

8. What factor can result of the skipping of the login banner being displayed?
   _____

Answers

1. Message of the Day (MOTD)
2. Login
3. Exec
4. To set the start and end of the banner text.
5. e – Try to use characters which will NOT appear in the text.
6. Answers vary, but can include warnings against unauthorized use.
7. None will be displayed at login.
8. If no password is configured for login.

Configuring the Password Encryption Service

In this lab we are going to configure password encryption on the router to prevent the passwords from being displayed as plain text.

Hardware & Configuration Required for this Lab
- One Cisco router
- One PC to console into the router
- One console cable

By default, the standard enable password as well as passwords that are entered on line interfaces are stored in clear text. A quick "show run" or "show running-configuration" command will reveal all of these passwords.

The "enable secret" is controlled differently. It is stored as an MD5 hash.

The first several lines of Cisco router and Cisco switch configurations define the services. For example, one service defines if timestamps will be included in log messages and if so what that format will be. Another service defines whether or not passwords will be encrypted in a configuration file.The "service password-encryption" commandencrypts the passwords in the configuration. It is reversible encryption and is not very secure, but it is enough to obscure and hinder easy viewing of the passwords. Encrypted passwords from one Cisco device's configuration can be entered encrypted into another Cisco device and it will work.

Router Configuration
Start with a clean configuration.

Lab Exercise
Set Passwords on VTY and Console Lines
Assign a password for console and VTY (telnet/SSH) access.

> Router(config)#**line con 0**
> Router(config-line)#**password cisco**
> Router(config-line)#**login**
> Router(config-line)#**line vty 0 4** (*You could type "exit" here and THEN "line vty 0 4", but the Cisco IOS CLI allows another line or interface or similar command to be specified WITHOUT typing "exit" first to return to what is called the "global configuration" prompt of "Router(config)#".*)
> Router(config-line)#**password cisco**

Router(config-line)#**end**

Show the running-configuraiton.

Router#**show running-config** (*You should already be in the habit of typing "show run" or "show running-config" after configuration has been entered to verify that the configuration is correct.*)

Current configuration:
! (*Your CLI output WILL vary slightly from this, including the comment lines which begin with an exclamation mark and some other lines. These are the variations between IOS versions, such as from 12.1 to 12.2 and 12.3. Look more towards the portions commented below.*)

version 12.4
no service timestampe log datetime msec
no service timestampe debug datetime msec
no service password-encryption
!
hostname Router
!
!
interface FastEthernet0/0
 no ip address
duplex auto
speed auto
shutdown
!
interface FastEthernet0/1
 no ip address
duplex auto
speed auto
shutdown
!
interface Serial0/1/0
 no ip address
clock rate 2000000
!
interface Serial0/1/1
 no ip address
 clock rate 2000000

!
interface Vlan1
no ipaddress
shutdown
!
ip classless

```
!
line con 0
 password cisco
login
line vty 0 4
password cisco
!
end
```

You will note that "password cisco" is in clear text and shown under "line con 0" and "line vty 0 4".

Enable Password Encryption

A single configuration command enables password encryption. Go into configuration mode.

> Router(config)#**service password-encryption**
> Router(config)#**end**

Now check the running-configuration and see how the passwords have been altered.

> Router#**show running-config** (*You should already be in the habit of typing "show run" or "show running-config" after configuration has been entered to verify that the configuration is correct.*)

> Current configuration:
> ! (*Your CLI output WILL vary slightly from this, including the comment lines which begin with an exclamation mark and some other lines. These are the variations between IOS versions, such as from 12.x to 15.x. Look more towards the portions commented below.*)

```
version 12.4
no service timestampe log datetime msec
no service timestampe debug datetime msec
service password-encryption
!
hostname Router
!
!
interface FastEthernet0/0
 no ip address
duplex auto
speed auto
shutdown
!
interface FastEthernet0/1
 no ip address
```

```
duplex auto
speed auto
shutdown
!
interface Serial0/1/0
 no ip address
clock rate 2000000
!
interface Serial0/1/1
 no ip address
 clock rate 2000000

!
interface Vlan1
no ipaddress
shutdown
!
ip classless
!
!
line con 0
 password 7 0822455D0A16
```
(This will vary, but note that there is a "7" then encrypted content.) line vty 0 4
```
password 7 0822455D0A16
```
(This will vary, but note that there is a "7" then encrypted content.)
```
!
end
```

Note that under "line con 0" the password is shown as "password 7 0822455D0A16". On your Cisco router this may appear different, but the important part to note is that the 7 indicates that the content following is encrypted. It is possible to enter the password unencrypted into the configuration like this:

Router(config)#**line con 0**
Router(config-line)#**password 0 cisco**

The 0 preceding the password indicates that clear-text is to follow. Whenever the password immediately follows the "password" keyword, without either a 0 or 7 being specified, the IOS CLI assumes that a clear-text password is being entered.

This reversible encryption makes it possible to copy-and-paste an encrypted password line like the ones shown above into another Cisco router or switch with the same effectiveness.

Note: On Cisco routers with higher version 12 IOS, the output of "show" commands can be filtered.   If your Cisco router or Cisco switch configuration starts getting to long, try this variation of the "show run" command:

Router#**show run | begin line con**

Whatever follows the pipe (shift backslash on most keyboards) and the keyword "begin" will skip all configuration output until that line is reached.

Password Encryption Service Review

Questions

1. What global configuration setting enables password encryption in the configuration?_____

2. What are the two values which can precede the password in a line password setting?_____

3. If a password is entered as "password 7 cisco", why will logins using "cisco" fail?_____

4. Can the encrypted version of passwords be copied and pasted to other Cisco devices?_____

5. What is the password if this configuration is entered: "password 0 030752180500"?_____

6. What happens to the unencrypted passwords in the configuration if the password-encryption service is enabled?

   _____

7. What happens to the encrypted passwords in the configuration if the password-encryption service is disabled?

   _____

8. Is the "enable secret" password modified by service password-encryption?

   _____

Answers

1. service password-encryption
2. 0 and 7
3. The password "cisco" will be considered to be the encrypted version of the actual password. This actually will not work properly since it is not a correct encrypted form of a password and the line will be unable to be accessed. Use "password 0 cisco" instead.
4. Yes, but only so long as the entire configuration line is copied exactly.
5. 030752180500
6. They stay become encrypted.
7. They stay encrypted, but new password entries are stored unencrypted.
8. no

Exec Timeout and Login Failure Rate

The objective of this lab is to specify an idel timeout on the console or VTY lines and limit the number of login attempts.

Hardware & Configuration Required for this Lab
- One Cisco router
- One PC to console into the router
- One console cable

Management access to Cisco devices can be limited, as shown by using access-lists to limit the hosts which can connect. Management access can become more secure by logging off idle telnet and SSH sessions as well as limiting the number of password attempts before disconnecting the client. This is effective in blocking brute force password hacking.

Router Configuration

Start with a clean configuration by erasing any configuration you may have. Go into configuration mode and then add the following management login configuration:

```
Router(config)#interface lo 0
Router(config-if)#ip address 10.1.1.1 255.255.255.0
Router(config-if)#no shut
Router(config-if)#exit
Router(config)#line con 0
Router(config-line)#password cisco
Router(config-line)#login
Router(config-line)#exit
Router(config)#line vty 0 15 (This is "line vty 0 15" on 2600 series or higher routers.)
Router(config-line)#password cisco
Router(config-line)#login
Router(config-line)#exit
```

Lab Exercise

Configure an Exec Timeout

Set the console to disconnect sessions idle for 30 seconds. This is extreme, but it quicker to test in a lab environment than a standard 15 minute idle timeout.

```
Router(config)#line con 0
Router(config-line)#exec- timeout 0 30 (The numbers represent minutes and seconds.)
```

Router(config-line)#**end**

Exit the current session. Go back in. Wait 30 seconds. The console will logout the console session. Login again and change this to a more tolerable 5 minutes.

Router(config)#**line con 0**
Router(config-line)#**exec- timeout 5 0** (*This is 5 minutes and 0 seconds.*)
Router(config-line)#**end**

Try this on the VTY as well.

Router(config)#**line vty 0 4** (*line vty 0 15 on some routers, but not required for this lab.*)
Router(config-line)#**exec- timeout 0 10** (*This is 0 minutes and 10 seconds.*)
Router(config-line)#**end**

Router#**telnet 10.1.1.1**
Router#telnet 10.1.1.1
Trying 10.1.1.1 ... Open

User Access Verification

Password:**cisco**
Router>   (*Wait 10 seconds.*)
[Connection to 10.1.1.1 closed by foreign host])

Router#(*Back to the original prompt after 10 seconds this appears.*)

Configure a Login Failure Rate
The limit for the number of login attempts is not configured under the line but rather in the global configuration mode. This is the normal "Router(config)#" prompt, as opposed to the prompt when configuring an interface, "Router(config-if)#", or a line "Router(config-line)#". You may only see these commands in Advanced IP Services or similar IOS feature sets.

Router(config)#**security authentication failure rate 2 log** (*Stops after 2 failed attempts.*)

The newer method using AAA to limit login attempts is shown below:

Router(config)#**aaa new-model**
Router(config)#**aaa authentication attempts login 2**

Configuring an Exec Timeout and Login Failure Rate Review

Questions

1. Which interfaces or lines can have an exec time-out value?

    _____

2. Within which configuration mode or configuration prompt is the login rate set?

    _____

3. What are the two values specified within the exec time-out setting?

    _____

4. What is the effect of "exec time-out 0 5"?

    _____

5. What happens to a console connection, once logged in, if no exec-timeout is set?

    _____

6. Can the console idle timeout and the VTY line timeout be different values?

    _____

7. Can each VTY line have a different idle timeout value?

    _____

8. What type of hacking is prevented by the login failure rate?

    _____

Answers

1. Console and VTY lines
2. global configuration mode – "Router(config)#"
3. minutes and seconds
4. The connection is disconnected after a mere 5 seconds of being idle. This is not advisable, but illustrates the danger in not knowing that these are not hours and minutes.
5. The console session will remain logged in indefinitely.
6. yes
7. yes – Try "line vty 0" and "exec-timeout 1 0" followed by "line vty 1" and "exec-timeout 2 0" followed by "line vty 3" and "exec-timeout 3 0" and so on.
8. brute force

Installing a TFTP Server & Overview

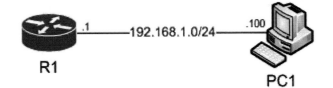

R1   PC1

The purpose of this lab is for you to learn what a TFTP server is and to go over some of the TFTP server setup options. We will also show you how to use the TFTP server to backup your running config file.

Hardware & Configuration Requirements for this Lab

- One Cisco router with one Ethernet port
- One PC running TFTP Server Software
- One crossover Cat 5 cable for a direct PC to router connection or connect the PC and router to a switch via two straight through Cat 5 cables

---

Commands Used in this Lab

copy running-config tftp: - Used to copy the device's running configuration to a TFTP server
copy tftp running-conifg - Used to copy an image from a TFTP to flash

---

TFTP Download and Install
The most common way to upgrade a router is to use a TFTP server as it's fast and convenient. So let's review where to get a copy of a TFTP server and how to install it. You can download a free copy of our TFTP server at www.CertificaitonKits.com/tftpserver/tftpserver.zip or you can install it off the CD we included in our kit.

In regards to the install process, simply take all the default options for the installation. You can then launch the TFTP Server from either the Start-Programs-CertificationKits-TFTP Server-CertificationKits TFTP Server icon or the corresponding shortcut on your desktop.

Below you will see a screen shot of the TFTP Server Console. So let's cover the various features of the TFTP server.

The first thing you will note is in the bottom left hand corner of the TFTP Server is whether or not the TFTP Service is running. If not, you will want to start the TFTP Server and you simply do so by clicking the **Server Start** button. Then you will see the service status as Running.

The next thing we want to look at is the **Local Network Endpoint** option. This is simply the IP address of the TFTP server. You may ask why do you have a drop down? Well if you have multiple NICs in the computer, you may want to bind the TFTP service to a specific NIC. Also if you don't remember the IP address of the computer, you simply select the drop down and you will see it.

The next option is the **Port**. This is the port the TFTP protocol runs over, so there really should be no need to change this.

Then finally we have the **Server Storage Folder**. This is the location on the computer where you want the program to default for storage of items like your IOS images and configuration files. This can be a local drive or a network drive on your computer. By default it is C:\TFTP-Storage. So you must remember to store a copy of your IOS file here before you attempt to do an IOS upgrade or it will fail.

Alert! – Any time you change any of the settings, you must click **Save Settings** for the new settings to bind to the TFTP server.

Configure our router with an IP of 192.168.1.1 and a hostname of R1.

Router>**enable**
Router#**config terminal**
Enter configuration commands, one per line. End with CNTL/Z.
Router(config)#**hostname R1**
R1(config)#**interface Fa0/0**
R1(config-if)#**ip address 192.168.1.1 255.255.255.0**
R1(config-if)#**no shutdown**
R1(config-if)#**end**
R1#**copy running-config startup-config**
Destination filename [startup-config]?
Building configuration...
[OK]
R1#

Then make sure you can you have connectivity over to the TFTP server. Make sure the IP on your PC (TFTP Server) is 192.168.1.100. Now we have to actually create a configuration file on the router.

R1# **ping 192.168.1.100**
Type escape sequence to abort.
Sending 5, 100-byte ICMP Echos to 192.168.1.100, timeout is 2 seconds:
!!!!!
Success rate is 100 percent (5/5), round-trip min/avg/max = 1/1/4 ms

Now that you have network connectivity, we will copy the local startup-config from the router to the TFTP server. This way if the router was to crash and if we have to replace it, we can simply retrieve a copy of the startup-config and copy back over to the router and we are back in business.

R1#**copy startup-config tftp**
Address or name of remote host []? **192.168.1.100**
Destination filename [r1-confg]? **<just hit enter>**
!!
1030 bytes copied in 2.489 secs (395 bytes/sec)
R1#

Now if you go to your computer and under the c:\TFTP-Storage folder you should see your startup-config file that was copied named r1-confg.

Upgrading the IOS on a Router

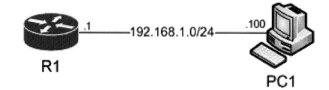

R1   .1 ——192.168.1.0/24—— .100   PC1

The purpose of this lab is for you to learn how to upgrade the IOS on a Cisco Router via a couple methods. Before starting this lab, it is recommended that you review setting up a TFTP server lab.

Since the process is virtually identical for upgrading routers and switches, this lab will just focus on routers.

Hardware & Configuration Requirements for this Lab

- One Cisco router
- One PC running TFTP Server software
- One crossover Cat 5 cable for a direct PC to router connection or connect the PC and router to a switch via two straight through Cat 5 cables
- **Note:** It is suggested to only try this lab after you complete all of the Chapter 2 labs so you are familiar with the commands

---

Commands Used in this Lab

copy flash:<image name> tftp - Used to copy the device's image to a TFTP server
copy tftp flash - Used to copy an image from a TFTP to flash
copy ftp flash - Used to copy an image from a FTP to flash
tftpdnld - ROMMON tool used to copy an image to flash from a TFTP server
xmodem - Used to copy an image via a console cable
confreg - Used to edit various ROMMON and console settings

The most common way to upgrade a router is to use a TFTP server as it's fast and convenient. In this lab we are using a 2611XM. However the process is pretty much the same for virtually any router absent the file names so don't fret is you do no have the same model. The first step is to configure the router with an IP address.

R1>**enable**

R1#**config terminal**
R1(config)#**int fa0/0**
R1(config-if)#**ip address 192.168.1.1 255.255.255.0**
R1(config-if)#**no shut**
R1(config-if)#**end**
R1#

Now let's make sure we can reach the host running as the TFTP server. We will assume you set the computer that is running as the TFTP Server with an IP address of 192.168.1.100. If you do not get a ping response, double check your cabling and the IP address on the TFTP Server (also make sure you have turned off Windows Firewall).

R1#**ping 192.168.1.100**
Type escape sequence to abort.
Sending 5, 100-byte ICMP Echos to 192.168.1.100, timeout is 2 seconds:
!!!!!
Success rate is 100 percent (5/5), round-trip min/avg/max = 1/1/4 ms

In the TFTP-Storage folder I have the following IOS image.

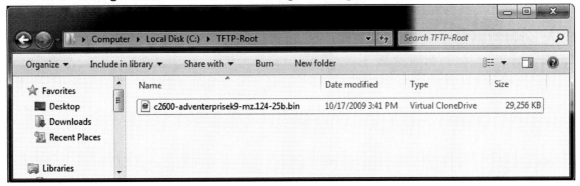

Checking the requirements on Cisco's website or via Google for the IOS image we can see we need 128MB of DRAM and 32MB of Flash.

Checking the output of **show version** we can see that we are currently running 12.4(17) and we do indeed have 128MB DRAM and 32MB Flash.
Note: It's very important to make sure the router can handle the new image before starting, otherwise the router may not boot as the process may erase the current IOS file.

R1#**show version**
Cisco IOS Software, C2600 Software (C2600-ADVENTERPRISEK9-M), Version 12.4(17), RELEASE SOFTWARE (fc1)
Technical Support: http://www.cisco.com/techsupport
Copyright (c) 1986-2007 by Cisco Systems, Inc.
Compiled Fri 07-Sep-07 16:05 by prod_rel_team
ROM: System Bootstrap, Version 12.2(8r) [cmong 8r], RELEASE SOFTWARE (fc1)

R1 uptime is 15 minutes
System returned to ROM by reload
System image file is "**flash:c2600-adventerprisek9-mz.124-17.bin**"
This product contains cryptographic features and is subject to United
States and local country laws governing import, export, transfer and
use. Delivery of Cisco cryptographic products does not imply
third-party authority to import, export, distribute or use encryption.
Importers, exporters, distributors and users are responsible for
compliance with U.S. and local country laws. By using this product you
agree to comply with applicable laws and regulations. If you are unable
to comply with U.S. and local laws, return this product immediately.
A summary of U.S. laws governing Cisco cryptographic products may be found at:
http://www.cisco.com/wwl/export/crypto/tool/stqrg.html
If you require further assistance please contact us by sending email to
export@cisco.com.
Cisco 2611XM (MPC860P) processor (revision 4.0) with **127110K**/3962K bytes of memory.
Processor board ID JMX0908L1GG
M860 processor: part number 5, mask 2
2 FastEthernet interfaces
2 Serial(sync/async) interfaces
32K bytes of NVRAM.
32768K bytes of processor board System flash (Read/Write)
Configuration register is 0x2102

It's also a good idea to keep a backup of the old IOS just in case something happens.
We'll use **copy flash:c2600-adventerprisek9-mz.124-17.bin tftp** to store a copy of the
IOS on the TFTP server.

R1#**copy flash:c2600-adventerprisek9-mz.124-17.bin tftp**
Address or name of remote host []? 192.168.1.100
Destination filename [c2600-adventerprisek9-mz.124-17.bin]?
!!
29925948 bytes copied in 159.048 secs (188157 bytes/sec)

On the TFTP server we see the the name of the IOS file and where it is being sent in the
console window.

To do the upgrade we use the **copy tftp flash** command. Notice that part of the process
is to erase the flash. That is why it is important to verify the new image will work
because the old one is usually wiped out and you can be left with no IOS to boot the
router.

Note: If you have enough room in flash you can storage multiple images, you can bypass
the erasing of flash by pressing any other key then Enter.

R1#**copy tftp flash**
Address or name of remote host []? 192.168.1.100
Source filename []? c2600-adventerprisek9-mz.124-25b.bin
Destination filename [c2600-adventerprisek9-mz.124-25b.bin]?
Accessing tftp://192.168.1.100/c2600-adventerprisek9-mz.124-25b.bin...
Erase flash: before copying? [confirm]
Erasing the flash filesystem will remove all files! Continue? [confirm]
Erasing device... eeeeeeeeeeeeeeeeeeeeeeeeeeeeeeeeeeeeeeeeeeeeeeeeeeeeeeeee ...erased
Erase of flash: complete
Loading c2600-adventerprisek9-mz.124-25b.bin from 192.168.1.100 (via FastEthernet0/0): !!!!!!!!!!!!!!
!!!
[OK - 29957284 bytes]
Verifying checksum... CCCCCCCCCCCCCCCCCCCCCCCCCCCCCCCCCCCCCCCCCCCCCCCCCCCCCC OK (0x3C42)
29957284 bytes copied in 315.629 secs (94913 bytes/sec)

The final step is to save the configuration and reload.
R1# **copy running-config startup-config**
Destination filename [startup-config]?
Building configuration...
[OK]
R1#**reload**
System configuration has been modified. Save? [yes/no]: **yes**
Building configuration...
[OK]
Proceed with reload? [confirm]
*Mar 23 06:56:00.787: %SYS-5-RELOAD: Reload requested by console. Reload Reason: Reload Command.
    System Bootstrap, Version 12.2(8r) [cmong 8r], RELEASE SOFTWARE (fc1)
    Copyright (c) 2003 by cisco Systems, Inc.

Here is the output of the reboot, if there were any problems with the image such as
download corruption or the router doesn't meet the IOS requirements you'll start to see
problems in the Smart Init section. Typically you will see UNKNOWN if there is a
requirement problem and it will take a very long time to decompress the image. Once
the IOS fully loads we can see that it is running the new version.

System Bootstrap, Version 12.2(8r) [cmong 8r], RELEASE SOFTWARE (fc1)
Copyright (c) 2003 by cisco Systems, Inc.
C2600 platform with 131072 Kbytes of main memory
program load complete, entry point: 0x80008000, size: 0x1c91b04
Self decompressing the image : ###
[OK]
Smart Init is enabled
smart init is sizing iomem
ID   MEMORY_REQ   TYPE
00036B   0X00103980 C2611XM Dual Fast Ethernet
000065   0X00031500 Four port Voice PM

0X00098670 public buffer pools
0X00211000 public particle pools
TOTAL: 0X003DE4F0
If any of the above Memory Requirements are
"UNKNOWN", you may be using an unsupported
configuration or there is a software problem and
system operation may be compromised.
Rounded IOMEM up to: 3Mb.
Using 3 percent iomem. [3Mb/128Mb]
Restricted Rights Legend
Use, duplication, or disclosure by the Government is
subject to restrictions as set forth in subparagraph
(c) of the Commercial Computer Software - Restricted
Rights clause at FAR sec. 52.227-19 and subparagraph
(c) (1) (ii) of the Rights in Technical Data and Computer
Software clause at DFARS sec. 252.227-7013.
cisco Systems, Inc.
170 West Tasman Drive
San Jose, California 95134-1706
Cisco IOS Software, C2600 Software (C2600-ADVENTERPRISEK9-M), Version 12.4(25b),
RELEASE SOFTWARE (fc1)
Technical Support: http://www.cisco.com/techsupport
Copyright (c) 1986-2009 by Cisco Systems, Inc.
Compiled Wed 12-Aug-09 10:59 by prod_rel_team

This product contains cryptographic features and is subject to United
States and local country laws governing import, export, transfer and
use. Delivery of Cisco cryptographic products does not imply
third-party authority to import, export, distribute or use encryption.
Importers, exporters, distributors and users are responsible for
compliance with U.S. and local country laws. By using this product you
agree to comply with applicable laws and regulations. If you are unable
to comply with U.S. and local laws, return this product immediately.
A summary of U.S. laws governing Cisco cryptographic products may be found at:
http://www.cisco.com/wwl/export/crypto/tool/stqrg.html
If you require further assistance please contact us by sending email to
export@cisco.com.
Cisco 2611XM (MPC860P) processor (revision 4.0) with 127110K/3962K bytes of memory.
Processor board ID JMX0908L1GG
M860 processor: part number 5, mask 2
2 FastEthernet interfaces
2 Serial(sync/async) interfaces
2 Voice FXO interfaces
2 Voice FXS interfaces
32K bytes of NVRAM.
32768K bytes of processor board System flash (Read/Write)
Slot is empty or does not support clock participate

WIC slot is empty or does not support clock participate

Press RETURN to get started!

You can also upgrade the IOS via FTP or HTTP with the commands: **copy ftp flash** and **copy http flash** respectively. The process is exactly the same except they require more configuration to allow the router to connect to an FTP or HTTP server. Since they aren't part of the CCNA exam, we won't look at them at this time.

Note: On routers with USB ports, you can also use a USB flash drive to upgrade the router.

So that's how we upgrade a router that is running fine. Let's create a problem where the router won't boot and see how we can fix that. It seems a Junior Network Admin on his first day of the job tragically decided to erase the flash on the router and reboot.

R1#**delete flash:c2600-adventerprisek9-mz.124-25b.bin**
Delete filename [c2600-adventerprisek9-mz.124-25b.bin]? **y**
Delete flash:c2600-adventerprisek9-mz.124-25b.bin? [confirm] **y**
R1#**reload**
Proceed with reload? [confirm]
*Mar 23 07:09:46.166: %SYS-5-RELOAD: Reload requested by console. Reload Reason: Reload Command.

Here is what we see if the router can't find a suitable IOS in its flash (this section does not apply to 2500 series routers, but you can follow the steps at www.certificationkits.com/cisco-2500-router-ios-upgrade/), we'd also see something similar if the router couldn't load the IOS due to corruption or memory isssues. After trying for a bit, it will automatically boot into rommon mode.

System Bootstrap, Version 12.2(8r) [cmong 8r], RELEASE SOFTWARE (fc1)
Copyright (c) 2003 by cisco Systems, Inc.
C2600 platform with 131072 Kbytes of main memory
boot: cannot determine first file name on device "flash:"
System Bootstrap, Version 12.2(8r) [cmong 8r], RELEASE SOFTWARE (fc1)
Copyright (c) 2003 by cisco Systems, Inc.
C2600 platform with 131072 Kbytes of main memory
boot: cannot determine first file name on device "flash:"
System Bootstrap, Version 12.2(8r) [cmong 8r], RELEASE SOFTWARE (fc1)
Copyright (c) 2003 by cisco Systems, Inc.
C2600 platform with 131072 Kbytes of main memory
rommon 1 >

ROMMON is a very simple and unfriendly operating system that can be used for repairing the router.

```
rommon 1 > ?
alias        set and display aliases command
boot          boot up an external process
break         set/show/clear the breakpoint
confreg        configuration register utility
cont          continue executing a downloaded image
context        display the context of a loaded image
cookie         display contents of cookie PROM in hex
dev           list the device table
dir           list files in file system
dis           display instruction stream
dnld          serial download a program module
frame          print out a selected stack frame
help          monitor builtin command help
history        monitor command history
meminfo          main memory information
repeat         repeat a monitor command
reset         system reset
set          display the monitor variables
stack          produce a stack trace
sync          write monitor environment to NVRAM
sysret         print out info from last system return
tftpdnld        tftp image download
unalias         unset an alias
unset         unset a monitor variable
xmodem          x/ymodem image download
```

The utility we need to use in this case is the **tftpdnld** command. TFTPDNLD is different
from any other Cisco command you have seen because it needs you to define variables
ahead of time.

```
rommon 10 > tftpdnld
Missing or illegal ip address for variable IP_ADDRESS
      Illegal IP address.
usage: tftpdnld [-r]
Use this command for disaster recovery only to recover an image via TFTP.
Monitor variables are used to set up parameters for the transfer.
(Syntax: "VARIABLE_NAME=value" and use "set" to show current variables.)
"ctrl-c" or "break" stops the transfer before flash erase begins.
      The following variables are REQUIRED to be set for tftpdnld:
      IP_ADDRESS: The IP address for this unit
      IP_SUBNET_MASK: The subnet mask for this unit
      DEFAULT_GATEWAY: The default gateway for this unit
      TFTP_SERVER: The IP address of the server to fetch from
      TFTP_FILE: The filename to fetch
      The following variables are OPTIONAL:
      TFTP_VERBOSE: Print setting. 0=quiet, 1=progress(default), 2=verbose
```

TFTP_RETRY_COUNT: Retry count for ARP and TFTP (default=12)
TFTP_TIMEOUT: Overall timeout of operation in seconds (default=7200)
TFTP_CHECKSUM: Perform checksum test on image, 0=no, 1=yes (default=1)
FE_SPEED_MODE: 0=10/hdx, 1=10/fdx, 2=100/hdx, 3=100/fdx, 4=Auto(deflt)
Command line options:
  -r: do not write flash, load to DRAM only and launch image

You set variables in ROMMON with the following syntax: **name=value**

The variables you need to set are:

IP_ADDRESS
IP_SUBNET_MASK
DEFAULT_GATEWAY
TFTP_SERVER
TFTP_FILE

I personally recommend using a text editor for this and copying and pasting rather then typing on the CLI. **Note:** These commands are case sensitive.

rommon 11 > **IP_ADDRESS=192.168.1.1**
rommon 12 > **IP_SUBNET_MASK=255.255.255.0**
rommon 13 > **DEFAULT_GATEWAY=192.168.1.1**
rommon 14 > **TFTP_SERVER=192.168.1.100**
rommon 15 > **TFTP_FILE=c2600-adventerprisek9-mz.124-25b.bin**

Once all the variables are set, launching tftpdnld will immediately begin the upgrade process, if you say Yes flash will be erased. Note: this takes a good 20 minutes.

rommon 20 > **tftpdnld**
 IP_ADDRESS: 192.168.1.1
    IP_SUBNET_MASK: 255.255.255.0
    DEFAULT_GATEWAY: 192.168.1.1
    TFTP_SERVER: 192.168.1.100
    TFTP_FILE: c2600-adventerprisek9-mz.124-25b.bin
Invoke this command for disaster recovery only.
    WARNING: all existing data in all partitions on flash will be lost!
    Do you wish to continue? y/n: [n]: **y**
Receiving c2600-adventerprisek9-mz.124-25b.bin from 192.168.1.100
!!!
File reception completed.
Copying file c2600-adventerprisek9-mz.124-25b.bin to flash.
Erasing flash at 0x61fc0000
program flash location 0x61c90000

You can exit rommon mode with the **boot** command which boots the router.
rommon 21 > **boot**

The final method you can use to upgrade a router is **xmodem** which downloads the IOS image through the console cable. As you might imagine, it will take quite a while and should only be used when you have no other option...or when you are paid by the hour (kidding).

rommon 22 > **xmodem**
usage: xmodem [-cyrx] <destination filename>
-c CRC-16
-y ymodem-batch protocol
-r copy image to dram for launch
-x do not launch on download completion

rommon 23 > **xmodem -c c2600-adventerprisek9-mz.124-25b.bin**
Do not start the sending program yet...
File size   Checksum   File name
29957284 bytes (0x1c91ca4) 0x3c42   c2600-adventerprisek9-mz.124-25b.bin
WARNING: All existing data in bootflash will be lost!
Invoke this application only for disaster recovery.
Do you wish to continue? y/n [n]: **y**
Ready to receive file c2600-adventerprisek9-mz.124-25b.bin ...

nd the router starts receiving the image. In just 11 hours and 40 minutes the router will be back up...Yikes!!!

Ready to receive file c2600-adventerprisek9-mz.124-25b.bin ...
Starting xmodem transfer. Press Ctrl+C to cancel.
Transferring c2600-adventerprisek9-mz.124-25b.bin...
0%   41 KB   0 KB/s 11:40:39 ETA   0 Errors

Since the default console speed is 9600 bps, you can make things a bit faster by changing the console speed to a higher value. You can change the console speed from ROMMON by using the **confreg** command.

rommon 28 > **confreg**
Configuration Summary
(Virtual Configuration Register: 0x2102)
enabled are:
load rom after netboot fails
console baud: 9600
boot: image specified by the boot system commands
or default to: cisco2-C2600
do you wish to change the configuration? y/n [n]: y

enable "diagnostic mode"? y/n [n]:
enable "use net in IP bcast address"? y/n [n]:
disable "load rom after netboot fails"? y/n [n]:
enable "use all zero broadcast"? y/n [n]:
enable "break/abort has effect"? y/n [n]:
enable "ignore system config info"? y/n [n]:
change console baud rate? y/n [n]: y
enter rate: 0 = 9600, 1 = 4800, 2 = 1200, 3 = 2400
4 = 19200, 5 = 38400, 6 = 57600, 7 = 115200 [0]: 7
change the boot characteristics? y/n [n]:
 Configuration Summary
(Virtual Configuration Register: 0x3922)
enabled are:
load rom after netboot fails
console baud: 115200
boot: image specified by the boot system commands
or default to: cisco2-C2600
do you wish to change the configuration? y/n [n]:

You must reset or power cycle for new config to take effect.
rommon 29 > **reset**

Remember after you change the console speed you'll need to reconnect with the new settings in your terminal emulator console session. Now our ETA is much lower.

rommon 1 > **xmodem -c c2600-adventerprisek9-mz.124-25b.bin**
Do not start the sending program yet...
File size   Checksum   File name
29957284 bytes (0x1c91ca4) 0x3c42   c2600-adventerprisek9-mz.124-25b.bin
WARNING: All existing data in bootflash will be lost!
Invoke this application only for disaster recovery.
Ready to receive file c2600-adventerprisek9-mz.124-25b.bin ...
Starting xmodem transfer. Press Ctrl+C to cancel.
Transferring c2600-adventerprisek9-mz.124-25b.bin...
1%   157 KB   3 KB/s **02:25:10 ETA** 2 Errors

Cisco Licensing

R1

The purpose of this lab is to explore the basics of Cisco licensing.

Hardware & Configuration Required for this Lab

- One 1841 Cisco router running IOS 15.x

Commands Used in this Lab

license install – Installs a license file to the router or switch
license boot – Tells the router what feature set to boot into
show license udi – Shows the router's serial number and Product ID
show license – Shows detailed licensing information

Inital Configs – Because this lab deals with licensing on a router, the configuration doesn't matter.

R1
!
line con 0
logging synch
exit

In the old days Cisco would handle IOS feature sets by having several different IOS versions each with their own set of features. The main IOS trains that we are concerned with under the CCNA level are:

IP Base – least amount of features
IP Services

Advanced IP Services

Advanced Enterprise Services – The most amount of features

There are other feature sets by they are used for things like VoIP or Service Provider stuff.

By now you're probably wondering "Ok, so what features are in the IP Base feature set and what do I get if I upgrade to Advanced IP Services?" Great question! Cisco has a handy tool that lets you know exactly what features are in each IOS release. It also helps you pick the right IOS for your needs.

Here is the link for the Cisco Feature Navigator
http://tools.cisco.com/ITDIT/CFN/jsp/SearchBySoftware.jsp

The downside to this system is that if you want to change feature sets you have to load the IOS on the router and perform a software upgrade.

With Cisco's latest IOS version 15.x, they borrowed a page from Microsoft's Windows Server playbook and started embracing a Universal image concept. What that means is that you only have to install a universal version of IOS on a Cisco router or switch and then you use license keys to activate the feature set you require. **Note:** Not all Cisco devices running a 15.x IOS use the universal image. It is mainly on this generation of routers: 1900, 2900, 3900 etc.

Once you order a license from Cisco they will send you an email like the one below.

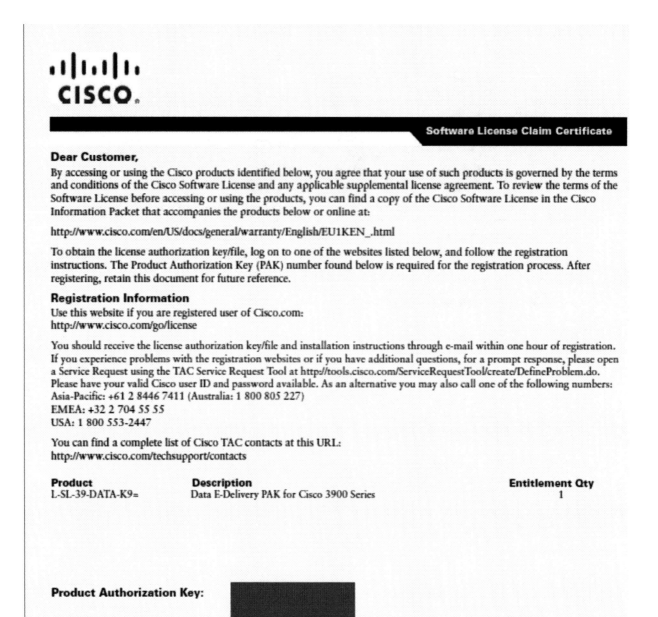

In the email is a Product Activation Key (blocked out sorry!). Next you need go to: www.cisco.com/go/licensing and log in with your Cisco CCO account. Click on **Get New** and then enter your PAK and click **Fulfill**.

Tools & Resources
Product License Registration

View in French   Contact Us   Feedback   Help

| Quickstart | Get New ▾ | Get Existing ▾ | Get Demo | Transfer ▾ | Device Management ▾ | My Information ▾ | Related Tools ▾ |

Get New Licenses From PAKs or Tokens

| 1. Specify PAK | 2. Assign SKUs to Devices | 3. Review |

˅ Get New Licenses From PAKs or Tokens

Enter a Single PAK or Token to fulfill: [Fulfill Single]   How do I ...
                                    Load More PAKs....

˅ Get New Licenses by Loading and Selecting Multiple PAKs

Specify Multiple PAKs to load into the PAKs list to Fulfill: [Load More PAKs]

[Fulfill Selected PAKs]

Group by PAK ▾

PAK	PAK Status	Product Family	SKU Name	Qty	Search
search pak...	search pak status...	search product...	search sku...		

1 Show 10 ▾ records

[Fulfill Selected PAKs]

On the next page you will have supply your routers serial number and your device
Product ID. This can be found with the **show license udi** command.

PDC-EDGE(config)#**do show license udi**

Device# PID   SN   UDI
----

*0   C3900-SPE100/K9   <serial>   C3900-SPE100/K9:<serial>

After going through the process, Cisco will email you a license file with a .lic extension that you will have to load on the router with either a usb thumb drive or via file transfer (TFTP,FTP,HTTP). Then you can use the **license install <path>/<file>** command. **Note:** This command is under the privileged level not the configure level.

Installing licenses from "tftp://10.212.0.115/cisco-pdcedge.lic"

Loading cisco-pdcedge.lic from 10.212.0.115 (via GigabitEthernet0/2): !
[OK - 1152 bytes]
Installing...Feature:datak9...Successful:Supported
1/1 licenses were successfully installed
0/1 licenses were existing licenses
0/1 licenses were failed to install

Finally go into configure mode and type: *license boot module <router type> technology-package <feature set>*. Then save and reboot. Optionally you can use the command *license accept end user agreement* to agree to any EULA messages when you activate features.

PDC-EDGE(config)#**license accept end user agreement**
PDC-EDGE(config)#**license boot module c3900 technology-package datak9**
% use 'write' command to make license boot config take effect on next boot

We can verify what licenses are on the router by looking at the output of a **show version**. Here is the output from the router before I added the license. We can see that a Data Evaluation license was on the router.

PDC-EDGE(config)#**do sh ver | be License**

License Info:

Technology Package License Information for Module:'c3900'

Technology   Technology-package   Technology-package
            Current   Type   Next reboot
----

ipbase   ipbasek9   Permanent   ipbasek9
security   securityk9 Permanent   securityk9
uc   None   None   None
data   datak9   Evaluation   datak9

After the reboot we can see that the data license is now permanent!

PDC-EDGE(config)#**do sh ver | be License**

License Info:

Technology Package License Information for Module:'c3900'

Technology   Technology-package   Technology-package
            Current   Type   Next reboot
----

ipbase   ipbasek9   Permanent   ipbasek9
security   securityk9 Permanent   securityk9
uc   None   None   None
data   datak9   Permanent   datak9

The last useful command for licensing is the *show license* command which shows detailed information on the licenses on the router.

PDC-EDGE#**show license**

Index 1 Feature: ipbasek9
    Period left: Life time
    License Type: Permanent
    License State: Active, In Use
    License Count: Non-Counted
    License Priority: Medium
Index 2 Feature: securityk9
    Period left: Life time
    License Type: Permanent
    License State: Active, In Use
    License Count: Non-Counted
    License Priority: Medium
Index 3 Feature: uck9
    Period left: Not Activated
    Period Used: 0 minute 0 second
    License Type: Evaluation
    License State: Not in Use, EULA not accepted
    License Count: Non-Counted
    License Priority: None
Index 4 Feature: datak9
    Period left: Life time
    License Type: Permanent
    License State: Active, In Use
    License Count: Non-Counted
    License Priority: Medium
Index 5 Feature: gatekeeper
    Period left: Not Activated
    Period Used: 0 minute 0 second
    License Type: Evaluation
    License State: Not in Use, EULA not accepted
    License Count: Non-Counted
    License Priority: None
Index 6 Feature: LI
Index 7 Feature: SSL_VPN
    Period left: Not Activated
    Period Used: 0 minute 0 second
    License Type: Evaluation

License State: Not in Use, EULA not accepted

License Count: 5000/0/0 (Active/In-use/Violation)

License Priority: None

Index 8 Feature: ios-ips-update

Period Used: 0 minute 0 second

License Type: Evaluation

Start Date: N/A, End Date: Dec 31 2025

License State: Not in Use, EULA not accepted

License Count: Non-Counted

License Priority: None

Index 9 Feature: SNASw

Period left: Not Activated

Period Used: 0 minute 0 second

License Type: Evaluation

License State: Not in Use, EULA not accepted

License Count: Non-Counted

License Priority: None

Index 10 Feature: hseck9

Terminal Server Setup

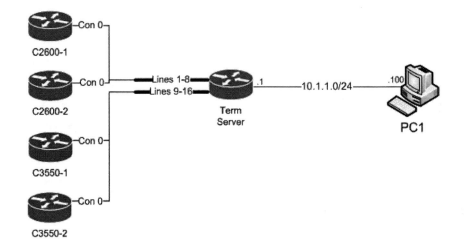

The purpose of this lab is to explore basic terminal services on a Cisco 2509, 2511 or 2512 router. Many people use the term Terminal Server and Access Server to describe the functionality we are about to cover. **Please do not jump to this lab first.** You need the background from the other labs to really understand what is happening in this lab. Even then, it is frustrating and confusing for some at this point in your studies. If that is the case, simply skip the lab and come back to it after chapter 9.

Hardware & Configuration Required for this Lab

- A Cisco terminal server, typically a 2509, 2510, 2511 or 2512 router
- At least one octal cable for a standard terminal server or an 8 pack of rollover cables for the RJ version of the terminal server
- One AUI transceiver if you will telnet into the terminal server (you can simply console in if you do not have a transciever for the terminal server's AUI port)
- One crossover Cat 5 cable for a direct PC to router connection or connect the PC and router to a switch via two straight through Cat 5 cables
- At least one other Cisco device to connect to the terminal server octal cable

---

Commands Used in Lab

show line – Shows the lines on the terminal server, state and stats.
ip hosts - Used to make host entries on the router.
Ctrl+Shift+6 then X – Toggle between devices connected to the terminal server.
clear line #- Used to reset a line and kick off users.

show sessions – Keep track of the devices you are connected.

Initial Configs – Where you see *Initial Configs,* these are basic configuration steps that by now you should be able to perform on the devices by yourself without us detailing them step by step. Generally you simply go into enable and then configuration mode and start the configuration.

Term Server
hostnameTerm-Server
line console 0
logging synch
transport input none
line 1 16
no exec *(stops rouge exec sessions and helps you keep your sanity)*
transport input all
exec-timeout 0 0
interface e0
ip address 10.1.1.1 255.255.255.0
no shut

PC1

In most non SOHO production environments you will use either a terminal server or a trusted host to centrally manage devices. This is sometimes also referred to as reverse telnet. This lab focuses on getting started with Cisco terminal servers which are lightweight routers that are solely used to connect to other devices through their console ports. The advantage of terminal servers is that they are the only means where you can remotely reboot a device and stay connected to it (an example is when you are upgrading the device).

Logging into a terminal server for the first time is pretty much idential to other Cisco devices. The first main task we need to do is create a loopback interface which will be used for reverse telnet into the device.

Term-Server(config)#**int lo0**
Term-Server(config-if)#**ip add 1.1.1.1 255.255.255.255**

Because you will almost never via the console port into a terminal server to do work(except in a lab environment like this which is perfectly fine), we'll take a minute and setup telnet on the device. Then you can use telnet to the terminal server or just connect the console port to the terminal server directly. We will use local authentication to give it a bit more security then otherwise.

Term-Server(config)#**line vty 0 4**
Term-Server(config-line)#**login local**

Next we'll make a username and password, we'll use certificationkits / cisco123 for the login.

Term-Server(config)#**username certificationkits password cisco123**

Let's first review a couple of commands and what they are used for in a terminal server before we cover our actual configuration. The first question students will ask is how do we know which lead is what line? Well, terminal servers use the concept of TTY lines for configuration of each of the octal cable leads. Each one of the numbered octal leads cooresponds to a TTY line on the terminal server. Here is a picture of an octal cable.

Please note if you have two octal cables, line one on the second octal cable will actually be line 9 in the show line output below.

You can view the lines on the terminal server with the **show line** command.

Term-Server#**show line**

	Tty Typ	Tx/Rx	A	Modem	Roty	AccO	Accl	Uses	Noise	Overruns	Int
	0 CTY		-	-	-	-	0	0	0/0		-
*	1 TTY	9600/9600	-	-	-	-	-	1	111	8070/24210	-
	2 TTY	9600/9600	-	-	-	-	-	0	1	0/0	-
	3 TTY	9600/9600	-	-	-	-	-	0	0	0/0	-
*	4 TTY	9600/9600	-	-	-	-	-	0	109	8338/25009	-
	5 TTY	9600/9600	-	-	-	-	-	0	0	0/0	-
	6 TTY	9600/9600	-	-	-	-	-	0	0	0/0	-
	7 TTY	9600/9600	-	-	-	-	-	0	0	0/0	-
	8 TTY	9600/9600	-	-	-	-	-	0	0	0/0	-
	9 TTY	9600/9600	-	-	-	-	-	0	1	0/0	-
	10 TTY	9600/9600	-	-	-	-	-	1	16	24/75	-
	11 TTY	9600/9600	-	-	-	-	-	0	0	0/0	-
	12 TTY	9600/9600	-	-	-	-	-	0	0	0/0	-
	13 TTY	9600/9600	-	-	-	-	-	0	0	0/0	-
	14 TTY	9600/9600	-	-	-	-	-	0	0	0/0	-
	15 TTY	9600/9600	-	-	-	-	-	0	0	0/0	-
	16 TTY	9600/9600	-	-	-	-	-	0	0	0/0	-
	17 AUX	9600/9600	-	-	-	-	-	0	0	0/0	-
*	18 VTY		-	-	-	-	4	0	0/0		-
	19 VTY		-	-	-	-	1	0	0/0		-
	20 VTY		-	-	-	-	0	0	0/0		-
	21 VTY		-	-	-	-	0	0	0/0		-
	22 VTY		-	-	-	-	0	0	0/0		-

By default each line will have a transmit and receive of 9600 bps (this is the speed you have to enter to connect to a Cisco router). The speed can be adjusted if you are trying to connect to other vendor's equipment but we won't get into that for the moment. Because I have two octal cables it shows 16 lines, if you just have one it will just show only 8. Also all TTY lines are in the 20xx range. So if you have a device in TTY 01 you would connect to port 2001. Finally the * means that line is in use, when a line is in use the **Uses** column will change to 1. Only one person can use a console connection at a time.

If you need to clear a line (kick out a user or in otherwords). Reset the line so you can use it. You can use the **clear line** command followed by the line number. We suggest anytime you connect to an access server to go through and clear all the lines. You may have to do it more than once as per Cisco's site as this is sometimes problematic.

Term-Server#**clear line 1**

```
  [confirm]
[OK]
Term-Server#show line
Tty Typ    Tx/Rx    A Modem  Roty AccO Accl  Uses  Noise  Overruns  Int
0 CTY         -  -  -  -  -   0    0    0/0    -
1 TTY  9600/9600 -  -   -  -  -    1   116  8119/24356  -
2 TTY  9600/9600 -  -   -  -  -    0    1    0/0    -
3 TTY  9600/9600 -  -   -  -  -    0    0    0/0    -
*   4 TTY  9600/9600 -  -   -  -  -    0   109  8387/25157  -
5 TTY  9600/9600 -  -   -  -  -    0    0    0/0    -
6 TTY  9600/9600 -  -   -  -  -    0    0    0/0    -
7 TTY  9600/9600 -  -   -  -  -    0    0    0/0    -
8 TTY  9600/9600 -  -   -  -  -    0    0    0/0    -
9 TTY  9600/9600 -  -   -  -  -    0    1    0/0    -
10 TTY  9600/9600 -  -   -  -  -    1   16   24/75    -
11 TTY  9600/9600 -  -   -  -  -    0    0    0/0    -
12 TTY  9600/9600 -  -   -  -  -    0    0    0/0    -
13 TTY  9600/9600 -  -   -  -  -    0    0    0/0    -
14 TTY  9600/9600 -  -   -  -  -    0    0    0/0    -
15 TTY  9600/9600 -  -   -  -  -    0    0    0/0    -
16 TTY  9600/9600 -  -   -  -  -    0    0    0/0    -
```

Now that you know how to mover around a little on a terminal seriver, let's do an actual configuration. We will want to create an IP Host entries on the terminal server that point to the loopback address and the TTY line number you want to connect to. If you are using an octal cable, you will see that they are numbered 1 through 8. .

The syntax for the **ip host** command is: **ip host** <host name> <optional port number> <IP address>. The command can also be used to make quick host tables for your devices to make things like pinging easier if making a proper DNS server is not practical for your needs.

Term-Server(config)#**ip host C2600-1 2001 1.1.1.1**
Term-Server(config)#**ip host C2600-2 2002 1.1.1.1**
Term-Server(config)#**ip host C3550-1 2003 1.1.1.1**
Term-Server(config)#**ip host C3550-2 2004 1.1.1.1**

So for the configuration above you will insert octal cable number 1 into the C2600-1, cable number 2 into the C2600-2, cable number 3 into the C3550-1, and cable number 4 into the C3550-2. Starting to make sense? Finally I recommend setting a password so people may not enter configuration mode and effectively just allow the terminal server to be used as a jump point.

Term-Server(config)#**enable secret Super!!!!S3cr3t**

Let's try this out. Telnet to the terminal server and try to connect to your first device. If you do not have a transceiver to convert the AUI port to an RJ-45 style Ethernet port for your terminal server, simply do this via your serial console session.

User Access Verification
Username: **certificationkits**
Password:
Term-Server#**C2600-1**
Trying C2600-1 (1.1.1.1, 2001)...
% Connection refused by remote host
Term-Server#**clear line 1**
                           ^

% Invalid input detected at '^' marker.

Looks like we have a slight problem, looks like someone has connected to line 1 **again** but the certificationkits user can't clear the line without going into privileged enable mode since you probably don't want someone phoning you everytime they need a line cleared, we can give them permission to clear lines. Permissions are out of the CCNA scope and probably CCNA Security's scope as well. So no need to study this unless it interests you.

Term-Server(config)# **privilege exec level 0 clear line**

The basic logic of the privilege command is to tell the router what commands can run at each privilege level, if you recall there are 2 default privilege levels in Cisco, 0 which is for those in exec mode and 15 for those in privileged exec mode (enable mode). So what we are doing is saying that the **clear line** command can be run in exec mode...Cool, huh?

Term-Server#**clear line 1**
[confirm]
 [OK]

Now it works, back to what we doing originally. The next concept is very important. The way you make your **initial** connection to the remote device is via the **host name**.

Term-Server#**c2600-1**
 Trying C2600-1 (1.1.1.1, **2001**)... Open
2611XM>

Once we are connected to the first device, in my case its one of my 2611XMs, we can configure it however we need to. If we need to connect to another device we can use the following key sequence **Ctrl + Shift + 6** then press **X**. That brings you **back** to your **Terminal Server**. This is a very important concept.

The **Ctrl + Shift + 6** then press **X** key sequence takes a little bit of time to get used to the key strokes. It is probably the most difficult thing for a new terminal or access server administrator to get used to. So again, that brought us **back** to the terminal server.

```
2611XM>
Term-Server#c3550-1
Trying C3550-1 (1.1.1.1, 2003)... Open
        C3550-1>
Term-Server#
```

You can keep track of what you are connected to with **show sessions**.

```
Term-Server#show sessions
   Conn Host        Address      Byte  Idle Conn Name
     1 c2600-1      1.1.1.1        0    1   c2600-1
   * 2 c3550-1      1.1.1.1        0    0   c3550-1
```

The Next Two Paragraphs Are Super Important!
When you need to reconnect to a device once you started a session you can use the **resume** command followed by either the connection number or the host name.

Important note – If you use the host name here(for example: c2600-1), you will get a %Connection refused by remote host error. Why? Because the terminal server already has an open connection with the router as we simply suspened the session when we bounced back to the terminal server with the **Ctrl + Shift + 6** then press **X** key sequence. Now if we would have terminated the session then you would have needed to recreate it by using the host name. This concept will save you hours of pulling your hair out on why you can sometimes connect to a remote device and other times cannot.

```
Term-Server#resume 1
 [Resuming connection 1 to c2600-1 ... ]
2611XM>
```

When you are done, you will need to disconnect from the devices to avoid people having to clear the line afterwards. This is done with the **disconnect** command, just like the resume command you can either enter the connection number or the host name.

```
Term-Server#disconnect 1
Closing connection to c2600-1 [confirm]
Term-Server#disconnect c3550-1
Closing connection to c3550-1 [confirm]

Term-Server#show sessions
% No connections open
```

And that is a terminal server in a nut shell. You won't be tested on them very much if at all in the CCNA exam. However you will eventually use them in the real world and it's handy to know how to at least setup the basics.

Troubleshooting Procedure

Follow these instructions to troubleshoot your configuration.

If you cannot connect to the router of your choice with a name configured in the **ip host** command check:

1. Check whether the port address is configured correctly.
2. Verify whether the address (interface) used for the reverse Telnet is up/up. The output of the **show ip interface brief**command provides this information. Cisco recommends you to use loopbacks because they are always up.
3. Ensure that you have the correct type of cabling. For example, you are using rollover cables with an RJ version access server and not patch cables.
4. Establish a Telnet connection to the IP address port to test direct connectivity. You must telnet from both an external device and the terminal server. For example, **telnet 172.21.1.1 2003**.
5. Ensure that you have the **transport input telnet** command under the line for the target device. The target device is the device that is connected to the terminal server.
6. Use a PC/dumb terminal to connect directly to the console of the target router. The target router is the device connected to the terminal server. This step helps you identify the presence of a port issue.
7. If you are disconnected, check timeouts. You can remove or adjust timeouts.

Static Routing

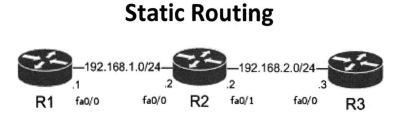

R1 fa0/0 —192.168.1.0/24— fa0/0 R2 fa0/1 —192.168.2.0/24— fa0/0 R3
.1 .2 .2 .3

The purpose of this lab is to explore basic routing and active connectivity between several routers. Please make sure you erase any configuration on your routers before starting this lab.

Hardware & Configuration Required for this Lab

- One Cisco router with two Ethernet interfaces
- Two Cisco routers with one Ethernet interface
- Two Ethernet crossover cables

The first step in getting connectivity is configuring IP addresses on all the interfaces and enabling them. In this lab, we are going to configure the routers to talk to each other over the Ethernet interfaces. This is considered a LAN port. You will see in the RIP Routing lab we will use a combination of LAN and WAN(the WAN ports are serial interfaces) interfaces which require some different configuration steps. Finally, you see that we will use combinations of LAN and WAN interfaces to communicate between routers in our labs to provide you with a more real world scenario and experience.

Note: When you connect the routers via LAN ports, you do not need to set which side will be DCE via the clock rate command. But when we get to WAN ports, you will need to set the DCE device via the clock rate command.

R1(config)#**int fa0/0**
R1(config-if)#**ip add 192.168.1.1 255.255.255.0**
R1(config-if)#**no shut**
R1(config-if)#
*Mar 1 00:07:49.403: %LINK-3-UPDOWN: Interface FastEthernet0/0, changed state to up
*Mar 1 00:07:50.403: %LINEPROTO-5-UPDOWN: Line protocol on Interface FastEthernet0/0, changed state to up

By default console output will not be synchronous meaning that log messages will be merged with your command line as seen above when we typed the **exit** command it was merged with the interface status. To stop this annoying behavior we can add the command **logging synchronous** under **line console 0**, most people add this to all routers for convenience.

R1(config)#**line console 0**
R1(config-line)#**logging synch**

Let's finish up configuring the other routers.

R2(config)#**line con 0**
R2(config-line)#**logging synch**
R2(config-line)#**exit**
R2(config)#**int fa0/0**
R2(config-if)#**ip add 192.168.1.2 255.255.255.0**
R2(config-if)#**no shut**
R2(config-if)#
*Mar 1 00:15:47.619: %LINK-3-UPDOWN: Interface FastEthernet0/0, changed state to up
*Mar 1 00:15:48.619: %LINEPROTO-5-UPDOWN: Line protocol on Interface FastEthernet0/0, changed state to up
R2(config-if)#**int fa0/1**
R2(config-if)#**ip add 192.168.2.2 255.255.255.0**
R2(config-if)#**no shut**
R2(config-if)#
*Mar 1 00:16:08.319: %LINK-3-UPDOWN: Interface FastEthernet0/1, changed state to up
*Mar 1 00:16:09.319: %LINEPROTO-5-UPDOWN: Line protocol on Interface FastEthernet0/1, changed state to up

And finally R3.
R3(config)#**line console 0**
R3(config-line)#**logging synch**
R3(config-line)#**exit**
R3(config)#**int fa0/0**
R3(config-if)#**ip add 192.168.2.3 255.255.255.0**
R3(config-if)#**no shut**
R3(config-if)#
*Mar 1 00:20:22.063: %LINK-3-UPDOWN: Interface FastEthernet0/0, changed state to up
*Mar 1 00:20:23.063: %LINEPROTO-5-UPDOWN: Line protocol on Interface FastEthernet0/0, changed state to up

Checking the routing table
Now that we have the links up, let's have a look at the routing tables.
R1#**show ip route**
   Codes: C - connected, S - static, R - RIP, M - mobile, B - BGP
   D - EIGRP, EX - EIGRP external, O - OSPF, IA - OSPF inter area
   N1 - OSPF NSSA external type 1, N2 - OSPF NSSA external type 2
   E1 - OSPF external type 1, E2 - OSPF external type 2
   i - IS-IS, su - IS-IS summary, L1 - IS-IS level-1, L2 - IS-IS level-2
   ia - IS-IS inter area, * - candidate default, U - per-user static route

  o - ODR, P - periodic downloaded static route
Gateway of last resort is not set
C   192.168.1.0/24 is directly connected, FastEthernet0/0

The routing table is heart of any router. It provides a list of all the routes the router knows about along with the next-hop used to reach them. Initially a router will only know about its directly connected interfaces. These routes will have a **C** next to so show it is a connected route.

If we try to ping R2 from R1 we can see that is successful because the two interfaces are directly connected and in the same subnet.

R1#**ping 192.168.1.2**
Type escape sequence to abort.
  Sending 5, 100-byte ICMP Echos to 192.168.1.2, timeout is 2 seconds:
  .!!!!
  Success rate is 80 percent (4/5), round-trip min/avg/max = 108/147/192 ms

But if we were to try to ping R3 from R1 we can see that it fails because R1's routing table has no knowledge of the 192.168.2.0/24 network

R1#**ping 192.168.2.2**
Type escape sequence to abort.
  Sending 5, 100-byte ICMP Echos to 192.168.2.2, timeout is 2 seconds:
  .....
  Success rate is 0 percent (0/5)

If we enable debugging on R1 we can see confirm that the pings are failing because of no route.

R1#**debug ip packet**
  IP packet debugging is on
 R1#ping 192.168.2.2
Type escape sequence to abort.
  Sending 5, 100-byte ICMP Echos to 192.168.2.2, timeout is 2 seconds:
IP: s=0.0.0.0 (local), d=192.168.2.2, len 128, unroutable
IP: s=0.0.0.0 (local), d=192.168.2.2, len 128, unroutable
IP: s=0.0.0.0 (local), d=192.168.2.2, len 128, unroutable
IP: s=0.0.0.0 (local), d=192.168.2.2, len 128, unroutable
IP: s=0.0.0.0 (local), d=192.168.2.2, len 128, unroutable
  Success rate is 0 percent (0/5)

Debugging is very useful for troubleshooting issues as it shows what is actually happening on the router. Care must be taken when using on production environments as if the network is busy the debug can quickly overrun the router.

Default Routing and Static Routes

To solve our reachability issue we need to tell R1 now to reach the networks it doesn't know about. One of the simplest ways to do so is with default routing. Default routing is simply a route that says *"If I don't know how to reach something, send it to this directly connected neighbor"* Default routes are actually very common, in fact pretty much any residential ISP service will send customers a default route via the modem to allow connectivity this is much more efficient then sending all their customer's the full internet routing table which is currently over 280,000 routes!!!

To configure a default route, you would use the command **ip route 0.0.0.0 0.0.0.0 next-hop <next-hop ip>.** The command is actually a static route (we'll get to those later) that says to get to 0.0.0.0/0 (means all routes) send it to this next hop.

R1(config)#**ip route 0.0.0.0 0.0.0.0 192.168.1.2**

Checking the routing table for R1 again we can see that there is now a static route listed, and it says the Gateway of last resort is 192.168.1.2.

Important Note: We are about to introduce below the **do** command. This command became available in some of the 12.2 releases. So if you are running an IOS version that does not support the do command, simply upgrade to a newer version of IOS and you will more than likely see it work. **Exam Alert:** The do command allows you to run privileged commands in **global configuration** mode. We do this as it is much easier to run the various show and ping commands in this manner than backing all the way out of the IOS hierarchy and then coming back in. But be aware of the context in which you would generally perform these commands in privileged mode so you do not get tripped up on the exam.

R1(config)#**do show ip route**
  Codes: C - connected, S - static, R - RIP, M - mobile, B - BGP
  D - EIGRP, EX - EIGRP external, O - OSPF, IA - OSPF inter area
  N1 - OSPF NSSA external type 1, N2 - OSPF NSSA external type 2
  E1 - OSPF external type 1, E2 - OSPF external type 2
  i - IS-IS, su - IS-IS summary, L1 - IS-IS level-1, L2 - IS-IS level-2
  ia - IS-IS inter area, * - candidate default, U - per-user static route
  o - ODR, P - periodic downloaded static route
Gateway of last resort is 192.168.1.2 to network 0.0.0.0
C   192.168.1.0/24 is directly connected, FastEthernet0/0
  S* 0.0.0.0/0 [1/0] via 192.168.1.2

Now if we try to ping R2's Fa0/1 interface we can see that it is now successful.

R1(config)#**do ping 192.168.2.2**
Type escape sequence to abort.
  Sending 5, 100-byte ICMP Echos to 192.168.2.2, timeout is 2 seconds:

!!!!!

However if we try to ping R3 we find it still fails.

R1(config)#**do ping 192.168.2.3**
Type escape sequence to abort.
   Sending 5, 100-byte ICMP Echos to 192.168.2.3, timeout is 2 seconds:
   .....

Hmm let's think for a minute about why that isn't working. Let's turn on a debug on R1
to see if we can figure out whats happening.

R1#**debug ip packet**
IP packet debugging is on
R1#**ping 192.168.2.3**
Type escape sequence to abort.
   Sending 5, 100-byte ICMP Echos to 192.168.2.3, timeout is 2 seconds:
IP: tableid=0, s=192.168.1.1 (local), d=192.168.2.3 (FastEthernet0/0), routed via FIB
IP: s=192.168.1.1 (local), d=192.168.2.3 (FastEthernet0/0), len 128, sending.
IP: tableid=0, s=192.168.1.1 (local), d=192.168.2.3 (FastEthernet0/0), routed via FIB
IP: s=192.168.1.1 (local), d=192.168.2.3 (FastEthernet0/0), len 128, sending.
IP: tableid=0, s=192.168.1.1 (local), d=192.168.2.3 (FastEthernet0/0), routed via FIB
IP: s=192.168.1.1 (local), d=192.168.2.3 (FastEthernet0/0), len 128, sending.
IP: tableid=0, s=192.168.1.1 (local), d=192.168.2.3 (FastEthernet0/0), routed via FIB
IP: s=192.168.1.1 (local), d=192.168.2.3 (FastEthernet0/0), len 128, sending.
IP: tableid=0, s=192.168.1.1 (local), d=192.168.2.3 (FastEthernet0/0), routed via FIB
IP: s=192.168.1.1 (local), d=192.168.2.3 (FastEthernet0/0), len 128, sending.
   Success rate is 0 percent (0/5)

Looking at the debug output we can see that it is sending a ping with a source of
192.168.1.1 to the destination 192.168.2.3 and its being sent out the interface Fa0/0,
that looks alright, let's check out R3 and see what it's doing.

R3#**debug ip packet**
   IP packet debugging is on
   R3#
   IP: tableid=0, s=192.168.1.1 (FastEthernet0/0), d=192.168.2.3 (FastEthernet0/0), routed via
RIB
   IP: s=192.168.1.1 (FastEthernet0/0), d=192.168.2.3 (FastEthernet0/0), len 128, rcvd 3
   IP: s=192.168.2.3 (local), d=192.168.1.1, len 128, **unroutable**

We can see that when R3 tries to respond to R1's pings it has no idea how to send them
back because it doesn't have a route to 192.168.1.0 thus the packets are unroutable.
This is a good lession because routing needs to be bi-directional for routing to work. To
fix this lets have add a static route.

The syntax for a static route is the same as a default route except it is more specific. You simply replace the 0.0.0.0 0.0.0.0 with the network and the subnet mask of what you want to reach.

R3(config)#**ip route 192.168.1.0 255.255.255.0 192.168.2.2**

Checking the routing table on R3 we can see that the 192.168.1.0 route is now listed but the gateway of last resort is not set.

R3(config)#**do show ip route**
  Codes: C - connected, S - static, R - RIP, M - mobile, B - BGP
 D - EIGRP, EX - EIGRP external, O - OSPF, IA - OSPF inter area
 N1 - OSPF NSSA external type 1, N2 - OSPF NSSA external type 2
 E1 - OSPF external type 1, E2 - OSPF external type 2
 i - IS-IS, su - IS-IS summary, L1 - IS-IS level-1, L2 - IS-IS level-2
 ia - IS-IS inter area, * - candidate default, U - per-user static route
 o - ODR, P - periodic downloaded static route
Gateway of last resort is not set
S   192.168.1.0/24 [1/0] via 192.168.2.2
  C   192.168.2.0/24 is directly connected, FastEthernet0/0

Now if we try to ping from R1 to R3 we can see it works just fine.

R1#**ping 192.168.2.3**
Type escape sequence to abort.
  Sending 5, 100-byte ICMP Echos to 192.168.2.3, timeout is 2 seconds:
  !!!!!
  Success rate is 100 percent (5/5), round-trip min/avg/max = 316/326/352 ms

Static Routes Review

Questions:

1. When there is a single link in or out of the network, it is known as a _____ _____.

2. At the end of an 'ip route' static route command, it is possible to add a parameter to assign this particular static route a higher administrative distance than the default administrative distance of 1. This is called a _____ _____ _____.

3. If an administrative distance is not specified, a Cisco router uses the _____ _____ _____ for static route (1).

4. The best way to verify a static or default route configuration is by checking that the route is in the _____ _____.

5. The command to view the IP routing table is _____ _____ _____.

6. Enter the command to set up a static route to 192.168.1.0/24, where the next hop address is 192.168.2.2: _____.

7. What is the default administrative distance of a static route where the next hop specified is the IP address of a neighboring router? _____.

Answers:

1. stub network
2. floating static route
3. default administrative distance
4. routing table
5. show ip route
6. Ip route 192.168.1.0 255.255.255.0 192.168.2.2
7. The default administrative distance of a static route pointing to a neighbor's IP address is 1.

Default Routing

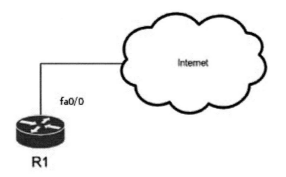

The purpose of this lab is to explore a common default routing scenario

---

Hardware & Configuration Required for this Lab

- One Cisco router with one Ethernet interface
- One straight through Cat 5 cable
- Internet connection

Commands Used in this Lab

ip address dhcp- Tells the router to get its IP via DHCP
ip route - Used to configure static and default routes
show ip route- Displays the routing table

Initial Configs - Where you see *Initial Configs,* these are basic configuration steps that by now you should be able to perform on the devices by yourself without us detailing them step by step. Generally you simply go into enable and then configuration mode and start the configuration.

R1
hostname R1
line console 0
logging synch

A default route on a router is simply a route that the router uses when it doesn't know how to get to something. PCs usually call these default gateways where if the PC doesn't know how to reach a network it sends the packets to the default gateway router and hopes for the best. Most internet connections use this as well where the ISP modem will simply assign you an IP address and a default gateway to allow you to get access to the internet.

This is a simple real world lab to show you how to configure basic internet connectivity. Most residential internet connections are configured via DHCP for simplicity for the customer who normally isn't very intelligent when it comes to technology. So routers have the ability for interfaces to be configured via DHCP, rather than statically setting the address. This is done with the **ip address dhcp** command under the interface.

R1(config)#**int fa0/0**
R1(config-if)#**ip address dhcp**
R1(config-if)#**no shut**
*Mar 1 00:01:36.499: %LINK-3-UPDOWN: Interface FastEthernet0/0, changed state to up
*Mar 1 00:01:37.499: %LINEPROTO-5-UPDOWN: Line protocol on Interface FastEthernet0/0, changed state to up
*Mar 1 00:01:48.811: %DHCP-6-ADDRESS_ASSIGN: Interface FastEthernet0/0 **assigned DHCP address 10.10.2.63**

After you receive an IP address via DHCP, the router will also add a default route to the routing table. We will talk about DHCP in later labs, but whatever is setup as the default gateway in the DHCP offer will be the router's default route. We can see this by checking **show ip route** notice that there is a 0.0.0.0/0 static route and the **gateway of last resort** is set to 10.10.2.1 which is my Internet router.

Office(config-if)#**do sh ip route**
    Codes: C - connected, S - static, R - RIP, M - mobile, B - BGP
    D - EIGRP, EX - EIGRP external, O - OSPF, IA - OSPF inter area
    N1 - OSPF NSSA external type 1, N2 - OSPF NSSA external type 2
    E1 - OSPF external type 1, E2 - OSPF external type 2
    i - IS-IS, su - IS-IS summary, L1 - IS-IS level-1, L2 - IS-IS level-2
    ia - IS-IS inter area, * - candidate default, U - per-user static route
    o - ODR, P - periodic downloaded static route
Gateway of last resort is 10.10.2.1 to network 0.0.0.0
    10.0.0.0/24 is subnetted, 1 subnets
C   10.10.2.0 is directly connected, FastEthernet0/0
S* 0.0.0.0/0 [254/0] via 10.10.2.1

Now we can ping stuff on the internet such as google.com.
Office#**ping google.com**
Translating "google.com"...domain server (4.2.2.2) [OK]
Type escape sequence to abort.
Sending 5, 100-byte ICMP Echos to 74.125.47.104, timeout is 2 seconds:
!!!!!

Success rate is 100 percent (5/5), round-trip min/avg/max = 76/95/112 ms

Now let's add the default route, but first we will remove the previous IP information with the **no ip address** command as this will remove all of the DHCP configuration.

R1(config)#**int fa0/0**
R1(config-if)#**no ip add**

Notice how the **Gateway of last resort** is no longer set.

Office(config-if)#**do sh ip route**
    Codes: C - connected, S - static, R - RIP, M - mobile, B - BGP
    D - EIGRP, EX - EIGRP external, O - OSPF, IA - OSPF inter area
    N1 - OSPF NSSA external type 1, N2 - OSPF NSSA external type 2
    E1 - OSPF external type 1, E2 - OSPF external type 2
    i - IS-IS, su - IS-IS summary, L1 - IS-IS level-1, L2 - IS-IS level-2
    ia - IS-IS inter area, * - candidate default, U - per-user static route
    o - ODR, P - periodic downloaded static route
Gateway of last resort is not set

Now let's add a static IP on our interface.

R1(config)#**int fa0/0**
R1(config-if)#**ip address 10.10.2.63 255.255.255.0**
R1(config-if)#**no shut**

To add a default route we simply need to configure a static route like normal but the network and mask will be all zeros.

R1(config)#**ip route 0.0.0.0 0.0.0.0 10.10.2.1**

Now we can see our default route is back.

R1(config-if)#**do sh ip route**
    Codes: C - connected, S - static, R - RIP, M - mobile, B - BGP
    D - EIGRP, EX - EIGRP external, O - OSPF, IA - OSPF inter area
    N1 - OSPF NSSA external type 1, N2 - OSPF NSSA external type 2
    E1 - OSPF external type 1, E2 - OSPF external type 2
    i - IS-IS, su - IS-IS summary, L1 - IS-IS level-1, L2 - IS-IS level-2
    ia - IS-IS inter area, * - candidate default, U - per-user static route
    o - ODR, P - periodic downloaded static route
Gateway of last resort is 10.10.2.1 to network 0.0.0.0
    10.0.0.0/24 is subnetted, 1 subnets
C   10.10.2.0 is directly connected, FastEthernet0/0
S* 0.0.0.0/0 [254/0] via 10.10.2.1

We won't have DNS anymore because it was configured with DHCP earlier, we can manually add DNS servers on the router with the **ip name-server <DNS1> <DNS2>**. I personally use 4.2.2.2 and 4.2.2.3 for DNS servers on the job because it's easy to remember.

R1(config)#**ip name-server 4.2.2.2 4.2.2.3**

And we can ping on the internet again.

R1(config)#**do ping google.com**
Translating "google.com"...domain server (4.2.2.2) [OK]
Type escape sequence to abort.
Sending 5, 100-byte ICMP Echos to 74.125.45.100, timeout is 2 seconds:
!!!!!
Success rate is 100 percent (5/5), round-trip min/avg/max = 80/94/112 ms

Default routing can also be handy in branch office scenarios where rather then configuring full routing which might require expensive equipment; you can send a smaller cheaper router with a default route to the main office to establish connectivity.

EIGRP Routing

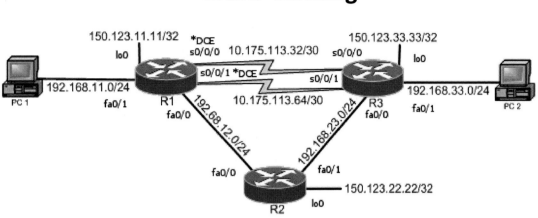

The purpose of this lab is to explore the functionality of the EIGRP routing protocol.

Hardware & Configuration Required for this Lab

- Two Cisco routers with two Fast Ethernet interfaces and two serial ports
- One Cisco router with two Fast Ethernet interfaces
- Two crossover Cat 5 cables for router to router
- Two DTE/DCE back to back cables
- Two PCs to connect to the routers
- Two crossover Cat 5 cables for PC to Router or four straight through Cat 5 cables if you put a switch in between them
- **Special Note:** If you do not have three routers with dual Ethernet ports and two PCs, it's ok. Simply do not configure the 192.168.11.0 subnet on R1 and the 192.168.33.0 subnet on R3. Then do your pings from R1 & R3 respectively in place of the PCs and the lab will still work fine.

Commands Used in this Lab

router eigrp – Enables eigrp on the router
show ip eigrp topology - Displays the eigrp topology table and route information
clock rate – Sets clock speed on a WAN serial link
bandwidth – Logial setting of the bandwidth metric on a link
delay – Logical setting of the delay metric on a link
variance <multiplier> - Used to tell the router what multiple of the feasible distance should be considered for unequal load balancing

ip hello-interval eigrp – sets the hello time on an eigrp interface
ip hold-time eigrp – sets the hold time on an eirgrp interface
debug ip eigrp – Displays route table updates and associated messages

---

Initial Configs - Where you see *Initial Configs,* these are basic configuration steps that by now you should be able to perform on the devices by yourself without us detailing them step by step. Generally you simply go into enable and then configuration mode and start the configuration. Keep in mind the way to address your interfaces may be a bit different than what we have here. You can always use the show interface command to see what the nomenclature is for the serial ports you have installed.

R1
hostname R1
line con 0
logging synch
exit
int loopback 0
ip add 150.123.11.11 255.255.255.255
int fa0/0
ip add 192.168.12.1 255.255.255.0
no shut
int fa0/1
ip add 192.168.11.1 255.255.255.0
no shut
int s0/0/0
ip add 10.175.113.33 255.255.255.252
clock rate 128000 (if you have a WIC-1DSU-TI module(don't confuse this with a WIC-1T, use the *service-module T1 clock source internal* command instead)).
no shut
int s0/0/1
ip add 10.175.113.65 255.255.255.252
clock rate 128000 (if you have a WIC-1DSU-TI module(don't confuse this with a WIC-1T, use the *service-module T1 clock source internal* command instead)).
no shut

R2
hostname R2
line con 0
logging synch
exit
int loopback 0
ip add 150.123.22.22 255.255.255.255
int fa0/0

ip add 192.168.12.2 255.255.255.0
no shut
int fa0/1
ip add 192.168.23.2 255.255.255.0
no shut

R3
hostname R3
line con 0
logging synch
exit
int loopback 0
ip add 150.123.33.33 255.255.255.255
int fa0/0
ip add 192.168.23.3 255.255.255.0
no shut
int fa0/1
ip add 192.168.33.1 255.255.255.0
no shut
int s0/0/0
ip add 10.175.113.34 255.255.255.252
(If you have a WIC-1DSU-TI module(don't confuse this with a WIC-1T, use the *service-module T1 clock source line* command here)).
no shut
int s0/0/1
ip add 10.175.113.66 255.255.255.252
(If you have a WIC-1DSU-TI module(don't confuse this with a WIC-1T, use the *service-module T1 clock source line* command here)).
no shut

| PC-1 | PC-2 |

EIGRP is Cisco's proprietary routing protocol. It is a hybrid protocol meaning it is a mix between distance vector (i.e. RIP) and link state protocols (i.e. OSPF, ISIS).

To enable EIGRP on a router you use its router command **router eigrp <AS>**. EIGRP requires an Autonomous system number because that is how it determines what routers belong to the same EIGRP routing domain. For example a router with an EIGRP AS of 1 and another with an AS of 150 will not form adjacency they will simply ignore each other.

Note: AS numbers are unique to your own network, so you pick whatever number makes sense to you.

Like RIP, EIGRP is easy to configure basic functionality once again it uses the **network** statement to control what interfaces are going to run EIGRP.

The network statement uses the following syntax:
network <classful network>

The network statement is still classful so if you enter **network 10.0.0.0** any interface with an IP in the range of 10.0.0.1 - 10.255.255.254 will be added to EIGRP. You can optionally add a wildcard mask to the network statement to be more selective. **network 10.1.1.1 0.0.0.0** for example will only enable EIGRP on an interface with the IP 10.1.1.1 instead of the whole range.

Wildcard masks are used with Access-lists and several other functions as well. They are the inverse of a subnet mask excluding the network bit. In a subnet mask the 1 bit is ignored, in a wildcard the 0 bit is ignored. Here is a table showing the common Class C wildcard masks.

Subnet Mask	Size of Network	Wildcard Mask
255.255.255.0	256	0.0.0.255
255.255.255.128	128	0.0.0.127
255.255.255.192	64	0.0.0.63
255.255.255.224	32	0.0.0.31
255.255.255.240	16	0.0.0.15
255.255.255.248	8	0.0.0.7
255.255.255.252	4	0.0.0.3
255.255.255.254	2	0.0.0.1
255.255.255.255	1	0.0.0.0

Let's enable EIGRP on all of routers for all interfaces. We will use EIGRP AS 123. For now let's just use the classful statements. To prove it's using classful statements lets enter R1's 10 network as 10.10.10.0.

```
R1(config)#router eigrp 123
R1(config-router)#network 10.10.10.0
R1(config-router)#network 192.168.11.0
R1(config-router)#network 192.168.12.0
R1(config-router)#network 150.123.0.0

R2(config)#router eigrp 123
R2(config-router)#network 10.0.0.0
R2(config-router)#network 192.168.12.0
R2(config-router)#network 192.168.23.0
R2(config-router)#network 150.123.0.0

R3(config)#router eigrp 123
R3(config-router)#network 10.0.0.0
R3(config-router)#network 192.168.23.0
R3(config-router)#network 192.168.33.0
R3(config-router)#network 150.123.0.0
```

One thing you will notice is that EIGRP is a very fast protocol. It almost immediately forms adjacency once it's configured on both ends. When EIGRP adjacencies are formed, messages similar to the following will be displayed.

```
%DUAL-5-NBRCHANGE: IP-EIGRP 123: Neighbor 10.175.113.34 (Serial0/0/0) is up: new adjacency
%DUAL-5-NBRCHANGE: IP-EIGRP 123: Neighbor 10.175.113.66 (Serial0/0/1) is up: new adjacency
```

A quick way to show which interfaces are participating in EIGRP is with the **show ip protocol** command. Example output is below:

```
  R1#show ip protocol
 Routing Protocol is "eigrp  123 "
   Outgoing update filter list for all interfaces is not set
   Incoming update filter list for all interfaces is not set
   Default networks flagged in outgoing updates
   Default networks accepted from incoming updates
   EIGRP metric weight K1=1, K2=0, K3=1, K4=0, K5=0
   EIGRP maximum hopcount 100
   EIGRP maximum metric variance 1
 Redistributing: eigrp 123
   Automatic network summarization is in effect
   Automatic address summarization:
     150.123.0.0/16 for FastEthernet0/0, FastEthernet0/1, Serial0/0/1, Serial0/0/0
       Summarizing with metric 128256
     10.0.0.0/8 for Loopback0, FastEthernet0/0, FastEthernet0/1
       Summarizing with metric 2169856
 Output truncated
```

A handy command to see what adjacencies are up and running is: **show ip eigrp neighbors**. It will show the neighbor IP, what interface it was learned on. Troubleshooting wise the most useful column is the **Q Cnt** which is the Queue Count, basically if the number is not zero something is wrong in your network.

```
 R1#show ip eigrp neighbors
 IP-EIGRP neighbors for process 123
 H  Address          Interface    Hold Uptime    SRTT  RTO  Q  Seq
                                   (sec)          (ms)       Cnt Num
 0  192.168.12.2     Fa0/0        12   00:02:30 40     1000 0  8
 1  10.175.113.66 Se0/0/1         10   00:02:22 40     1000 0  14
 2  10.175.113.34 Se0/0/0         14   00:02:22 40     1000 0  16
```

You can also use **show ip eigrp interfaces** to see a quick summary of what interfaces are running EIGRP and how many peers are learned on each interface.

```
 R1#show ip eigrp interfaces
```

Interface	Peers	Xmit Queue Un/Reliable	Mean SRTT	Pacing Time Un/Reliable	Multicast Flow Timer	Pending Routes
Lo0	0	0/0	1236	0/10	0	0
Fa0/0	1	0/0	1236	0/10	0	0
Fa0/1	0	0/0	1236	0/10	0	0
Se0/0/1	1	0/0	1236	0/10	0	0
Se0/0/0	1	0/0	1236	0/10	0	0

Another somewhat helpful show command is: **show ip eigrp traffic** which shows traffic statistics for EIGRP.

R3#**show ip eigrp traffic 123**
IP-EIGRP Traffic Statistics for process 123
  Hellos sent/received: 494/295
  Updates sent/received: 9/11
  Queries sent/received: 0/0
  Replies sent/received: 0/0
  Acks sent/received: 11/6
  Input queue high water mark 1, 0 drops
  SIA-Queries sent/received: 0/0
  SIA-Replies sent/received: 0/0

Finally let's have a look at the routing table, we can see by default EIGRP is auto-summarizing routes to their classful boundary, let's take a minute and see what kind of fun this causes. EIGRP routes will start with a **D** you can also just show EIGRP routes with **show ip route eigrp. Important Note:** If you do not have as many interfaces on your routers, your output may be slightly different.

R1#**show ip route**
Codes: C - connected, S - static, I - IGRP, R - RIP, M - mobile, B - BGP
       D - EIGRP, EX - EIGRP external, O - OSPF, IA - OSPF inter area
       N1 - OSPF NSSA external type 1, N2 - OSPF NSSA external type 2
       E1 - OSPF external type 1, E2 - OSPF external type 2, E - EGP
       i - IS-IS, L1 - IS-IS level-1, L2 - IS-IS level-2, ia - IS-IS inter area
       * - candidate default, U - per-user static route, o - ODR
       P - periodic downloaded static route

Gateway of last resort is not set

     10.0.0.0/8 is variably subnetted, 3 subnets, 2 masks
D   10.0.0.0/8 is a summary, 00:08:37, Null0
C   10.175.113.32/30 is directly connected, Serial0/0/0
C   10.175.113.64/30 is directly connected, Serial0/0/1
     150.123.0.0/16 is variably subnetted, 2 subnets, 2 masks
D   150.123.0.0/16 is a summary, 00:08:37, Null0
C   150.123.11.11/32 is directly connected, Loopback0
C   192.168.11.0/24 is directly connected, FastEthernet0/1
C   192.168.12.0/24 is directly connected, FastEthernet0/0
D   192.168.23.0/24 [90/30720] via 192.168.12.2, 00:08:36, FastEthernet0/0
D   192.168.33.0/24 [90/33280] via 192.168.12.2, 00:08:36, FastEthernet0/0

Let's focus on 2 routes, the 192.168.23.0 route and the loopback network. From R1 we can see that we can reach the 192.168.23.0 network with a ping which is what we would expect.

R1#**ping 192.168.23.3**
Type escape sequence to abort.
Sending 5, 100-byte ICMP Echos to 192.168.23.3, timeout is 2 seconds:
!!!!!
Success rate is 100 percent (5/5), round-trip min/avg/max = 0/2/6 ms

However we can see that we can't reach either of the loopback networks from R1.

R1#**ping 150.123.22.22**
Type escape sequence to abort.
    Sending 5, 100-byte ICMP Echos to 150.123.22.22, timeout is 2 seconds:
    .....
Success rate is 0 percent (0/5)

R1#**ping 150.123.33.33**
Type escape sequence to abort.
    Sending 5, 100-byte ICMP Echos to 150.123.33.33, timeout is 2 seconds:
    .....
Success rate is 0 percent (0/5)

To figure out why this is happening, let's have another look at the routing table, this time, just the loopback networks. We see two routes, one for our loopback0 interface and the other a summary route pointing to Null0.

Null0 is a special interface that simply discards anything sent to it, EIGRP uses it when making summaries because the idea is that with longest match routing. The router will never use its own summary routes but instead will use any shorter route. The problem is that with auto-summary, we don't have any longer match routes. In the next few show commands, we are going to just show you the portion of the output to focus on starting now.

R1#**show ip route | begin 150.123.0.0** *(on most 12.4 and later IOS, use the | sec command)*
    150.123.0.0/16 is variably subnetted, 2 subnets, 2 masks
D   150.123.0.0/16 is a summary, 19:12:40, Null0
C   150.123.11.11/32 is directly connected, Loopback0

Since the loopback is directly connected, the router will make a summary route to advertise to R2 and R3 and point it to Null0. When it receives the 150.123.0.0/16 route from the other routes, R1 sees it already has a directly connected network with the address 150.123.0.0/16 (The Null0 interface) and it simply ignores the update. The 192.168.23.0 route works because R1 doesn't have an interface with the 192.168.23.0 network configured on it, so there isn't a summary route for it.

R1#**show ip route 150.123.22.0**
Routing entry for 150.123.0.0/16

Known via "eigrp 123", distance 5, metric 128256, type internal
  Redistributing via eigrp 123
  Last update from 0.0.0.0 on Null0, 19:16:10 ago
  Routing Descriptor Blocks:
  * 0.0.0.0, from 0.0.0.0, 19:16:10 ago, via Null0
      Route metric is 128256, traffic share count is 1
      Total delay is 5000 microseconds, minimum bandwidth is 8000000 Kbit
      Reliability 255/255, minimum MTU 1500 bytes
      Loading 1/255, Hops 0

Here's a debug showing R1 routing the packets to oblivion.
IP: tableid=0, s=150.123.11.11 (local), d=150.123.33.33 (Null0), routed via RIB
IP: s=150.123.11.11 (local), d=150.123.33.33 (Null0), len 100, sending.
IP: tableid=0, s=150.123.11.11 (local), d=150.123.33.33 (Null0), routed via RIB
IP: s=150.123.11.11 (local), d=150.123.33.33 (Null0), len 100, sending.
IP: tableid=0, s=150.123.11.11 (local), d=150.123.33.33 (Null0), routed via RIB

Note: When you try this on our own your output might not be exactly the same.

While the above is a bit of an extreme case, it is another reason why summaries need to be carefully considered as it has the potential for routing loops and the loss of route visibility. This means that if one of R3's serial interfaces had a problem (10.0.0.0 network) the other routes wouldn't realize there was an issue. The solution is to disable auto-summary with the **no auto-summary** command. It is a best practice to always immediately disable auto-summary unless you have a good reason for using it.

R1(config)#**router eigrp 123**
R1(config-router)#**no auto-summary**
%DUAL-5-NBRCHANGE: IP-EIGRP 123: Neighbor 10.175.113.66 (Serial0/0/1) is up: new adjacency
%DUAL-5-NBRCHANGE: IP-EIGRP 123: Neighbor 10.175.113.34 (Serial0/0/0) is up: new adjacency
%DUAL-5-NBRCHANGE: IP-EIGRP 123: Neighbor 192.168.12.2 (FastEthernet0/0) is up: new adjacency

R2(config)#**router eigrp 123**
R2(config-router)#**no auto-summary**
%DUAL-5-NBRCHANGE: IP-EIGRP 123: Neighbor 192.168.23.3 (FastEthernet0/1) is up: new adjacency
%DUAL-5-NBRCHANGE: IP-EIGRP 123: Neighbor 192.168.12.1 (FastEthernet0/0) is up: new adjacency

R3(config)#**router eigrp 123**
R3(config-router)#**no auto-summary**
%DUAL-5-NBRCHANGE: IP-EIGRP 123: Neighbor 192.168.23.2 (FastEthernet0/0) is up: new adjacency
%DUAL-5-NBRCHANGE: IP-EIGRP 123: Neighbor 10.175.113.65 (Serial0/0/1) is up: new adjacency
%DUAL-5-NBRCHANGE: IP-EIGRP 123: Neighbor 10.175.113.33 (Serial0/0/0) is up: new adjacency

After the EIGRP resyncs the routing table, we can now see the individual /32 routes for the loopbacks. Please focus on the route below in the output.

R1#show ip route | sec 150.123.0.0 *(on most 12.4 and later IOS, use the | sec command)*
    150.123.0.0/32 is subnetted, 3 subnets
C   150.123.11.11 is directly connected, Loopback0
D   150.123.22.22 [90/156160] via 192.168.12.2, 00:02:03, FastEthernet0/0
D   150.123.33.33 [90/158720] via 192.168.12.2, 00:00:39, FastEthernet0/0

And we can reach all of them from R1.

R1#ping 150.123.22.22
Type escape sequence to abort.
    Sending 5, 100-byte ICMP Echos to 150.123.22.22, timeout is 2 seconds:
    !!!!!
    Success rate is 100 percent (5/5), round-trip min/avg/max = 0/3/19 ms

R1#ping 150.123.33.33
Type escape sequence to abort.
    Sending 5, 100-byte ICMP Echos to 150.123.33.33, timeout is 2 seconds:
    !!!!!
    Success rate is 100 percent (5/5), round-trip min/avg/max = 0/0/0 ms

As mentioned above, EIGRP is a very fast protocol that can detect issues very quickly. It does this with the concept of successors and feasible successors; the successor is the route that is chosen for the routing table. This is chosen by the best metric (Bandwidth + Delay by default) routes also have to pass EIGRPs loop prevention rule which says that the Advertised Distance of a route (R2 -> R3) will be lower than the Feasible Distance (R1 -> R2 -> R3). EIGRP also stores a number of feasible successors so that in case something goes wrong with the successor it can switch routes as soon as it knows there is a problem.

R1#show ip eigrp topology
IP-EIGRP Topology Table for AS 123

Codes: P - Passive, A - Active, U - Update, Q - Query, R - Reply,
    r - Reply status

P 150.123.11.11/32, 1 successors, FD is 128256
    via Connected, Loopback0
P 192.168.12.0/24, 1 successors, FD is 28160
    via Connected, FastEthernet0/0
P 192.168.11.0/24, 1 successors, FD is 28160
    via Connected, FastEthernet0/1
P 10.175.113.32/30, 1 successors, FD is 2169856
    via Connected, Serial0/0/0
P 10.175.113.64/30, 1 successors, FD is 2169856
    via Connected, Serial0/0/1
P 192.168.33.0/24, 1 successors, FD is 33280
    via 192.168.12.2 (33280/30720), FastEthernet0/0

P 192.168.23.0/24, 1 successors, FD is 30720
        via 192.168.12.2 (30720/28160), FastEthernet0/0
        via 10.175.113.66 (2172416/28160), Serial0/0/1
        via 10.175.113.34 (2172416/28160), Serial0/0/0
P 150.123.22.22/32, 1 successors, FD is 156160
        via 192.168.12.2 (156160/128256), FastEthernet0/0
P 150.123.33.33/32, 1 successors, FD is 158720
        via 192.168.12.2 (158720/156160), FastEthernet0/0
        via 10.175.113.34 (2297856/128256), Serial0/0/0
        via 10.175.113.66 (2297856/128256), Serial0/0/1

Let's test this out, according to the topology table R1 is prefering the Fa0/0 interface to reach R3's loopback. After a bit, I disabled R3's Fa0/0 interface by simply unplugging it (you can also issue the **shutdown** command from interface configuration mode on Fa0/0). Notice how it takes about 7 packets to figure out there is a problem and switch over?

R1#**ping 150.123.33.33 repeat 1000** *(if the repeat command does not work for you as you are running an older version of IOS, simply type ping with no ip address. You will then be prompted for the protocol, IP address and how many times to send with the repeat option where you can enter 1000).*
Type escape sequence to abort.
        Sending 100000, 100-byte ICMP Echos to 150.123.33.33, timeout is 2 seconds:
        !!
Success rate is **99 percent (840/847)**, round-trip min/avg/max = 1/9/80 ms

To demonstrate how fast the switch over actually is lets debug the routing table with **debug ip routing.** Debug ip routing is not really a CCNA command but it is pretty useful to see any changes to the routing table in real time. Notice that as soon as EIGRP detects the R3 interface is down and removes the route, within the same second it has switched to the serial links to route the traffic. You will have to plug the cable back in and remove it to see this actually happen.

R1# **debug ip routing**
IP routing debugging is on
R1#**ping 150.123.33.33 repeat 1000**
Type escape sequence to abort.
        Sending 1000, 100-byte ICMP Echos to 150.123.33.33, timeout is 2 seconds:
        !!!
        !!!!!!!!!!!!!!!!!!!!!!!!!!!!!......
RT: delete network route to 150.123.33.33
RT: NET-RED 150.123.33.33/32
RT: SET_LAST_RDB for 150.123.33.33/32
     NEW rdb: via 10.175.113.34
RT: add 150.123.33.33/32 via 10.175.113.34, eigrp metric [90/2297856]
RT: NET-RED 150.123.33.33/32
RT: SET_LAST_RDB for 150.123.33.33/32

NEW rdb: via 10.175.113.66
RT: add 150.123.33.33/32 via 10.175.113.66, eigrp metric [90/2297856]
NEW rdb: via 10.175.113.66!!!!!!!!!!!!!

Checking the table now we can see that EIGRP is now load balancing between both
serial links because they have equal metrics. Focus on this portion of the output.

R1# **show ip route | begin 150.123.33.33** *(on most 12.4 and later IOS, use the | sec command)*
D   150.123.33.33 [90/2297856] via 10.175.113.34, 00:15:48, Serial0/0/0
              [90/2297856] via 10.175.113.66, 00:15:48, Serial0/0/1

Let's bring R3's Fa0/0 link back up by plugging the cable back in (or issuing a **no
shutdown** command from within interface configuration mode).

R3(config)#**int fa0/0**
R3(config-if)#**no shutdown**
%LINK-5-CHANGED: Interface FastEthernet0/0, changed state to up
%LINEPROTO-5-UPDOWN: Line protocol on Interface FastEthernet0/0, changed state to up
%DUAL-5-NBRCHANGE: IP-EIGRP 123: Neighbor 192.168.23.2 (FastEthernet0/0) is up: new adjacency

Let's examine the topology table a bit more closely. Specifically 150.123.33.33/32.
R1#**show ip eigrp topology | begin 150.123.33.33/32** *(on most 12.4 and later IOS, use the | sec command)*
P 150.123.33.33/32, 1 successors, FD is 158720
        via 192.168.12.2 (158720/156160), FastEthernet0/0
        via 10.175.113.66 (2297856/128256), Serial0/0/1
        via 10.175.113.34 (2297856/128256), Serial0/0/0

If you want to load balance between unequal links (like for example a FastEthernet and
a Serial interface) you have two options. One is to modify the bandwidth and delay on
the interface so that its equal with the other interfaces the other is to use
the **variance** command. In either case it's helpful to look at the detailed topology info
for the routes you're interested in. You can do this with the **show ip eigrp topology
<route>** command. The command will show you the complete metric info for each
interface that knows about the route and also the FD/AD.

R1#**show ip eigrp topology 150.123.33.33/32**
IP-EIGRP (AS 123): Topology entry for 150.123.33.33/32
  State is Passive, Query origin flag is 1, 1 Successor(s), FD is 158720
  Routing Descriptor Blocks:
  192.168.12.2 (FastEthernet0/0), from 192.168.12.2, Send flag is 0x0
    Composite metric is (158720/156160), Route is Internal
    Vector metric:
      Minimum bandwidth is 100000 Kbit
      Total delay is 5200 microseconds
      Reliability is 255/255
      Load is 1/255
      Minimum MTU is 1500

Hop count is 2
10.175.113.34 (Serial0/0/0), from 10.175.113.34, Send flag is 0x0
  Composite metric is (2297856/128256), Route is Internal
  Vector metric:
  Minimum bandwidth is 1544 Kbit
  Total delay is 25000 microseconds
  Reliability is 255/255
  Load is 1/255
  Minimum MTU is 1500
  Hop count is 1
10.175.113.66 (Serial0/0/1), from 10.175.113.66, Send flag is 0x0
  Composite metric is (2297856/128256), Route is Internal
  Vector metric:
  Minimum bandwidth is 1544 Kbit
  Total delay is 25000 microseconds
  Reliability is 255/255
  Load is 1/255
  Minimum MTU is 1500
  Hop count is 1

To change the metric info on interface, we can do this with the **bandwidth** and **delay** commands. It is important to remember that the bandwidth command is purely logical - meaning it's only used by protocols such as EIGRP or QoS to determine the link bandwidth. It will not affect the actual **speed** of a link, only the speed command can do that.

However, it's a bit of a painful trial and error process to fine tune the metrics on the interfaces and can affect other protocols that rely on the bandwidth command. Below shows how to adjust the metrics. But do **NOT** run these commands now.
R1(config)#**int s0/0/0**
R1(config-if)#**bandwidth 100000**
R1(config-if)#**delay 55**

The better way to do it is using the **variance** command. The variance command is used to tell the router what multiple of feasible distance is should be considered for unequal load balancing.
The syntax is: **variance <multiplier>**

For example if R1's Fa0/0 interface has a Feasible Distance of 158720 if we were to configure a variance of 2 then R1 would accept anything with a Feasible Distance between the range of 158720 - 317440 will be used for load balancing. It's worth noting that unequal load balancing isn't 1 to 1 between the interfaces but instead quoting Cisco, "the router distributes traffic proportionately to the ratios of the metrics that are associated with different routes." Which simply means the router will intelligently send more traffic across the faster links then the slower ones.

So looking at the FD for the Ethernet link is 158720 and the Serial links have a FD of 2297856. To find the value of variance you take the highest interface FD and divide it by the lowest interface FD (the successor). Look for the info in the output below.

R1#**show ip eigrp topology | begin 150.123.33.33/32** *(on most 12.4 and later IOS, use the | sec command)*
P 150.123.33.33/32, 1 successors, FD is 158720
        via 192.168.12.2 (158720/156160), FastEthernet0/0
        via 10.175.113.66 (2297856/128256), Serial0/0/1
        via 10.175.113.34 (2297856/128256), Serial0/0/0

The highest FD is 2297856 and the successor FD is 158720.

R1(config)#**router eigrp 123**
R1(config-router)#**variance 14**

You'll notice that nothing changed in the routing table, this is because 14 is a clean divide. It's actually too small, we will need to increase the variance to 15 instead.
R1#**show ip route eigrp**
      150.123.0.0/32 is subnetted, 3 subnets
D   150.123.22.22 [90/156160] via 192.168.12.2, 00:00:30, FastEthernet0/0
D   150.123.33.33 [90/158720] via 192.168.12.2, 00:00:30, FastEthernet0/0
D   192.168.23.0/24 [90/30720] via 192.168.12.2, 00:00:30, FastEthernet0/0
D   192.168.33.0/24 [90/33280] via 192.168.12.2, 00:00:30, FastEthernet0/0

After we change the variance to 15 we see the routes being added to the routing table since we still have **debug ip routing** on.
R1(config)#**router eigrp 123**
R1(config-router)#**variance 15**
R1(config-router)#**exit**
R1#**clear ip eigrp neighbors**
RT: add 150.123.33.33/32 via 10.175.113.34, eigrp metric [90/2297856]
RT: NET-RED 150.123.33.33/32
RT: add 150.123.33.33/32 via 10.175.113.66, eigrp metric [90/2297856]
RT: NET-RED 150.123.33.33/32

You **must** run the *clear ip eigrp neighbors* command every time you change the variance on most pre 12.4 IOS routers. You will then see the route changes. Now we can we see the other paths for R3's loopback. Look for this in the output.
R1#**show ip route**
D   150.123.33.33 [90/158720] via 192.168.12.2, 00:00:12, FastEthernet0/0
                    [90/2297856] via 10.175.113.34, 00:00:11, Serial0/0/0
                    [90/2297856] via 10.175.113.66, 00:00:11, Serial0/0/1

EIGRP communicates with its peers by sending hello packets every 5 seconds for high speed broadcast links and every 60 seconds for slow speed NBMA links (Frame-relay). If you need to adjust the timers (perhaps you want EIGRP to detect link failures more quickly) you can use the **ip hello-interval eigrp <AS> <seconds>** command. When you change the hello time, you'll also need to adjust the **hold-timer** with the **ip hold-time eigrp <AS> <seconds>**. As a rule of thumb the hold time should be 3 times as much as the hello interval.

Note: If you are going to change timers it is important to make sure the other side of the link also is configured for the same value to avoid any issues.

Let's change the hello time on the Fast Ethernet links to be 1 second instead of 5, we'll also adjust the hold time.

R1(config)#**int fa0/0**
R1(config-if)#**ip hello-interval eigrp 123 1**
R1(config-if)#**ip hold-time eigrp 123 3**

R2(config)#**int fa0/1**
R2(config-if)#**ip hello-interval eigrp 123 1**
R2(config-if)#**ip hold-time eigrp 123 3**
R2(config-if)#**int fa0/0**
R2(config-if)#**ip hello-interval eigrp 123 1**
R2(config-if)#**ip hold-time eigrp 123 3**

R3(config)#**int fa0/0**
R3(config-if)#**ip hello-interval eigrp 123 1**
R3(config-if)#**ip hold-time eigrp 123 3**

Now let's try our ping test again with a timeout of 1 second which is our hello time. I'll ping R3's loopback then disconnect R3's Fa0/0 cable (or administratively shut it down). Notice that this time we only lost 3 ping packets which is what we would expect, after R1 misses 3 hellos from the Fa0/0 path it switches over to the serial links. The repeat command may not work on 12.3 or older IOS versions.

R1#**ping 150.123.33.33 repeat 1000 timeout 1**
Type escape sequence to abort.
    Sending 100000, 100-byte ICMP Echos to 150.123.33.33, timeout is 1 seconds:
    !!
    !!
    !!
    Success rate is 98 percent (278/281), round-trip min/avg/max = 1/12/64 ms

Failover time is great when there is a feasible successor for a route because EIGRP simply switches over to the new one. But what happens when EIGRP doesn't have a feasible successor and there is a problem? When EIGRP doesn't have a backup route it will send a query out to all of its neighbors asking if they know of a way to get to the downed network. This process is called the Active state because the router is actively trying to solve reachability problems, this is the opposite of passive state where everyone is in sync and there is not a lot of chatter in the network. When neighbors receive a query they will do one of two things: Either they will have a route and respond with an UPDATE packet or if the router doesn't it will send out its own query to all of its neighbors to see if it can figure out the route.

The downside of this system is that a router will only send out one query packet per neighbor in an effort to minimize redundant chatter, while it is waiting the router will keep the router an Active state until it receives either a reply or an update packet from each neighbor. During this time route is still kept in the routing table. In large EIGRP networks it may take awhile for all the query packets to be answered or worse yet if the QUERY or the REPLY packet is lost in transit due for whatever reason every router looking for the route will need to wait for the hold time to expire and everyone to resync before the network turns passive again. This can be a massive waste of bandwidth as well as be a lengthy outage considering the hold-time on NBMA links is 180 seconds or 3 minutes. This issue is called Stuck in Active.

To help explore this we'll change the timers on the Fast Ethernet links to 60/180 and we'll change the S0/0/0 links to 1/3.

```
R1(config-if)#int s0/0/0
R1(config-if)# ip hello-interval eigrp 123 1
R1(config-if)# ip hold-time eigrp 123 3
R1(config-if)#int fa0/0
R1(config-if)# ip hello-interval eigrp 123 60
R1(config-if)# ip hold-time eigrp 123 180

R2(config-if)#int fa0/0
R2(config-if)# ip hello-interval eigrp 123 60
R2(config-if)# ip hold-time eigrp 123 180
R2(config-if)#int fa0/1
R2(config-if)# ip hello-interval eigrp 123 60
R2(config-if)# ip hold-time eigrp 123 180

R3(config-if)#int s0/0/0
R3(config-if)# ip hello-interval eigrp 123 1
R3(config-if)# ip hold-time eigrp 123 3
R3(config-if)#int fa0/0
R3(config-if)# ip hello-interval eigrp 123 60
R3(config-if)# ip hold-time eigrp 123 180
```

Next we'll apply a standard ACL on R1's Fa0/0 to block all traffic and shut down R3's S0/0/0.

```
R1(config)#access-list 5 deny any
R1(config)#int fa0/0
R1(config-if)#ip access-group 5 in
```

R3(config-if)#**int s0/0/0**
R3(config-if)#**shut**

If we turn on **debug ip eigrp** we can see looking for the serial network.

R1#**debug ip eigrp**
IP-EIGRP(Default-IP-Routing-Table:123): 10.175.113.32/30 - not in IP routing table
IP-EIGRP(Default-IP-Routing-Table:123): Int 10.175.113.32/30
metric 4294967295 - 0 4294967295

On R2 we can see the QUERY packet and a few milliseconds later it receives a REPLY packet from R3 confirming there is no other route.

IP-EIGRP(Default-IP-Routing-Table:123): Processing incoming QUERY packet

IP-EIGRP(Default-IP-Routing-Table:123): Processing incoming REPLY packet

Since we are blocking any traffic on R1's Fa0/0 interface it will not receive R2's REPLY so it will remain in active, we can see this by checking show ip eigrp topology.

R1#**show ip eigrp topology**
        IP-EIGRP Topology Table for AS 123
Codes: P - Passive, A - Active, U - Update, Q - Query, R - Reply,
        r - reply Status
P 192.168.33.0/24, 1 successors, FD is 33280
        via 192.168.12.2 (33280/30720), FastEthernet0/0
        P 192.168.11.0/24, 1 successors, FD is 28160
        via Connected, FastEthernet0/1
        P 192.168.12.0/24, 1 successors, FD is 28160
        via Connected, FastEthernet0/0
        P 192.168.23.0/24, 1 successors, FD is 30720
        via 192.168.12.2 (30720/28160), FastEthernet0/0
        P 150.123.22.22/32, 1 successors, FD is 156160
        via 192.168.12.2 (156160/128256), FastEthernet0/0
        P 150.123.33.33/32, 1 successors, FD is 158720
        via 192.168.12.2 (158720/156160), FastEthernet0/0
        P 150.123.11.11/32, 1 successors, FD is 128256
        via Connected, Loopback0
        A 10.175.113.32/30, 1 successors, FD is Inaccessible, Q
        1 replies, active 00:00:17, query-origin: Local origin
        Remaining replies:
        via 192.168.12.2, r, FastEthernet0/0

Eventually the hold-time expires and the route is removed.

R1#
%DUAL-5-NBRCHANGE: IP-EIGRP(0) 123: Neighbor 192.168.12.2
 (FastEthernet0/0) is down: holding time expired

Now shut off the debug and review the topology table to see that the route has been removed.

R1#**debug ip eigrp**

Finally EIGRP can be a bit of a chatty protocol with all its hellos and various other packets it sends frequently it's possible on some slow WAN links that EIGRP can drown out actual data traffic if EIGRP is busy enough. By default EIGRP may take up to 80% of a link for its own communications. You can adjust this value with the **ip bandwidth-percent eigrp <AS> <percent>** command under an interface.

Note: The bandwidth-percent command replies on the configured bandwidth on the interface, if this value is wrong the command won't work as expected.

R1(config)#**int s0/0/0**
R1(config-if)#**ip bandwidth-percent eigrp 123 20**
Examine the routing tables of all three routers starting with Router1 and then going to Router2 and Router3.

EIGRP Review Questions
1) What is the administrative distance of EIGRP?_____

2) Does EIGRP support load balancing by default? _____

3) From the Router1 router, what would be the command to display the EIGRP topology table?_____

4) What command would save the current configuration of all the routers?_____

Answers

1) 90 is for internal EIGRP and 170 for external EIGRP.
2) Yes, only equal cost load balancing. Unequal cost load balancing can be enabled using the variance command.
3) show ip eigrp topology
4) copy run start

Split-Horizon: EIGRP

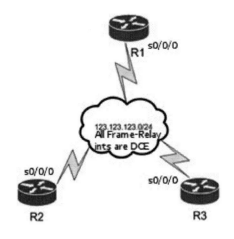

The purpose of this lab explores the Split-Horizon rule for EIGRP. We put this lab in the EIGRP section, but we suggest you come back to it after you do the labs in Chapter 12 so you fully understand the Frame-Relay setup above. We used a 2801 as our Frame-Relay router which will help explain our Serial numbering in this lab as it may be different for you. In our next Frame-Relay lab we will use a 1841 so you can see the difference.

Hardware & Configuration Required for this Lab

- Three Cisco routers with one serial port
- One Cisco router with at least three serial ports
- Three DCE/DTE back to back cables
- **Note:** If you do not have a third router, simply strip R3 out of your lab and you can still follow the logic of the lab

---

Commands Used in this Lab

no ip split-horizon eigrp <AS> - Disables Split-horizon on an interface

---

Initial Configs - Where you see *Initial Configs,* these are basic configuration steps that by now you should be able to perform on the devices by yourself without us detailing them step by step. Keep in mind the way to address your interfaces may be a bit different than what we have here. You can always use the show interface command to see what the nomenclature is for the serial ports you have installed.

FRAME
host FRAME
frame-relay switching
interface Serial0/1/0
  encapsulation frame-relay
  clock rate 64000
  frame-relay intf-type dce
  frame-relay route 102 interface Serial0/2/0 201
  frame-relay route 103 interface Serial0/3/0 301
  no shut
interface Serial0/2/0
  encapsulation frame-relay
  clock rate 64000
  frame-relay intf-type dce
  frame-relay route 201 interface Serial0/1/0 102
  no shut
interface Serial0/3/0
  encapsulation frame-relay
  clock rate 64000
  frame-relay intf-type dce
  frame-relay route 301 interface Serial0/1/0 103
  no shut

R1
line console 0
logging synch
int s0/0/0
encapsulation frame-relay
no frame inverse
no shut
int s0/0/0.123 multi
ip add 123.123.123.1 255.255.255.0
frame map ip 123.123.123.2 102 broadcast
frame map ip 123.123.123.3 103 broadcast
host R1

R2
line console 0
logging synch
int s0/0/0
encapsulation frame-relay
no frame inverse
no shut
int s0/0/0.123 multi
ip add 123.123.123.2 255.255.255.0
frame map ip 123.123.123.1 201 broadcast
host R2

R3
line console 0
logging synch
int s0/0/0
encapsulation frame-relay
no frame inverse
no shut
int s0/0/0.123 multi
ip add 123.123.123.3 255.255.255.0
frame map ip 123.123.123.1 301 broadcast
no shut
host R3

Distance routing protocols have a simple loop prevention rule called Split-horizon. The split-horizon rule says that a routing protocol will not send out an update on the same interface it received an update on. This is a particular problem on Frame-relay Hub and Spoke networks because the hub will receive an update from one spoke but due to split-horizon will not forward the update to the other spokes since it's the same interface.

First let's add a loopback interface on each router. We will use the 150.101.123.x/32 scheme where X is the router number.

R1(config)#**int lo0**
R1(config-if)#**ip add 150.101.123.1 255.255.255.255**

R2(config)#**int lo0**
R2(config-if)#**ip add 150.101.123.2 255.255.255.255**

R3(config)#**int lo0**
R3(config-if)#**ip add 150.101.123.3 255.255.255.255**

Next let's enable EIGRP AS 123 on the frame network and add the loopbacks.
R1(config)#**router eigrp 123**
R1(config-router)#**no auto**
R1(config-router)#**network 123.123.123.0 255.255.255.0**
*Mar 1 00:46:48.711: %DUAL-5-NBRCHANGE: IP-EIGRP(0) 123: Neighbor 123.123.123.2 (Serial0/0/0.123) is up: new adjacency
*Mar 1 00:46:48.735: %DUAL-5-NBRCHANGE: IP-EIGRP(0) 123: Neighbor 123.123.123.3 (Serial0/0/0.123) is up: new adjacency
R1(config-router)#**network 150.101.123.0 255.255.255.0**

R2(config)#**router eigrp 123**
R2(config-router)#**no auto**
R2(config-router)#**network 123.123.123.0 255.255.255.0**
*Mar 1 00:46:48.335: %DUAL-5-NBRCHANGE: IP-EIGRP(0) 123: Neighbor 123.123.123.1

(Serial0/0/0.123) is up: new adjacency
R2(config-router)#**network 150.101.123.0 255.255.255.0**

R3(config)#**router eigrp 123**
R3(config-router)#**no auto**
R3(config-router)#**network 123.123.123.0 255.255.255.0**
*Mar 1 00:46:47.743: %DUAL-5-NBRCHANGE: IP-EIGRP(0) 123: Neighbor 123.123.123.1
(Serial0/0/0.123) is up: new adjacency
R3(config-router)#**network 150.101.123.0 255.255.255.0**

We can see that R1 has learned both R2 & R3 as expected.
R1(config)#**do show ip route eigrp**
　　　150.101.0.0/32 is subnetted, 3 subnets
D　　　150.101.123.2 [90/2297856] via 123.123.123.2, 00:01:28, Serial0/0/0.123
D　　　150.101.123.3 [90/2297856] via 123.123.123.3, 00:01:28, Serial0/0/0.123

R2 & R3 however only learned the R1 route due to the split-horizon rule.
R2(config)#**do show ip route eigrp**
　　　150.101.0.0/32 is subnetted, 2 subnets
D　　　150.101.123.1 [90/2297856] via 123.123.123.1, 00:01:28, Serial0/0/0.123

R3(config)#**do show ip route eigrp**
　　　150.101.0.0/32 is subnetted, 2 subnets
D　　　150.101.123.1 [90/2297856] via 123.123.123.1, 00:01:28, Serial0/0/0.123

We can disable split-horizon by using the **no ip split-horizon eigrp <AS>** command under the interface.
R1(config)#**int s0/0/0.123**
R1(config-subif)#**no ip split-horizon eigrp 123**
R1(config-subif)#
*Mar 1 00:50:57.875: %DUAL-5-NBRCHANGE: IP-EIGRP(0) 123: Neighbor 123.123.123.3
(Serial0/0/0.123) is resync: split horizon changed
*Mar 1 00:50:57.875: %DUAL-5-NBRCHANGE: IP-EIGRP(0) 123: Neighbor 123.123.123.2
(Serial0/0/0.123) is resync: split horizon changed

Now if we check the routing table on R2 & R3 we can see we are learning all routes.
R2(config)#**do show ip route eigrp**
　　　150.101.0.0/32 is subnetted, 3 subnets
D　　　150.101.123.1 [90/2297856] via 123.123.123.1, 00:04:29, Serial0/0/0.123
D　　　150.101.123.3 [90/2809856] via 123.123.123.1, 00:00:35, Serial0/0/0.123

R3(config)#**do show ip route eigrp**
　　　150.101.0.0/32 is subnetted, 3 subnets
D　　　150.101.123.1 [90/2297856] via 123.123.123.1, 00:04:38, Serial0/0/0.123
D　　　150.101.123.2 [90/2809856] via 123.123.123.1, 00:00:43, Serial0/0/0.123

OSPF Routing

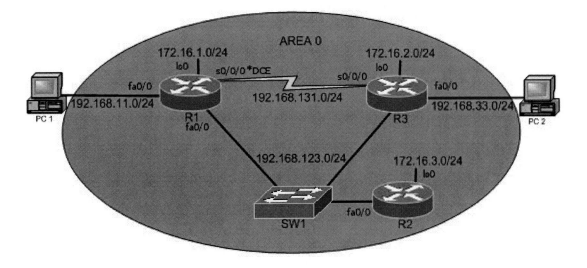

The purpose of this lab is to explore the functionality of OSPF using a single area. This lab focuses many on the basics concepts of OSPF.

Hardware & Configuration Required for this Lab

- Two Cisco routers with two Fast Ethernet interfaces and one serial port
- One Cisco router with one Fast Ethernet interface
- One DCE/DTE back to back cable
- One switch to connect the routers
- Three straight through Cat 5 cables to connect the routers to the switch
- Two PCs to connect to the routers
- Two crossover Cat 5 cables for PC to Router or four straight through Cat 5 cables if you put a switch in between them
- **Special Note:** If you do not have two routers with dual Ethernet ports and two PCs, that is ok. Simply configure the 192.168.11.0 subnet on R1 using a loopback interface and the 192.168.33.0 subnet on R3 using a loopback interface. Then do your pings from R1 & R3 respectively using an extended ping specifying the source address of the ping in place of issuing the ping from the PCs and the lab will still work fine.

Commands Used in this Lab

router ospf <process> - Used to enable ospf on the router

network <network> <wildcard mask> area – Adds networks to the OSPF database
ip ospf <process> area <area>- Used to enable ospf on an interface
ip ospf hello-interval <x> - Used to configure the ospf hello timer value
show ip ospf neighbor – Provides neighbor IDs, state, address, dead time and interface

---

Initial Configs - Where you see *Initial Configs,* these are basic configuration steps that by now you should be able to perform on the devices by yourself without us detailing them step by step. Generally you simply go into enable and then configuration mode and start the configuration. Keep in mind the way to address your interfaces may be a bit different than what we have here. You can always use the show interface command to see what the nomenclature is for the serial ports you have installed.

R1

host R1
line con 0
logging synch
exit
int lo0
ip add 172.16.1.1 255.255.255.0
int fa0/0
ip add 192.168.123.1 255.255.255.0
no keep
no shut
int fa0/1 (Note: loopback1 can be used if either your router does not have dual fastethernet interfaces or you do not have two PCs)
ip add 192.168.11.1 255.255.255.0
no shut (Note: command not needed if loopback interface is used)
int s0/0/0
ip add 192.168.131.1 255.255.255.0
clock rate 64000 (if you have a WIC-1DSU-TI module(don't confuse this with a WIC-1T, use the *service-module T1 clock source internal* command instead)).
no shut
exit

R2
host R2
line con 0
logging synch

exit
int lo0
ip add 172.16.2.1 255.255.255.0
int fa0/0
ip add 192.168.123.2 255.255.255.0
no shut
exit

R3
host R3
line con 0
logging synch
exit
int lo0
ip add 172.16.3.1 255.255.255.0
int fa0/0
ip add 192.168.123.3 255.255.255.0
no keep
no shut
int fa0/1 (Note: loopback can be used if either your router does not have dual
fastethernet interfaces or you do not have two PCs)
ip add 192.168.33.1 255.255.255.0
no shut (Note: command not needed if loopback interface is used)
int s0/0/0
ip add 192.168.131.3 255.255.255.0
(If you have a WIC-1DSU-TI module(don't confuse this with a WIC-1T, use the *service-module T1 clock source line* command here)).
no shut
exit

PC-1

Internet Protocol Version 4 (TCP/IPv4) Properties

General

You can get IP settings assigned automatically if your network supports this capability. Otherwise, you need to ask your network administrator for the appropriate IP settings.

○ Obtain an IP address automatically
◉ Use the following IP address:

IP address: 192 . 168 . 11 . 100
Subnet mask: 255 . 255 . 255 . 0
Default gateway: 192 . 168 . 11 . 1

○ Obtain DNS server address automatically
◉ Use the following DNS server addresses:

Preferred DNS server: .   .
Alternate DNS server: .   .

☐ Validate settings upon exit

Advanced...

OK   Cancel

PC-2

Internet Protocol Version 4 (TCP/IPv4) Properties

General

You can get IP settings assigned automatically if your network supports this capability. Otherwise, you need to ask your network administrator for the appropriate IP settings.

○ Obtain an IP address automatically
◉ Use the following IP address:

IP address: 192 . 168 . 33 . 100
Subnet mask: 255 . 255 . 255 . 0
Default gateway: 192 . 168 . 33 . 1

○ Obtain DNS server address automatically
◉ Use the following DNS server addresses:

Preferred DNS server: .   .
Alternate DNS server: .   .

☐ Validate settings upon exit

Advanced...

OK   Cancel

OSPF is an Interior Gateway Protocol used to distribute routing information within a single Autonomous System. It is the routing protocol of choice for mid-sized to large companies as it can be used to design and build large and complicated networks. It is considerably more scalable than RIP as RIP has a limit of 15 hops whereas OSPF can scale to almost a limitless amount of routers. The reason it is more scalable then distance vector protocols is because it is hierarchical, groups of routers are put into their own area which only talk outside of their area when they need to. This is more efficient than RIP or EIGRP where a router needs to sync routing tables with every other peer.

Note: While OSPF doesn't technically have a device limit there are complex design considerations that are required to run OSPF on large networks. Also as with any routing protocol there are other factors that will affect scalability such as the router's cpu and memory.

To enable OSPF on a router you use the **router ospf <process id>** command. The process command simply keeps track of what OSPF process is running on the router as you can have multiple OSPF processes running if you need to (this is commonly used in ISPs) It is entirely locally significant so it doesn't matter if you choose 3 as a process on one router and 44444 as a process on another. Most people just use **router ospf 1** everywhere to keep things simple.

You can add networks into OSPF in two ways; the first way is via the **network** command. The **network** command is a bit more complicated then with the other routing protocols we looked at earlier.
The syntax is: **network <network> <wildcard mask> area <area>**.

Since OSPF is entirely a classless protocol it doesn't support classful network statements like RIP version 1 does so a wildcard mask must be used.   The same concept applies though; any interfaces that match the network/wildcard range will be added into OSPF under the configured area. Here is a quick reminder of some wildcard masks.

Subnet Mask	Size of Network	Wildcard Mask
255.255.255.0	256	0.0.0.255
255.255.255.128	128	0.0.0.127
255.255.255.192	64	0.0.0.63
255.255.255.224	32	0.0.0.31
255.255.255.240	16	0.0.0.15
255.255.255.248	8	0.0.0.7
255.255.255.252	4	0.0.0.3
255.255.255.254	2	0.0.0.1
255.255.255.255	1	0.0.0.0

I briefly mentioned the concepts of Areas in the beginning of the lab, OSPF is a hierarchical protocol where routers are logically grouped together in OSPF Areas, all areas have to connect to area 0 which is called the backbone area. This lab is going to just focus on Area 0 for now but you can either enter the area as a decimal value or in an IP address format. The range of configurable areas you can use is: 0 - 4294967295 which is more then you'll ever need.

R1(config)#**router ospf 1**
R1(config-router)#**network 192.168.123.1 0.0.0.0 area 0**

The second way is to configure OSPF directly on an interface.
The syntax is: **ip ospf <process> area <area>**

R1(config)#**int fa0/0**
R1(config-if)#**ip ospf 1 area 0**

Both ways will achieve the same goal so use whatever works for you but it's a good idea to know them both well for testing purposes and in the real world. Let's enable OSPF on all interfaces. We will use the network statements method because it's more fun.

R1(config)#**router ospf 1**
R1(config-router)#**network 192.168.131.0 0.0.0.255 area 0**
R1(config-router)#**network 192.168.123.0 0.0.0.255 area 0**
R1(config-router)#**network 192.168.11.0 0.0.0.255 area 0**
R1(config-router)#**network 172.16.1.0 0.0.0.255 area 0**

R2(config)#**router ospf 1**
R2(config-router)#**network 192.168.123.0 0.0.0.255 area 0**

R2(config-router)#**network 172.16.2.0 0.0.0.255 area 0**

R3(config)#**router ospf 1**
R3(config-router)#**network 192.168.131.0 0.0.0.255 area 0**
R3(config-router)#**network 192.168.123.0 0.0.0.255 area 0**
R3(config-router)#**network 192.168.33.0 0.0.0.255 area 0**
R3(config-router)#**network 172.16.3.0 0.0.0.255 area 0**

As usual the first thing we'll look at is the **show ip protocols** output.

R1#**show ip protocols**

Routing Protocol is "ospf 1"
  Outgoing update filter list for all interfaces is not set
  Incoming update filter list for all interfaces is not set
  Router ID 192.168.131.1
  Number of areas in this router is 1. 1 normal 0 stub 0 nssa
  Maximum path: 4
  Routing for Networks:
    172.16.1.0 0.0.0.255 area 0
    192.168.11.0 0.0.0.255 area 0
    192.168.123.0 0.0.0.255 area 0
    192.168.131.0 0.0.0.255 area 0
  Reference bandwidth unit is 100 mbps
  Routing Information Sources:
    Gateway   Distance   Last Update
    192.168.123.2   110   00:00:59
    192.168.131.3   110   00:00:16
  Distance: (default is 110)

We can show a brief summary of neighbor information with **show ip ospf neighbor**. This is actually a pretty useful command as it will show you the neighbor's router-id/IP address, election priority, adjacency state, the router type, and the dead time. If you do not have a real node for PC2, you may not see the .33 entries below.

R1#**show ip ospf neighbor**

Neighbor ID   Pri State   Dead Time Address   Interface
192.168.123.2 1 FULL/BDR   00:00:33 192.168.123.2 FastEthernet0/0
192.168.131.3 1 FULL/DROTHER 00:00:32 192.168.123.3 FastEthernet0/0
192.168.131.3 0 FULL/ -   00:00:33 192.168.131.3 Serial0/0/0

It's worth taking a minute to talk about the State column. Here is a description of the various OSPF States.

Down

This is the first OSPF neighbor state. It means that the router hasn't received any hello packets. During the fully adjacent neighbor state, if a router doesn't receive hello packet from a neighbor within the Dead time. The neighbor will return to a downed state and be removed from the configuration.

Attempt

This state is only valid for manually configured neighbors in an NBMA (Frame-relay) environment. In Attempt state, the router sends unicast hello packets every poll interval to the neighbor, from which hellos have not been received within the dead interval.

Init

This state specifies that the router has received a hello packet from its neighbor, but the receiving router's ID was not included in the hello packet. When a router receives a hello packet from a neighbor, it will reply back with a hello packet that contains its router id.

2-way

This state designates that 2-way or bi-directional communication has been established between two routers. Bi-directional means that each router has seen the other's hello packet. This state is attained when the router receiving the hello packet sees its own Router ID within the received hello packet's neighbor field. At this state, a router decides whether to become adjacent with this neighbor. On broadcast media and non-broadcast multiaccess networks, a router becomes full only with the designated router (DR) and the backup designated router (BDR); it stays in the 2-way state with all other neighbors. On Point-to-point and Point-to-multipoint networks, a router becomes full with all connected routers. At the end of this stage, the DR and BDR for broadcast and non-broadcast multiacess networks are elected.

Exstart

Once the DR and BDR are elected, the actual process of exchanging link state information can start between the routers and their DR and BDR.

In this state, the routers and their DR and BDR establish a master-slave relationship and choose the initial sequence number for adjacency formation. The router with the higher router ID becomes the master and starts the exchange, and as such, is the only router that can increment the sequence number. The master/slave election is on a per-neighbor basis.

Exchange

In the exchange state, OSPF routers exchange database descriptor (DBD) packets. Database descriptors contain link-state advertisement (LSA) headers only and describe the contents of the entire link-state database. Each DBD packet has a sequence number which can be incremented only by master which is explicitly acknowledged by slave. Routers also send link-state request packets and link-state update packets (which contain the entire LSA) in this state. The contents of the DBD received are compared to the information contained in the routers link-state database to check if new or more current link-state information is available with the neighbor.

Loading

In this state, the actual exchange of link state information occurs. Based on the information provided by the DBDs, routers send link-state request packets. The neighbor then provides the requested link-state information in link-state update packets. During the adjacency, if a router receives an outdated or missing LSA, it requests that LSA by sending a link-state request packet. All link-state update packets are acknowledged.

Full

In this state, routers are fully adjacent with each other. All the router and network LSAs are exchanged and the routers' databases are fully synchronized. Everything is working just fine.

Full is the normal state for an OSPF router. If a router is stuck in another state, it's an indication that there are problems in forming adjacencies. The only exception to this is the 2-way state, which is normal in a broadcast network. Routers achieve the full state with their DR and BDR only. Neighbors always see each other as 2-way.

The other part of the State column shows the router role. The roles can be:

-	This means the interface type doesn't support DR elections.
DR	This means the neighbor is the Designated Router.
BDR	This means the neighbor is the Backup Designated Router.
DROTHER	This means the neighbor is neither the DR or the BDR.

Looking at the **show ip ospf neighbor** output we can see that for subnet 192.168.123.0/24, R1 is the DR, R2 is the BDR, and R3 is just another router. Note: Your lab may vary with regards to which router is the DR and BDR. Also keep in mind the order and interface type may vary based upon if you have a built-in serial port, WIC-1T, WIC-1DSU-T1, WIC-2t, WIC-2A/S, or NM-4A/S module. But you should be able to figure it out.

The OSPF Network Type determines whether or not a link will participate in the DR election and also what default timers the interface will use. You can see what network type is configured on an interface; as well as check the interface timers with: **show ip ospf interfaces**

Loopback0 is up, line protocol is up
  Internet Address 172.16.1.1/24, Area 0
  Process ID 1, Router ID 192.168.131.1, **Network Type LOOPBACK**, Cost: 1
  Loopback interface is treated as a stub Host
FastEthernet0/1 is up, line protocol is up
  Internet Address 192.168.11.1/24, Area 0
  Process ID 1, Router ID 192.168.131.1, **Network Type BROADCAST**, Cost: 1
  Transmit Delay is 1 sec, State DR, Priority 1
  Designated Router (ID) 192.168.131.1, Interface address 192.168.11.1
  No backup designated router on this network
  Timer intervals configured, Hello 10, Dead 40, Wait 40, Retransmit 5
    oob-resync timeout 40
    Hello due in 00:00:02
  Supports Link-local Signaling (LLS)
  Cisco NSF helper support enabled
  IETF NSF helper support enabled
  Index 3/3, flood queue length 0
  Next 0x0(0)/0x0(0)
  Last flood scan length is 0, maximum is 0
  Last flood scan time is 0 msec, maximum is 0 msec
  Neighbor Count is 0, Adjacent neighbor count is 0
  Suppress hello for 0 neighbor(s)
FastEthernet0/0 is up, line protocol is up
  Internet Address 192.168.123.1/24, Area 0
  Process ID 1, Router ID 192.168.131.1, **Network Type BROADCAST**, Cost: 1
  Transmit Delay is 1 sec, State DR, Priority 1
  Designated Router (ID) 192.168.131.1, Interface address 192.168.123.1
  Backup Designated router (ID) 192.168.123.2, Interface address 192.168.123.2
  Timer intervals configured, Hello 10, Dead 40, Wait 40, Retransmit 5
    oob-resync timeout 40
    Hello due in 00:00:08
  Supports Link-local Signaling (LLS)
  Cisco NSF helper support enabled

IETF NSF helper support enabled
Index 2/2, flood queue length 0
Next 0x0(0)/0x0(0)
Last flood scan length is 1, maximum is 1
Last flood scan time is 0 msec, maximum is 0 msec
Neighbor Count is 2, Adjacent neighbor count is 2
  Adjacent with neighbor 192.168.123.2 (Backup Designated Router)
  Adjacent with neighbor 192.168.131.3
Suppress hello for 0 neighbor(s)
Serial0/0/0 is up, line protocol is up
  Internet Address 192.168.131.1/24, Area 0
  Process ID 1, Router ID 192.168.131.1, **Network Type POINT_TO_POINT**, Cost: 64
  Transmit Delay is 1 sec, State POINT_TO_POINT
  Timer intervals configured, Hello 10, Dead 40, Wait 40, Retransmit 5
   oob-resync timeout 40
   Hello due in 00:00:06
  Supports Link-local Signaling (LLS)
  Cisco NSF helper support enabled
  IETF NSF helper support enabled
  Index 1/1, flood queue length 0
  Next 0x0(0)/0x0(0)
  Last flood scan length is 1, maximum is 1
  Last flood scan time is 0 msec, maximum is 0 msec
  Neighbor Count is 1, Adjacent neighbor count is 1
   Adjacent with neighbor 192.168.131.3
  Suppress hello for 0 neighbor(s)

When checking the routing table, OSPF routes are shown with an **O**.

R1#**show ip route ospf**

     172.16.0.0/16 is variably subnetted, 3 subnets, 2 masks

O   172.16.3.1/32 [110/2] via 192.168.123.3, 00:03:51, FastEthernet0/0

O   172.16.2.1/32 [110/2] via 192.168.123.2, 00:04:34, FastEthernet0/0
O   192.168.33.0/24 [110/2] via 192.168.123.3, 00:17:24, FastEthernet0/0

Now let's make sure we can ping everyone.

R1#**ping 192.168.33.1**
Type escape sequence to abort.
Sending 5, 100-byte ICMP Echos to 192.168.33.1, timeout is 2 seconds:
!!!!!
Success rate is 100 percent (5/5), round-trip min/avg/max = 28/28/28 ms

R1#**ping 172.16.2.1**
Type escape sequence to abort.

Sending 5, 100-byte ICMP Echos to 172.16.2.1, timeout is 2 seconds:
!!!!!
Success rate is 100 percent (5/5), round-trip min/avg/max = 28/28/28 ms

So it looks like our routes are working!

If you need to adjust the OSPF network timers you can use the **ip ospf hello-interval** interface command. When you change the hello timer the dead timer will automatically change to 4x the hello value. But you can also manually change it with the **ip ospf dead-interval** interface command.

R1(config)#**int fa0/0**
R1(config-if)#**ip ospf hello-interval 5**
R1(config-if)#**do sh ip ospf int fa0/0**
FastEthernet0/0 is up, line protocol is up
  Internet Address 192.168.123.1/24, Area 0
  Process ID 1, Router ID 192.168.131.1, Network Type BROADCAST, Cost: 1
  Transmit Delay is 1 sec, State DR, Priority 1
  Designated Router (ID) 192.168.131.1, Interface address 192.168.123.1
  Backup Designated router (ID) 192.168.123.2, Interface address 192.168.123.2
  Timer intervals configured, **Hello 5, Dead 20, Wait 20**, Retransmit 5
   oob-resync timeout 40
   Hello due in 00:00:00
  Supports Link-local Signaling (LLS)
  Cisco NSF helper support enabled
  IETF NSF helper support enabled
  Index 2/2, flood queue length 0
  Next 0x0(0)/0x0(0)
  Last flood scan length is 1, maximum is 1
  Last flood scan time is 0 msec, maximum is 0 msec
  Neighbor Count is 2, Adjacent neighbor count is 2
    Adjacent with neighbor 192.168.123.2 (Backup Designated Router)
    Adjacent with neighbor 192.168.131.3
  Suppress hello for 0 neighbor(s)

Remember, timers need to match for adjacency to form. The full requirements are:

1. Subnet mask on network must match
2. Neighbors must be in common network.
3. Hello inteval must match
4. Dead interval must match
5. Must be in the same OSPF area.
6. MTU must match
7. Must pass authentication if configured.

Also the 2 neighbors must compatible network types, if you try to peer a broadcast network interface with a point-to-point. The adjacency will come up but you will never learn any routes.

OSPF Review Questions

1. OSPF routers run the _____ algorithm.
2. OSPF routers identify each other with a _____ _____.
3. _____ _____ denotes multiple devices accessing a medium in which broadcasts and multicasts are heard by all devices sharing that medium.
4. _____ _____ are devices that cannot hear each other's broadcasts because the medium is separated by other routers, such as with Frame Relay.
5. OSPF uses _____ as a metric.
6. An OSPF's router ID is based on _____.
7. OSPF hellos are sent every _____ seconds on a multi-access medium.
8. The OSPF process ID is _____.
9. When examining routes in the routing table, enter the code used to represent OSPF routes: _____.

Match the Router Types & Area Types below to the cooresponding definition.
Router Types
A. Internal Router
B. Area Border Router(ABR)
C. Backbone Router
D. AS Boundry Router(ASBR)
10. _____ A router with an interface in area 0
11. _____ Connects to additional routing domains
12. _____ All interfaces reside within the same area
13. _____ Connects two or more areas

Area Types
A. Standard Area
B. Stub Area
C. Totally Stubby Area
D. Not So Stubby Area (NSSA)
14. _____ External link (type 5) LSAs are replaced with a default route
15. _____ A stub area containing an ASBR; type 5 LSAs are converted to type 7 there
16. _____ Default OSPF area type
17. _____ Type 3, 4, and 5 LSAs are replaced with a default route

Answers:

1. Dijkstra
2. router ID
3. Broadcast multi-access
4. Nonbroadcast multi-access
5. OSPF uses cost as metric.
6. AN OSPF's router ID is based on the highest IP address on its loopback interface. If configured, or the highest IP address on its active interfaces.
7. OSPF hellos are sent every 10 seconds.
8. The OSPF process ID is locally significant.
9. The code used to represent OSPF routes is 'o'. The letter 'o' is used to represent OSPF routes in an IP routing table.
10. C
11. B
12. A
13. D
14. B
15. D
16. A
17. C

Multi Area OSPF Routing

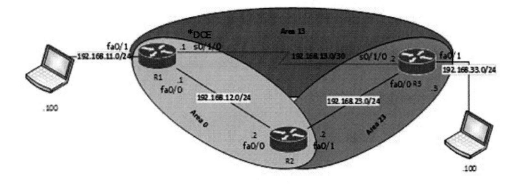

The purpose of this lab is to explore the functionality of OSPF using multiple areas. This lab focuses on many on the basic concepts of OSPF.

Hardware & Configuration Required for this Lab

- Two Cisco routers with two Fast Ethernet interfaces and one serial port
- One Cisco router with two Fast Ethernet interfaces or one Fast Ethernet if you want to use a switch to connect R2 instead.
- One DCE/DTE back to back cable
- Two PCs to connect to the routers
- Three straight through Cat 5 cable
- **Note:** If you do not have two routers with dual Ethernet ports and two PCs, that is ok. Simply configure the PC subnets as loopback interfaces and source your pings from the loopback network when you want to test.

Commands Used in this Lab

router ospf <process> - Used to enable ospf on the router
network <network> <wildcard mask> area – Adds networks to the OSPF database
ip ospf <process> area <area>- Used to enable ospf on an interface
ip ospf hello-interval <x> - Used to configure the ospf hello timer value
show ip ospf neighbor – Provides neighbor IDs, state, address, dead time and interface

---

Inital Configs - Where you see *Initial Configs,* these are basic configuration steps that by now you should be able to perform on the devices by yourself without us detailing them step by step. Generally you simply go into enable and then configuration mode and start the configuration. **Note:** If your interfaces don't match the configs, simply change the interface names to what matches your lab.

R1

hostname R1
line con 0
logging synch
exit
interface FastEthernet0/0
 ip address 192.168.12.1 255.255.255.0
 no shut

interface FastEthernet0/1 (Note: loopback1 can be used if either your router does not have dual fastethernet interfaces or you do not have two PCs)
 ip address 192.168.11.1 255.255.255.0
 no shut (Note: command not needed if loopback interface is used)

interface Serial0/1/0
 ip address 192.168.13.1 255.255.255.252
 no shut
 clock rate 128000 (if you have a WIC-1DSU-TI module(don't confuse this with a WIC-1T, use the *service-module T1 clock source internal* command instead)).
 exit

R2

hostname R2
line con 0
logging synch
exit
interface FastEthernet0/0
 ip address 192.168.12.2 255.255.255.0
 no shut

interface FastEthernet0/1
 ip address 192.168.23.2 255.255.255.0
 no shut

R3

hostname R3
line con 0
logging synch
exit

interface FastEthernet0/0
 ip address 192.168.23.3 255.255.255.0
 no shut

interface FastEthernet0/1 (Note: loopback3 can be used if either your router does not
have dual fastethernet interfaces or you do not have two PCs)
 ip address 192.168.33.3 255.255.255.0
 no shut (Note: command not needed if loopback interface is used)

interface Serial0/1/0
 ip address 192.168.13.2 255.255.255.252
 no shut
 clock rate 128000 (If you have a WIC-1DSU-TI module(don't confuse this with a WIC-1T, use the
service-module T1 clock source line command here)).

PC-1   **PC-2**

OSPF is by far the most preferred enterprise class routing protocol. It has many more
design and scalability options than EIGRP. In fact, due to OSPF's hierarchical nature, it
can easily and efficiently scale to thousands of routers. However OSPF is more
complicated than EIGRP because there are quite a few more design decisions that have
to be made.

One of the main reasons companies prefer OSPF over EIGRP is that EIGRP is propriety to
Cisco. Thus it can only be run on Cisco equipment. If your company has a couple Juniper
routers in the mix, you will most likely pick OSPF rather than deal with managing
multiple routing protocols.

Next we will enable OSPF on the routers utilizing the respective areas depicted in the figure at the beginning of the lab. From a design perspective, ALL areas need to be directly connected to area 0. The lab in question has three areas, namely 0, 13 and 23 of which 13 and 23 are directly connected to 0. Area 0 is a special area known as the backbone area. Note: Respective commands to enable OSPF on respective interfaces were described in the previous lab. If you need a refresher, please refer to the previous lab. We will utilize the **network** statement under the **router ospf <process ID>** command to enble OSPF on the respective routers.

R1(config)#**router ospf 1**
R1(config-router)#**network 192.168.11.0 0.0.0.255 area 0**
R1(config-router)#**network 192.168.12.0 0.0.0.255 area 0**
R1(config-router)#**network 192.168.13.0 0.0.0.3 area 13**

R2(config)#**router ospf 1**
R2(config-router)#**network 192.168.12.0 0.0.0.255 area 0**
R2(config-router)#**network 192.168.23.0 0.0.0.255 area 23**

R3(config)#**router ospf 1**
R3(config-router)#**network 192.168.33.0 0.0.0.255 area 23**
R3(config-router)#**network 192.168.13.0 0.0.0.3 area 13**
R3(config-router)#**network 192.168.23.0 0.0.0.255 area 23**

After entering your configs, you should start seeing adjacency messages similar to the following:
%OSPF-5-ADJCHG: Process 1, Nbr 192.168.33.3 on Serial0/1/0 from LOADING to FULL, Loading Done

Now that OSPF Multi-Area has been configured, the first thing we will look at is the output from the **show ip protocols** command. Some output may vary based upon if you used a loopback interface or not. Simply focus on the concept at hand.

R1#**show ip protocols**

Routing Protocol is "ospf 1"
  Outgoing update filter list for all interfaces is not set
  Incoming update filter list for all interfaces is not set
  Router ID 192.168.11.1
  Number of areas in this router is 2. 2 normal 0 stub 0 nssa
  Maximum path: 4
  Routing for Networks:
    192.168.11.0 0.0.0.255 area 0
    192.168.12.0 0.0.0.255 area 0

    192.168.13.0 0.0.0.3 area 13
Routing Information Sources:
  Gateway   Distance   Last Update
  192.168.11.1   110   00:27:16
  192.168.23.2   110   00:28:16
  192.168.33.3   110   00:27:16
Distance: (default is 110)

As with the signal area OSPF configuration, we can show a brief summary of neighbor information with the **show ip ospf neighbor** command. It will show you the neighbor's router-id/IP address, election priority, adjacency state, the router type, and the dead time. If you do not have a node on the 33 network, you will not see it in the output below.

R1#**show ip ospf neighbor**

Neighbor ID Pri State   Dead Time Address   Interface
192.168.23.2 1 FULL/BDR   00:00:30 192.168.12.2 FastEthernet0/0
192.168.33.3 0 FULL/ -   00:00:39 192.168.13.2 Serial0/1/0

The OSPF Network Type determines whether or not a link will participate in the DR election and also what default timers the interface will use. You can see what network type is configured on an interface; as well as check the interface timers with: **show ip ospf interfaces** command.

R1#**show ip ospf interface**
Loopback1 is up, line protocol is up
  Internet address is 192.168.11.1/24, Area 0
  Process ID 1, Router ID 192.168.11.1, Network Type LOOPBACK, Cost: 1
  Loopback interface is treated as a stub Host
FastEthernet0/0 is up, line protocol is up
  Internet address is 192.168.12.1/24, Area 0
  Process ID 1, Router ID 192.168.11.1, Network Type BROADCAST, Cost: 1
  Transmit Delay is 1 sec, State DR, Priority 1
  Designated Router (ID) 192.168.11.1, Interface address 192.168.12.1
  Backup Designated Router (ID) 192.168.23.2, Interface address 192.168.12.2
  Timer intervals configured, Hello 10, Dead 40, Wait 40, Retransmit 5
    Hello due in 00:00:09
  Index 2/2, flood queue length 0
  Next 0x0(0)/0x0(0)
  Last flood scan length is 1, maximum is 1
  Last flood scan time is 0 msec, maximum is 0 msec
  Neighbor Count is 1, Adjacent neighbor count is 1
    Adjacent with neighbor 192.168.23.2 (Backup Designated Router)
  Suppress hello for 0 neighbor(s)

Serial0/1/0 is up, line protocol is up
  Internet address is 192.168.13.1/30, Area 13
  Process ID 1, Router ID 192.168.11.1, Network Type POINT-TO-POINT, Cost: 64
  Transmit Delay is 1 sec, State POINT-TO-POINT, Priority 0
  No designated router on this network
  No backup designated router on this network
  Timer intervals configured, Hello 10, Dead 40, Wait 40, Retransmit 5
    Hello due in 00:00:05
  Index 3/3, flood queue length 0
  Next 0x0(0)/0x0(0)
  Last flood scan length is 1, maximum is 1
  Last flood scan time is 0 msec, maximum is 0 msec
  Neighbor Count is 1, Adjacent neighbor count is 1
    Adjacent with neighbor 192.168.33.3
  Suppress hello for 0 neighbor(s)

When checking the routing table, OSPF routes are shown with an **O**. If you did not configure the loopback interface and you simply configured the FA0/0 interface on R3 but do not have a node on it, it will not show up in the output below as it is not active.

R1#show ip route ospf
O IA 192.168.23.0 [110/2] via 192.168.12.2, 00:46:47, FastEthernet0/0
      192.168.33.0/32 is subnetted, 1 subnets
O IA   192.168.33.3 [110/3] via 192.168.12.2, 00:45:32, FastEthernet0/0

Cisco 2900/3500 Switch Password Recovery

We will enter ROMMON mode on the switch and rename the startup-configuration in order to bypass it on the next boot. Boot, get enabled/privileged access, load the saved configuration, set new passwords, rename the file back, then save the configuration.

Hardware & Configuration Requirements for this Lab
- One Cisco 2950, 2960, 3550, or 3560 series switch

Just like routers, sometimes the password or login for managing a switch becomes lost or unknown. Very similar to entering ROMMON on a router via the console, switches perform password recovery by renaming the configuration file prior to loading the startup configuration.

Switch Configuration

Start with a clean configuration on the switch. This can be accomplished by executing "write erase" from enabled (privilege level 15) mode, then reloading the switch.

> Switch> **enable**
> Switch# **write erase**
> Switch# **reload**
> System configuration has been modified. Save? [yes/no]: **n**
> Proceed with reload? [confirm]

Lab Exercise
Set the Login and Enable Passwords

Although this step is not necessary, it adds realism. These passwords can be replaced with anything since they will be circumvented by the password recovery process.

> Switch(config)# **enable secret 0c$** (*Always use "enable secret" and never "enable password" because "enable password" stores the enable password in the config as clear text*).
> Switch(config)# **no enable password**
> Switch(config)# **!** (*Documents sometimes separate configuration commands with an exclamation point. Just note that the CLI ignores input beginning with a !.*)
> Switch(config)# **line con 0**
> Switch (config-line)# **password 0c$1C**
> Switch (config-line)# **exit**
> Switch (config)# **copy running-config startup-config**

Boot and Enter ROMMON

Exit the console ssession and try to log back in and verify you are prompted for the passwords configured above. Now power down the switch. Make a console connection and start with the switch powered off. Hold down the MODE button on the front of the switch while connecting the power cord. Continue holding the mode button until the ROMMON prompt appears in the terminal or after about 15 seconds have passed, at which time the ROMMON prompt will appear after the mode button is released. You may need to try this more than once to get thet sequence and timing correct.

> Rommon 1>

Rename the Startup Configuration

Read both possible scenarios below before proceeding. Rename the startup configuration file, "config.text", using the **ren** command. Note the new filename.

> Rommon 1> **ren flash:config.text flash:config.old**
> Rommon 2> **boot**

On some switches, the flash file system must be initialized with the FLASH_INIT command.

> Rommon 1> **flash_init**
> Rommon 2> **ren flash:config.text flash:config.old**
> Rommon 3> **boot**

In ROMMON, the command "boot" will resume the IOS load and switch boot.

Load the Configuration and Set New Passwords

Allow the switch to boot, load the IOS image, perform power on-self tests (POST), and provide the command line interface (CLI) exec/unprivileged mode prompt. Enter enabled/privileged mode, load the startup-configuration, then enter configuration mode to enter new passwords once already in enabled/privileged mode. Reboot to test.

Enable mode commands and config t commands are assumed to reach this point:

> SW1(config)# **enable secret cisco**
> SW1(config)# **line con 0**
> SW1(config-line)# **password cisco**
> SW1(config-line)# **end**
> SW1#**copy running-config startup-config**

Reboot the unit and verify the password changes are active.

Switching and VLAN Introduction

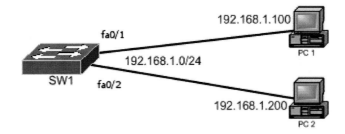

This is a simple lab that explores basic switching concepts while also introducing VLANs.

Hardware & Configuration Required for this Lab

- One Cisco switch
- Two PCs to connect to the switch
- Two straight through Cat 5 cables

Commands Used in this Lab

show ip int brief – Displays the status of all the interfaces on a switch
show mac-address-table - Displays the mac address table
show vlan - Shows full information for VLANs configured on the switch
show vlan brief- Displays a brief summary of the VLANs configured on a switch
show vlan id <#>- Displays full information for a given vlan on a switch
vlan <#>-Configures a vlan on a modern switch
vlan database-Enters the vlan database
switchport access vlan <#>-Configures a vlan on an interface

Initial Configs - Where you see *Initial Configs,* these are basic configuration steps that by now you should be able to perform on the devices by yourself without us detailing them step by step. Generally you simply go into enable and then configuration mode and start the configuration.

SW1
line console 0
logging synch

Patch PC1 to Fa0/1
Patch PC2 to Fa0/2

PC-1   **PC-2**

Just like with a hub, there is no special configuration required for the switch to provide connectivity between PC1 and PC2 saying that it's a pretty safe bet that Cisco certifications and your future employers will expect a bit more knowledge with switches. Let's have a look at the interface summary; comparing this with a router we can see several differences at first glance.

- There are many more ports. 24 on this switch, but they can range in the hundreds for bigger switches.
- There is a logical Vlan1 interface, more on this later.
- All ports unused ports are in the down/down state. A port will come up when something is plugged into it. A router interface is administratively down by default.

C3550-1#**sh ip int br**

Interface	IP-Address	OK?	Method	Status	Protocol
Vlan1	unassigned	YES	manual	administratively down	down
FastEthernet0/1	unassigned	YES	manual	up	up
FastEthernet0/2	unassigned	YES	manual	up	up
FastEthernet0/3	unassigned	YES	manual	down	down
FastEthernet0/4	unassigned	YES	manual	down	down
FastEthernet0/5	unassigned	YES	manual	down	down
FastEthernet0/6	unassigned	YES	manual	down	down
FastEthernet0/7	unassigned	YES	manual	down	down

FastEthernet0/8	unassigned	YES	manual	down	down
FastEthernet0/9	unassigned	YES	manual	down	down
FastEthernet0/10	unassigned	YES	manual	down	down
FastEthernet0/11	unassigned	YES	manual	down	down
FastEthernet0/12	unassigned	YES	manual	down	down
FastEthernet0/13	unassigned	YES	manual	down	down
FastEthernet0/14	unassigned	YES	manual	down	down
FastEthernet0/15	unassigned	YES	manual	down	down
FastEthernet0/16	unassigned	YES	manual	down	down
FastEthernet0/17	unassigned	YES	manual	down	down
FastEthernet0/18	unassigned	YES	manual	down	down
FastEthernet0/19	unassigned	YES	manual	down	down
FastEthernet0/20	unassigned	YES	manual	down	down
FastEthernet0/21	unassigned	YES	manual	down	down
FastEthernet0/22	unassigned	YES	manual	down	down
FastEthernet0/23	unassigned	YES	manual	down	down
FastEthernet0/24	unassigned	YES	manual	down	down
GigabitEthernet0/1	unassigned	YES	manual	down	down
GigabitEthernet0/2	unassigned	YES	manual	down	down

A fundamental difference between hubs and switches is that switches keep track of source mac addresses it learns and records them into its mac-address-table. This table can be viewed on most switches with the command: **show mac-address-table**. The output will show static and dynamic learnings. Static macs are the actual switch interfaces and any macs you statically define whereas dynamic macs are those learned from other sources. As an example, the two PCs connected to the switch.

```
C3550-1#show mac-address-table
    Mac Address Table
    -------------------------------------------

Vlan    Mac Address    Type      Ports
----    -----------    --------  -----
    All  000b.46c9.6e00  STATIC    CPU
    All  000b.46c9.6e01  STATIC    CPU
    All  000b.46c9.6e02  STATIC    CPU
    All  000b.46c9.6e03  STATIC    CPU
    All  000b.46c9.6e04  STATIC    CPU
    All  000b.46c9.6e05  STATIC    CPU
    All  000b.46c9.6e06  STATIC    CPU
        Total Mac Addresses for this criterion: 49
```
Output truncated

Keep in mind that this switch isn't in production and only has two PCs connected to it at the moment. However the mac-address-table is already somewhat large. Thankfully you can also filter the mac-address-table output by whether it was dynamically or statically learned and also by interface and by vlan. Example options on the **show mac-address-table** command are as follows:

```
C3550-1# show mac-address-table ?
  address     address keyword
  aging-time  aging-time keyword
  count       count keyword
  dynamic     dynamic entry type
  interface   interface keyword
  multicast   multicast info for selected wildcard
  notification  MAC notification parameters and history table
  static      static entry type
  vlan        VLAN keyword
  |           Output modifiers
  <cr>
```

Here is the output from the **show mac-address-table dynamic** command:

```
C3550-1# show mac-address-table dynamic
Mac Address Table
-------------------------------------------

Vlan  Mac Address      Type      Ports
-----  ---------------  --------  --------
1      0015.b751.1be9   DYNAMIC   Fa0/2
1      001b.2418.3bc9   DYNAMIC   Fa0/1
```

Another major topic for switches is VLANs. Most switch topics involve VLANs in one way or another. Fortunately the concept of a VLAN is actually pretty simple and doesn't require too much thought (although the technologies that use VLANs do!!!).

As a quick refresher VLANs or Virtual LANs are just logical networks that allow you to connect various devices in the same broadcast domain.   So in simple terms, a VLAN is essentially equivalent to an IP subnet. For example, if your company's Sales department is located on several floors and across several switches, you can simply put them all in the same VLAN to provide them the same connectivity.

You can view all the VLANs defined on a switch with the **show vlan** command, by default all ports will be in VLAN 1 which is what we see below.

```
C3550-1#show vlan
VLAN Name                     Status    Ports
------------- ------------------------------- --------- -------------------------------
1   default                   active    Fa0/1, Fa0/2, Fa0/3, Fa0/4
                                        Fa0/5, Fa0/6, Fa0/7, Fa0/8
                                        Fa0/9, Fa0/10, Fa0/11, Fa0/12
                                        Fa0/13, Fa0/14, Fa0/15, Fa0/16
```

```
                                   Fa0/17, Fa0/18, Fa0/19, Fa0/20
                                   Fa0/21, Fa0/22, Fa0/23, Fa0/24
                                   Gi0/1, Gi0/2
1002 fddi-default            act/unsup
1003 token-ring-default      act/unsup
1004 fddinet-default         act/unsup
1005 trnet-default           act/unsup
```

VLAN	Type	SAID	MTU	Parent	RingNo	BridgeNo	Stp	BrdgMode	Trans1	Trans2
1	enet	100001	1500	-	-	-	-	-	0	0
1002	fddi	101002	1500	-	-	-	-	-	0	0
1003	tr	101003	1500	-	-	-	-	-	0	0
1004	fdnet	101004	1500	-	-	-	ieee	-	0	0
1005	trnet	101005	1500	-	-	-	ibm	-	0	0

```
Remote SPAN VLANs
-----------------------------------------------------------------------


Primary Secondary Type          Ports
-------------- --------- ---------------- ----------------------------------------
```

Like most things with Cisco, you also have the option of reducing the output with **show vlan brief**.

C3550-1#**show vlan brief**
VLAN Name	Status	Ports
1 default	active	Fa0/1, Fa0/2, Fa0/3, Fa0/4 Fa0/5, Fa0/6, Fa0/7, Fa0/8 Fa0/9, Fa0/10, Fa0/11, Fa0/12 Fa0/13, Fa0/14, Fa0/15, Fa0/16 Fa0/17, Fa0/18, Fa0/19, Fa0/20 Fa0/21, Fa0/22, Fa0/23, Fa0/24 Gi0/1, Gi0/2
1002 fddi-default	act/unsup	
1003 token-ring-default	act/unsup	
1004 fddinet-default	act/unsup	
1005 trnet-default	act/unsup	

If you are only interested in a certain VLAN you can use the **show vlan id <#>** command to filter the output to the VLAN you need to see.

C3550-1#**show vlan id 1**
VLAN Name	Status	Ports
1 default	active	Fa0/1, Fa0/2, Fa0/3, Fa0/4

```
                           Fa0/5, Fa0/6, Fa0/7, Fa0/8
                           Fa0/9, Fa0/10, Fa0/11, Fa0/12
                           Fa0/13, Fa0/14, Fa0/15, Fa0/16
                           Fa0/17, Fa0/18, Fa0/19, Fa0/20
                           Fa0/21, Fa0/22, Fa0/23, Fa0/24
                           Gi0/1, Gi0/2
VLAN Type  SAID      MTU  Parent  RingNo  BridgeNo  Stp  BrdgMode  Trans1  Trans2
---- ----- --------- ----- ------ ------ -------------------------------------------------- ---- -------- ------ ------

1     enet  100001   1500  -        -       -            -    -          0       0
```

To create a VLAN you use the **vlan** command from global configuration mode followed by the VLAN number.

C3550-1(config)#**vlan ?**
  WORD   ISL VLAN IDs 1-4094

By default you may create VLANs between 2-1001 when we get a little deeper into switching, we will see that you can use the extended VLANs range which allows you to create VLANs from 2-1001,1006-4094. Vlan 1 is the industry standard for switch management among other things which is why by default all ports are in Vlan 1 and there is a vlan1 interface. It is good practice to use vlans other that vlan 1 when assigning interfaces to vlans.

Vlans 1002-1005 are special purpose VLANs that are never used anymore and only exist so Cisco can comply with industry standards (and to provide some excellent CCNA exam questions of course). They are mostly used for token ring networks (when have you seen those around lately?) and in fact you can't even use them on Ethernet ports.

C3550-1(config-if)#**switchport access vlan 1005**
% Warning: port will be inactive in non-ethernet VLAN

Before we play with making VLANs let's first make sure PC1 and PC2 can ping each other. BTW generally speaking if you ping from PC1 and receive a reply from PC2 this implies 2-way communication and there is no need to ping PC1 from PC2.

Now we will make 2 VLANs and add the interfaces that connect the PCs into separate VLANs. When making VLANs you can optionally name each VLAN, this is just a visual aid for you and doesn't affect any configuration. BTW you **MUST** type **exit** after configuring multiple VLANs or the switch will discard your last VLAN.

C3550-1(config)#**vlan 100**
C3550-1(config-vlan)#**name PC-1**
C3550-1(config-vlan)#**vlan 101**
C3550-1(config-vlan)#**name PC-2**
C3550-1(config-vlan)#**exit**

Checking **show vlan** again we can see we now have VLANs 100 and 101 and each have a name but no ports are assigned.

C3550-1(config)#**do show vlan brief**

VLAN	Name	Status	Ports
1	default	active	Fa0/1, Fa0/2, Fa0/3, Fa0/4
			Fa0/5, Fa0/6, Fa0/7, Fa0/8
			Fa0/9, Fa0/10, Fa0/11, Fa0/12
			Fa0/13, Fa0/14, Fa0/15, Fa0/16
			Fa0/17, Fa0/18, Fa0/19, Fa0/20
			Fa0/21, Fa0/22, Fa0/23, Fa0/24
			Gi0/1, Gi0/2
100	**PC-1**	**active**	
101	**PC-2**	**active**	
1002	fddi-default	act/unsup	
1003	token-ring-default	act/unsup	
1004	fddinet-default	act/unsup	
1005	trnet-default	act/unsup	

Note: If you are running older switches in your network like the popular Cisco 2924 models, then you'll find that they don't have a **vlan** command from global configuration mode.

C2900-1(config)#**vlan ?**
% Unrecognized command

They actually use a different configuration mode called **vlan database** which has been deprecated in newer switches. **Note:** Cisco doesn't test the **vlan database**, as it has been deprecated but it is nice to know in the real workd that it exists in the event you are maintaining older switches. An example configuration on an a 2900 series switch is as follows:

C2900-1#**vlan database**
C2900-1(vlan)#

Here are the various commands you can use inside the VLAN database. You will mostly use the **abort, exit, vlan, and show** commands.

C2900-1(vlan)#**?**
VLAN database editing buffer manipulation commands:
  abort Exit mode without applying the changes
  apply Apply current changes and bump revision number
  exit   Apply changes, bump revision number, and exit mode
  no   Negate a command or set its defaults
  reset Abandon current changes and reread current database
  show   Show database information
  vlan   Add, delete, or modify values associated with a single VLAN
  vtp   Perform VTP administrative functions.

You add a vlan with the **vlan** command, you can optionally name the vlan with the **name** option.

The syntax is: **vlan <#> name <optional name>**
C2900-1(vlan)#**vlan 100**
VLAN 100 added:
  Name: VLAN0100

C2900-1(vlan)#**vlan 100 name PC-1**
VLAN 100 added:
  Name: PC-1

Let's add the other vlan as well.
C2900-1(vlan)#**vlan 101 name PC-2**
VLAN 101 added:
  Name: PC-2

You can view the configured VLANs directly from the vlan database with
the **show** command. Most switches support the **show vlan** command as well but
sometimes checking the VLANs from the vlan database is the only option.

```
C2900-1(vlan)#show
    VLAN ISL Id: 1
    Name: default
    Media Type: Ethernet
    VLAN 802.10 Id: 100001
    State: Operational
    MTU: 1500
VLAN ISL Id: 100
    Name: PC-1
    Media Type: Ethernet
    VLAN 802.10 Id: 100100
    State: Operational
    MTU: 1500
VLAN ISL Id: 101
    Name: PC-2
    Media Type: Ethernet
    VLAN 802.10 Id: 100101
    State: Operational
    MTU: 1500
VLAN ISL Id: 1002
    Name: fddi-default
    Media Type: FDDI
    VLAN 802.10 Id: 101002
    State: Operational
    MTU: 1500
    Bridge Type: SRB
    Ring Number: 0
VLAN ISL Id: 1003
    Name: token-ring-default
    Media Type: Token Ring
    VLAN 802.10 Id: 101003
    State: Operational
    MTU: 1500
    Bridge Type: SRB
    Ring Number: 0
VLAN ISL Id: 1004
    Name: fddinet-default
    Media Type: FDDI Net
    VLAN 802.10 Id: 101004
    State: Operational
    MTU: 1500
    STP Type: IEEE
```

VLAN ISL Id: 1005
    Name: trnet-default
    Media Type: Token Ring Net
    VLAN 802.10 Id: 101005
    State: Operational
    MTU: 1500
    STP Type: IBM

The new VLANs aren't actually made active until you type **apply or exit**, Apply is used when you are still configuring things in the vlan database and **exit** is used when you are done and want to save your changes.

C2900-1(vlan)#**exit**
APPLY completed.
Exiting....

If you try to enter the vlan database on a newer switch that supports the global **vlan** command then you'll get a warning message saying that support for the database has ended. You can still use it however.

C3550-1#**vlan database**
% Warning: It is recommended to configure VLAN from config mode,
as VLAN database mode is being deprecated. Please consult user
documentation for configuring VTP/VLAN in config mode.

To assign a vlan to a port we need to go under the interface and type **switchport access vlan** and the vlan number.

C3550-1(config)#**int fa0/1**
C3550-1(config-if)#**switchport access vlan 100**
C3550-1(config-if)#**int fa0/2**
C3550-1(config-if)#**switchport access vlan 101**

There is a third way to configure VLANs on a switch and that is by adding a new vlan directly to an interface.

C3550-1(config)#**int fa0/10**
C3550-1(config-if)#**switchport access vlan 555**
% Access VLAN does not exist. Creating vlan 555

If we check the configured VLANs again we can see now the ports are bound to the new VLANs.

C3550-1#**show vlan brief**

VLAN	Name	Status	Ports
1	default	active	Fa0/3, Fa0/4, Fa0/5, Fa0/6
			Fa0/7, Fa0/8, Fa0/9, Fa0/11
			Fa0/12, Fa0/16, Fa0/17, Fa0/18
			Fa0/19, Fa0/20, Fa0/21, Fa0/22
			Fa0/23, Fa0/24, Gi0/1, Gi0/2
100	PC-1	active	Fa0/1
101	PC-2	active	Fa0/2
555	VLAN0555	active	Fa0/10
1002	fddi-default	act/unsup	
1003	token-ring-default	act/unsup	
1004	fddinet-default	act/unsup	
1005	trnet-default	act/unsup	

If we try to ping from PC1 again we can see PC2 is no longer reachable even though it is in the same IP subnet because it is now in a different broadcast domain.

We can confirm it is in a different broadcast domain by checking a packet capture of PC1 we can see that it isn't able to ARP PC2 at all.

If we check the mac-address-table we can see that it is noting what vlan the macs are learned from.

C3550-1#show mac-address-table dynamic
```
    Mac Address Table
  -------------------------------------------

Vlan    Mac Address       Type        Ports
----    -----------       --------    -----
 100    001b.2418.3bc9    DYNAMIC     Fa0/1
 101    0015.b751.1be9    DYNAMIC     Fa0/2
 Total Mac Addresses for this criterion: 2
```

There is much more to switching then this lab shows, other labs will go into things like Trunking, Spanning Tree Protocol, VLAN management, and Security in some depth.

VLAN Review

Questions:

1. You've connected your switches together with a crossover cable. What would be a possible reason for a switching loop to occur?

   _____

2. What is not a similarity between STP and RSTP?

   _____

3. What occurs when a link fails in an EtherChannel bundle?

   _____

4. The SYSTEM LED will be _____ if the switch has experienced a malfunction.

5. Enter the switch command that allows you to see the contents of the port address table: _____

6. A connection that supports multiple VLANs is called a _____

7. The _____ is a proprietary Cisco protocol used to share VLAN configuration information between Cisco switches on trunk connections.

8. The root switch is the one elected with the _____

9. The switch port that is chosen to forward traffic for a segment is called a

   _____

10. How many port states are there in RSTP? _____

Answers:

1. When PortFast is enabled, you must not connect a switch, bridge, or hub to that interface, or loops may occur

2. In RSTP, BPDUs originate from each switch and act as a keepalive. STP BPDUs originate from the root bridge and are forwarded by other switches.

3. When a link fails in an EtherChannel bundle, the traffic is redistributed over the remaining links.

4. The system LED will be amber if the switch has experienced a malfunction

5. Show mac-address-table

6. Trunk

7. VTP

8. The switch with the lowest switch ID is elected as the root switch.

9. The switch port that is chosen to forward traffic for a segment is called a designated port.

10. There are 3 port states in RSTP: discarding, learning, and forwarding.

Trunking

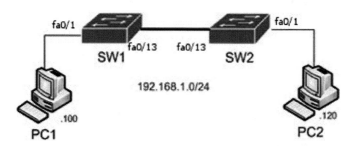

The purpose of this lab is to explore basic trunking in a switch environment.

Hardware & Configuration Required for this Lab

- Two Cisco switches
- One crossover Cat5 cables to connect the switches via port 13
- Two PCs to connect to the switches
- Two straight through Cat 5 cables

Commands Used in Lab

show interface trunk - Shows a summary of all trunking information
show interface <port> switchport-Displays detailed informaton about the switchport
switchport mode dynamic - Changes DTP's operating mode
switchport nonegotiate-Disables DTP on interface
switchport trunk encapsulation- Manually selects trunking protocol
switchport mode trunk-Manually sets the port as trunking
switchport trunk native vlan - Changes native vlan for 802.1Q
switchport trunk allowed vlan-Controls what vlans are allowed across a trunk link

---

Initial Configs - Where you see *Initial Configs,* these are basic configuration steps that by now you should be able to perform on the devices by yourself without us detailing them step by step. Generally you simply go into enable and then configuration mode and start the configuration.

SW1

hostname SW1
line console 0
logging synch

SW2
hostname SW2
line console 0
logging synch

PC-1   **PC-2**

Trunking is often said to be connecting multiple switches together, which is true but a better definition is allowing multiple VLANs across an interface. It's important to remember that a switch can trunk with many devices including routers, switches, firewalls, servers, and more.

Trunking for the most part is an easy topic. For a switch to be considered a useful switch in an enterprise environment, it must support at least some kind of trunking. In this lab we have connected two Cisco switches together via port 13.

We can quickly view the status of all ports on a switch by issuing the following command.

SW1#**sho ip interface brief**

Interface	IP-Address	OK?	Method	Status	Protocol
Vlan1	unassigned	YES	unset	administratively down	down
FastEthernet0/1	unassigned	YES	unset	up	up
FastEthernet0/2	unassigned	YES	unset	down	down

FastEthernet0/3	unassigned	YES	unset	down	down
FastEthernet0/4	unassigned	YES	unset	down	down
FastEthernet0/5	unassigned	YES	unset	down	down
FastEthernet0/6	unassigned	YES	unset	down	down
FastEthernet0/7	unassigned	YES	unset	down	down
FastEthernet0/8	unassigned	YES	unset	down	down
FastEthernet0/9	unassigned	YES	unset	down	down
FastEthernet0/10	unassigned	YES	unset	down	down
FastEthernet0/11	unassigned	YES	unset	down	down
FastEthernet0/12	unassigned	YES	unset	down	down
FastEthernet0/13	unassigned	YES	unset	up	up
FastEthernet0/14	unassigned	YES	unset	down	down
FastEthernet0/15	unassigned	YES	unset	down	down
FastEthernet0/16	unassigned	YES	unset	down	down
FastEthernet0/17	unassigned	YES	unset	down	down
FastEthernet0/18	unassigned	YES	unset	down	down
FastEthernet0/19	unassigned	YES	unset	down	down
FastEthernet0/20	unassigned	YES	unset	down	down
FastEthernet0/21	unassigned	YES	unset	down	down
FastEthernet0/22	unassigned	YES	unset	down	down
FastEthernet0/23	unassigned	YES	unset	down	down
FastEthernet0/24	unassigned	YES	unset	down	down
GigabitEthernet0/1	unassigned	YES	unset	down	down
GigabitEthernet0/2	unassigned	YES	unset	down	down

Before doing any changes to a switch network it's usually a good idea to have an up-to-date diagram and to verify it with **show cdp neighbor.** This can save a lot of troubleshooting down the road when things get more complex.

SW1#**show cdp neighbor**
    Capability Codes: R - Router, T - Trans Bridge, B - Source Route Bridge
    S - Switch, H - Host, I - IGMP, r - Repeater, P - Phone

Device ID	Local Intrfce	Holdtme	Capability	Platform	Port ID
SW2	Fas 0/13	153	S	WS-C3550-2	Fas 0/13

Now we need to configure FastEthernet 0/13 on both switches to be a trunk port. This is accomplished by issuing the **switchport mode trunk** command from within interface configuration mode for FastEthernet 0/13. This command needs to be performed on both switches.

SW1(config)#**int fa0/13**
SW1(config-if)#**switchport mode trunk**

Now that trunking is enabled on FastEthernet 0/13 we can verify the configuration utilizing the **show interfaces trunk** command. This shows us a summary of pretty much all the trunking information covered on the CCNA exam.

SW1#show interface trunk

Port	Mode	Encapsulation	Status	Native vlan
Fa0/13	on	802.1q	trunking	1

Port	Vlans allowed on trunk
Fa0/13	1-1005

Port	Vlans allowed and active in management domain
Fa0/13	1,100,101

Port	Vlans in spanning tree forwarding state and not pruned
Fa0/13	1,100,101

There is a lot here, so let's go over it. A handy command for looking into trunking config is **show interface <port> switchport** although it's a little overkill in most cases.
Note: Some switches don't have the show interface trunk command so you'll have to settle for this one.

SW1#show interface fa0/13 switchport
Name: Fa0/13
Switchport: Enabled
Administrative Mode: trunk
Operational Mode: trunk
Administrative Trunking Encapsulation: dot1q
Operational Trunking Encapsulation: dot1q
Negotiation of Trunking: On
Access Mode VLAN: 1 (default)
Trunking Native Mode VLAN: 1 (default)
Voice VLAN: none
Administrative private-vlan host-association: none
Administrative private-vlan mapping: none
Administrative private-vlan trunk native VLAN: none
Administrative private-vlan trunk encapsulation: dot1q
Administrative private-vlan trunk normal VLANs: none
Administrative private-vlan trunk private VLANs: none
Operational private-vlan: none
Trunking VLANs Enabled: ALL
Pruning VLANs Enabled: 2-1001
Capture Mode Disabled
Capture VLANs Allowed: ALL
Protected: false
Appliance trust: none

We can see from the output from both the **show interface trunk** and looking at Fa0/13's switchport information that the switch is utilizing dot1q trunking between the switches. There are two main trunking protocols in the industry: Inter-Swtich Link (ISL) and 802.1Q (also called dot1q or Vlan tagging).

ISL is Cisco proprietary and only available on older platforms as Cisco has phased it out over the years. It adds a header to each frame with the VLAN information.   When the other side receives the frame, it removes the header and passes the frame along to its destination. It supports up to 1000 vlans.

802.1Q is the standards based trunking protocol. It adds a 4 byte tag in each frame with the VLAN value except for the configured native vlan. In general, dot1q supports 4094 vlans.

A Native VLAN is simply a frame without a 802.1Q tag. It's around because some devices don't support vlan tagging. When the switch receives a frame from a 802.1Q trunk without a vlan tag, it simply assumes it belongs to the native VLAN (by default the native vlan is 1).

The switch figures out what protocol to trunk with via the Dynamic Trunking Protocol (DTP).

DTP has two modes:
Desirable - The interface will actively try to negotiate trunking with its directly connected neighbor.
Auto - The interface will not actively send out DTP packets but will respond to any it receives and form a trunk.

You can control this behavior with **switchport mode dynamic <mode>** under an interface.

SW1(config-if)#**switchport mode dynamic ?**
  auto   Set trunking mode dynamic negotiation parameter to AUTO
  desirable   Set trunking mode dynamic negotiation parameter to DESIRABLE

You can also disable DTP entirely with: **switchport nonegotiate** (must have statically set trunking first).
SW1(config)#**int fa0/13**
SW1(config-if)#**switchport nonegotiate**

If you don't statically set trunking before you try to turn off DTP you'll get:
C3550-1(config)#**int fa0/13**
C3550-1(config-if)#**switchport nonegotiate**
Command rejected: Conflict between 'nonegotiate' and 'dynamic' status.

Now that we have Fa0/13 configured as a trunk port and we have explained what trunking is, let's get a little deeper into trunking.

Checking the switchport information on Fa0/13 we can see the link is still trying to negotiate trunking even though we statically set everything because we left DTP on.

SW1(config)#**do sh int fa0/13 sw**
Name: Fa0/13
Switchport: Enabled
Administrative Mode: trunk
Operational Mode: trunk
Administrative Trunking Encapsulation: dot1q
Operational Trunking Encapsulation: dot1q

Negotiation of Trunking: On
Access Mode VLAN: 1 (default)
Trunking Native Mode VLAN: 1 (default)
Voice VLAN: none
Administrative private-vlan host-association: none
Administrative private-vlan mapping: none
Administrative private-vlan trunk native VLAN: none
Administrative private-vlan trunk encapsulation: dot1q
Administrative private-vlan trunk normal VLANs: none
Administrative private-vlan trunk private VLANs: none
Operational private-vlan: none
Trunking VLANs Enabled: ALL
Pruning VLANs Enabled: 2-1001
Capture Mode Disabled
Capture VLANs Allowed: ALL
Protected: false
Appliance trust: none

If we turn on nonegotiate, we can see the status changes in the switchport output.
SW1(config)#**int fa0/13**
SW1(config-if)#**sw nonegotiate**

SW1(config)#**do sh int fa0/13 sw**
Name: Fa0/13
Switchport: Enabled
Administrative Mode: trunk
Operational Mode: trunk
Administrative Trunking Encapsulation: dot1q
Operational Trunking Encapsulation: dot1q

Negotiation of Trunking: Off
Access Mode VLAN: 1 (default)

Trunking Native Mode VLAN: 1 (default)
Voice VLAN: none
Administrative private-vlan host-association: none
Administrative private-vlan mapping: none
Administrative private-vlan trunk native VLAN: none
Administrative private-vlan trunk encapsulation: dot1q
Administrative private-vlan trunk normal VLANs: none
Administrative private-vlan trunk private VLANs: none
Operational private-vlan: none
Trunking VLANs Enabled: ALL
Pruning VLANs Enabled: 2-1001
Capture Mode Disabled
Capture VLANs Allowed: ALL
Protected: false
Appliance trust: none

Let's start adding vlans into the network.

SW1(config)#**vlan 50**   (repeat for VLANs 51 – 59)
SW1(config-vlan)#**exit**

SW2(config)#**vlan 50**   (repeat for VLANs 51 – 59)
SW2(config-vlan)#**exit**

Assign Fa0/1 on SW1 and Fa0/2 on SW2 to be in VLAN 50.

SW1(config)#**int fa0/1**
SW1(config-if)#**switchport access vlan 50**

SW2(config)#**int fa0/2**
SW2(config-if)#**switchport access vlan 50**

After we add the vlans we can see that the vlan range is added to the allowed and active part of the trunking output which means that PC-1 should be able to ping PC-2.

C3550-2(config)#**do show interface trunk**

Port	Mode	Encapsulation	Status	Native vlan
Fa0/13	on	802.1q	trunking	1

Port	Vlans allowed on trunk
Fa0/13	1-1005

Port	Vlans allowed and active in management domain
Fa0/13	1,**50,51,52,53,54,55,56,57,58,59**,100,101

Port	Vlans in spanning tree forwarding state and not pruned
Fa0/13	1,**50,51,52,53,54,55,56,57,58,59**,100,101

Before, PC-1 and PC-2 were connected to switchports in VLAN 1, now the ports on switchports in VLAN 50. As we can see from the output below, PC-1 is still able to ping PC-2 since VLAN 50 is being trunked across SW1 and SW2 on interface Fa0/13.

A quick note on native vlans; there is not a lot of telltale signs of the native vlan in a production network. The best way to verify it via packet capturing is checking the CDP frames.

If necessary you can change the native vlan under an interface with the **switchport trunk native vlan** command. Note: You must change the native vlan on each end o the trunk or you will receive native vlan mismatch errors. Below is an example of changing the native vlan on FA0/13 to VLAN 59. Again, the change needs to be performed on both SW1 and SW2. Once the native vlan is changed on SW1 and prior to it being changed on SW2, a CDP error similar to the following will appear:

%CDP-4-NATIVE_VLAN_MISMATCH: Native VLAN mismatch discovered on FastEthernet0/13 (59), with SW2 FastEthernet0/13 (1).

SW1(config)#**int fa0/13**
SW1(config-if)#**switchport trunk native vlan 59**

SW2(config)#**int fa0/13**
SW2(config-if)#**switchport trunk native vlan 59**

SW1(config)#**do sh int trunk**

Port	Mode	Encapsulation	Status	Native vlan
Fa0/13	**on**	**802.1q**	**trunking**	**59**

Port	Vlans allowed on trunk
Fa0/13	1-1005

Port	Vlans allowed and active in management domain
Fa0/13	1,50,51,52,53,54,55,56,57,58,59,100,101

Port	Vlans in spanning tree forwarding state and not pruned
Fa0/13	1,50,51,52,53,54,55,56,57,58,59,100,101

The last think we'll look at with trunking is Allowed vlans on the trunk. This is controlled with the interface **switchport trunk allowed vlan** command. This is mostly used for security and basic traffic engineering purposes where you may not want all vlans to be learned by all switches.

SW1(config-if)#**switchport trunk allowed vlan ?**

WORD	VLAN IDs of the allowed VLANs when this port is in trunking mode
add	add VLANs to the current list
all	all VLANs
except	all VLANs except the following
none	no VLANs
remove	remove VLANs from the current list

For example let's configure the switches so that only vlans 1, 50, 51 and 52 are allowed across the trunk.

SW1(config)#**int fa0/13**
SW1(config-if)#**switchport trunk allowed vlan 1, 50-52**

SW2(config)#**int fa0/13**
SW2(config-if)#**sw tr allowed vlan remove 50**
C3550-2(config-if)#**int fa0/14**
C3550-2(config-if)#**switchport trunk allowed vlan 1, 50-52**

Checking the trunk output we can see that only VLANs 1, 50, 51 and 52 are allowed on the trunk.

SW1#**show int trunk**
Port   Mode   Encapsulation Status   Native vlan
Fa0/13 on   802.1q   trunking   59

Port   Vlans allowed on trunk

Fa0/13   1,50-52

Port   Vlans allowed and active in management domain

Fa0/13   1,50,51,52

Port   Vlans in spanning tree forwarding state and not pruned

Fa0/13   1,50,51,52

VTP

SW1   SW2   SW3

The purpose of this lab is to explore using VTP in a switch environment.

Hardware & Configuration Required for this Lab

- Three Cisco switches
- Two crossover Cat5 cables to connect between the switches
- Review the configuration below to figure out which ports to connect between switch 1 and switch 2.
- **Delete vlan.dat** if there is vlan configuration on the switch via the *delete flash:vlan.dat* command.

Commands Used in Lab

show vtp status- Shows a summary of all VTP information
vtp mode server-Sets VTP to run in Server mode
vtp mode client-Sets VTP to run in Client mode
vtp mode transparent-Sets VTP to run in Transparent mode
vtp domain <name> -Changes the VTP domain on a switch
vtp password <word>-Sets a MD5 password on the VTP domain

Initial Configs - Where you see *Initial Configs,* these are basic configuration steps that by now you should be able to perform on the devices by yourself without us detailing them step by step. Generally you simply go into enable and then configuration mode and start the configuration.

SW1
hostname SW1
line console 0
logging synch
int fa0/1
description to SW2

SW2
hostname SW2
line console 0
logging synch
int fa0/1
description to SW1
int fa0/2
description to SW3
shutdown

SW3
hostname SW3
line console 0
logging synch
int fa0/2
description to SW2

VLAN Trunking Protocol (VTP) is a Cisco proprietary VLAN management solution for switches. Its purpose is to ensure that all switches in a domain have the same VLAN information by having the VTP server send out any VTP changes across the network. Since VTP works on Cisco devices only, the rest of the world uses the GARP VLAN Registration Protocol (GVRP) but that is outside of the scope of the CCNA exam.

Here is some prep work we have to do manually on Switch3 to make the lab work correctly at the end.

SW3(config)#**vlan 50-59**
SW3(config-vlan)#**vlan 60**
SW3(config-vlan)#**vlan 80**
SW3(config-vlan)#**vlan 400-409**
SW3(config-vlan)#**vlan 410**
SW3(config-vlan)#**vlan 411-415**
SW3(config-vlan)#**exit**
SW3(config)#**vtp domain certificationkits**
Changing VTP domain name from NULL to certificationkits

There really isn't much to VTP. But a good place to start is checking the default VTP config with **show vtp status**

SW1#**sh vtp status**
VTP Version   : 2
Configuration Revision   : 0
Maximum VLANs supported locally   : 1005
Number of existing VLANs   : 5

```
VTP Operating Mode              : Server
VTP Domain Name                 :
VTP Pruning Mode                : Disabled
VTP V2 Mode                     : Disabled
VTP Traps Generation            : Disabled
MD5 digest                      : 0x7D 0x5A 0xA6 0x0E 0x9A 0x72 0xA0 0x3A
Configuration last modified by 0.0.0.0 at 0-0-00 00:00:00
Local updater ID is 0.0.0.0 (no valid interface found)
```

To activate VTP we first need to assign a VTP domain name. This is done with the **vtp domain** command. Let's assign a domain name of **certification** on SW1 and SW2.

SW1(config)#**vtp domain certification**
Changing VTP domain name from NULL to certification

Once we enter in the domain name, we can see that our SW2 has learned about the domain name and made the change for us. This is because in VTP v2 the switch will broadcast out the domain name and as a time saver any switch without a domain name set will join the domain.

SW1#**show vtp status**
```
VTP Version                     : 2
Configuration Revision          : 0
Maximum VLANs supported locally : 1005
Number of existing VLANs        : 5
VTP Operating Mode              : Server
```
VTP Domain Name   : certification
```
VTP Pruning Mode                : Disabled
VTP V2 Mode                     : Disabled
VTP Traps Generation            : Disabled
MD5 digest                      : 0x7D 0x5A 0xA6 0x0E 0x9A 0x72 0xA0 0x3A
Configuration last modified by 0.0.0.0 at 0-0-00 00:00:00
Local updater ID is 0.0.0.0 (no valid interface found)
```

Let's add some vlans to the mix on SW1.
SW1(config)#**vlan 10-20**
SW1(config-vlan)#**exit**

Notice that the revision version has went up by one to show us we made a change to the vlan database and the number of vlans have increased to 16.

SW1(config)#**do show vtp status**
```
VTP Version                     : 2
```
Configuration Revision   : 1
```
Maximum VLANs supported locally : 1005
```
Number of existing VLANs   : 16

```
VTP Operating Mode            : Server
VTP Domain Name               : certificationkits
VTP Pruning Mode              : Disabled
VTP V2 Mode                   : Disabled
VTP Traps Generation          : Disabled
MD5 digest                    : 0x7D 0x5A 0xA6 0x0E 0x9A 0x72 0xA0 0x3A
Configuration last modified by 0.0.0.0 at 3-1-93 16:53:46
Local updater ID is 0.0.0.0 (no valid interface found)
```

On SW2 we see identical information.

```
SW2#show vtp status
VTP Version                       : 2
Configuration Revision            : 1
Maximum VLANs supported locally   : 1005
Number of existing VLANs          : 16
VTP Operating Mode                : Server
VTP Domain Name                   : certificationkits
VTP Pruning Mode                  : Disabled
VTP V2 Mode                       : Disabled
VTP Traps Generation              : Disabled
MD5 digest                        : 0x71 0x22 0xF0 0xF7 0xE1 0xAE 0x44 0x09
Configuration last modified by 0.0.0.0 at 3-1-93 16:53:46
Local updater ID is 0.0.0.0 (no valid interface found)
```

And we can see that SW2 has learned about the new vlans. It's good to point out that even though the switch has learned about the vlans, you still need to apply them to interfaces to use them. However it is very handy in trunking situations since the switches on both ends of a trunk link need to know about the new vlan.

```
SW2#show vlan brief
VLAN  Name                      Status    Ports
----  ------------------------- --------- -------------------------------
 1    default                   active    Fa0/1, Fa0/2, Fa0/3, Fa0/4
                                          Fa0/5, Fa0/6, Fa0/7, Fa0/8
                                          Fa0/9, Fa0/10, Fa0/11, Fa0/12
                                          Fa0/16, Fa0/17, Fa0/18, Fa0/19
                                          Fa0/20, Fa0/21, Fa0/22, Fa0/23
                                          Fa0/24, Gi0/1, Gi0/2
 10   VLAN0010                  active
 11   VLAN0011                  active
 12   VLAN0012                  active
 13   VLAN0013                  active
 14   VLAN0014                  active
 15   VLAN0015                  active
 16   VLAN0016                  active
 17   VLAN0017                  active
```

18	VLAN0018	active
19	VLAN0019	active
20	VLAN0020	active
1002	fddi-default	act/unsup
1003	token-ring-default	act/unsup
1004	fddinet-default	act/unsup
1005	trnet-default	act/unsup

There are **3 modes of VTP**.

Server - The switch can add or remove vlans as it pleases, changes are propagated throughout the network.

Client - The switch is not allowed to add or remove vlans, learns changes from other switches.

Transparent - The switch can made changes but does not propagate them. Basically VTP is turned off (it will still pass updates it receives to other switches).

Because SW2 is in server mode it can also make changes. So if we remove a few vlans, SW1 should remove them as well.

SW2(config)#**no vlan 15-20**

And we can see it is removed.

SW1(config)#**do sh vlan**

VLAN	Name	Status	Ports
1	default	active	Fa0/1, Fa0/2, Fa0/3, Fa0/4
			Fa0/5, Fa0/6, Fa0/7, Fa0/8
			Fa0/9, Fa0/10, Fa0/11, Fa0/12
			Fa0/16, Fa0/17, Fa0/18, Fa0/19
			Fa0/20, Fa0/21, Fa0/22, Fa0/23
			Fa0/24, Gi0/1, Gi0/2
10	VLAN0010	active	
11	VLAN0011	active	
12	VLAN0012	active	
13	VLAN0013	active	
14	VLAN0014	active	

Let's change SW2 to client mode and try the same thing. We can change vtp modes with the **vtp mode** command.

SW2(config)#**vtp mode client**
Setting device to VTP CLIENT mode.

Now under VTP status we can see its operating mode is Client.

SW2(config)#**do show vtp status**
VTP Version   : 2
Configuration Revision   : 2
Maximum VLANs supported locally   : 1005
Number of existing VLANs   : 10
VTP Operating Mode   **: Client**
VTP Domain Name   : certificationkits
VTP Pruning Mode   : Disabled
VTP V2 Mode   : Disabled
VTP Traps Generation   : Disabled
MD5 digest   : 0xAD 0x65 0x84 0x9D 0x38 0x8B 0x71 0x22
Configuration last modified by 0.0.0.0 at 3-1-93 17:07:23

So if we try to add a vlan now, we get a message saying it is not allowed.
SW2(config)#**vlan 20**
VTP VLAN configuration not allowed when device is in CLIENT mode.

Let's bring the link between SW2 and SW3 online.
SW2(config)#**int fa0/2**
SW2(config-if)#**no shut**

SW3 is an old switch that has quite a few vlans configured on it. If they had the same
VTP domain name, they would have overwrote our database. But since they do not
have the same VTP domain name we are safe. Let's look.

SW2(config)#**do show vtp status**
VTP Version   : 2
Configuration Revision   : 2
Maximum VLANs supported locally   : 1005
Number of existing VLANs   : 10
VTP Operating Mode   **: Client**
VTP Domain Name   : certification
VTP Pruning Mode   : Disabled
VTP V2 Mode   : Disabled
VTP Traps Generation   : Disabled
MD5 digest   : 0xAD 0x65 0x84 0x9D 0x38 0x8B 0x71 0x22
Configuration last modified by 0.0.0.0 at 3-1-93 17:07:23

Now let's change our VTP domain name to certificationktis and see what happens.
SW2(config)#**vtp domain certificationkits**
Now you are going to see trunk lines going down for the switch in the VTP certification domain and the

trunk line go up for the certificationkits VTP domain. So give it a few seconds.
SW2(config)#**do show vtp status**
VTP Version   : 2
Configuration Revision   : 6

Maximum VLANs supported locally : 1005
Number of existing VLANs   : 33
VTP Operating Mode   : Client
VTP Domain Name   : certificationkits
VTP Pruning Mode   : Disabled
VTP V2 Mode   : Disabled
VTP Traps Generation   : Disabled
MD5 digest   : 0x7E 0x4C 0x93 0xD8 0xAB 0xCA 0x39 0x53
Configuration last modified by 0.0.0.0 at 3-1-93 22:32:02

Unfortunately it seems that our old vlans in the 10-15 range have been wiped out?!?!?!

SW2(config-if)#**do sh vlan brief**

VLAN	Name	Status	Ports
1	default	active	Fa0/3, Fa0/4, Fa0/5, Fa0/6
			Fa0/7, Fa0/8, Fa0/9, Fa0/10
			Fa0/11, Fa0/12, Fa0/13, Fa0/14
			Fa0/15, Fa0/16, Fa0/17, Fa0/18
			Fa0/19, Fa0/20, Fa0/21, Fa0/22
			Fa0/23, Fa0/24, Gi0/1, Gi0/2
50	VLAN0050	active	
51	VLAN0051	active	
52	VLAN0052	active	
53	VLAN0053	active	
54	VLAN0054	active	
55	VLAN0055	active	
56	VLAN0056	active	
57	VLAN0057	active	
58	VLAN0058	active	
59	VLAN0059	active	
60	VLAN0060	active	
80	VLAN0080	active	
400	VLAN0400	active	
401	VLAN0401	active	

VLAN	Name	Status	Ports
402	VLAN0402	active	
403	VLAN0403	active	
404	VLAN0404	active	
405	VLAN0405	active	
406	VLAN0406	active	
407	VLAN0407	active	
408	VLAN0408	active	
409	VLAN0409	active	
410	VLAN0410	active	

```
411  VLAN0411              active
412  VLAN0412              active
413  VLAN0413              active
414  VLAN0414              active
415  VLAN0415              active
1002 fddi-default          act/unsup
1003 token-ring-default       act/unsup
1004 fddinet-default       act/unsup
1005 trnet-default         act/unsup
```

This is because of how VTP works. It treats the highest Configuration Revision # to be the most trusted switch in the network. Since SW3 had a config revision of 6 and the other switch had a revision of 2, VTP will replace all other VTP information with SW3's VTP information. In the real world this is actually a common issue. What happens is an old switch gets plugged into the network either by a tired network admin about to have a bad day, an office worker that wants to plug in an extra laptop or even an evil hacker.

Note: This will happen if the switch is in server or client mode.

SW3#**show vtp status**

```
VTP Version                      : 2
Configuration Revision           : 6
Maximum VLANs supported locally  : 68
Number of existing VLANs         : 33
VTP Operating Mode               : Server
VTP Domain Name                  : certificationkits
VTP Pruning Mode                 : Disabled
VTP V2 Mode                      : Disabled
VTP Traps Generation             : Disabled
MD5 digest                       : 0x7E 0x4C 0x93 0xD8 0xAB 0xCA 0x39 0x53
```

The way to clear the revision counter is to change the switches domain name. By the way, older switches use the vlan database to configure vtp. The commands are otherwise the same.

SW3#**vlan database**
SW3(vlan)#**vtp domain test**
Changing VTP domain name from certificationkits to test
SW3(vlan)#**exit**

We can confirm the status changed with **show vtp status**.

SW3#**show vtp status**

```
VTP Version                      : 2
Configuration Revision           : 0
Maximum VLANs supported locally  : 1005
```

```
Number of existing VLANs        : 33
VTP Operating Mode              : Server
VTP Domain Name                 : test
VTP Pruning Mode                : Disabled
VTP V2 Mode                     : Disabled
VTP Traps Generation            : Disabled
MD5 digest                      : 0x2E 0x57 0xA0 0xCF 0xFF 0x8D 0xD5 0xE7
Configuration last modified by 0.0.0.0 at 3-1-93 22:32:02
```

Notice how that set back our configuration revision number. Now let's remove our vlans, add a few then bring us back into the certificationkits domain to see it overwrite again.

SW3(config)#**no vlan 2-999**
SW3(config)#**vlan 10-15**
SW3(config-vlan)#**end**

SW3#**vlan database**
SW3(vlan)#**vtp domain certificationkits**
Changing VTP domain name from test to certificationkits
SW3(vlan)#**exit**
APPLY completed.
Exiting....

After the lines come back up, now everything is back to normal. Though this can be considerably more painful in a production environment.

SW3#**show vtp status**
```
VTP Version                          : 2
Configuration Revision               : 6
Maximum VLANs supported locally  : 1005
Number of existing VLANs             : 33
VTP Operating Mode                   : Server
VTP Domain Name                      : certificationkits
VTP Pruning Mode                     : Disabled
VTP V2 Mode                          : Disabled
VTP Traps Generation                 : Disabled
MD5 digest                           : 0x28 0x57 0xA4 0xC0 0x99 0x38 0x45 0xDF
Configuration last modified by 0.0.0.0 at 3-1-93 17:37:20
```

A good practice used by most of the world to prevent this situation is to set a VTP password in the network so rogue switches can't bring down the network so easily. This is done with the **vtp password** command. Being a security nut, let's choose the uncrackable password of cisco. But first we have to bring SW1 into the certificationkits domain.

SW1#**vlan database**
SW1(vlan)#**vtp domain certificationkits**
SW1(config)#**vtp password cisco**
Setting device VLAN database password to cisco

SW2(config)#**vtp password cisco**
Setting device VLAN database password to cisco

SW3(vlan)#**vtp password cisco**
Setting device VLAN database password to cisco.
SW3(vlan)#**exit**
APPLY completed.
Exiting....

If everything is happy with the passwords, the MD5 digest should match on all switches. If you ever get a situation where the digest doesn't match, check the passwords. Sometimes it just takes you to flap a trunk interface between the switches to get it going.

SW1(config)#**do show vtp status**
VTP Version   : 2
Configuration Revision   : 8
Maximum VLANs supported locally   : 1005
Number of existing VLANs   : 11
VTP Operating Mode   : Server
VTP Domain Name   : certificationkits
VTP Pruning Mode   : Disabled
VTP V2 Mode   : Disabled
VTP Traps Generation   : Disabled
MD5 digest   **: 0x65 0xAE 0xE7 0x73 0xDB 0x8C 0x4D 0x06**

SW2(config)#**do show vtp status**
VTP Version   : 2
Configuration Revision   : 8
Maximum VLANs supported locally   : 1005
Number of existing VLANs   : 11
VTP Operating Mode   : Client
VTP Domain Name   : certificationkits
VTP Pruning Mode   : Disabled
VTP V2 Mode   : Disabled
VTP Traps Generation   : Disabled
MD5 digest   **: 0x65 0xAE 0xE7 0x73 0xDB 0x8C 0x4D 0x06**

SW3#**show vtp status**
VTP Version   : 2
Configuration Revision   : 8
Maximum VLANs supported locally   : 68

```
Number of existing VLANs        : 11
VTP Operating Mode              : Server
VTP Domain Name                 : certificationkits
VTP Pruning Mode                : Disabled
VTP V2 Mode                     : Disabled
VTP Traps Generation            : Disabled
```
MD5 digest   : 0x65 0xAE 0xE7 0x73 0xDB 0x8C 0x4D 0x06

The last thing worth talking about in VTP is transparent mode. As mentioned in the basic switching lab there is the standard vlan range: 1-1005 and the extended range 1006-4094. To use the extended range the switch must be in vtp transparent mode because you don't want the switch advertising vlans that the downstream switch might not know about. If you try to make one, you get a message like this...

SW1(config)#**vlan 4000**
SW1(config-vlan)#**exit**
% Failed to create VLANs 4000
VLAN(s) not available in Port Manager.
%Failed to commit extended VLAN(s) changes.

First we need to set the vtp mode to transparent with **vtp mode transparent.**
SW1(config)#**vtp mode transparent**
Setting device to VTP TRANSPARENT mode.

And now we can add it.
SW1(config)#**vlan 4000**
SW1(config-vlan)#**exit**

SW1(config)#**do sh vlan id 4000**
VLAN   Name   Status   Ports
---- ------------------------------- -------- ------------------------------
4000   VLAN4000   active   Fa0/13, Fa0/14, Fa0/15

Finally we can see on SW2 that it doesn't know about this vlan.
SW2(config)#**do sh vlan id 4000**
VLAN id 4000 not found in current VLAN database

This is because SW1 is in transparent mode and any changes performed are locally changed only and not propogated to other switches.

Switching Review

Questions:

1. What VTP modes save their VLAN information to NVRAM? (List 2) _____

    _____

2. You want to connect your Cisco Catalyst switch to a Nortel switch. What must be true? _____

3. How do you associate VLANs to an interface in a router-on-a-stick configuration?

    _____

Give the terms below that correspond with the definitions provided.

4. _____ Carrying multiple VLANs over the same physical connection

5. _____ By default, frames in this VLAN are untagged when sent across a trunk

6. _____ The VLAN to which an access port is assigned

7. _____ If configured, enables minimal trunking to support voice traffic in addition to data traffic on an access port

8. _____ Can be used to automatically establish trunks between capable ports (insecure)

9. _____ A virtual interface which provides a routed gateway into and out of a VLAN

10. _____ Forms an unconditional trunk

11. _____ Attempts to negotiate a trunk with the far end

12. _____ Forms a trunk only if requested by the far end

13. _____ Will never form a trunk

14. _____ Provides for the establishment, configuration, and maintenance of a PPP link.

15. _____ A separate NCP is used to negotiate the configuration of each network layer protocol (such as IP) carried by PPP.

16. _____ Original, obsolete authentication protocol which relies on the exchange of a plaintext key to authenticate peers (RFC 1334).

17. _____ Authenticates peers using the MD5 checksum of a pre-shared secret key (RFC 1994).

Answers:

1. Server and Transparent VTP modes are the only modes that save their VLAN configuration to NVRAM.
2. Because you are connecting a Nortel switch, you must use a standard method of trunking (IEEE 802.1q). ISL and VTP are Cisco proprietary functions.
3. The 'encapsulation' command is used to assign VLANs to a subinterface.
4. Trunking
5. Native VLAN
6. Access VLAN
7. Voice VLAN
8. Dynamic Trunking Protocol
9. Switched Virtual Interface
10. Trunk
11. Dynamic Desirable
12. Dynamic auto
13. Access
14. Link Control Protocol (LCP)
15. Network Control Protocol (NCP)
16. Plaintext Authentication Protocol (PAP)
17. Challenge Handshake Authentication Protocol (CHAP)

Spanning Tree Protocol

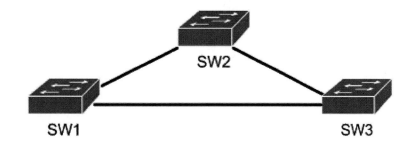

SW2

SW1   SW3

The purpose of this lab is to explore using STP in a switch environment.

Hardware & Configuration Required for this Lab

- Three Cisco switches
- Five crossover Cat5 cables to connect switches(although you can get by with three for most of the lab)
- **Note:** Read the Initial Configs to figure out the topology connections

---

Commands Used in Lab

show cdp neigbors- Shows a summary of all neighboring devices and how they are connected
show spanning-Shows STP statistics such as priority, age, delay and various timers
spanning-tree vlan 1 root primary-Sets switch priority one lower than current root
spanning-tree cost x- Modifies the port cost of an interface
spanning-tree portfast –Enables portfast on a spanning-tree interface
spanning-tree bpduguard enable-Enables bpduguard on a spanning-tree interface

---

Initial Configs - Where you see *Initial Configs,* these are basic configuration steps that by now you should be able to perform on the devices by yourself without us detailing them step by step. Generally you simply go into enable and then configuration mode and start the configuration. ****Special Note**** Some Cisco switches do not support ISL and dot1q. In those instances in which the switch only supports dot1q the command to set that encapsulation type will error out as it is the only type available and thus does not need to be set.

SW1

hostname SW1
line console 0
logging synch
int fa0/1
description to SW2
switchport trunk encapsulation dot1q
switchport mode trunk
switchport nonegotiate
int fa0/3
description to SW3
switchport trunk encapsulation dot1q
switchport mode trunk
switchport nonegotiate
int fa0/4
description Second connection to SW2
switchport trunk encapsulation dot1q
switchport mode trunk
switchport nonegotiate

SW2

hostname SW2
line console 0
logging synch
int fa0/1
description to SW1
switchport trunk encapsulation dot1q
switchport mode trunk
switchport nonegotiate
int fa0/2
description to SW3
switchport trunk encapsulation dot1q
switchport mode trunk
switchport nonegotiate
int fa0/4
description Second connection to SW1
switchport trunk encapsulation dot1q
switchport mode trunk
switchport nonegotiate

SW3

hostname SW3
line console 0
logging synch
int fa0/2

description to SW2
switchport trunk encapsulation dot1q
switchport mode trunk
switchport nonegotiate
int fa0/3
description to SW1
switchport trunk encapsulation dot1q
switchport mode trunk
switchport nonegotiate

Spanning Tree Protocol is probably the most difficult subject on the switching side of the CCNA exam. It's complex and can be confusing with so many concepts flying around. If you haven't read up on STP before the lab, I recommend you give it a quick once over (you really should review the theory before you do any of the lab topics).

STP is a switches loop prevention protocol. The idea is that by a switch's nature, it will send on broadcasts and also if a switch doesn't know the destination, it will send a frame out each port. The problem with that is illustrated in this lab topology. If SW1 sends out a broadcast it will be received by SW2 and SW3, SW2 and SW3 upon receiving the broadcast will not forward the broadcast back to SW1 because it received it on that link, but will forward the broadcast to each other SW2 -> SW3 and SW3 -> SW2. From there the switches will forward the broadcast to SW1 and round and round it goes. This is called a broadcast storm.

It is actually a very serious problem and the broadcast storm usually gets so severe it will freeze workstation computers because the CPU is loaded with NIC requests.

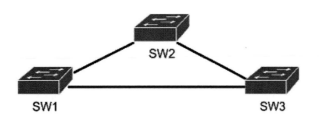

What STP does in a nutshell, is selectively block un-needed links between switches to prevent loops. So in the above example, STP would block traffic on a link to prevent traffic from looping from switch to switch.

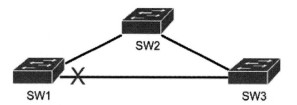

STP has had many revisions over the years. One such revision is Per Vlan Spanning Tree (PVST+). Originally Spanning tree only worked as a single instance which doesn't work so well with many different vlans on the network. That is because now all traffic has to follow a single path which is bad because all those redundant links between your switches are no longer being used. With PVST+ a different spanning tree runs for each vlan. So you can fine tune the network however you see fit. Before starting let's verify our topology using CDP.

Here's the CDP information. As mentioned before, it is a good idea to check CDP before doing any work on a network to see what devices are connected and to what interfaces.

SW1#show cdp neighbors
Capability Codes: R - Router, T - Trans Bridge, B - Source Route Bridge
                  S - Switch, H - Host, I - IGMP, r - Repeater, P - Phone

Device ID	Local Intrfce	Holdtme	Capability	Platform	Port ID
SW3	Fas 0/3	144		3560	Fas 0/3
SW2	Fas 0/1	158		3560	Fas 0/1
SW2	Fas 0/4	158		3560	Fas 0/4

SW2(config)#do show cdp neighbors
Capability Codes: R - Router, T - Trans Bridge, B - Source Route Bridge
                  S - Switch, H - Host, I - IGMP, r - Repeater, P - Phone

Device ID	Local Intrfce	Holdtme	Capability	Platform	Port ID
SW3	Fas 0/2	130		3560	Fas 0/2
SW1	Fas 0/1	144		3560	Fas 0/1
SW1	Fas 0/4	144		3560	Fas 0/4

SW3#show cdp neighbors
Capability Codes: R - Router, T - Trans Bridge, B - Source Route Bridge
                  S - Switch, H - Host, I - IGMP, r - Repeater, P - Phone

Device ID	Local Intrfce	Holdtme	Capability	Platform	Port ID
SW1	Fas 0/3	134		3560	Fas 0/3
SW2	Fas 0/2	125		3560	Fas 0/2

The main output you'll be looking at for STP is: **show spanning-tree** which shows you pretty much everything you need to know at this level.

SW1#show spanning-tree
VLAN0001

Spanning tree enabled protocol ieee
Root ID   Priority   32769
           Address   000D.BD19.43EE

           This bridge is the root
           Hello Time 2 sec Max Age 20 sec Forward Delay 15 sec

Bridge ID Priority   32769 (priority 32768 sys-id-ext 1)
           Address   000D.BD19.43EE
           Hello Time 2 sec Max Age 20 sec Forward Delay 15 sec
           Aging Time 20

Interface	Role Sts	Cost	Prio.Nbr	Type
Fa0/1	Desg FWD	19	128.1	P2p
Fa0/3	Desg FWD	19	128.3	P2p
Fa0/4	Desg FWD	19	128.4	P2p

Based on the output from the **show spanning-tree** command, we can see that SW1 is the root bridge and has two ports in forwarding state, ports Fa0/1 and Fa0/3.

We can see from the output that SW3 is not the root bridge but rather the path to the root bridge is via Fa0/3. The STP root is elected based on the lowest bridge priority. If all switches have the same bridge priority then the switch with the lowest MAC address is elected the root bridge. Thus your output may not match what we have here.

SW3#show spanning-tree
VLAN0001
  Spanning tree enabled protocol ieee
  Root ID   Priority   32769
             Address   000D.BD19.43EE
             Cost   **19**
             Port   3(FastEthernet0/3)
             Hello Time 2 sec Max Age 20 sec Forward Delay 15 sec

  Bridge ID Priority   32769 (priority 32768 sys-id-ext 1)
             Address   00D0.5801.6D1B
             Hello Time 2 sec Max Age 20 sec Forward Delay 15 sec
             Aging Time 20

Interface	Role Sts	Cost	Prio.Nbr	Type
Fa0/2	Altn BLK	19	128.2	P2p
Fa0/3	Root FWD	19	128.3	P2p

You can control what switch wins the election by changing the switch priority with the **spanning-tree vlan <# or range> priority** command. The command accepts increments of 4096 where lower is better. Entering a value that is not an increment of 4096 will show you the acceptable values if you arre too lazy to the math :)

SW3(config)#**spanning-tree vlan 1 priority 5**
% Bridge Priority must be in increments of 4096.
% Allowed values are:
  0   4096 8192 12288 16384 20480 24576 28672
  32768 36864 40960 45056 49152 53248 57344 61440

Let's make SW3 the root by using a lower priorit Like 16384.
  SW3(config)#**spanning-tree vlan 1 priority 16384**

Checking SW2 we can see that the root switch is connected to port Fa0/2 which we know from CDP is SW3.

SW2#**show spanning-tree**
VLAN0001
  Spanning tree enabled protocol ieee
  Root ID   Priority   16385
             Address   00D0.5801.6D1B
             Cost   **19**
             Port   2(FastEthernet0/2)
             Hello Time 2 sec Max Age 20 sec Forward Delay 15 sec

  Bridge ID Priority   32769 (priority 32768 sys-id-ext 1)
             Address   0090.0C69.E4C0
             Hello Time 2 sec Max Age 20 sec Forward Delay 15 sec
             Aging Time 20

Interface   Role Sts   Cost   Prio.Nbr Type
--------------- ---- --- --------- -------- --------------------------------
Fa0/1   Altn BLK 19   128.1   P2p
Fa0/4   Altn BLK 19   128.4   P2p
Fa0/2   Root FWD 19   128.2   P2p

Checking SW3 we can confirm the switch is the root.
SW3#**show spanning-tree**
VLAN0001
  Spanning tree enabled protocol ieee
  Root ID   Priority   16385
             Address   00D0.5801.6D1B

             This bridge is the root
             Hello Time 2 sec Max Age 20 sec Forward Delay 15 sec

```
Bridge ID  Priority    16385  (priority 16384 sys-id-ext 1)
     Address    00D0.5801.6D1B
     Hello Time  2 sec  Max Age 20 sec  Forward Delay 15 sec
     Aging Time  20


Interface       Role Sts  Cost    Prio.Nbr Type
--------------- ---- ---  --------- -------- --------------------------------
Fa0/2           Desg FWD 19        128.2    P2p
Fa0/3           Desg FWD 19        128.3    P2p
```

A more convenient way to make a switch the root of STP is the **spanning-tree vlan 1 root primary** command.

SW2(config)#**spanning-tree vlan 1 root primary**

The root priority command works by looking at the current root switch's priority and sets the switch priority to be lower.

SW2#**show spanning-tree**
VLAN0001
  Spanning tree enabled protocol ieee
  Root ID   Priority   12289
             Address   0090.0C69.E4C0

             This bridge is the root
             Hello Time 2 sec Max Age 20 sec Forward Delay 15 sec

  Bridge ID Priority   12289 (priority 12288 sys-id-ext 1)
             Address   0090.0C69.E4C0
             Hello Time 2 sec Max Age 20 sec Forward Delay 15 sec
             Aging Time 20

```
Interface       Role Sts   Cost    Prio.Nbr Type
--------------- ---- ---  --------- -------- -------------------------------
Fa0/1           Desg FWD  19        128.1    P2p
Fa0/4           Desg FWD  19        128.4    P2p
Fa0/2           Desg FWD  19        128.2    P2p
```

Spanning tree has 5 states an interface can be in and needs to transition between all states before an interface will forward traffic.
Disabled- STP is not enabled on the interface, not shown in output.
Blocking - STP is blocking all frames.
Listening - STP is sending and receiving BPDUs
Learning - STP is learning information from other switches and building a loop free

topology.

Forwarding - STP is forwarding all frames.

If you ever noticed that it takes a little while after you plug an interface into a switch before it starts working. That is due to STP. All in all it takes approximately 50 seconds for a port to move from blocking to forwarding. 20 seconds to move out of blocking, 15 seconds to move from listening and another 15 seconds to transition from learning into forwarding.

After the STP election chooses a root bridge, the next task is for the other switches to find the shortest path to the root switch since all switch traffic must be sent to the root switch. This is why it's a bad idea to have an older switch as the root in a production network.

STP chooses the root port in a few ways. First it will use interface cost, then if they match it will use port priority, then finally it will just simply pick the lowest port number. Here is a table that shows the interface costs for various interface speeds.

Bandwidth	Cost
4 Mbps	250
10 Mbps	100
16 Mbps	62
45 Mbps	39
100 Mbps	19
155 Mbps	14
622 Mbps	6
1 Gbps	4
10 Gbps	2

Looking at SW1 we know from CDP that Fa0/1 and Fa0/4 connects to SW2. We can see from the spanning-tree output that both interfaces have a cost of 19 since they are both 100mbs. Next, both interfaces have the default port-priority of 128. So Fa0/1 is chosen as the root port because it is a lower port number. Fa0/4 is blocked because it is a redundant link.

Fa0/3 is a Designated link because it connects to SW3 and doesn't cause any loops.

```
SW1#show spanning-tree
VLAN0001
  Spanning tree enabled protocol ieee
  Root ID    Priority    12289
             Address     0090.0C69.E4C0
             Cost        19
             Port        1(FastEthernet0/1)
```

Hello Time 2 sec Max Age 20 sec Forward Delay 15 sec

Bridge ID Priority   32769 (priority 32768 sys-id-ext 1)
        Address   000D.BD19.43EE
        Hello Time   2 sec Max Age 20 sec Forward Delay 15 sec
        Aging Time 20

Interface	Role	Sts	Cost	Prio.Nbr	Type
Fa0/1	Root	FWD	19	128.1	P2p
Fa0/3	Desg	FWD	19	128.3	P2p
Fa0/4	Altn	BLK	19	128.4	P2p

You can modify the port cost with the interface **spanning-tree cost** command. The lower cost the better.

SW1(config-if)#**spanning-tree cost ?**
 <1-200000000> port path cost

Let's change the cost of SW1's Fa0/4 so it will be the forwarding versus blocking and become the root port.
Note: Changing the cost of spanning-tree only affects the local switch.

SW1(config)#**int fa0/4**
SW1(config-if)#**spanning-tree cost 1**

After we change the cost we can see that Fa0/4 is the new root port.

SW1#**show spanning-tree**
VLAN0001
 Spanning tree enabled protocol ieee
 Root ID   Priority   12289
        Address   0090.0C69.E4C0
        Cost   19
        Port   **1(FastEthernet0/4)**
        Hello Time 2 sec Max Age 20 sec Forward Delay 15 sec

 Bridge ID Priority   32769 (priority 32768 sys-id-ext 1)
        Address   000D.BD19.43EE
        Hello Time   2 sec Max Age 20 sec Forward Delay 15 sec
        Aging Time 20

Interface	Role	Sts	Cost	Prio.Nbr	Type
Fa0/1	Desg	ALT	19	128.1	P2p
Fa0/3	Desg	FWD	19	128.3	P2p

```
Fa0/4        Root FWD 19      128.4    P2p
```

At this point let's add some vlans into the mix. Add the vlans on all three switches.
SW1(config)#**vlan 50-53**
SW1(config-vlan)#**exit**

SW2(config)#**vlan 50-53**
SW2(config-vlan)#**exit**

SW3(config)#**vlan 50-53**
SW3(config-vlan)#**exit**

Using the **show spanning-tree** command we can see there is a STP instance for each vlan.

SW1#**show spanning-tree**
VLAN0001
  Spanning tree enabled protocol ieee
  Root ID   Priority   12289
            Address   0090.0C69.E4C0
            Cost   19
            Port   1(FastEthernet0/1)
            Hello Time 2 sec Max Age 20 sec Forward Delay 15 sec

  Bridge ID Priority   32769 (priority 32768 sys-id-ext 1)
            Address   000D.BD19.43EE
            Hello Time 2 sec Max Age 20 sec Forward Delay 15 sec
            Aging Time 20

```
Interface      Role Sts  Cost   Prio.Nbr Type
---------------- ---- --- --------- -------- --------------------------------
Fa0/1          Altn  BLK  19     128.1    P2p
Fa0/3          Desg FWD 19      128.3    P2p
Fa0/4          Root FWD 19      128.4    P2p
```

VLAN0050
  Spanning tree enabled protocol ieee
  Root ID   Priority   32818
            Address   000D.BD19.43EE
            This bridge is the root
            Hello Time 2 sec Max Age 20 sec Forward Delay 15 sec

  Bridge ID Priority   32818 (priority 32768 sys-id-ext 50)
            Address   000D.BD19.43EE
            Hello Time 2 sec Max Age 20 sec Forward Delay 15 sec
            Aging Time 20

Interface	Role	Sts	Cost	Prio.Nbr	Type
Fa0/1	Desg	FWD	19	128.1	P2p
Fa0/3	Desg	FWD	19	128.3	P2p
Fa0/4	Desg	FWD	19	128.4	P2p

VLAN0051

Spanning tree enabled protocol ieee
Root ID   Priority   32819
           Address   000D.BD19.43EE
           This bridge is the root
           Hello Time 2 sec Max Age 20 sec Forward Delay 15 sec

Bridge ID Priority   32819 (priority 32768 sys-id-ext 51)
           Address   000D.BD19.43EE
           Hello Time 2 sec Max Age 20 sec Forward Delay 15 sec
           Aging Time 20

Interface	Role	Sts	Cost	Prio.Nbr	Type
Fa0/1	Desg	FWD	19	128.1	P2p
Fa0/3	Desg	FWD	19	128.3	P2p
Fa0/4	Desg	FWD	19	128.4	P2p

VLAN0052

Spanning tree enabled protocol ieee
Root ID   Priority   32820
           Address   000D.BD19.43EE
           This bridge is the root
           Hello Time 2 sec Max Age 20 sec Forward Delay 15 sec

Bridge ID Priority   32820 (priority 32768 sys-id-ext 52)
           Address   000D.BD19.43EE
           Hello Time 2 sec Max Age 20 sec Forward Delay 15 sec
           Aging Time 20

Interface	Role	Sts	Cost	Prio.Nbr	Type
Fa0/1	Desg	FWD	19	128.1	P2p
Fa0/3	Desg	FWD	19	128.3	P2p
Fa0/4	Desg	FWD	19	128.4	P2p

VLAN0053

Spanning tree enabled protocol ieee

```
   Root ID   Priority    32821
             Address     000D.BD19.43EE
             This bridge is the root
             Hello Time  2 sec  Max Age 20 sec  Forward Delay 15 sec

   Bridge ID  Priority    32821  (priority 32768 sys-id-ext 53)
             Address     000D.BD19.43EE
             Hello Time  2 sec  Max Age 20 sec  Forward Delay 15 sec
             Aging Time  20

Interface       Role Sts Cost    Prio.Nbr Type
---------------- ---- --- --------- -------- --------------------------------
Fa0/1           Desg FWD 19       128.1   P2p
Fa0/3           Desg FWD 19       128.3   P2p
Fa0/4           Desg FWD 19       128.4   P2p
```

Since this can potentially show a lot of output, we can filter the STP output to a specific VLAN with the **show spanning-tree vlan** command. Let's focus on vlan 50 for now.

```
SW1#show spanning-tree vlan 50
VLAN0050
  Spanning tree enabled protocol ieee
  Root ID   Priority    32818
            Address     000D.BD19.43EE
            This bridge is the root
            Hello Time  2 sec  Max Age 20 sec  Forward Delay 15 sec

   Bridge ID  Priority    32818  (priority 32768 sys-id-ext 50)
             Address     000D.BD19.43EE
             Hello Time  2 sec  Max Age 20 sec  Forward Delay 15 sec
             Aging Time  20

Interface       Role Sts   Cost    Prio.Nbr Type
---------------- ---- --- --------- -------- --------------------------------
Fa0/1           Desg FWD 19       128.1   P2p
Fa0/3           Desg FWD 19       128.3   P2p
Fa0/4           Desg FWD 19       128.4   P2p
```

The cost command we entered earlier is affecting all vlans. We can refine most STP configuration to a given vlan. We can change the cost command with **spanning-tree vlan <#> cost**. Let's remove our previous command and refine it to vlan 1.

```
SW1(config)#int fa0/4
SW1(config-if)#no spanning-tree cost
SW1(config-if)#spanning vlan 1 cost 1
```

After we make the change we can see that vlan 1 still has a cost of 1 for Fa0/4.

SW1#**show spanning vlan 1**
VLAN0001
  Spanning tree enabled protocol ieee
  Root ID   Priority   12289
            Address   0090.0C69.E4C0
            Cost   19
            Port   1(FastEthernet0/4)
            Hello Time 2 sec Max Age 20 sec Forward Delay 15 sec

  Bridge ID Priority   32769 (priority 32768 sys-id-ext 1)
            Address   000D.BD19.43EE
            Hello Time 2 sec Max Age 20 sec Forward Delay 15 sec
            Aging Time 20

Interface   Role Sts   Cost   Prio.Nbr Type
---------------- ---- --- --------- -------- --------------------------------
Fa0/1   Altn BLK   19   128.1   P2p
Fa0/3   Desg FWD 19   128.3   P2p

Fa0/4   Root FWD 1   128.4   P2p

But vlan 50 has the default cost of 19.

SW1#**show spanning vlan 50**
VLAN0050
  Spanning tree enabled protocol ieee
  Root ID   Priority   32818
            Address   000D.BD19.43EE
            This bridge is the root
            Hello Time 2 sec Max Age 20 sec Forward Delay 15 sec

  Bridge ID Priority   32818 (priority 32768 sys-id-ext 50)
            Address   000D.BD19.43EE
            Hello Time 2 sec Max Age 20 sec Forward Delay 15 sec
            Aging Time 20

Interface   Role Sts   Cost   Prio.Nbr Type
---------------- ---- --- --------- -------- --------------------------------
Fa0/1   Desg FWD 19   128.1   P2p
Fa0/3   Desg FWD 19   128.3   P2p
Fa0/4   Desg FWD **19**   128.4   P2p

The other configurable way to modify the interface selection in STP is port-priority. Like cost lower is better. However it only affects downstream switches. It does not affect the interface selection on the switch it is configured on. To configure port-priority, use the **spanning-tree port-priority** command or the **spanning-tree vlan # port-**

priority command under an interface.

For example let's influence SW2 to use Fa0/4 for vlan 50 traffic. This will be configured on SW1. Port-priority values increment by 16.

A **show spanning-tree vlan 50** command on SW2 prior to making the change reveals the following.

```
SW2#show spanning-tree vlan 50
VLAN0050
  Spanning tree enabled protocol ieee
  Root ID   Priority   32818
            Address    000D.BD19.43EE
            Cost       19
            Port       1(FastEthernet0/1)
            Hello Time  2 sec  Max Age 20 sec  Forward Delay 15 sec

  Bridge ID  Priority   32818 (priority 32768 sys-id-ext 50)
            Address     0090.0C69.E4C0
            Hello Time  2 sec  Max Age 20 sec  Forward Delay 15 sec
            Aging Time  20

Interface      Role Sts   Cost    Prio.Nbr Type
---------------- ---- --- --------- -------- --------------------------------
Fa0/1          Root FWD 19       128.1    P2p
Fa0/4          Altn BLK  19       128.4    P2p
Fa0/2          Desg FWD 19       128.2    P2p
```

Let's jump back to switch 1 for now.

```
SW1(config)#int fa0/4
SW1(config-if)#spanning-tree vlan 50 port-priority 16
```

After we make a change we can see the priority for Fa0/4 is now 16.

```
SW1#show spanning-tree vlan 50
VLAN0050
  Spanning tree enabled protocol ieee
  Root ID   Priority   32818
            Address    000D.BD19.43EE
            This bridge is the root
            Hello Time  2 sec  Max Age 20 sec  Forward Delay 15 sec

  Bridge ID  Priority   32818 (priority 32768 sys-id-ext 50)
            Address     000D.BD19.43EE
            Hello Time  2 sec  Max Age 20 sec  Forward Delay 15 sec
            Aging Time  20
```

Interface	Role Sts	Cost	Prio.Nbr	Type
Fa0/1	Desg FWD	19	128.1	P2p
Fa0/3	Desg FWD	19	128.3	P2p
Fa0/4	Desg FWD	19	**16**.4	P2p

Now we can see SW2 is using Fa0/4 as the root port.

SW2#**show spanning-tree vlan 50**
VLAN0050
  Spanning tree enabled protocol ieee
  Root ID   Priority   32818
               Address   000D.BD19.43EE
               Cost   19
               Port   1(FastEthernet0/1)
               Hello Time 2 sec Max Age 20 sec Forward Delay 15 sec

  Bridge ID Priority   32818 (priority 32768 sys-id-ext 50)
             Address   0090.0C69.E4C0
             Hello Time 2 sec Max Age 20 sec Forward Delay 15 sec
             Aging Time 20

Interface	Role	Sts	Cost	Prio.Nbr	Type
Fa0/1	Altn	BLK	19	128.1	P2p
Fa0/4	**Root**	**FWD**	19	128.4	P2p
Fa0/2	Desg	FWD	19	128.2	P2p

The next thing we will look at is the portfast feature. Portfast is used to allow workstations and routers to avoid the 50 second STP delay when a port is enabled and immediately transition to the forwarding stage. For example, a PC typically tries to get an IP via DHCP while booting. If the STP delay was not disabled, the computer would not be able to get a DHCP lease and would assign a 169.254.x.x APIPA IP.

You can enable portfast on an interface with the **spanning-tree portfast** command. You'll get a message warning you to only use this command on ports that do not connect switches because it essentially shuts off STP for that port and can introduce loops into the network.

SW2(config)#**int fa0/10**
SW2(config-if)#**spanning-tree portfast**
%Warning: portfast should only be enabled on ports connected to a single
host. Connecting hubs, concentrators, switches, bridges, etc... to this
interface when portfast is enabled, can cause temporary bridging loops.
Use with CAUTION

%Portfast has been configured on FastEthernet0/10 but will only have effect when the interface is in a non-trunking mode.

There is companion features to portfast called BPDUguard and BPDUfilter. BPDU Filter will tell the switch that if it receives spanning-tree BPDU frames, it should simply ignore them and allow other traffic to pass. The downside is that you won't be notified when someone plugs a switch into their PC Ethernet port.

The command for BPDU Guard is **spanning-tree bpdufilter enable**
SW2(config)#**int fa0/10**
SW2(config-if)#**spanning-tree bpdufilter enable**

We'll test this out by connecting a router to SW Fa0/10 and enabling bridging on it.
Note: Briding is not in the CCNA exam, this is just a handy verification. Configure the router's

FastEthernet port with an IP and bring it up connecting it to SW2.
Router(config)#**bridge 1 protocol ieee**
Router(config)#**int fa0/0**
Router(config)#**no shut**
Router(config-if)#**bridge-group 1**

Give it about 60 seconds and then we can see that the router has sent out 24 BPDU frames to SW2 but hasn't received anything.

Router#**show spanning-tree**
 Bridge group 1 is executing the ieee compatible Spanning Tree protocol
     Bridge Identifier has priority 32768, address 0012.80cb.e8e0
     Configured hello time 2, max age 20, forward delay 15
     We are the root of the spanning tree
     Topology change flag not set, detected flag not set
     Number of topology changes 1 last change occurred 00:00:39 ago
     from FastEthernet0/0
     Times: hold 1, topology change 35, notification 2
     hello 2, max age 20, forward delay 15
     Timers: hello 1, topology change 0, notification 0, aging 300
 Port 4 (FastEthernet0/0) of Bridge group 1 is forwarding
     Port path cost 19, Port priority 128, Port Identifier 128.4.
     Designated root has priority 32768, address 0012.80cb.e8e0
     Designated bridge has priority 32768, address 0012.80cb.e8e0
     Designated port id is 128.4, designated path cost 0
     Timers: message age 0, forward delay 0, hold 0
     Number of transitions to forwarding state: 1
     BPDU: sent 24, received 0

Checking STP detail on SW2's Fa0/10 we can see it hasn't received any BPDUs so we know its ignoring them.

SW2#**sh spanning interface fa0/10 detail**
 Port 1 (FastEthernet0/10) of VLAN0001 is forwarding
   Port path cost 19, Port priority 128, Port Identifier 128.1.
   Designated root has priority 24577, address 000b.46c9.6e00
   Designated bridge has priority 24577, address 000b.46c9.6e00
   Designated port id is 128.1, designated path cost 0
   Timers: message age 0, forward delay 0, hold 0
   Number of transitions to forwarding state: 1
   The port is in the portfast mode
   Link type is point-to-point by default
   Bpdu guard is enabled
   Bpdu filter is enabled
   BPDU: sent 0, **received 0**

A more aggressive approach is to enable BPDU Guard. This disables the interface as soon as it receives a BPDU. This is a more common option as you will likely be made aware of an interface being shutdown from several different messages.

The command for this is: **spanning-tree bpduguard enable** under the interface.

SW2(config)#**int fa0/10**
SW2(config-if)#**no spanning-tree bpdufilter**
SW2(config-if)#**spanning-tree bpduguard enable**

As soon as the router sends a BPDU to SW2, BPDU Guard shuts down the port.

 1d07h: %SPANTREE-2-BLOCK_BPDUGUARD: Received BPDU on port FA0/10 with BPDU Guard enabled.
 1d07h: %PM-4-ERR_DISABLE: bpduguard error detected on Fa0/10, putting Fa0/10 in err-disable state
 1d07h: %LINEPROTO-5-UPDOWN: Line protocol on Interface FastEthernet0/10, changed state to down
 1d07h: %LINK-3-UPDOWN: Interface FastEthernet0/10, changed state to down

If you don't happen to see the disable message, you can check **show ip int brief** and you will simply see the interface is down.

SW2(config-if)#**do sh ip int br | in FastEthernet0/10**
FastEthernet0/10   unassigned   YES unset down   down

You'll have to check **show interface** to see why the port was disabled.
SW2#**show int fa0/10**
FastEthernet0/10 is down, line protocol is down **(err-disabled)**
   Hardware is Fast Ethernet, address is 000b.46c9.6e01 (bia 000b.46c9.6e01)
   MTU 1500 bytes, BW 10000 Kbit, DLY 1000 usec,
     reliability 255/255, txload 1/255, rxload 1/255

It's also a good idea to check the log which will show you the bpdu information.

SW2#**show log**
Syslog logging: enabled (0 messages dropped, 2 messages rate-limited, 0 flushes, 0 overruns)
   Console logging: level debugging, 129 messages logged
   Monitor logging: level debugging, 0 messages logged
   Buffer logging: level debugging, 131 messages logged
   Exception Logging: size (4096 bytes)
   File logging: disabled
   Trap logging: level informational, 133 message lines logged

1d07h: %SPANTREE-2-BLOCK_BPDUGUARD: Received BPDU on port FastEthernet0/10 with BPDU Guard enabled.
1d07h: %PM-4-ERR_DISABLE: bpduguard error detected on Fa0/10, putting Fa0/10 in err-disable state
1d07h: %LINEPROTO-5-UPDOWN: Line protocol on Interface FastEthernet0/10, changed state to down
1d07h: %LINK-3-UPDOWN: Interface FastEthernet0/10, changed state to down

To re-enable the port you must do a shutdown and then a no shutdown. Of course since the router is still sending BPDUs, it is immediately brought down again.

SW2(config)#**int fa0/10**
SW2(config-if)#**shut**
1d07h: %LINK-5-CHANGED: Interface FastEthernet0/10, changed state to administratively down
SW2(config-if)#**no shut**
1d07h: %LINK-3-UPDOWN: Interface FastEthernet0/10, changed state to up
1d07h: %SPANTREE-2-BLOCK_BPDUGUARD: Received BPDU on port FastEthernet0/10 with BPDU Guard enabled.
1d07h: %PM-4-ERR_DISABLE: bpduguard error detected on Fa0/1, putting Fa0/10 in err-disable state
1d07h: %LINK-3-UPDOWN: Interface FastEthernet0/10, changed state to down

A more automatic way of dealing with BPDU Guard shutdowns is using **err-disable** to turn the port back on in x amount of time. There are two parts to err-disable; the cause and the interval. To enable the feature, first use the **errdisable recovery cause bpduguard** command. This tells err-disable to turn back on BPDU Guard port shutdowns and the **errdisable recovery interval** command specifies how long it will leave the port down.

Let's set the switch to turn the port back on after 3 minutes.

SW2(config)#**errdisable recovery cause bpduguard**
SW2(config)#**errdisable recovery interval 180**

After the timer is up, we see the port is back up (I removed the bridging configuration).

SW2(config)#
1d07h: %PM-4-ERR_RECOVER: Attempting to recover from bpduguard err-disable state on Fa0/10
1d07h: %LINK-3-UPDOWN: Interface FastEthernet0/10, changed state to up

Switching Review
Questions:

1. What two components make up a Bridge ID? (List two) _____ _____
2. What is the purpose of configuring a default gateway in a Catalyst switch?

    _____

3. You just connected your interface to a hub. What two things must be true?

    _____   _____

Put the action on the right in order on the left(steps 1 through 4) based on switch path selection.

4. ____(1st)   A. Prefer the neighbor with the lowest cost to root
5. ____(2nd)   B. Prefer the lowest sender port ID
6. ____(3rd)   C. Prefer the neighbor with the lowest bridge ID
7. ____(4th)   D. Bridge with lowest root ID becomes the root

Fill in the terms below that correspond with the definitions provided.

8. _____ Enables immediate transition into the forwarding state (designates edge ports under MST)
9. _____ Enables switches to maintain backup paths to root
10. _____ Enables immediate expiration of the Max Age timer in the event of an indirect link failure
11. _____ Prevents a port from becoming the root port
12. _____ Error-disables a port if a BPDU is received
13. _____ Prevents a blocked port from transitioning to listening after the Max Age timer has expired
14. _____ Blocks BPDUs on an interface (disables STP)
15. _____ Connects to exactly one other bridge (full duplex)
16. _____ Potentially connects to multiple bridges (half duplex)
17. _____ Connects to a single host; designated by PortFast

Put the items on the right in order on the left(steps 1 through 4) based on Spanning Tree operation.

18.____(1st)   A. Select designated ports – One designated port is selected per segment

19.____(2nd) B. Select root port - Each bridge selects its primary port facing the root

20.____(3rd) C. Determine root bridge – The bridge advertising the lowest bridge ID becomes the root bridge

21.____(4th) D. Block ports with loops - All non-root and non-desginated ports are blocked

Answers:

1. The Bridge ID comprises the bridge priority plus the MAC address of the switch.
2. The default gateway is the IP address of the Layer 3 routing device that is used when devices are issuing Telnet, SSH, HTTP, and SNMP requests to the switch. To respond to these requests, the switch must send the responses to the router who in turn will route them back to the end devices.
3. When connecting to a hub, you have to be able to detect collisions; thus, you must be running half duplex.
4. D
5. A
6. C
7. B
8. PortFast
9. UplinkFast
10. BackboneFast
11. Root Guard
12. BPDU Guard
13. Loop Guard
14. BPDU Filter
15. Point-to-point
16. Shared
17. Edge
18. C
19. B
20. A
21. D

Rapid Spanning Tree Protocol

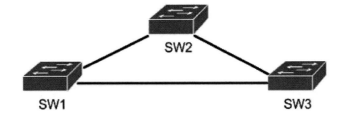

SW2

SW1   SW3

The purpose of this lab is to explore using STP in a switch environment.

Hardware & Configuration Required for this Lab

- Three Cisco switches
- Eleven crossover Cat5 cables to connect switches to fully mimic the lab, but you can get by with three
- You will read the show cdp neighbors in the lab to figure out the topology

---

Commands Used in this Lab

spanning-tree mode rapid-pvst- Changes the STP mode to RSTP

Physical Cabling Reference - Read the show cd neighbor to figure out the topology.

SW1#**show cdp neighbor**
Capability Codes: R - Router, T - Trans Bridge, B - Source Route Bridge
                  S - Switch, H - Host, I - IGMP, r - Repeater, P - Phone

Device ID	Local Intrfce	Holdtme	Capability	Platform	Port ID
Switch	Fas 0/13	143		3560	Fas 0/13
Switch	Fas 0/14	143		3560	Fas 0/14
Switch	Fas 0/15	143		3560	Fas 0/15
Switch	Fas 0/16	143		3560	Fas 0/16
Switch	Fas 0/21	143		3560	Fas 0/21
Switch	Fas 0/22	143		3560	Fas 0/22
Switch	Fas 0/23	143		3560	Fas 0/23
Switch	Fas 0/24	143		3560	Fas 0/24

SW2#**show cdp neighbor**

Capability Codes: R - Router, T - Trans Bridge, B - Source Route Bridge
                  S - Switch, H - Host, I - IGMP, r - Repeater, P - Phone

Device ID	Local Intrfce	Holdtme	Capability	Platform	Port ID
Switch	Fas 0/13	172		3560	Fas 0/13
Switch	Fas 0/14	172		3560	Fas 0/14
Switch	Fas 0/15	172		3560	Fas 0/15
Switch	Fas 0/16	172		3560	Fas 0/16
Switch	Fas 0/17	150		3560	Fas 0/17
Switch	Fas 0/18	150		3560	Fas 0/18
Switch	Fas 0/19	150		3560	Fas 0/19

SW3#**show cdp neighbor**
Capability Codes: R - Router, T - Trans Bridge, B - Source Route Bridge
                  S - Switch, H - Host, I - IGMP, r - Repeater, P - Phone

Device ID	Local Intrfce	Holdtme	Capability	Platform	Port ID
Switch	Fas 0/21	133		3560	Fas 0/21
Switch	Fas 0/22	133		3560	Fas 0/22
Switch	Fas 0/23	133		3560	Fas 0/23
Switch	Fas 0/24	133		3560	Fas 0/24
Switch	Fas 0/17	172		3560	Fas 0/17
Switch	Fas 0/18	172		3560	Fas 0/18
Switch	Fas 0/19	172		3560	Fas 0/19

Initial Configs

SW1
line console 0
logging synch
hostname SW1
int range fa0/13 - 16 , fa0/21 - 24
switchport trunk encapsulation dot1q
switchport mode trunk
switchport nonegotiate

SW2
line console 0
logging synch
hostname SW2
int range fa0/13 - 16 , fa0/21 - 24
switchport trunk encapsulation dot1q
switchport mode trunk
switchport nonegotiate

SW3
line console 0
logging synch

```
hostname SW3
int range fa0/17 - 19, fa0/23 - 24
switchport trunk encapsulation dot1q
switchport mode trunk
switchport nonegotiate
```

Rapid Spanning Tree Protocol is the replacement for normal STP. As the name suggests, it operates much faster then the 50 second converenge times that STP offers. It does this by combining a number of Cisco proprietry STP features such as UplinkFast, PortFast and Backbonefast. Another name for this form of RSTP is Rapid PVST, as it also supports multiple vlans.

RSTP is enabled on a switch with the **spanning-tree mode rapid-pvst** command.

SW1(config)#**spanning-tree mode rapid-pvst**

SW2(config)#**spanning-tree mode rapid-pvst**

SW3(config)#**spanning-tree mode rapid-pvst**

It's important to note that older switches such as Cisco 2924XL does not support RSTP.

If you recall from the STP lab, there are 5 port states that STP transitions through before a port will be active. RSTP only uses 3 port states: Discarding (same as blocking), Learning, and Forwarding. Here is a table from Cisco comparing the varous states.

STP (802.1D) State	RSTP (802.1w) State	Included in Active Topology?	Learns MAC Addresses?
Disabled	Discarding	No	No
Blocking	Discarding	No	No
Listening	Discarding	Yes	No
Learning	Learning	Yes	Yes
Forwarding	Forwarding	Yes	Yes

We still use **show spanning-tree** to view most of the information about RSTP. Notice that the **Spanning tree enabled protocol** is showing rstp.

```
SW2#show spanning-tree
VLAN0001

  Spanning tree enabled protocol rstp
  Root ID    Priority    32769
             Address     000D.BD19.43EE
             Cost        19
```

Port   13(FastEthernet0/13)
Hello Time 2 sec Max Age 20 sec Forward Delay 15 sec

Bridge ID Priority   32769 (priority 32768 sys-id-ext 1)
           Address   0090.0C69.E4C0
           Hello Time   2 sec Max Age 20 sec Forward Delay 15 sec
           Aging Time   20

Interface	Role Sts	Cost	Prio.Nbr	Type
Fa0/18	Desg FWD	19	128.18	P2p
Fa0/16	Altn BLK	19	128.16	P2p
Fa0/19	Desg FWD	19	128.19	P2p
Fa0/17	Desg FWD	19	128.17	P2p
Fa0/14	Altn BLK	19	128.14	P2p
Fa0/15	Altn BLK	19	128.15	P2p
Fa0/13	Root FWD	19	128.13	P2p

RSTP does have a few new port roles that should be explained.

Root Port: Just like STP, this is the port used to reach the root switch. Root port is shown on the diagram with the red circles.

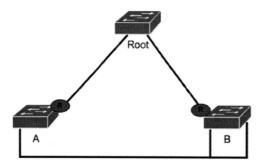

Designated Port: Just like STP, this is the port used to link switches together. It is highlighted in the diagram as a light blue circle.

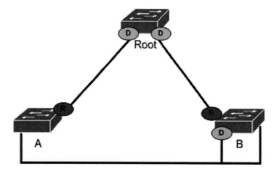

Alternate Port: Rather then having a blocking port RSTP instead uses Alternate and Backup ports. Alternate ports are where if the switch B receives a superior BPDU from A it can immediately choose that port as the new root path.

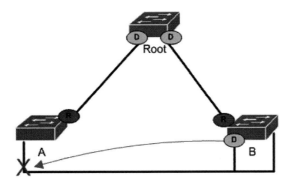

Backup Port: Similar to Alternate ports except the backup port is a blocked port on the same switch.

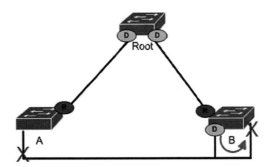

On SW2, let's disable Fa0/13 and we can see that immediately Fa0/14 becomes the root port.

SW2(config-if)#**int fa0/13**
SW2(config-if)#**shut**
SW1(config-if)#do show spanning
1w6d: %LINK-5-CHANGED: Interface FastEthernet0/13, changed state to administratively down
1w6d: %LINEPROTO-5-UPDOWN: Line protocol on Interface FastEthernet0/13, changed state to down
SW1(config-if)#**do show spanning**
VLAN0001
  Spanning tree enabled protocol rstp
  Root ID   Priority   32769
             Address   000D.BD19.43EE
             Cost   19
             Port   14(FastEthernet0/14)

```
                Hello Time  2 sec  Max Age 20 sec  Forward Delay 15 sec
Bridge ID  Priority    32769 (priority 32768 sys-id-ext 1)
          Address      0090.0C69.E4C0
          Hello Time  2 sec  Max Age 20 sec  Forward Delay 15 sec
          Aging Time  20


Interface       Role Sts   Cost    Prio.Nbr Type
---------------- ---- --- --------- -------- --------------------------------
Fa0/18          Desg FWD 19     128.18    P2p
Fa0/16          Altn BLK  19    128.16    P2p
Fa0/19          Desg FWD 19     128.19    P2p
Fa0/17          Desg FWD 19     128.17    P2p

Fa0/14          Root FWD 19     128.14    P2p
Fa0/15          Altn BLK  19    128.15    P2p
```

When Fa0/13 comes back, it immediately becomes the root port again.

```
SW2(config)#int fa0/13
SW2(config-if)#no shut
SW2(config-if)#do show spanning
1w6d: %LINK-3-UPDOWN: Interface FastEthernet0/13, changed state to up
1w6d: %LINEPROTO-5-UPDOWN: Line protocol on Interface FastEthernet0/13, changed state to up
SW1(config-if)#do show spanning
VLAN0001
 Spanning tree enabled protocol rstp
 Root ID   Priority    32769
           Address     000D.BD19.43EE
           Cost        19
           Port        13(FastEthernet0/13)
           Hello Time  2 sec  Max Age 20 sec  Forward Delay 15 sec

 Bridge ID  Priority    32769  (priority 32768 sys-id-ext 1)
           Address     0090.0C69.E4C0
           Hello Time  2 sec  Max Age 20 sec  Forward Delay 15 sec
           Aging Time  20


Interface       Role Sts   Cost    Prio.Nbr Type
---------------- ---- --- --------- -------- --------------------------------
Fa0/18          Desg FWD 19     128.18    P2p
Fa0/16          Altn BLK  19    128.16    P2p
Fa0/19          Desg FWD 19     128.19    P2p
Fa0/17          Desg FWD 19     128.17    P2p
Fa0/14          Altn BLK  19    128.14    P2p
Fa0/15          Altn BLK  19    128.15    P2p

Fa0/13          Root FWD 19     128.13    P2p
```

Everything else pretty much works the same as STP, so it's not worth going through again.

Per VLAN Spanning Tree Protocol

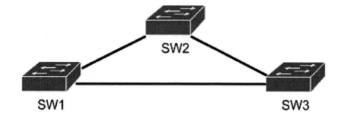

The purpose of this lab is to explore using Per VLAN STP in a switch environment.

Hardware & Configuration Required for this Lab

- Three Cisco switches.
- Nine crossover Cat5 cables to connect switches to fully mimic the lab, but you can get by with three.
- You will read the show cdp neighbors in the lab to figure out the topology.

Commands Used in this Lab

spanning-tree mode pvst- Changes the STP mode to PVSTP (default)

Physical Cabling Reference - Read the show cd neighbor to figure out the topology.

SW1#**show cdp ne**
Capability Codes: R - Router, T - Trans Bridge, B - Source Route Bridge
                   S - Switch, H - Host, I - IGMP, r - Repeater, P - Phone

Device ID	Local Intrfce	Holdtme	Capability	Platform	Port ID
SW2	Fas 0/14	170		3560	Fas 0/14
SW2	Fas 0/15	170		3560	Fas 0/15
SW3	Fas 0/21	165		3560	Fas 0/21
SW3	Fas 0/23	165		3560	Fas 0/23
SW3	Fas 0/22	165		3560	Fas 0/22
SW2	Fas 0/13	170		3560	Fas 0/13

SW2#**show cdp neighbor**
Capability Codes: R - Router, T - Trans Bridge, B - Source Route Bridge
                   S - Switch, H - Host, I - IGMP, r - Repeater, P - Phone

Device ID	Local Intrfce	Holdtme	Capability	Platform	Port ID
SW3	Fas 0/18	125		3560	Fas 0/18
SW3	Fas 0/19	125		3560	Fas 0/19
SW3	Fas 0/17	125		3560	Fas 0/17
SW1	Fas 0/13	130		3560	Fas 0/13
SW1	Fas 0/14	130		3560	Fas 0/14
SW1	Fas 0/15	130		3560	Fas 0/15

SW3#show cdp neighbor
Capability Codes: R - Router, T - Trans Bridge, B - Source Route Bridge
                  S - Switch, H - Host, I - IGMP, r - Repeater, P - Phone

Device ID	Local Intrfce	Holdtme	Capability	Platform	Port ID
SW2	Fas 0/17	145		3560	Fas 0/17
SW2	Fas 0/18	145		3560	Fas 0/18
SW2	Fas 0/19	145		3560	Fas 0/19
SW1	Fas 0/21	145		3560	Fas 0/21
SW1	Fas 0/22	145		3560	Fas 0/22
SW1	Fas 0/23	145		3560	Fas 0/23

Initial Configs

SW1
line console 0
logging synch
hostname SW1
int range fa0/13 - 15, fa0/21 - 23
switchport trunk encapsulation dot1q
switchport mode trunk
switchport nonegotiate

SW2
line console 0
logging synch
hostname SW2
int range fa0/13 - 15, fa0/17 - 19
switchport trunk encapsulation dot1q
switchport mode trunk
switchport nonegotiate

SW3
line console 0
logging synch
hostname SW3
int range fa0/17 - 19, fa0/21 - 23
switchport trunk encapsulation dot1q
switchport mode trunk

switchport nonegotiate

Per-VLAN Spanning Tree is the default Spanning Tree Protocol on modern Cisco switches. It is very similar to the plain old STP, except for it creates a different instance for every vlan created on the switch. This is useful to Network Engineers because it is both more scalable than the regular STP. It also is more flexible when it comes to traffic engineering.

PVSTP is enabled on a switch by default, but you can also use the **spanning-tree mode pvst** command to enable it.

To view information on STP, we still use the **show spanning-tree** command. The output is almost identical to the plain STP, except for the system-id field. Because PVSTP creates a new instance per VLAN on the switch, STP needs a way to tell between the potential 4094 spanning-tree instances. It does this by appending the vlan value to the sys-id-ext field. This also modifies the Bridge priority.

SW2# **show spanning-tree**
VLAN0001
  Spanning tree enabled protocol ieee
  Root ID   Priority   32769
               Address   000D.BD19.43EE
               Cost   19
               Port   13(FastEthernet0/13)
               Hello Time 2 sec Max Age 20 sec Forward Delay 15 sec

  Bridge ID Priority   32769 (priority 32768 sys-id-ext 1)
             Address   0090.0C69.E4C0
             Hello Time 2 sec Max Age 20 sec Forward Delay 15 sec
             Aging Time 20

Interface	Role	Sts	Cost	Prio.Nbr	Type
Fa0/18	Desg	FWD	19	128.18	P2p
Fa0/19	Desg	FWD	19	128.19	P2p
Fa0/17	Desg	FWD	19	128.17	P2p
Fa0/14	Altn	BLK	19	128.14	P2p
Fa0/15	Altn	BLK	19	128.15	P2p
Fa0/13	Root	FWD	19	128.13	P2p

Since looking at PVSTP would be pretty boring without creating some vlans, let's take a moment to create VLANs 100, 200, 300 using VTP. We will use a VTP domain of CISCO.

SW1(config)#**vtp domain CISCO**
Changing VTP domain name from NULL to CISCO
*Mar 1 01:08:21.710: %SW_VLAN-6-VTP_DOMAIN_NAME_CHG: VTP domain name changed to CISCO.
SW1(config)#**vlan 100,200,300**
SW1(config-vlan)#**exit**

Vlan Trunking Protocol will automatically propagate information across its trunks as soon as you define a vtp domain name.

SW2#**show vlan**

VLAN	Name	Status	Ports
1	default	active	Fa0/1, Fa0/2, Fa0/3, Fa0/4
			Fa0/5, Fa0/6, Fa0/7, Fa0/8
			Fa0/9, Fa0/10, Fa0/11, Fa0/12
			Fa0/16, Fa0/17, Fa0/20, Fa0/21
			Fa0/22, Fa0/23, Fa0/24, Gig0/1
			Gig0/2
100	VLAN0100	active	
200	VLAN0200	active	
300	VLAN0300	active	
1002	fddi-default	act/unsup	
1003	token-ring-default	act/unsup	
1004	fddinet-default	act/unsup	
1005	trnet-default	act/unsup	

VLAN	Type	SAID	MTU	Parent	RingNo	BridgeNo	Stp	BrdgMode	Trans1	Trans2
1	enet	100001	1500	-	-	-	-	-	0	0
100	enet	100100	1500	-	-	-	-	-	0	0
200	enet	100200	1500	-	-	-	-	-	0	0
300	enet	100300	1500	-	-	-	-	-	0	0
1002	fddi	101002	1500	-	-	-	-	-	0	0
1003	tr	101003	1500	-	-	-	-	-	0	0
1004	fdnet	101004	1500	-	-	-	ieee	-	0	0
1005	trnet	101005	1500	-	-	-	ibm	-	0	0

Remote SPAN VLANs

Primary Secondary Type   Ports

------- --------- ---------------- --

Now if we check spanning tree again, we should see the other vlan instances.

SW1(config)#**do show spanning**

VLAN0001
  Spanning tree enabled protocol rstp
  Root ID   Priority   32769
             Address   000D.BD19.43EE
             This bridge is the root
             Hello Time 2 sec Max Age 20 sec Forward Delay 15 sec

  Bridge ID Priority   32769 (priority 32768 sys-id-ext 1)
             Address   000D.BD19.43EE
             Hello Time 2 sec Max Age 20 sec Forward Delay 15 sec
             Aging Time 20

Interface   Role Sts Cost   Prio.Nbr Type
---------------- ---- --- --------- -------- --------------------------------
Fa0/21   Desg FWD 19   128.21 P2p
Fa0/22   Desg FWD 19   128.22 P2p
Fa0/23   Desg FWD 19   128.23 P2p
Fa0/13   Desg FWD 19   128.13 P2p
Fa0/14   Desg FWD 19   128.14 P2p
Fa0/15   Desg FWD 19   128.15 P2p

VLAN0100
  Spanning tree enabled protocol rstp
  Root ID   Priority   32868
             Address   000D.BD19.43EE
             This bridge is the root
             Hello Time 2 sec Max Age 20 sec Forward Delay 15 sec

  Bridge ID Priority   32868 (priority 32768 sys-id-ext 100)
             Address   000D.BD19.43EE
             Hello Time 2 sec Max Age 20 sec Forward Delay 15 sec
             Aging Time 20

Interface   Role Sts Cost   Prio.Nbr Type
---------------- ---- --- --------- -------- --------------------------------
Fa0/21   Desg FWD 19   128.21 P2p
Fa0/22   Desg FWD 19   128.22 P2p
Fa0/23   Desg FWD 19   128.23 P2p
Fa0/13   Desg FWD 19   128.13 P2p
Fa0/14   Desg FWD 19   128.14 P2p
Fa0/15   Desg FWD 19   128.15 P2p

VLAN0200

Spanning tree enabled protocol rstp
Root ID   Priority   32968
           Address   000D.BD19.43EE
           This bridge is the root
           Hello Time 2 sec Max Age 20 sec Forward Delay 15 sec

Bridge ID Priority   32968 (priority 32768 sys-id-ext 200)
           Address   000D.BD19.43EE
           Hello Time 2 sec Max Age 20 sec Forward Delay 15 sec
           Aging Time 20

Interface	Role	Sts	Cost	Prio.Nbr	Type
Fa0/21	Desg	FWD	19	128.21	P2p
Fa0/22	Desg	FWD	19	128.22	P2p
Fa0/23	Desg	FWD	19	128.23	P2p
Fa0/13	Desg	FWD	19	128.13	P2p
Fa0/14	Desg	FWD	19	128.14	P2p
Fa0/15	Desg	FWD	19	128.15	P2p

VLAN0300

Spanning tree enabled protocol rstp
Root ID   Priority   33068
           Address   000D.BD19.43EE
           This bridge is the root
           Hello Time 2 sec Max Age 20 sec Forward Delay 15 sec

Bridge ID Priority   33068 (priority 32768 sys-id-ext 300)
           Address   000D.BD19.43EE
           Hello Time 2 sec Max Age 20 sec Forward Delay 15 sec
           Aging Time 20

Interface	Role	Sts	Cost	Prio.Nbr	Type
Fa0/21	Desg	FWD	19	128.21	P2p
Fa0/22	Desg	FWD	19	128.22	P2p
Fa0/23	Desg	FWD	19	128.23	P2p
Fa0/13	Desg	FWD	19	128.13	P2p
Fa0/14	Desg	FWD	19	128.14	P2p
Fa0/15	Desg	FWD	19	128.15	P2p

That gives us a lot of output. Fortunately we can filter by the vlan we are interested in. Let's look at Vlan 200.

SW1(config)#**do show spanning vlan 200**

VLAN0200
  Spanning tree enabled protocol rstp
  Root ID   Priority   32968
            Address   000D.BD19.43EE
            This bridge is the root
            Hello Time 2 sec Max Age 20 sec Forward Delay 15 sec

  Bridge ID Priority   32968 (priority 32768 sys-id-ext 200)
            Address   000D.BD19.43EE
            Hello Time 2 sec Max Age 20 sec Forward Delay 15 sec
            Aging Time 20

```
Interface        Role Sts  Cost   Prio.Nbr Type
---------------- ---- ---  ------- -------- --------------------------------
Fa0/21           Desg FWD  19       128.21  P2p
Fa0/22           Desg FWD  19       128.22  P2p
Fa0/23           Desg FWD  19       128.23  P2p
Fa0/13           Desg FWD  19       128.13  P2p
Fa0/14           Desg FWD  19       128.14  P2p
Fa0/15           Desg FWD  19       128.15  P2p
```

Everything else pretty much works the same as STP, so it's not worth going through again. The only exception is that you can specify the vlan when changing features like cost. This will allow you to adjust STP for only the vlan you want, rather than affecting the whole STP network.

SW2(config)#**int f0/13**
SW2(config-if)#**spanning-tree vlan 200 cost 20**

SW2(config-if)#**do show spanning-tree vlan 200**

VLAN0200
  Spanning tree enabled protocol rstp
  Root ID   Priority   32968
            Address   000D.BD19.43EE
            Cost   19
            Port   13(FastEthernet0/13)
            Hello Time 2 sec Max Age 20 sec Forward Delay 15 sec

  Bridge ID Priority   32968 (priority 32768 sys-id-ext 200)
            Address   0090.0C69.E4C0
            Hello Time 2 sec Max Age 20 sec Forward Delay 15 sec
            Aging Time 20

```
Interface        Role Sts  Cost    Prio.Nbr Type
```

```
----------------- ---- --- --------- -------- --------------------------------
Fa0/13      Altn  BLK  20     128.13  P2p

Fa0/14      Root  FWD 19      128.14  P2p
Fa0/15      Altn  BLK  19     128.15  P2p
Fa0/18      Desg FWD 19      128.18  P2p
Fa0/19      Desg FWD 19      128.19  P2p
```

Inter-VLAN Routing

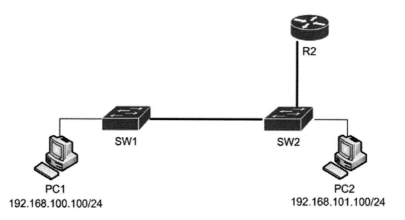

The purpose of this lab is to explore using STP in a switch environment.

Hardware & Configuration Required for this Lab

- Two Cisco switches, SW1 should be a Layer 3 switch for the SVI section. If you do not have one, you can skip that part of the lab
- One Cisco 100mb router
- Four crossover Cat5 cables to connect the switches
- Two PCs
- Three straight through Cat5 cables to connect the PC and router
- Read the show cdp neighbors below to figure out the topology connections

---

Commands Used in this Lab

interface <ethernet>.<sub> - Creates a subinterface on a router for trunking
encapsultion <encap> <vlan> - Sets what encapsulation mode and vlan the subinterface will use
ip routing - Enables L3 routing on a switch
interface vlan <#> - Creates a SVI on a switch

Physical Cabling Reference - Read the show cdp neighbors to figure out the topology.

SW1#**show cdp neighbors**
Capability Codes: R - Router, T - Trans Bridge, B - Source Route Bridge
                 S - Switch, H - Host, I - IGMP, r - Repeater, P - Phone

Device ID	Local Intrfce	Holdtme	Capability	Platform	Port ID
SW2	Fas 0/13	138		3560	Fas 0/13
SW2	Fas 0/14	138		3560	Fas 0/14
SW2	Fas 0/15	138		3560	Fas 0/15
SW2	Fas 0/16	138		3560	Fas 0/16

Note: PC-1 is connected to Fa0/10

SW2#**show cdp neighbors**
Capability Codes: R - Router, T - Trans Bridge, B - Source Route Bridge
                 S - Switch, H - Host, I - IGMP, r - Repeater, P - Phone

Device ID	Local Intrfce	Holdtme	Capability	Platform	Port ID
R2	Fas 0/2	172	R	C1841	Fas 0/0
SW1	Fas 0/13	140		3560	Fas 0/13
SW1	Fas 0/15	140		3560	Fas 0/15
SW1	Fas 0/16	140		3560	Fas 0/16
SW1	Fas 0/14	140		3560	Fas 0/14

Note: PC-2 is connected to Fa0/10

Initial Configs - Where you see *Initial Configs,* these are basic configuration steps that by now you should be able to perform on the devices by yourself without us detailing them step by step. Generally you simply go into enable and then configuration mode and start the configuration.

SW1
hostname SW1
line console 0
logging synch
vtp domain certificationkits
int range fa0/13 - 16
switchport trunk encapsulation dot1q
switchport mode trunk
switchport nonegotiate

SW2
hostname SW2
line console 0
logging synch
vtp domain certificationkits

int range fa0/13 - 16
switchport trunk encapsulation dot1q
switchport mode trunk
switchport nonegotiate

PC-1   **PC-2**

Internet Protocol Version 4 (TCP/IPv4) Properties		Internet Protocol Version 4 (TCP/IPv4) Properties	
General		**General**	
You can get IP settings assigned automatically if your network supports this capability. Otherwise, you need to ask your network administrator for the appropriate IP settings.		You can get IP settings assigned automatically if your network supports this capability. Otherwise, you need to ask your network administrator for the appropriate IP settings.	
○ Obtain an IP address automatically		○ Obtain an IP address automatically	
● Use the following IP address:		● Use the following IP address:	
IP address:	192 . 168 . 100 . 100	IP address:	192 . 168 . 101 . 100
Subnet mask:	255 . 255 . 255 . 0	Subnet mask:	255 . 255 . 255 . 0
Default gateway:	192 . 168 . 100 . 1	Default gateway:	192 . 168 . 101 . 1
○ Obtain DNS server address automatically		○ Obtain DNS server address automatically	
● Use the following DNS server addresses:		● Use the following DNS server addresses:	
Preferred DNS server:	. .	Preferred DNS server:	. .
Alternate DNS server:	. .	Alternate DNS server:	. .
☐ Validate settings upon exit	Advanced...	☐ Validate settings upon exit	Advanced...
	OK Cancel		OK Cancel

An obvious question you may have asked yourself when going through the vlan labs is; "If every vlan is in its own broadcast domain, how do you get VLANs to communicate with each other?" Well, there are two ways a switch can route between vlans. One is a method called **Router on a Stick** and the other uses SVI interfaces on a layer 3 switch.

Let's look at **Router on a Stick** first. It's called that because basically the switches send all traffic to the router which does the routing between the vlans and then sends it back. First things first, let's add PC-1 into vlan 100 and PC-2 into vlan 101.

SW1(config)#**int fa0/10**
SW1(config-if)#**switchport access vlan 100**
% Access VLAN does not exist. Creating vlan 100

SW2(config)#**int fa0/10**
SW2(config-if)#**sw ac vl 101**
% Access VLAN does not exist. Creating vlan 101

The **Router on a Stick** configuration is actually pretty easy. All we need to do on the switches is configure the port connecting R2 to be a dot1q trunk.

SW2(config)#**int fa0/2**
SW2(config-if)#**switchport trunk encapsulation dot1q**
SW2(config-if)#**switchport mode trunk**
1w6d: %LINEPROTO-5-UPDOWN: Line protocol on Interface FastEthernet0/2, changed state to down
1w6d: %LINEPROTO-5-UPDOWN: Line protocol on Interface FastEthernet0/2, changed state to up

However, on the router there is a bit more configuration. It is a best practice not to have any IP configuration on the physical router interface. So I recommend setting the interface back to defaults with: **default interface <int>**.

Note: The router will work fine if you leave IP info on the physical router interface. It just can be very confusing to someone unfamiliar with the network.

R2(config)#**default int fa0/0**
Building configuration...
Interface FastEthernet0/0 set to default configuration

The first step is to create a logical interface on the router for the vlan to trunk to. This is done by adding a number to the interface.
Note: While you can use any number you feel like for a logical interface, its best to use the vlan number to avoid confusion.

R2(config)#**int fa0/0?**
 . : <0-1>

R2(config)#**int fa0/0.?**
  <0-4294967295> FastEthernet interface number

Lets start with vlan 100.
R2(config)#**int fa0/0.100**
R2(config-subif)#

Next we have to set what encapsulation the sub interface will use. This is done with the **encapsulation** command. Depending on the router you're using, it may or may not support ISL. It is always a safe bet to use dot1q.

R2(config-subif)#**encapsulation ?**
  dot1Q IEEE 802.1Q Virtual LAN

This part of the encapsulation command is setting what vlan will be allowed on the trunk. In this case its 100.

R2(config-subif)#**encapsulation dot1Q ?**
  <1-4094> IEEE 802.1Q VLAN ID

R2(config-subif)#**encapsulation dot1Q 100**

After we set the encapsulation we are able to set an IP address on the sub interface.
Note: This configuration does have an order of operations, if you try to add an IP before you set the encapsulation you receive an error.

Now let's set the IP address. We will set 192.168.100.1/24 on the fa0/0.100 interface.
R2(config-subif)#**ip add 192.168.100.1 255.255.255.0**

And we'll also configure vlan 101 on another subinterface. We'll use the IP address 192.168.101.1/24.
Note: You may only set one vlan per sub interface on a router. If you want to trunk multiple vlans, you must make multiple sub interfaces.

R2(config)#**int fa0/0.101**
R2(config-subif)#**encapsulation dot1q 101**
R2(config-subif)#**ip add 192.168.101.1 255.255.255.0**

Now we can see that PC-1 and PC-2 can ping each other even though they are in different vlans.

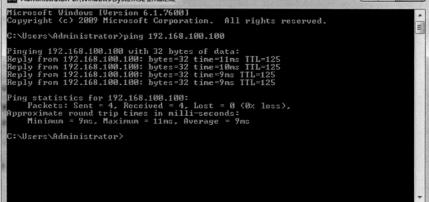

The problem with this method is that it is a single point of failure for the network. If anything happens to the link between R2 and SW2, all inter-vlan communication stops. Plus it adds strain and delay to the network as every frame needs to be sent to the router trunk link and then back to its destination.

Let's shutdown the link on SW2 that connects to R2. Now the PCs can no longer ping each other.

SW2(config)#**int fa0/2**
SW2(config-if)#**shut**
1w6d: %LINK-5-CHANGED: Interface FastEthernet0/2, changed state to administratively down
1w6d: %LINEPROTO-5-UPDOWN: Line protocol on Interface FastEthernet0/2, changed state to down

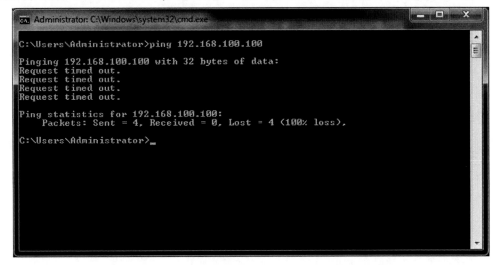

Basically we enable routing on layer 3 switches so it can route between the vlans itself. Let's keep this simple and just use one switch. We'll disable the trunk links on SW1 and plug PC-2 into Fa0/11.

SW1(config)#**int range fa0/12 - 24**
SW1(config-if-range)#**shut**

SW1(config)#**int fa0/11**
SW1(config-if)#**sw ac vl 101**

The topology will look something like this afterwards.

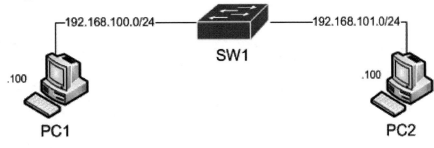

Next we will configure vlan interfaces for each vlan.

SW1(config)#**int vlan 100**
1w6d: %LINEPROTO-5-UPDOWN: Line protocol on Interface Vlan100, changed state to up
SW1(config-if)#ip add 192.168.100.1 255.255.255.0

SW1(config)#**int vlan 101**
1w6d: %LINEPROTO-5-UPDOWN: Line protocol on Interface Vlan101, changed state to up
SW1(config-if)#ip add 192.168.101.1 255.255.255.0

To enable L3 routing on a switch you use the **ip routing** command.
Note: Layer 3 switches are more expensive then L2 switches so you may not have
choosen to purchase them for your studies.

SW1(config)#**ip routing**

At this point the switch behaves like a router. Let's check the routing table. We can see
both vlan interfaces as directly connected.

SW1(config)#**do show ip route**
Codes: C - connected, S - static, I - IGRP, R - RIP, M - mobile, B - BGP
      D - EIGRP, EX - EIGRP external, O - OSPF, IA - OSPF inter area
      N1 - OSPF NSSA external type 1, N2 - OSPF NSSA external type 2
      E1 - OSPF external type 1, E2 - OSPF external type 2, E - EGP
      i - IS-IS, L1 - IS-IS level-1, L2 - IS-IS level-2, ia - IS-IS inter area
      * - candidate default, U - per-user static route, o - ODR
      P - periodic downloaded static route
Gateway of last resort is not set
C   192.168.100.0/24 is directly connected, Vlan100
C   192.168.101.0/24 is directly connected, Vlan101

Now we are able to ping between vlans again.

```
Administrator: C:\Windows\system32\cmd.exe

Microsoft Windows [Version 6.1.7600]
Copyright (c) 2009 Microsoft Corporation.  All rights reserved.

C:\Users\Administrator>ping 192.168.100.100

Pinging 192.168.100.100 with 32 bytes of data:
Reply from 192.168.100.100: bytes=32 time=11ms TTL=125
Reply from 192.168.100.100: bytes=32 time=10ms TTL=125
Reply from 192.168.100.100: bytes=32 time=9ms TTL=125
Reply from 192.168.100.100: bytes=32 time=9ms TTL=125

Ping statistics for 192.168.100.100:
    Packets: Sent = 4, Received = 4, Lost = 0 (0% loss),
Approximate round trip times in milli-seconds:
    Minimum = 9ms, Maximum = 11ms, Average = 9ms

C:\Users\Administrator>
```

Configuring an EtherChannel Link

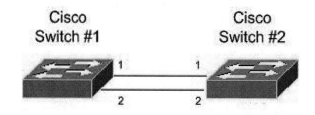

In this lab we will configure a two interface EtherChannel between two Cisco Ethernet switches. If the switches used have 100mb/s interfaces, then this will create a connection that could potentially provide 200mb/s of bandwidth between the Ethernet switches.

Hardware & Configuration Required for this Lab

- Two Cisco switches
- Two crossover Cat 5 cables
- Connect Switch #1 interface FastEthernet0/1 to Switch #2 interface FastEthernet0/1
- Connect Switch #1 interface FastEthernet0/2 to Switch #2 interface FastEthernet0/2
- Begin with the default configuration on both switches. If a configuration is in place, erase the startup-configuration and restart the switch. After restarting, set the hostname on both switches.

The available bandwidth for interconnecting two Ethernet switches is not limited to the speed of single interfaces. If two Ethernet switches only have 100mb/s then 100mb/s is not the actual limit for uplinking one switch into another. While some Ethernet switches might have 12, 24, 48, or more switchports at one speed, many Cisco switches might have 1, 2, 4, or more uplink ports, often fiber-optic ports, at higher speeds such as GigabitEthernet or TenGigabitEthernet. Without investing in the costs for that equipment, or using those ports, multiple Ethernet switchports can be combined into an EtherChannel. An EtherChannel combines multiple switchports, most often up to eight, into a combined single connection.

Switch Configurations

Switch #1
Switch(config)#**hostname SW1**

Switch #2
Switch(config)#**hostname SW2**

Configure EtherChannel on the Interfaces

Configure interface FastEthernet0/1 and FastEthernet0/2 on both switches to use EtherChannel.

Switch #1
SW1(config)#**interface FastEthernet0/1**
SW1(config-if)#**channel-group 1 mode on**
SW1(config-if)#**interface FastEthernet0/2** (*This step could be skipped with "interface range".*)
SW1(config-if)#**channel-group 1 mode on**

Switch #2
SW2(config)#**interface range FastEthernet0/1 - 2**
SW2(config-if)#**channel-group 1 mode on**

Enter configuration mode for the PortChannel interface for group 1 which contains group members FastEthernet0/1 and FastEthernet0/2.

Switch #1
SW1(config)#**interface Port-Channel 1**

Switch #2
SW1(config)#**interface Port-Channel 1**

Verify the EtherChannel status with the show EtherChannel command and see the number of ports assigned to the channel:

SW1(config)#**show EtherChannel**
Channel-group listing:

Group: 1

Group state = L2
Ports: 2   Maxports = 8
Port-channels: 1 Max Port-channels = 1
Protocol: -
SW1#

Configuring an EtherChannel Link Review
Questions

1. What is the main purpose of using EtherChannel?

   _____

2. What is the limit to the number of interfaces that can be in an interface group?

   _____

3. What interface configuration adds an interface to EtherChannel 7?

   _____

4. What is the older version of the interface configuration for adding interfaces to EtherChannel group 8?

   _____

5. After adding interfaces to an EtherChannel, what interface is created?

   _____

6. What is difference in the color of the link lights on the switches after EtherChannel?

   _____

7. How fast of an EtherChannel could be created with all GigabitEthernet interfaces?

   _____

8. Is EtherChannel enabled by default on Cisco switchports?

   _____

Answers

1. EtherChannel combines interfaces to increase bandwidth in interconnections.
2. 8
3. channel-group 7
4. port group 8
5. PortChannel
6. One of the switchports was orange/amber due to spanning-tree blocking the loop by disabling the port. After enabling EtherChannel, it re-enabled the port and the link light went green.
7. 8gb/s
8. no

Configuring EtherChannel using PAgP

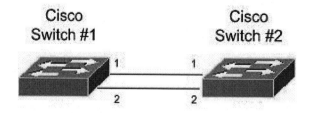

In this lab we will configure a two interface EtherChannel between two Cisco Ethernet switches using PAgP. If the switches used have 100mb/s interfaces, then this will create a connection that could potentially provide 200mb/s of bandwidth between the Ethernet switches.

Hardware & Configuration Required for this Lab

- Two Cisco switches
- Two crossover Cat 5 cables
- Connect Switch #1 interface FastEthernet0/1 to Switch #2 interface FastEthernet0/1
- Connect Switch #1 interface FastEthernet0/2 to Switch #2 interface FastEthernet0/2
- Begin with the default configuration on both switches. If a configuration is in place, erase the startup-configuration and restart the switch. After restarting, set the hostname on both switches.

Port aggregation protocol (PAgP) aids in the automatic creation of EtherChannel links. PAgP packets are sent between Fast EtherChannel-capable ports in order to negotiate the forming of a channel. PAgP is a Cisco proprietary protocol. It will only work on Cisco Ethernet switches and adds two modes beyond regular EtherChannel.

EtherChannel can either be "on" or the default setting of "off" on switchport interfaces. PAgP provides the ability to detect the presence of PAgP configured EtherChannel interfaces on another Cisco switch and also adds the "dynamic" and "auto" modes. Switchports assigned to an EtherChannel group and using PAgP in dynamic mode actively attempt to seek out a PAgP dynamic mode or auto mode device on the interface. If either is connected, the interfaces on both Ethernet switches join the EtherChannel group.

PAgP desirable actively send packets to negotiate with other PAgP interfaces and listens for packets from other PAgP desirable and auto interfaces to EtherChannel with other interfaces.

PAgP auto passively listens for packets initiated from a PAgP dynamic interface to negotiate EtherChannel with other PAgP interfaces.

Switch Configuration

Configure EtherChannel on the Interfaces

Configure interface FastEthernet0/1 and FastEthernet0/2 on SW1 to attempt to form a PAgP EtherChannel while configuring SW2 with the mode auto command which will attempt to negotiate a PAgp EtherChannel only.

Switch #1
SW1(config)#**interface FastEthernet0/1**
SW1(config-if)#**channel-group 1 mode desirable**
SW1(config-if)#**interface FastEthernet0/2** (*This step could be skipped with "interface range".*)
SW1(config-if)#**channel-group 1 mode desirable**

Switch #2
SW2(config)#**interface range FastEthernet0/1 - 2**
SW2(config-if)#**channel-group 1 mode auto**

Verify that the PAgP EtherChannel negotiated correctly below in bold.

SW1#**show EtherChannel summary**
Flags: D - down   P - in port-channel
          I - stand-alone   s - suspended
          H - Hot-standby (LACP only)
          - Layer3   S - Layer2
          u - unsuitable for bundling
          U - in use   f - failed to allocate aggregator
          d - default port

Number of channel-groups in use: 1
Number of aggregators: 1
Group Port-channel Protocol   Ports
------+-------------+-----------+---
1   Po1(SU)   **PAgP**   Fa0/1(P)   Fa0/2(Pd)

Configuring EtherChannel using PAgP Review
Questions

1. What is the main purpose of using PAgP?

   _____

2. What are the two modes which PAgP uses to negotiate?

   _____

3. Which mode does PAgP only listen for PAgP advertisement packets?

   _____

4. What is the result of PAgP dynamic and PAgP dynamic on EtherChannel interfaces?

   _____

5. What is the result of PAgP dynamic and PAgP auto on EtherChannel interfaces?

   _____

6. What is the result of PAgP auto and PAgP auto on EtherChannel interfaces?

   _____

7. Can PAgP be used to negotiate EtherChannel on interfaces to non-Cisco switches?

   _____

8. Is PAgP enabled by default on Cisco switchports?

   _____

Answers

1. Automatic enabling of EtherChannel on interfaces between switches.
2. Dynamic and Auto
3. auto
4. PAgP will negotiate an EtherChannel connection on the interconnected interfaces.
5. PAgP will negotiate an EtherChannel connection on the interconnected interfaces.
6. PAgP will not negotiate an EtherChannel connection and not join the channel-group.
7. No
8. No

Configuring EtherChannel using LACP

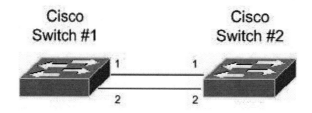

In this lab we will configure a two interface EtherChannel between two Cisco Ethernet switches using LACP. If the switches used have 100mb/s interfaces, then this will create a connection that could potentially provide 200mb/s of bandwidth between the Ethernet switches.

Hardware & Configuration Required for this Lab

- Two Cisco 4000 series or better switches. Thus you may read through it.
- Two crossover Cat 5 cables
- Connect Switch #1 interface FastEthernet0/1 to Switch #2 interface FastEthernet0/1
- Connect Switch #1 interface FastEthernet0/2 to Switch #2 interface FastEthernet0/2
- Begin with the default configuration on both switches. If a configuration is in place, erase the startup-configuration and restart the switch. After restarting, set the hostname on both switches.

Link Aggregation Control Protocol (LACP) aids in the automatic creation of EtherChannel links. LACP packets are sent between EtherChannel-capable ports in order to negotiate the forming of a channel. LACP is an industry standard, so it can work with connections to non-Cisco switches and can even be used on some servers with multiple network cards.

EtherChannel can either be "on" or the default setting of "off" on switchport interfaces. LACP which provides the ability to detect the presence of LACP configured EtherChannel interfaces on another switch or device, adds "active" and "passive" modes. Switchports assigned to an EtherChannel group and using LACP in active mode actively attempt to seek out a LACP dynamic mode or passive mode devices on the interface. If either is connected, the interfaces on both Ethernet switches join the EtherChannel group.

LACP active actively send packets to negotiate with other LACP interfaces and listens for packets from other LACP desirable and auto interfaces to EtherChannel with other interfaces.

LACP passive passively listens for packets initiated from a LACP active interface to negotiate EtherChannel with other LACP interfaces.

Switch Configuration

Begin with the default configuration on both switches. If a configuration is in place, erase the startup-configuration and restart the switch.

Switch#**erase startup-config**
Erasing the nvram filesystem will remove all configuration files! Continue? [confirm] (*Press Enter*)
Switch#**reload**

System configuration has been modified. Save? [yes/no]: **no**
Proceed with reload? [confirm] (*Press Enter*)

After restarting, set the hostname on both switches.

Switch #1
Switch(config)#**hostname SW1**

Switch #2
Switch(config)#**hostname SW2**

Configure EtherChannel on the Interfaces

Configure interface FastEthernet0/1 and FastEthernet0/2 on both switches to use EtherChannel.

Switch #1
SW1(config)#**interface FastEthernet0/1**
SW1(config-if)#**channel-group 1 protocol LACP**
SW1(config-if)#**channel-group 1 mode active**
SW1(config-if)#**interface FastEthernet0/2** (*This step could be skipped with "interface range".*)
SW1(config-if)#**channel-group 1 protocol LACP**
SW1(config-if)#**channel-group 1 mode active**

Switch #2
SW2(config)#**interface range FastEthernet0/1 - 2**
SW2(config-if)#**channel-group 1 protocol LACP**
SW2(config-if)#**channel-group 1 mode active**

Enter configuration mode for the PortChannel interface for group 1 which contains group members FastEthernet0/1 and FastEthernet0/2.

Switch #1
SW1(config)#**interface PortChannel 1**

Switch #2
SW2(config)#**interface PortChannel 1**

Verify that the EtherChannel status has negotiated:

SW1(config)#**show EtherChannel**

NOTE: If the "channel-group" interface configuration is not supported by your Ethernet switch, then you cannot perform this lab on your Ethernet switches.

Configuring EtherChannel using LACP Review

Questions

1. What is the main purpose of using LACP?

   _____

2. What are the two modes which LACP uses to negotiate?

   _____

3. Which mode does LACP only listen for LACP advertisement packets?

   _____

4. What is the result of LACP active and LACP passive on EtherChannel interfaces?

   _____

5. What is the result of LACP active and LACP passive on EtherChannel interfaces?

   _____

6. What is the result of LACP passive and LACP passive on EtherChannel interfaces?

   _____

7. Can LACP be used to negotiate EtherChannel on interfaces to non-Cisco switches?

   _____

8. Is LACP enabled by default on Cisco switchports?

   _____

Answers

1. Automatic enabling of EtherChannel on interfaces to switches and/or servers.
2. Active and Passive
3. Active
4. LACP will negotiate an EtherChannel connection on the interconnected interfaces.
5. LACP will negotiate an EtherChannel connection on the interconnected interfaces.
6. LACP will not negotiate an EtherChannel connection and not join the channel-group.
7. No
8. No

Configuring a PortChannel Interface

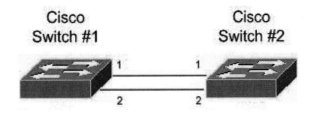

In this lab we will configure a two interface EtherChannel between two Cisco Ethernet switches to use trunking. If the switches used have 100mb/s interfaces, then this will create a connection that could potentially provide 200mb/s of bandwidth between the Ethernet switches.

Hardware & Configuration Required for this Lab

- Two Cisco switches
- Two crossover Cat 5 cables
- Connect Switch #1 interface FastEthernet0/1 to Switch #2 interface FastEthernet0/1
- Connect Switch #1 interface FastEthernet0/2 to Switch #2 interface FastEthernet0/2
- Begin with the default configuration on both switches. If a configuration is in place, erase the startup-configuration and restart the switch. After restarting, set the hostname on both switches.

EtherChannel groups are controlled overall by their PortChannel interfaces. If six FastEthernet switchports are assigned to channel-group 9, then there is an interface PortChannel 9 which controls settings for the channel-group. The individual interfaces can all be configured for speed, duplex, CDP, and similar settings; but must all match to be eligible for the channel-group.

Switch Configurations

Switch #1
Switch(config)#**hostname SW1**
SW1(config)#**interface range FastEthernet0/1 - 2**
SW1(config-if)#**channel-group 1 mode on**

Switch #2
Switch(config)#**hostname SW2**
SW2(config)#**interface range FastEthernet0/1 - 2** (*If your switch cannot use the range specification, configure each interface individually.*)
SW2(config-if)#**channel-group 1 mode on**

Configure the PortChannel Interfaces

Configure the PortChannel interface to trunk between switches.

Switch #1
SW1(config)#**interface port-channel 1**
SW1(config-if)#**switchport trunk encapsulation dot1q** (*this command may not work if your switch does not support both ISL and dot1q and in that case you can skip it*)
SW1(config-if)#**switchport mode trunk**

Switch #2
SW2(config)#**interface port-channel 1**
SW2(config-if)#**switchport trunk encapsulation dot1q**
SW2(config-if)#**switchport mode trunk**

Verify that the EtherChannel status has negotiated and that the trunk has established.

SW1#**show etherchannel**
     Channel-group listing:

Group: 1

Group state = L2
Ports: 2   Maxports = 8
Port-channels: 1 Max Port-channels = 1
Protocol: -

SW1#**show interface trunk**

Port	Mode	Encapsulation	Status	Native vlan
Po1	on	802.1q	trunking	1
Port	Vlans allowed on trunk			
Po1	1-4094			
Port	Vlans allowed and active in management domain			
Po1	1			
Port	Vlans in spanning tree forwarding state and not pruned			
Po1	1			

Now issue a show run to see the configuration in the running-config.

SW1#**show running-config**
interface FastEthernet0/1
 channel-group 1 mode on
 switchport mode trunk
!
interface FastEthernet0/2

channel-group 1 mode on
switchport mode trunk
!
...
!
interface Port-channel 1
switchport trunk encapsulation dot1q
switchport mode trunk

Now shutdown the port channel and then bring it back up to see the interface status changes.

SW1(config)#**int port-channel 1**
SW1(config-if)#**shutdown**
00:15:38: %LINEPROTO-5-UPDOWN: Line protocol on Interface Port-channel1, changed state to down
00:15:39: %LINK-5-CHANGED: Interface FastEthernet0/1, changed state to administratively down
00:15:39: %LINK-5-CHANGED: Interface FastEthernet0/2, changed state to administratively down
00:15:39: %LINK-5-CHANGED: Interface Port-channel1, changed state to administratively down
00:15:40: %LINEPROTO-5-UPDOWN: Line protocol on Interface FastEthernet0/1, changed state to down
00:15:40: %LINEPROTO-5-UPDOWN: Line protocol on Interface FastEthernet0/2, changed state to down

SW1(config-if)#**no shut**
00:16:19: %LINK-3-UPDOWN: Interface Port-channel1, changed state to down
00:16:19: %LINK-3-UPDOWN: Interface FastEthernet0/1, changed state to up
00:16:19: %LINK-3-UPDOWN: Interface FastEthernet0/2, changed state to up
00:16:22: %LINEPROTO-5-UPDOWN: Line protocol on Interface FastEthernet0/1, changed state to up
00:16:22: %LINEPROTO-5-UPDOWN: Line protocol on Interface FastEthernet0/2, changed state to up
00:16:23: %LINK-3-UPDOWN: Interface Port-channel1, changed state to up
00:16:24: %LINEPROTO-5-UPDOWN: Line protocol on Interface Port-channel1, changed state to up

Configuring PortChannel Interface Review

Questions

1. What is a requirement for switchports to be part of a channel-group?

   _____

2. What is the interface that controls the EtherChannel for channel-group 11?

   _____

3. What happens to the EtherChannel if one of the two interfaces is shutdown?

   _____

4. What happens if the PortChannel interface is shutdown?

   _____

5. What does CDP report when 2 interfaces are added to an EtherChannel?

   _____

6. Can an EtherChannel still use IEEE802.1Q trunking?

   _____

7. What happens to the EtherChannel if one cables between switches is unplugged?

   _____

8. Research EtherChannel further and find what methods can be specified to determine how network traffic is selected to use one of the multiple connections in the group.

   _____

Answers

1. Same port settings regarding speed
2. Interface PortChannel 11
3. The EtherChannel continues over the remaining interface.
4. The configured interfaces stay up, but go back to their original configure mode.
5. CDP reports on the connection on each interface, not over the PortChannel interface.
6. Yes
7. The same occurs if a port was shutdown, the EtherChannel continues over the other remaining interfaces up within the channel group.
8. Source IP Address, Destination IP Address, Source MAC Address, Destination MAC Address

Standard ACL

The purpose of this lab is to cover using standard access-lists.

Hardware & Configuration Required for this Lab

- One Cisco router with two Fast Ethernet ports
- Two Cisco switches. This can also be done with one switch if need be.
- At least two PCs. If you don't have a second PC, then just add multiple IP addresses on the NIC of your PC.
- Four straight-through Cat 5 cables
- **Note:** You could still complete this lab by removing the two switches and two of the patch cables and replacing them with two crossover cables. Another option would be if you do not have a router with two Ethernet interfaces is to have two single Ethernet routers connected back to back via the serial ports and having the Ethernet port on each available for the switch/PCs.

Commands Used in this Lab

access-list <number> - Defines an access list and associates it with a number.
ip access-group <number> <direction>- Applies an access list and it's contents to a particular interface and direction.

Initial Configs

R1
hostname R1

line console 0
logging synch
int fa0/0
ip add 172.16.232.1 255.255.255.0
no shutdown
int fa0/1
ip add 172.16.244.1 255.255.255.240
no shutdown

SW1
hostname SW1
line console 0
logging synch
int fa0/1
switchport mode access
sw ac vl 100
int fa0/10
switchport mode access
switchport access vlan 100

SW2
hostname SW2
line console 0
logging synch
int fa0/1
switchport mode access
switchport access vlan 200
int fa0/10
switchport mode access
switchport access vlan 200

PC-1

PC-2

Access-lists are one of those things that absolutely must be mastered in order to be successful. Nothing will get you hot water faster than applying an ACL to the wrong interface or accidently denying all traffic in the network. A common misconception is that access-lists are purely for security. This is not true as they can be used for literally dozens of things from controlling routing policy to filtering debug output. However in this lab we are just focusing on security.

Before getting started with anything related to security, it's important to check to make sure you have proper communication between your hosts to save troubleshooting time later. Here we can see that PC1 and PC2 can ping each other.

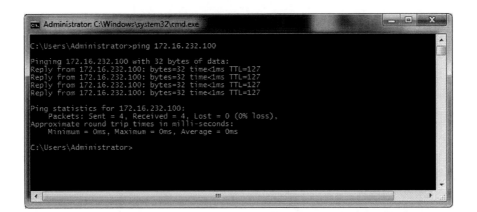

To define an access-list on a router, you use the **access-list <number>** command. There are many kinds of access-lists available that are controlled by the access-list number you pick. For example, in this lab we are focusing on standard access-lists. So if we enter a number between the ranges of 1-99 or 1300-1999 it will be a standard ACL. If we type **access-list 123** it would be an extended access-list because 123 falls in the extended access-list range. We'll pick **access-list 25**.

R1(config)#**access-list ?**
  <1-99>   IP standard access list
  <100-199>   IP extended access list
  <1100-1199>   Extended 48-bit MAC address access list
  <1300-1999>   IP standard access list (expanded range)
  <200-299>   Protocol type-code access list
  <2000-2699>   IP extended access list (expanded range)
  <700-799>   48-bit MAC address access list
  dynamic-extended Extend the dynamic ACL absolute timer
  rate-limit   Simple rate-limit specific access list

So what is a Standard Access-list? The standard type is a very simple access-list that matches traffic only by source traffic. After we pick the ACL number, we need to choose whether traffic it matches is permitted or denied.

Note: You can also use the remark option to make a quick note about the ACL for your reference later.

R1(config)#**access-list 25 ?**
  deny   Specify packets to reject
  permit Specify packets to forward
  remark Access list entry comment

Let's permit traffic only from PC2 to anywhere in the network. So we will choose the **permit** option. Now we have three options; match by a network, match anything, or match a single host.

R1(config)#**access-list 25 permit ?**
  Hostname or A.B.C.D Address to match
  any   Any source host
  host   A single host address

For now we are going to choose the **host** option which just selects one IP.
 R1(config)#**access-list 25 permit host 172.16.244.10**

At this point the ACL will be permitting only the IP 172.16.244.10. It is very important to remember that there is an implicit deny statement at the bottom of all access-lists which matches if no other access-list statement matches. Forgetting about the implicit deny could be very bad as the list is blocking **ALL** traffic not explicitly permitted.

Now that we have an access-list, we need to apply it to an interface. This is done with the **ip access-group** command under the interface. The syntax is: **ip access-group <acl #> <direction>**

When applying an access-list it is important to consider the direction of traffic from the router's perspective. Is the traffic coming in the interface or is it going out of the interface? We'll look at both. For now we'll apply the access-list to the Fa0/1 interface inbound.

 R1(config)#**int fa0/1**
 R1(config-if)#**ip access-group 25 in**

Rather then setup multple PCs for the 172.16.244.0/28 network, I added several IPs on my Windows PC.   These are 172.16.244.10-14.

```
Administrator: C:\Windows\system32\cmd.exe

C:\Users\Administrator>netsh interface ipv4 show addresses LAB

Configuration for interface "LAB"
    DHCP enabled:                      No
    IP Address:                        172.16.244.10
    Subnet Prefix:                     172.16.244.0/28 (mask 255.255.255.240)
    IP Address:                        172.16.244.11
    Subnet Prefix:                     172.16.244.0/28 (mask 255.255.255.240)
    IP Address:                        172.16.244.12
    Subnet Prefix:                     172.16.244.0/28 (mask 255.255.255.240)
    IP Address:                        172.16.244.13
    Subnet Prefix:                     172.16.244.0/28 (mask 255.255.255.240)
    IP Address:                        172.16.244.14
    Subnet Prefix:                     172.16.244.0/28 (mask 255.255.255.240)
    Default Gateway:                   172.16.244.1
    Gateway Metric:                    1
    InterfaceMetric:                   20

C:\Users\Administrator>_
```

We can see that if we ping from PC2 with a source address of 172.16.244.10, the ping is successful but if we try with .11 the ping fails.

We can see how many packets are matching with the **show access-list** command.

R1#**show access-list 25**
Standard IP access list 25
    10 permit 172.16.244.10 (5001 matches)

If we want to see how many packets are being denied, we will need to add a **deny any** statement to the ACL so it shows up in the **show access-list** output.
Note: Many people add "deny any" to the bottom of the ACL so they don't forgot about the implicit deny and so they can see how many packets are being denied.

R1(config)#**access-list 25 deny any**
R1(config)#**do show access-list 25**
Standard IP access list 25
    10 permit 172.16.244.10 (5008 matches)
    20 deny   any (12 matches)

Let's remove the access-list and add a loopback on R1.

R1(config)#**int fa0/1**
R1(config-if)#**no ip access-group 25 in**
R1(config-if)#**int lo0**
R1(config-if)#**ip add**
*Mar 24 05:18:34.105: %LINEPROTO-5-UPDOWN: Line protocol on Interface Loopback0, changed state to up
R1(config-if)#**ip add 111.111.111.111 255.255.255.255**

At this point PC1 and PC2 can ping the loopback network just fine.

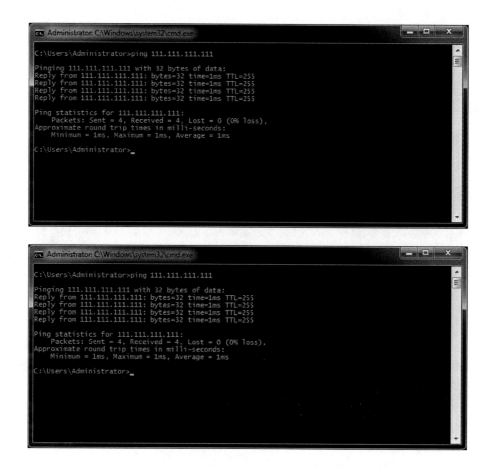

Let's make an access-list that will block PC1 & PC2 from talking to each other, but will allow them to talk to the loopback address. Remember that standard access-lists can only match source addresses not destinations. So we will have to solve this by ACL placement. In fact, for this scenario we can just use an access-list that denies all traffic!!

R1(config)#**access-list 10 deny any**
R1(config)#**int fa0/0**
R1(config-if)#**ip access-group 10 out**
R1(config-if)#**int fa0/1**
R1(config-if)#**ip access-group 10 out**

We can see this works. The reason why it works is because the packets don't transit the router to reach a logical interface.

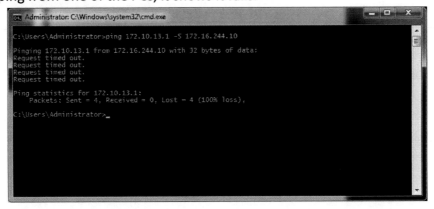

However, all other traffic trying to transit, the router will be blocked. For example, this router has an active serial interface.

R1(config)#**do show ip int br**

Interface	IP-Address	OK?	Method	Status	Protocol
FastEthernet0/0	172.16.232.1	YES	manual	up	up
Serial0/0	172.10.13.2	YES	TFTP	up	up
FastEthernet0/1	172.16.244.1	YES	manual	up	up
Serial0/1	unassigned	YES	TFTP	administratively down	down
NVI0	unassigned	NO	unset	up	up
Loopback0	111.111.111.111	YES	manual	up	up

R1(config)#**do ping 172.10.13.1**
Type escape sequence to abort.
Sending 5, 100-byte ICMP Echos to 172.10.13.1, timeout is 2 seconds:
!!!!!
Success rate is 100 percent (5/5), round-trip min/avg/max = 16/16/16 ms

Trying to ping from one of the PCs, it shows it fails.

Let's adjust the scenario so that the PCs can reach the serial network but not each other. We'll need to remove the access-list and start over.

R1(config)#**no access-list 10**

For each access-list we'll deny the opposite network and permit everything else.

R1(config)#**access-list 10 deny 172.16.244.0 0.0.0.15**
R1(config)#**access-list 10 permit any**
R1(config)#**access-list 11 deny 172.16.232.0 0.0.0.255**
R1(config)#**access-list 11 permit any**

Now we will apply them to the interfaces closest to the destination. This is because since standard access-lists can only match by source, you want to put them as close to the destination as possible to avoid them causing any unwanted issues. We will apply the access-group outbound because we only want to affect traffic leaving the interface, not coming in.

R1(config)#**int fa0/0**
R1(config-if)#**ip access-group 10 out**
R1(config-if)#**int fa0/1**
R1(config-if)#**ip access-group 11 out**

And now we can ping as expected.

Cisco Access Lists Review

Questions:

1. You want to create an access list to filter all traffic from the 172.16.16.0 255.255.240.0 network. What wildcard mask is appropriate? _____

2. You need to temporarily remove access list 101 from one of your interfaces what command is appropriate?_____

Answers:

1. 0.0.15.255 affects the 172.16.16.0 255.255.240.0 network. In the third octet, the first four bits are checked in binary, resulting in 00000000.00000000.00001111.11111111.

2. The correct syntax is 'no ip access-group 101'. This removes the access list from the interface.

Extended ACL

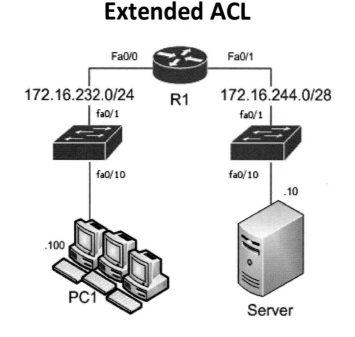

In this lab we will cover using extended access-lists.

Hardware & Configuration Required for this Lab

- One Cisco router with two Fast Ethernet ports
- Two Cisco switches. This can also be done with one switch if need be.
- At least two PCs. If you don't have a second PC, then just add multiple IP addresses to the NIC of your PC.
- At least one PC that can be used to run server services
- Four straight through Cat 5 cables
- **Note:** You could still complete this lab by removing the two switches and two of the patch cables and replacing them with two crossover cables. Another option would be if you do not have a router with two Ethernet interfaces is to have two single Ethernet routers connected back to back via the serial ports and having the Ethernet port on each available for the switch/PCs.

Commands Used in Lab

access-list <100-199 or 2000-2699><permit/deny><protocol><source><destination>
- Defines a extended access-list.
access-list <2000-2699> - Defines a extended access-list using the expanded range

Initial Configs - Where you see *Initial Configs,* these are basic configuration steps that by now you should be able to perform on the devices by yourself without us detailing them step by step. Generally you simply go into enable and then configuration mode and start the configuration.

R1
hostname R1
line console 0
logging synch
int fa0/0
ip add 172.16.232.1 255.255.255.0
no shut
int fa0/1
ip add 172.16.244.1 255.255.255.240
no shut

SW1
hostname SW1
line console 0
logging synch
int fa0/1
switchport mode access
switchport access vlan 100
int fa0/10
switchport mode access
switchport access vlan 100

SW2
hostname SW2
line console 0
logging synch
int fa0/1
switchport mode access
switchport access vlan 200
int fa0/10
switchport mode access
switchport access vlan 200

PC-1

Internet Protocol Version 4 (TCP/IPv4) Properties

General

You can get IP settings assigned automatically if your network supports this capability. Otherwise, you need to ask your network administrator for the appropriate IP settings.

○ Obtain an IP address automatically
◉ Use the following IP address:

IP address: 172 . 16 . 232 . 100
Subnet mask: 255 . 255 . 255 . 0
Default gateway: 172 . 16 . 232 . 1

○ Obtain DNS server address automatically
◉ Use the following DNS server addresses:

Preferred DNS server: .   .   . |
Alternate DNS server: .   .   .

☐ Validate settings upon exit   Advanced...

OK   Cancel

PC-2

Internet Protocol Version 4 (TCP/IPv4) Properties

General

You can get IP settings assigned automatically if your network supports this capability. Otherwise, you need to ask your network administrator for the appropriate IP settings.

○ Obtain an IP address automatically
◉ Use the following IP address:

IP address: 172 . 16 . 244 . 10
Subnet mask: 255 . 255 . 255 . 240
Default gateway: 172 . 16 . 244 . 1

○ Obtain DNS server address automatically
◉ Use the following DNS server addresses:

Preferred DNS server: | .   .   .
Alternate DNS server: .   .   .

☐ Validate settings upon exit   Advanced...

OK   Cancel

We saw from the previous lab that standard access-lists are easy to configure but aren't very flexible in how they match packets. Because of this, special care must be taken when placing the access-lists as because they only match by source packets, you can get some unexpected results. Extended Access-Lists, just as the name implies, has extended match criteria to help better filter the packets you want.

Extended Access-Lists can match by a packets source, destination, or by protocol which gives you a lot more flexibility. Extended ACLs are defined in the same way as standard ones. It is determined by what range the number of the access-list lands in. Extended Access-Lists use the ranges: 100-199 and 2000-2699.

The syntax is: **access-list <100-199 or 2000-2699> <permit/deny> <protocol> <source> <destination>**

R1(config)#**access-list ?**
  <1-99>   IP standard access list
  <100-199>   IP extended access list
  <1100-1199>   Extended 48-bit MAC address access list
  <1300-1999>   IP standard access list (expanded range)
  <200-299>   Protocol type-code access list
  <2000-2699>   IP extended access list (expanded range)
  <700-799>   48-bit MAC address access list
  dynamic-extended Extend the dynamic ACL absolute timer
  rate-limit   Simple rate-limit specific access list

Just like with the standard lists, we can choose to permit or deny the matched packets or add a remark.

Note: The dynamic option is used with a security option called Lock and Key Access-lists, we won't get into those.

R1(config)#**access-list 101 ?**
  deny   Specify packets to reject
  dynamic Specify a DYNAMIC list of PERMITs or DENYs
  permit   Specify packets to forward
  remark   Access list entry comment

After we choose what to do with the match packet, we must choose what protocol we are interested in. At the CCNA level, you will mostly be interested in: TCP, UDP, ICMP, and IP. IP is the equivalent of **any** as it will match any protocol. We'll choose **tcp** for now.

R1(config)#**access-list 101 permit ?**
  <0-255>   An IP protocol number
  ahp   Authentication Header Protocol
  eigrp   Cisco's EIGRP routing protocol
  esp   Encapsulation Security Payload
  gre   Cisco's GRE tunneling
  icmp   **Internet Control Message Protocol**
  igmp   Internet Gateway Message Protocol
  ip   **Any Internet Protocol**
  ipinip   IP in IP tunneling
  nos   KA9Q NOS compatible IP over IP tunneling
  ospf   OSPF routing protocol
  pcp   Payload Compression Protocol
  pim   Protocol Independent Multicast
  tcp   **Transmission Control Protocol**
  udp   **User Datagram Protocol**

The next section is where we can choose the source address or network. We can also choose **any** to match all source addresses.

R1(config)#**access-list 101 permit tcp ?**
  A.B.C.D Source address
  any   Any source host
  host   A single source host

After you enter the source criteria, you have an option to enter in port information and we will look at this in a little bit. If you don't need to enter any port or protocol information, then you can just enter info for the destination network.

R1(config)#**access-list 101 permit tcp any ?**
 A.B.C.D   Destination address
 any   Any destination host
 eq   Match only packets on a given port number
 gt   Match only packets with a greater port number
 host   A single destination host
 lt   Match only packets with a lower port number
 neq   Match only packets not on a given port number
 range   Match only packets in the range of port numbers

After the destination is entered, we again have the option to filter on port information. We also have various logging information that we will look at later.

R1(config)#**access-list 101 permit tcp any any ?**
 ack   Match on the ACK bit
 dscp   Match packets with given dscp value
 eq   Match only packets on a given port number
 established Match established connections
 fin   Match on the FIN bit
 fragments   Check non-initial fragments
 gt   Match only packets with a greater port number
 log   Log matches against this entry
 log-input   Log matches against this entry, including input interface
 lt   Match only packets with a lower port number
 neq   Match only packets not on a given port number
 option   Match packets with given IP Options value
 precedence   Match packets with given precedence value
 psh   Match on the PSH bit
 range   Match only packets in the range of port numbers
 rst   Match on the RST bit
 syn   Match on the SYN bit
 time-range   Specify a time-range
 tos   Match packets with given TOS value
 urg   Match on the URG bit

For the server in my lab, I have configured a Centos box to run a web server, an ftp server, and I have enabled telnet and SSH access to the box. We can see that the 172.16.232.0/24 network can reach the apache test page just fine.

And also the 172.16.232.0/24 network can ftp and telnet to the server just fine as well.

Our first scenario will be we only want the computer with an IP address of 172.16.232.15/24 to be able to access the web services at 172.16.244.10.   Before we begin we need to understand what traffic we are trying to block; webpages use the TCP port 80 for HTTP traffic.

To select port numbers in access lists, we have a few different operators we can use:
EQ = Equals a given port number
GT = All ports greater then the given port number
LT = All ports less then the given port number

RANGE = This is a port range, for example 1024 to 65535 to match all dynamic ports
NEQ = Not equal to the given port.

R1(config)#**access-list 101 permit tcp host 172.16.232.15 host 172.16.244.10 ?**
ack	Match on the ACK bit
dscp	Match packets with given dscp value
eq	Match only packets on a given port number
established	Match established connections
fin	Match on the FIN bit
fragments	Check non-initial fragments
gt	Match only packets with a greater port number
log	Log matches against this entry
log-input	Log matches against this entry, including input interface
lt	Match only packets with a lower port number
neq	Match only packets not on a given port number
option	Match packets with given IP Options value
precedence	Match packets with given precedence value
psh	Match on the PSH bit
range	Match only packets in the range of port numbers
rst	Match on the RST bit
syn	Match on the SYN bit
time-range	Specify a time-range
tos	Match packets with given TOS value
urg	Match on the URG bit
<cr>	

For CCNA we will usually use the equal **(EQ)** option for access-lists so that's what we will use here. We can see that IOS gives us names for some common ports so we can either type 80 for http or use the **www** keyword.
Note: The actual port number is shown in brackets when looking at ? output for eq.

R1(config)#**access-list 101 permit tcp host 172.16.232.15 host 172.16.244.1 eq ?**
<0-65535>	Port number
bgp	Border Gateway Protocol (179)
chargen	Character generator (19)
cmd	Remote commands (rcmd, 514)
daytime	Daytime (13)
discard	Discard (9)
domain	Domain Name Service (53)
drip	Dynamic Routing Information Protocol (3949)
echo	Echo (7)
exec	Exec (rsh, 512)
finger	Finger (79)
ftp	File Transfer Protocol (21)
ftp-data	FTP data connections (20)
gopher	Gopher (70)
hostname	NIC hostname server (101)

ident   Ident Protocol (113)
irc   Internet Relay Chat (194)
klogin   Kerberos login (543)
kshell   Kerberos shell (544)
login   Login (rlogin, 513)
lpd   Printer service (515)
nntp   Network News Transport Protocol (119)
pim-auto-rp PIM Auto-RP (496)
pop2   Post Office Protocol v2 (109)
pop3   Post Office Protocol v3 (110)
smtp   Simple Mail Transport Protocol (25)
sunrpc   Sun Remote Procedure Call (111)
tacacs   TAC Access Control System (49)
talk   Talk (517)
telnet   Telnet (23)
time   Time (37)
uucp   Unix-to-Unix Copy Program (540)
whois   Nicname (43)
www   World Wide Web (HTTP, 80)

R1(config)#**access-list 101 permit tcp host 172.16.232.15 host 172.16.244.10 eq 80**

Another good option when making access-lists is to add **access-list <#> deny ip any any log** to the bottom as it will show denied packets in the log.

R1(config)#**access-list 101 deny ip any any log**

Because Extended Access-lists are much more grandular then Standard ACLs, its best to place them as close to the traffic being affected as possible. Both because there is more overhead and because there is no reason to let packets that will be denied travel the network anymore then what is necessary.

R1(config)#**int fa0/0**
R1(config-if)#**ip access-group 101 in**

Now if we try to navigate to our server's webpage it no longer works.

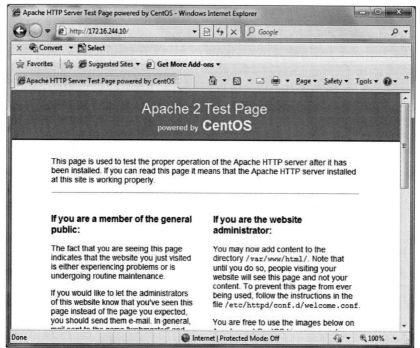

If we try to access the webpage from a host with the 172.16.232.15 address, it works just fine.

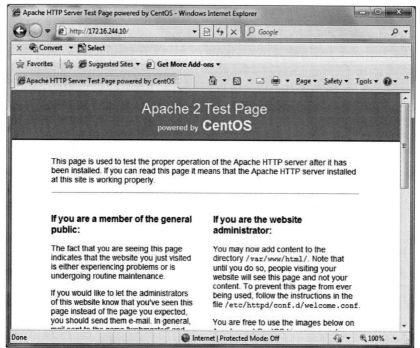

Checking **show access-list** we can see that packets are being both permited and denied.

R1(config)#**do sh access-list 101**
Extended IP access list 101

10 permit tcp host 172.16.232.15 host 172.16.244.10 eq www (28 matches)
20 deny ip any any log (36 matches)

Because we enabled logging on the **deny ip any any** line, we can go a bit deeper into what is being denied by checking the log to see information on the denied packets. The source address, destination address, protocol, and ports are recorded in the log which is handy to see if your accidently blocked a service you didn't mean to, or in production it can be handy to quickly see if someone is trying to access things in your network that they shouldn't be trying to access.

R1(config)#**do show log**
Syslog logging: enabled (11 messages dropped, 0 messages rate-limited,
0 flushes, 0 overruns, xml disabled, filtering disabled)
Console logging: level debugging, 7 messages logged, xml disabled,
filtering disabled
Monitor logging: level debugging, 0 messages logged, xml disabled,
filtering disabled
Buffer logging: level debugging, 3 messages logged, xml disabled,
filtering disabled
Logging Exception size (4096 bytes)
Count and timestamp logging messages: disabled
No active filter modules.
Trap logging: level informational, 43 message lines logged

Log Buffer (4096 bytes):
*Apr 7 08:31:25.540: %SEC-6-IPACCESSLOGP: list 101 denied tcp 172.16.232.100(49729)->172.16.244.10(80)
*Apr 7 08:31:40.232: %SEC-6-IPACCESSLOGP: list 101 denied tcp 172.16.232.100(49730)->172.16.244.10(80)
*Apr 7 08:32:05.069: %SEC-6-IPACCESSLOGP: list 101 denied tcp 172.16.232.100(49711)->172.16.244.10(80)
*Apr 7 08:35:05.068: %SEC-6-IPACCESSLOGP: list 101 denied tcp 172.16.232.100(49652)->172.16.244.10(23)
*Apr 7 08:36:49.223: %SEC-6-IPACCESSLOGDP: list 101 denied icmp 172.16.232.100->172.16.244.10 (8/0)

In the log we can see that telnet (port 23) and ICMP traffic is also being dropped by our access-lists. Let's modify the access-list to make sure those are permitted. Because we have added the **deny ip any any** explicitedly into the ACL anything we add afterwords would simply be denied by the statement since access-lists are read from the top down and stop as soon as a match is made.

R1(config)# **do show access-list**
Extended IP access list 101
    10 permit tcp host 172.16.232.15 host 172.16.244.10 eq www (28 matches)
    20 deny ip any any log (36 matches)

Unfortunately there isn't really a good way at the CCNA level to edit an access-list. So you have to remove the access-list list and reapply it. I recommend doing a **show run | in access-list <#>** to get the list, copy it to notepad and edit it from there.

R1(config)#**do show run | in access-list 101**
access-list 101 permit tcp host 172.16.232.15 host 172.16.244.10 eq www
access-list 101 deny   ip any any log

You can remove an entire access-list with **no access-list <#>**. You don't need to remove the access-group first.

R1(config)#**no access-list 101**

So let's add some more requirements to our access-list. Only 172.16.232.15 may access the web server in the 172.16.232.0/24 network. But hosts in the network can access any other network just fine. Because we want to deny specific destinations but allow traffic to go anywhere else, we need to have the most specific rules up top of the list and the general rules below.

R1(config)#**access-list 101 permit tcp host 172.16.232.15 host 172.16.244.10 eq 80**
R1(config)#**access-list 101 deny tcp 172.16.232.0 0.0.0.255 172.16.244.0 0.0.0.15 eq 80**
R1(config)#**access-list 101 permit tcp 172.16.232.0 0.0.0.255 any eq 80**

Now let's allow 172.16.232.15 to telnet to the server. No one else from 172.16.232.0/24 may telnet anything.
R1(config)#**access-list 101 permit tcp host 172.16.232.15 host 172.16.244.10 eq 23**

Finally, we will allow everyone in 172.16.232.0/24 to ping anything. Under the ICMP protocol, a ping is called an **echo** and and the reply is called **echo-reply**. You can see from the options you can be very flexible in what ICMP traffic you want to permit in your network.

R1(config)#**access-list 101 permit icmp any any ?**
  <0-255>   ICMP message type
  administratively-prohibited   Administratively prohibited
  alternate-address   Alternate address
  conversion-error   Datagram conversion
  dod-host-prohibited   Host prohibited
  dod-net-prohibited   Net prohibited
  dscp   Match packets with given dscp value
  echo   **Echo (ping)**
  echo-reply   **Echo reply**
  fragments   Check non-initial fragments
  general-parameter-problem   Parameter problem
  host-isolated   Host isolated
  host-precedence-unreachable Host unreachable for precedence
  host-redirect   Host redirect
  host-tos-redirect   Host redirect for TOS
  host-tos-unreachable   Host unreachable for TOS

host-unknown	Host unknown
host-unreachable	Host unreachable
information-reply	Information replies
information-request	Information requests
log	Log matches against this entry
log-input	Log matches against this entry, including input interface
mask-reply	Mask replies
mask-request	Mask requests
mobile-redirect	Mobile host redirect
net-redirect	Network redirect
net-tos-redirect	Net redirect for TOS
net-tos-unreachable	Network unreachable for TOS
net-unreachable	Net unreachable
network-unknown	Network unknown
no-room-for-option	Parameter required but no room
option	Match packets with given IP Options value
option-missing	Parameter required but not present
packet-too-big	Fragmentation needed and DF set
parameter-problem	All parameter problems
port-unreachable	Port unreachable
precedence	Match packets with given precedence value
precedence-unreachable	Precedence cutoff
protocol-unreachable	Protocol unreachable
reassembly-timeout	Reassembly timeout
redirect	All redirects
router-advertisement	Router discovery advertisements
router-solicitation	Router discovery solicitations
source-quench	Source quenches
source-route-failed	Source route failed
time-exceeded	All time exceededs
time-range	Specify a time-range
timestamp-reply	Timestamp replies
timestamp-request	Timestamp requests
tos	Match packets with given TOS value
traceroute	Traceroute
ttl-exceeded	TTL exceeded
unreachable	All unreachables
<cr>	

For now, we will just permit echo and echo-reply.

R1(config)#**access-list 101 permit icmp 172.16.232.0 0.0.0.255 any echo**
R1(config)#**access-list 101 permit icmp 172.16.232.0 0.0.0.255 any echo-reply**

```
Administrator: C:\Windows\system32\cmd.exe

C:\Users\Administrator>ping 172.16.244.10

Pinging 172.16.244.10 with 32 bytes of data:
Reply from 172.16.244.10: bytes=32 time=1ms TTL=63
Reply from 172.16.244.10: bytes=32 time=1ms TTL=63
Reply from 172.16.244.10: bytes=32 time=1ms TTL=63
Reply from 172.16.244.10: bytes=32 time=1ms TTL=63

Ping statistics for 172.16.244.10:
    Packets: Sent = 4, Received = 4, Lost = 0 (0% loss),
Approximate round trip times in milli-seconds:
    Minimum = 1ms, Maximum = 1ms, Average = 1ms

C:\Users\Administrator>
```

Here is our full access-list.

R1(config)#**do sh access-list 101**

Extended IP access list 101

    10 permit tcp host 172.16.232.15 host 172.16.244.10 eq www

    20 deny tcp 172.16.232.0 0.0.0.255 172.16.244.0 0.0.0.15 eq www

    30 permit tcp 172.16.232.0 0.0.0.255 any eq www (9 matches)

    40 permit tcp host 172.16.232.15 host 172.16.244.10 eq telnet (45 matches)

    50 deny tcp host 172.16.232.0 any eq telnet

    60 permit icmp 172.16.232.0 0.0.0.255 any echo (8 matches)

    70 permit icmp 172.16.232.0 0.0.0.255 any echo-reply

I recommend playing around with access-lists as much as possible until you get comfortable with them as they are something you definately need to master.

Named ACL

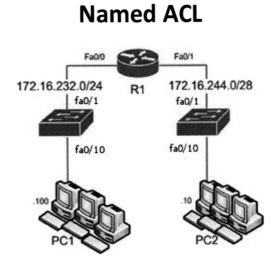

In this lab we will cover named access-lists.

Hardware & Configuration Required for this Lab

- One Cisco router with two Fast Ethernet ports
- Two Cisco switches. This can also be done with one switch if need be.
- At least two PCs. If you don't have a second PC, then just add multiple IP addresses to the NIC of your PC.
- At least one PC that can be used to run server services.
- At least 4 straight-through Cat 5 cables.
- **Note:** You could still complete this lab by removing the two switches and two of the patch cables and replacing them with two crossover cables. Another option would be if you do not have a router with two Ethernet interfaces is to have two single Ethernet routers connected back to back via the serial ports and having the Ethernet port on each available for the switch/PCs.

Commands Used in Lab

ip access-list <standard/extended> <name> - Defines a named access-list.

Initial Configs - Where you see *Initial Configs,* these are basic configuration steps that by now you should be able to perform on the devices by yourself without us detailing them step by step. Generally you simply go into enable and then configuration mode and start the configuration.

R1

hostname R1
line console 0
logging synch
int fa0/0
ip add 172.16.232.1 255.255.255.0
no shut
int fa0/1
ip add 172.16.244.1 255.255.255.240
no shut

SW1

hostname SW1
line console 0
logging synch
int fa0/1
switchport mode access
switchport access vlan 100
int fa0/10
switchport mode access
switchport access vlan 100

SW2

hostname SW2
line console 0
logging synch
int fa0/1
switchport mode access
switchport access vlan 200
int fa0/10
switchport mode access
switchport access vlan 200

PC-1   PC-2

Named Access-lists solve two issues with standard and extended access-lists. First, when you're troubleshooting in large networks it's not always easy to keep track what access-list 2653 does in your network. As the name implies, named ACLs allow you to use a logical name instead. Second, you can't remove a single line in a standard or extended access-list without first removing the entire list. Named ACLs allow you to edit specific lines rather then remove the entire list.

To define a named access-list you use the **ip access-list <standard/extended> <name>** command.

R1(config)#**ip access-list ?**
 extended   **Extended Access List**
 log-update   Control access list log updates
 logging   Control access list logging
 resequence Resequence Access List
 standard   **Standard Access List**

After you choose whether the list is standard or extended you can define a name for the access-list.
Note: You may choose to define a ACL#, we'll go over why you might do this later on.

R1(config)#**ip access-list standard ?**
 <1-99>   Standard IP access-list number
 <1300-1999> Standard IP access-list number (expanded range)
 WORD   Access-list name

R1(config)#**ip access-list extended ?**
 <100-199>   Extended IP access-list number

<2000-2699>   Extended IP access-list number (expanded range)
WORD   Access-list name

Let's make an extended ACL that will deny all ICMP traffic from 172.16.232.0/24 network. Because we are allowed to name the ACL, we can choose a name that tells us what the ACL is doing: NoPingsFrom232.

R1(config)#**ip access-list extended NoPingsFrom232**
R1(config-ext-nacl)#**deny icmp any any**
R1(config-ext-nacl)#**permit ip any any**

We can see I made a mistake with the above list. We wanted to block icmp from just 172.16.232.0/24, but this list is blocking all ICMP traffic. We can use the **show access-list** output to find out the sequence number we need. If you noticed from earlier outputs, there was always a number that imclemented by 10 with each access-list statement in the output; this is the sequence number. In the case of **deny icmp any any** it is 10. Please note in pre 12.4 IOS you may not see the numbers 10 and 20 and this may not work as expected.

R1(config-ext-nacl)#**do show access-list NoPingsFrom232**
Extended IP access list NoPingsFrom232
   10 deny icmp any any
   20 permit ip any any

Inside the named access-list configuration context, we can remove the line by doing a **no <sequence #>**. We can then add the replacement line by entering in the proper sequence number before our command.

R1(config)#**ip access-list extended NoPingsFrom232**
R1(config-ext-nacl)#**?**
Ext Access List configuration commands:
   <1-2147483647> Sequence Number
   default   Set a command to its defaults
   deny   Specify packets to reject
   dynamic   Specify a DYNAMIC list of PERMITs or DENYs
   evaluate   Evaluate an access list
   exit   Exit from access-list configuration mode
   no   Negate a command or set its defaults
   permit   Specify packets to forward
   remark   Access list entry comment

This is seen here.

R1(config)#**ip access-list extended NoPingsFrom232**
R1(config-ext-nacl)#**no 10**
R1(config-ext-nacl)#**10 deny icmp 172.16.232.0 0.0.0.255 any**

Now we can see line 10 has been changed to just match the 172.16.232.0 network.

R1(config-ext-nacl)#**do show access-list NoPingsFrom232**
Extended IP access list NoPingsFrom232
   10 deny icmp 172.16.232.0 0.0.0.255 any
   20 permit ip any any

If we decide that we want the host 172.16.232.10 to be able to use any ICMP traffic, we simply need to choose a lower sequence number then the deny statement.

R1(config)#**ip access-list extended NoPingsFrom232**
R1(config-ext-nacl)#**8 permit icmp host 172.16.232.10 any**

And we can see the new line is added above the deny statement.

R1(config-ext-nacl)#**do show access-list NoPingsFrom232**
Extended IP access list NoPingsFrom232
   8 permit icmp host 172.16.232.10 any
   10 deny icmp 172.16.232.0 0.0.0.255 any
   20 permit ip any any

We can also use the **ip access-list** command to edit particular lines in numbered access-lists as well. Let's consider this access-list where we have accidentally denied all traffic. We can use the same logic to edit a line rather then delete the list and readd it.

R1(config)#**access-list 123 deny ip any any**

First we check the **show access-list** output to see what sequence number is being used.

R1(config)#**do sh access-list 123**
Extended IP access list 123
   10 deny ip any any

Instead of defining a name for the access-list, we instead enter the numbered ACL #. Now we will add a statement that allows web traffic before the deny statement.

R1(config)#**ip access-list extended 123**
R1(config-ext-nacl)#**5 permit tcp any any eq 80**

And we can see web traffic is now allowed.

R1(config-ext-nacl)#**do show access-list 123**
Extended IP access list 123
   5 permit tcp any any eq www
   10 deny ip any any

Trusted Hosts

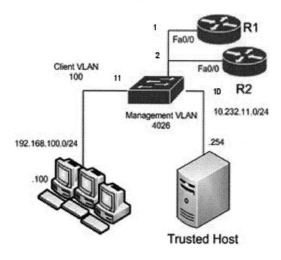

The purpose of this lab is to show you how to make a basic trusted host environment for your lab.

Hardware & Configuration Required for this Lab

- Two Cisco routers with a Fast Ethernet port
- One Cisco Layer 3 switch
- At least two PCs. One as a client. One as a Trusted Host
- Four straight-through Cat 5 cables

Commands Used in this Lab

access-list <100-199> - Defines a extended access-list
access-list <2000-2699> - Defines a extended access-list using the extended range

---

Initial Configs - Where you see *Initial Configs,* these are basic configuration steps that by now you should be able to perform on the devices by yourself without us detailing them step by step. Generally you simply go into enable and then configuration mode and start the configuration. Patch the client workstation to fa0/11. The trusted host to fa0/10, R1 to fa0/1 and R2 to fa0/2.

R1
line console 0
logging synch
hostname R1
int fa0/0
ip add 10.232.11.101 255.255.255.0
no shut

R2
line console 0
logging synch
hostname R2
int fa0/0
ip add 10.232.11.102 255.255.255.0
no shut

SW1
hostname SW1
line console 0
logging synch

PC1

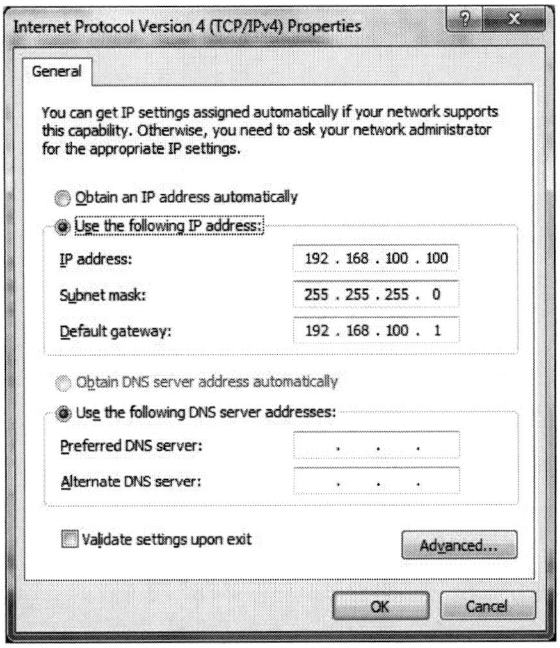

Most large corporations and ISPs in the world use the concept of Trusted Hosts to manage their network. Rather then allowing every PC in the network to access the company's core devices, they will instead give the IT staff permission to log into a central server that is allowed to access all devices. This has several benefits, but the most importent is user management. When adding or removing IT staff, you only need to create or delete a user on the trusted host. Along the same lines, it's easy to enforce password polcies built into the server to ensure that everyone changes their passwords once a month or whatever your security policy is for the company.

Additionally, it's much easier to secure your company's devices since there will only be a single IP that needs to be permitted in the access-lists. Most trusted hosts are using old SunOS servers or some other linux distribution with all but a few importent services disabled. In this lab I'm using CentOS for my server. Since this isn't a linux course, we won't go through locking down the server. So we won't look at it too much beyond setting an IP address as shown below.

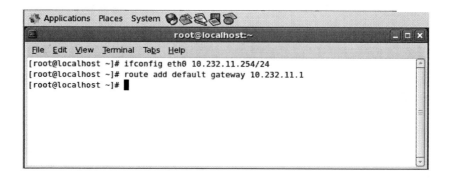

The first thing we need to do on our switch is set the device to transparent mode because we are using vlans above the standard range.

SW1(config)#**vtp mode transparent**
Setting device to VTP TRANSPARENT mode.

Next we will add the VLANs we will be using.
SW1(config)#**vlan 100**
SW1(config-vlan)#**name CLIENT**
SW1(config-vlan)#**vlan 4026**
SW1(config-vlan)#**name MANAGEMENT**
SW1(config-vlan)#**exit**

Next we will make vlan interfaces for our created vlans.
SW1(config)#**int vlan 100**
SW1(config-if)#**ip add 192.168.100.1 255.255.255.0**
SW1(config-if)#**exit**
SW1(config)#**int vlan 4026**
SW1(config-if)#**ip add 10.232.11.1 255.255.255.0**

Next we will assign the ports the routers and the trusted host that are connected on to vlan 4026 and the client ports into vlan 100.

```
SW1(config)#int range fa0/1 - 2 , fa0/10
SW1(config-if-range)#switchport access vlan 4026
SW1(config-if-range)#int fa0/11
SW1(config-if)#switchport access vlan 100
```

At this point I'm going to enable **ip routing** on the switch rather then setup router on a stick.

```
SW1(config)#ip routing
```

Now we need to make an access list that just permits the 192.168.100.0/24 network to ssh into our trusted host. We will allow the 10.232.11.0 s
ubnet to communicate freely with the vlan to ensure we don't break anything. Then we'll apply the access-list to the management vlan interface.

```
SW1(config)#ip access-list extended MGMT-ALLOW
SW1(config-ext-nacl)#permit tcp 192.168.100.0 0.0.0.255 host 10.232.11.254 eq 22
SW1(config-ext-nacl)#permit ip 10.232.11.0 0.0.0.255 10.232.11.0 0.0.0.255
SW1(config)#int vlan 4026
SW1(config-if)#ip access-group MGMT-ALLOW in
```

On the router end, we want to configure an access-list that only allows telnet traffic from our trusted host.

```
R1(config)#ip access-list extended MGMT-ALLOW
R1(config-ext-nacl)#permit tcp host 10.232.11.254 any eq 23
```

Next we'll make a username to log into the router with.
```
R1(config)#username ciscokits password ciscokits
```

Routers and switches have a special access-group called **access-class**. This specially controls what is allowed to telnet or ssh the device. It is applied under the **line vty 0 4** and controls access to the entire device rather then having to add the rule to every interface.

```
R1(config)#line vty 0 4
R1(config-line)#login local
R1(config-line)#access-class MGMT-ALLOW in
```

And we'll apply the same commands on R2.

R2(config)#**ip access-list extended MGMT-ALLOW**
R2(config-ext-nacl)#**permit tcp host 10.232.11.254 any eq 23**
R2(config)#**username ciscokits password ciscokits**
R2(config)#**line vty 0 4**
R2(config-line)#**login local**
R2(config-line)#**access-class MGMT-ALLOW in**

From one of PCs on the Client VLAN, we can see that we cannot telnet to the router on the Magement VLAN.

However we can see that if we first login to the Trusted Host, then we are able to Telnet and login to R1.

Controlling VTY Access

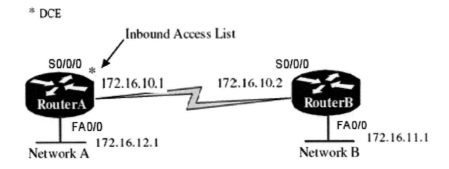

In this lab we'll be using a standard access lists to control VTY connections to RouterA. We will only allow the host 172.16.11.1 to telnet into RouterA and deny all other attempts.

Hardware & Configuration Required for this Lab
- Two Cisco routers with one Ethernet port and one serial port
- One back to back DTE/DCE serial cable

Router Configurations
RouterA
Logon to RouterA and enter the global configuration mode.
router>**en**
router#**config t**

Set the hostname of the router to RouterA
router(config)#**hostname RouterA**

Configure FA0/0 with an ip address of 172.16.12.1 using a 24 bit subnet mask. Bring the interface up using the no shut command.
RouterA(config)#**int fa0/0**
RouterA(config-if)#**ip address 172.16.12.1 255.255.255.0**
RouterA(config-if)#**no shut**

Disable the keepalives on int FA0/0 to allow the interface to stay up when not connected.
RouterA(config-if)#**no keepalive**

Configure serial0/0/0 on RouterA with the ip address of 172.16.10.1 and a 24 bit subnet mask. RouterA's serial0/0/0 also has the DCE end of the cable so set a clock rate of 64000. Bring the interface up using the no shut command.
RouterA(config)#**int s0/0/0**
RouterA(config-if)#**ip address 172.16.10.1 255.255.255.0**

RouterA(config-if)#**clockrate 64000**
RouterA(config-if)#**no shut**

Type in the no ip classless command.
RouterA(config-if)#**no ip classless**

Configure a static route for RouterA. Tell the router how to get over to the 172.16.11.0
network on RouterB.
RouterA(config)#**ip route 172.16.11.0 255.255.255.0 172.16.10.2**

Configure a standard access list using the number 1. Permit only traffic from the host
172.16.11.1. Deny all other traffic
RouterA(config)#**access-list 1 permit 172.16.11.1**

FYI: There is an implicit 'deny all' at the end of all access-lists statements. If a packet
cannot match up with the conditions of the access-list, the packet is denied. Because of
this implicit deny at the end of this specific access-list; any traffic that does not originate
from the host 172.16.11.1 will be denied.

Assign access list 1 to the VTY lines coming into RouterA using the access-class
command.
RouterA(config)#**line VTY 0 4**
RouterA(config-line)#**access-class 1 in** *(Applies standard access list 1 to all inbound)*
RouterA(config-line)# **password Cisco**

FYI: Using the access-class command allows only packets destined for telnetting into the
router to be looked at. All other packets will be ignored. The class command only works
at the VTY lines.

RouterB
Logon to RouterB and enter the global configuration mode.
router>**en**
router#**config t**

Set the hostname of the router to RouterB and define the source address of the telnet
packets from RouterB as Ethernet0
RouterB(config)#**hostname RouterB**
RouterB(config)# **ip telnet source-interface FA0/0**

Configure FA0/0 with an ip address of 172.16.11.1 using a 24 bit subnet mask. Bring the
interface up using the no shut command.
RouterB(config)#**int FA0/0**
RouterB(config-if)#**ip address 172.16.11.1 255.255.255.0**
RouterB(config-if)#**no shut**

Disable the keepalives on int FA0/0 to allow the interface to stay up when not connected.
RouterB(config-if)#**no keepalive**

Configure serial0/0/0 on RouterB with the ip address of 172.16.10.2 using a 24 bit subnet mask. Bring the interface up using the no shut command.
RouterB(config-if)#**int s0/0/0**
RouterB(config-if)#**ip address 172.16.10.2 255.255.255.**0
RouterB(config-if)#**no shut**

Type in the no ip classless command.
RouterB(config-if)#**no ip classless**

Configure a static route on RouterB. Tell the router how to get over to the 172.16.12.0 network on RouterA.
RouterB(config)#**ip route 172.16.12.0 255.255.255.0 172.16.10.1**

Test the Configuration
Test the configuring by establishing a telnet session with RouterA from Router B. The source address of the telnet packet is 172.16.11.1 which we defined on RouterB using the ip telnet source-interface FA0/0 command.
RouterB#**telnet 172.16.10.1**
Trying 172.16.10.1 . . . Open
User Access Verification
Password:

On RouterB, edit the configuration so that all telnet packets are sourced from the serial0/0/0 interface. Use the following command from the global configuration mode:
RouterB>**en**
RouterB#**config t**
RouterB(config)#**no ip telnet source-interface FA0/0**
RouterB(config)#**ip telnet source-interface serial0/0/0**

Try telnetting into RouterA again and this time the connection is refused because the address of the telnet packet does not match the access control list on router A
RouterB#**telnet 172.16.10.1**
Trying 172.16.10.1 . . .
% Connection refused by remote host

Cisco Discovery Protocol

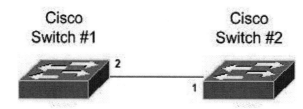

In this lab we will use CDP to identify connected Cisco devices. We will also learn how to disable CDP on switchports.

Hardware & Configuration Required for this Lab

- Two Cisco switches
- One crossover Cat 5 cable
- Connect Switch #1 interface FastEthernet0/2 to Switch #2 interface FastEthernet0/1
- Begin with the default configuration on both switches. If a configuration is in place, erase the startup-configuration and restart the switch. After restarting, set the hostname on both switches.

Connections between networking devices, such as all of the connections from switches to other switches, can become so complex that they become difficult to track. Even in documented network environments, it is extremely difficult to track all of the cabled connections between devices. Within Cisco network devices, Cisco Discovery Protocol (CDP) provides a solution by which routers and switches advertise their identity at regular intervals. A cabled connection between a switch and a router with CDP enabled allows the router to know what switch it is connected to and vice versa. If two switches are linked together, with interfaces up, CDP still communicates router identity information even if neither switch has a configured management IP address.

CDP may not be very useful on all end node connections, such as those going to user PCs or printers. However, when dealing with connections between Cisco switches and Cisco routers, CDP is very helpful. Device name, device type, configured IP address, and several other pieces of information are included in these multicast messages which Cisco devices transmit out all interfaces every 60 seconds. Using this information, a network administrator could learn of all connected Cisco devices to one device, connect to the next device using telnet or SSH, use CDP to learn off of the connected Cisco devices on that device, connect to the next device using telnet or SSH, and so on.

Switch Configuration

Start with a clean configuration on both switches.

> Switch#**erase startup-config**
> Erasing the nvram filesystem will remove all configuration files! Continue? [confirm]
> (*Press Enter*)
> Switch#**reload**
>
> System configuration has been modified. Save? [yes/no]: **no**
> Proceed with reload? [confirm] (*Press Enter*)

Configure the following on Switch #1:

> Switch(config)#**hostname SW1**
> SW1(config)#**interface vlan 1**
> SW1(config-if)#**ip address 192.168.0.11 255.255.255.0**
> SW1(config-if)#**no shutdown**
> SW1(config-if)#**enable secret cisco**
> SW1(config)#**line vty 0 15**
> SW1(config-line)#**password cisco**

Configure the following on Switch #2:

> Switch(config)#**hostname SW2**
> SW2(config)#**interface vlan 1**
> SW2(config-if)#**ip address 192.168.0.12 255.255.255.0**
> SW2(config-if)#**no shutdown**
> SW2(config-if)#**enable secret cisco**
> SW2(config)#**line vty 0 15**
> SW2(config-line)#**password cisco**

Ensure that the cable between switches produces a link light.

Show CDP Neighbors

CDP is enabled by default on all Cisco router and Cisco switch interfaces. Use the show command on Switch #1 to find connected Cisco devices which also have CDP enabled.

> SW1> **show cdp neighbors**
> Capability Codes: R - Router, T - Trans Bridge, B - Source Route Bridge
>   S - Switch, H - Host, I - IGMP, r - Repeater, P - Phone

Device ID	Local Intrfce	Holdtme	Capability	Platform	Port ID
SW2	Fas 0/2	133		3560	Fas 0/1

Note the device name, the local interface which the neighbor is connected, the model of the remote device, and the interface on the remote device for the connection.

Run the same command on Switch #2.

>   SW2> **show cdp neighbors**
>   Capability Codes: R - Router, T - Trans Bridge, B - Source Route Bridge
>   S - Switch, H - Host, I - IGMP, r - Repeater, P - Phone
>   Device ID   Local Intrfce   Holdtme   Capability   Platform   Port ID
>   SW1   Fas 0/1   159   3560   Fas 0/2

The output is reversed, still indicating the local interface and remote interface.

Show CDP Neighbors Detail

From either switch, add the keyword "detail" to the end of the command.

>   SW1#**show cdp neighbors detail**
>   Device ID: SW2
>   Entry address(es):
>   IP address : 192.168.0.12
>   Platform: cisco 3560, Capabilities:
>   Interface: FastEthernet0/2, Port ID (outgoing port): FastEthernet0/1
>   Holdtime: 134
>
>   Version :
>   Cisco IOS Software, C3560 Software (C3560-ADVIPSERVICESK9-M), Version 12.2(37)SE1,
>   RELEASE SOFTWARE (fc1)
>   Copyright (c) 1986-2007 by Cisco Systems, Inc.
>   Compiled Thu 05-Jul-07 22:22 by pt_team
>
>   advertisement version: 2
>   Duplex: full

There is much more information in this output. Most important is the connected device's IP address. This can be used to telnet from this switch to the next. From there, further network discovery via CDP can reveal the interconnection of all Cisco devices in a network.

Configuring Cisco Discovery Protocol Review

Questions

1. What does CDP stand for?_____

2. Is CDP normally on or off in the default configuration of a Cisco device?

   _____

3. How often does a router or switch interface send CDP messages?

   _____

4. Are CDP messages unicast, multicast, or broadcast frames?

   _____

5. What exec command shows connections learned through CDP?

   _____

6. What is the other variation of the CDP show command to obtain more information?

   _____

7. Name some information obtained from the detailed output not in the regular output.

   _____

8. What tasks can CDP help with?

   _____

Answers

1. Cisco Discovery Protocol
2. on
3. 60 seconds
4. Multicast – When using Ethernet, frames have a destination of 0100.0CCC.CCCC.
5. show cdp neighbor
6. show cdp neighbor detail
7. IP Address, detailed equipment model, IOS image revision and features, etc.
8. Network Discovery, learning device connections, troubleshooting IP mismatches,etc.

DHCP, DHCP Relay & DHCP Exclusions

The purpose of this lab is to explore configuring basic DHCP Relay on a Cisco router.

Hardware & Configuration Required for this Lab

- Two Cisco Routers with one serial port and one Ethernet port
- One DCE/DTE back to back serial cable
- Two PC to connect to the routers
- Two crossover Cat 5 cables

Commands Used in this Lab

service dhcp – Enables DHCP service on the router
ip dhcp pool <name> - Creates a DHCP pool on the router
default-router <ip address> - Sets the DHCP option for the default gateway on the host
ip helper-address <ip address> - Configures the DHCP relay service on the router

---

Initial Configs - Where you see *Initial Configs,* these are basic configuration steps that by now you should be able to perform on the devices by yourself without us detailing them step by step. Generally you simply go into enable and then configuration mode and start the configuration.

R1
    hostname R1
    line console 0
    logging synch
    int s0/0/0
    ip add 12.12.12.1 255.255.255.0

```
no shut
int fa0/0
ip add 192.168.110.1 255.255.255.0
no shut
ip route 0.0.0.0 0.0.0.0 12.12.12.2
```

R2
```
hostname R2
line console 0
logging synch
int s0/0/0
ip add 12.12.12.2 255.255.255.0
clock rate 64000
no shut
int fa0/0
ip add 192.168.111.1 255.255.255.0
no shut
ip route 0.0.0.0 0.0.0.0 12.12.12.1
```

When clients want an IP address, they will broadcast a DHCP Discover packet out its NIC looking for a DHCP server. So let's start by enabling the service on R1 and defining the pool of network address it can serve up to the clients. Then we will also configure the DHCP server to hand out optional DHCP settings such as the default router, the DNS server, and the domain suffix the clients should use in their configuration.

```
R1(config)#service dhcp
R1(config)#ip dhcp pool CLIENTS
R1(dhcp-config)#network 192.168.110.0 255.255.255.0
R1(dhcp-config)#default-router 192.168.110.1
R1(dhcp-config)#dns-server 192.168.110.50 192.168.110.51
R1(dhcp-config)#domain-name certificationkits.com
R1(dhcp-config)#lease 0 6
```

DHCP works well except when the network DHCP server is behind another router because routers block broadcasts from passing through. To get around this limitation, DHCP has a feature called DHCP-Relay which lets the router forward the DHCP broadcast as a unicast to the server.

DHCP Relay is actually very easy to configure. You just need to put the **ip helper-address** command on the interface that will be receiving the DHCP broadcasts. In our case, R1 is the DHCP server and the interface receiving the broadcast is FA0/0 on R2.

```
R2(config)#int fa0/0
```

R2(config-if)#**ip helper-address 12.12.12.1**

Now we can see that R1 is issuing IP addresses for R2's LAN.

R1(config)#**do sh ip dhcp binding**
Bindings from all pools not associated with VRF:
IP address   Client-ID/   Lease expiration   Type
Hardware address/
User name
192.168.111.2   0100.1b21.1d43.fa   May 31 2009 04:50 PM   Automatic

Configure DHCP Exclusion Ranges

Now let's try to make this a little more interesting by configuring a DHCP Exclusion range. First thing you will want to do is release the IP address from the PC. You can do that from a command prompt with the *ipconfig /release* command. You can then shut the PC down.

DHCP configuration takes place in the global section of the configuration. Not under the configuration for an interface. As a DHCP request is received on an interface configured for a specific subnet, DHCP leases are processed from the DHCP pool which matches the subnet configured on the interface.

R1(config)# **ip dhcp excluded-address 192.168.111.1 192.168.111.9** (*The syntax is to specify the starting IP address of exclusion followed by the ending IP address of exclusion.*)
R1(config)# **ip dhcp excluded-address 192.168.111.250 192.168.111.254** (*Multiple exclusions can be specified which match up to a DHCP pool or subnet.*)

The specific DHCP pool does not have to be named or referenced with excluded addresses.

Now boot the PC back up and once the PC receives an IP address, confirm the lease in the router.

R1#**show ip dhcp binding**
IP address   Client-ID/   Lease expiration   Type
Hardware address
192.168.111.10   0100.2368.b8c3.57   Jan 01 2012 01:30 AM   Automatic

The first available IP address in the DHCP pool following the exclusions, 192.168.111.10, should be leased to the DHCP client PC.

Configuring an DHCP Server Review
Questions

1. Why would IP addresses be excluded from a DHCP server range?

   _____

2. What configuration command sets exclusion ranges?

   _____

3. Can multiple exclusion ranges be configured for a subnet?

   _____

4. What type of network communication is a DHCP request? (uni/multi/broad-cast)

   _____

5. What would happen to a DHCP client if the DHCP pool has leased all IP addresses?

   _____

6. Research Cisco IOS configuration. Can a router's interface be a DHCP client?

   _____

7. Research Cisco IOS configuration. Can a switch interface VLAN 1 be a DHCP client?

   _____

8. Research the IP addresses beginning with 169.254. How do they relate to DHCP?

   _____

Answers

1. Network policy might desire that certain devices have static IP addresses in a subnet.

2. ip dhcp excluded-address

3. yes

4. broadcast

5. The DHCP client would fail to lease an IP address.

6. yes

7. yes

8. This is what Microsoft operating systems self-assign when DHCP leasing fails.

DNS

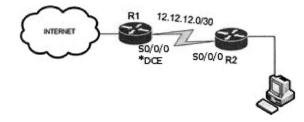

The purpose of this lab is to explore configuring a basic DNS server on a Cisco router.

Hardware & Configuration Required for this Lab

- Two Cisco Routers with one serial port and one Ethernet port
- One DCE/DTE back to back serial cable
- Two PC to connect to the routers
- Two crossover Cat 5 cables
- Advanced IP IOS Feature Set or better

Commands Used in this Lab

ip dns server – Enables the DNS service on the router
ip host <name> <ip address> - Creates a host entry in the DNS server
ip name server <ip address> - Specifies a Proxy DNS server for queries

---

Initial Configs - Where you see *Initial Configs,* these are basic configuration steps that by now you should be able to perform on the devices by yourself without us detailing them step by step. Generally you simply go into enable and then configuration mode and start the configuration.

R1
line console 0
logging synch
host R1
int s0/0/0
ip add 12.12.12.1 255.255.255.0
clock rate 64000 (if you have a WIC-1DSU-TI module(don't confuse this with a WIC-1T, use the *service-module T1 clock source internal* command instead)).

no shut
ip route 0.0.0.0 0.0.0.0 12.12.12.2
ip dhcp pool CLIENTS
network 192.168.110.0 255.255.255.0
default-router 192.168.110.1

R2
line console 0
logging synch
host R2
int s0/0/0
ip add 12.12.12.2 255.255.255.0
(If you have a WIC-1DSU-TI module(don't confuse this with a WIC-1T, use
the *service-module T1 clock source line* command here)).
no shut
ip route 0.0.0.0 0.0.0.0 12.12.12.1
int fa0/0
ip add 192.168.110.2 255.255.255.0
ip helper-address 12.12.12.1
no shut

Cisco routers can also be configured as basic DNS servers. The idea is that offices can
use the routers to provide DHCP and DNS services. This is helpful when the offices don't
have there own servers to provide DNS or DHCP services. Personally I feel that there is
not a great reason to run DHCP or DNS on your Cisco router in a corporate environment
as you do not want that over head on your router. This is really only useful in a small
business or home environment.

To enable your router as a DNS server you simply use the **ip dns server** command.
Please note that not all versions of IOS support this command. Please make sure you
are running at least Advanced IP Services IOS feature set or better.

R1(config)#**ip dns server**

There are two ways to handle DNS. Proxy DNS where the router makes DNS requests for
the computer's behalf and Authoritative where it actually creates records. First we'll
look at Proxy DNS. This is done simply by defining other DNS servers the router can
query with the **ip name-server command.**

R1(config)#**ip name-server 4.2.2.2 4.2.2.3**

For R2, we'll define R1 as its DNS server.
R2(config)#**ip name-server 12.12.12.1**

Now R2 can use R1 to resolve external DNS requests. This is assuming you have fully setup the router to work with your ISP provider which is outside the scope of this lab.
R2(config)#**do ping google.com**
Type escape sequence to abort.
Sending 5, 100-byte ICMP Echos to 64.233.169.104, timeout is 2 seconds:
!!!!!
Success rate is 100 percent (5/5), round-trip min/avg/max = 92/98/105 ms

Now in case you do not have your router connected to the Internet, let' still prove that this works as we can test out the authoritative DNS by making a loopback on R1.
R1(config)#**interface Loopback0**
R1(config-if)# **ip address 150.101.1.1 255.255.255.0**

R1(config-if)# **exit**

Next we will make a manual DNS entry with **ip host**.
R1(config)#**ip host Test 150.101.1.1**

Now from R2 we can ping "test" and it resolves verifying DNS is working!
R2(config)#**do ping test**
Translating "test"...domain server (12.12.12.1) [OK]
Type escape sequence to abort.
Sending 5, 100-byte ICMP Echos to 150.101.1.1, timeout is 2 seconds:
!!!!!
Success rate is 100 percent (5/5), round-trip min/avg/max = 16/16/20 ms

Configuring NTP

Network Time Protocol synchronizes the time and date between networked systems. It works on Cisco network devices, PCs, servers, and is an industry standard. Consistent time on devices is not only convenient in having the correct time in general, but also allows logs to be related between devices. In this lab we will configure a Cisco router as a NTP client.

Hardware & Configuration Required for this Lab
- Two Cisco Routers with at least one Fast Ethernet port
- One Cisco Switch
- Two straight through Cat 5 cables
- Connect Router #1 FastEthernet0/0 to Switch #1 interface FastEthernet0/1
- Connect Router #2 FastEthernet0/0 to Switch #1 interface FastEthernet0/2

Router and Switch Configurations

Begin with the default configuration on the routers and switch. If a configuration is in place, erase the startup-configuration and restart the switch.

Configure the Router #1 to connect into the 192.168.12.0/30 subnet.

Router(config)#**hostname R1**
R1(config)#**interface FastEthernet0/0**
R1(config-if)#**ip address 192.168.12.1 255.255.255.252**
R1(config-if)#**no shut**

Configure the Router #2 to connect into the 192.168.12.0/30 subnet and to act as an NTP server.

Router(config)#**hostname R2**
R2(config)#**interface FastEthernet0/0**
R2(config-if)#**ip address 192.168.12.2 255.255.255.252**
R2(config-if)#**no shut**

Test this by sending a PING from Router #1 to 192.168.12.2 or Router #2 to 192.168.12.1.

Configure the NTP Server
Configure Router #1 as an NTP server. Router #2 will be the NTP client.

R1(config)#**ntp master**
R1(config)#**exit**
R1#**clock set 17:00:30 Jan 1 2014** (*Set this to whatever time and date you wish.*)

R1#**show ntp association**

```
    address      ref clock   st when poll reach delay offset  disp
~127.127.7.1    127.127.7.1   7  -  64  0  0.0  0.00 16000.
 * master (synced), # master (unsynced), + selected, - candidate, ~ configured
```

Recall that 127.0.0.0/8 IP addresses are loopbacks, so Router #1 is stating that it is using itself as a clock source when it shows 127.127.7.1 as a reference clock.

Configure the NTP Client
Configure Router #2 as an NTP client using Router #1 as an NTP server.

R2(config)#**ntp server 192.168.12.1**
R2(config)#**exit**

Now lets check the time on Router2 and please note that there are a few caveats to this lab. If your time is off by more than 400 seconds between the two clocks; sometimes they will not synchronize. It also can take about 5 mintues for them to synchronize. So more than likely when you do your show ntp status you will see they are not synchronized yet. If they do not synchronize after about 5 mintues you might want to go back and set the time and date one after the other so they are only about 20 or 30 seconds off and they will have a much better chance of synchronizing. You will see the master in the show ntp association output.
R2#**show ntp status**
R2#**show ntp association**
R2#**show clock**

Configure the Stratum
The proximity of a clock from the true source of time is the stratum. Think of the Naval Observatory Atomic Clock or a GPS Satellite as stratum 0. A server which synchronizes from them is stratum 1, a server or host off of that is stratum 2, and so on. The configuration is pretty straight forward.

Configure Router #1 as a stratum 10 time server.

R1(config)#**ntp master 10**

Configure the Time Zone

Times are relative to the time zone and NTP information is not time zone specific, so in order for the correct local time to be displayed, the time zone must be configured.

R1(config)#**clock timezone EST -5**

Your actual time zone may vary, but enter the standard time, not the daylight savings time.

Configure Daylight Savings Time

Daylight Savings Time is observed in many areas with some exceptions, such as Arizona and parts of Indiana. The newest IOS versions understand the current start and end times for daylight savings time, but try configuring DST with the specific date settings.

R1(config)#**clock summer-time EDT recurring 2 Sun March 2:00 1 Sun November 2:00**
(*In daylight savings time, 1 hour difference by default, EST becomes EDT, CST becomes CDT, MST becomes MDT, and PST becomes PDT.*)

If daylight savings time is in effect, the Cisco device will correct the time based on the time zone and summertime information.

Configuring the Cisco IOS NTP Server Review

Questions

1. What is is the usual daylight savings time offset?_____

2. On what dates does daylight savings time start and end?_____

3. What time does daylight savings time change occur on those dates?_____

4. How does time change when daylight savings time starts and ends?

    _____

5. What happens to the time when daylight savings time starts / ends?

    _____

6. What command sets the proper time zone name and offset for USA Pacific time?

    _____

7. What term describes the number of times removed the time has been synchronized from another server to another back to the original time source?

    _____

8. What command sets a Cisco device to be a NTP source without an external clock?

    _____

Answers

1. 1 hour
2. 2nd Sunday in March to the 1st Sunday in November
3. 2:00am, local time
4. Jump 1 hour ahead in the Spring, 1 hour behind in the Fall
5. 2:00am to 2:59am is skipped (23 hour day) / 2:00am to 2:59am repeats (25 hour day)
6. clock timezone PST -8
7. stratum
8. ntp master

Configure Logging to a Remote Syslog Server

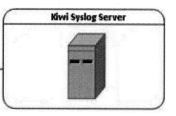

IP Address Schema

Device	Interface	IP Address	Connected to
Syslog Server	NIC	192.168.10.2/24	Switch - Fast Ethernet0/2
R1	FastEthernet 0/1	192.168.10.1/24	Switch – FastEthernet 0/1

Logging on a Cisco device is very important in researching recent events, ensuring proper operation, and when reviewing device history when troubleshooting problems.

Syslog is a client/server protocol used for forwarding log messages in an IP network. Messages produced by the device that usually go to the console can be collected by sending these messages to a device running a Syslog Server. Syslog enables you to gain information about device's performance, traffic and suspicious activity. The sender, also called client, sends small text messages to the server. These messages can be stored locally in buffer memory or sent to a Syslog Server that stores it.

Cisco devices will log events in a text log buffer within the device. While it is possible to connect to a Cisco network device and execute "show logging"; centralized logging servers have the capability of scanning log messages sent from many devices in the network and can alert or notify if certain messages are received. Additionally, it is less administrative overhead to have all logging viewable in one location.

Syslog service is a common network service to accomplish this task. A centralized Syslog Server could be part of a network management software package, a Linux or UNIX service, or even a reputable free download from well known organizations like Cisco, 3Com, and SolarWinds. For our lab, please download the Free Trial Kiwi Syslog Server available at www.Kiwisyslog.com.

Simple Network Management Protocol (SNMP) is a part of Transmission Control Protocol/Internet Protocol (TCP/IP) protocol suite that works on application layer and is mainly responsible for managing and monitoring network devices. Logging facilities are processes or categories which local logging messages can be categorized as when sent to external Syslog Servers. This is not normally necessary, but can be configured as an advanced feature to help better manage messages.

An example would be for messages from routers to use the classic Syslog category of "Local0" while switches use the category "Local1". That way there is a clear way to differentiate logging messages from different sources.

More useful is the severity of logging messages. This is a numeric system from severity 0, the most critical, to severity 7, which are just the most informative messages possible, like for diagnostic purposes.

0.	Emergency	Very critical and important messages, like a system failure.
1.	Alert attention.	Very important errors, something requiring immediate
2.	Critical etc.	Self-explanatory, critical problems, power supply failures,
3.	Error urgent	System faults, process failures, incorrect functions, but not
4.	Warning	Warnings, but not causing problems.
5.	Notice	Notifications, important but not worth responding to.
6.	Informational	Normal operational messages, useful for reporting.
7.	Debugging	Info useful for debugging the application, the most verbose.

Each Cisco device will already have a severity level for logging messages. For Cisco devices finding denials on an access-list with access-list logging enabled, those messages might be logged with severity level X. Then again, a power supply failure or operating outside of normal temperature environments might trigger a message with severity X.

Objective

Configure a Cisco router for internal buffered logging and to send logging information to the Kiwi Syslog Server.

Setup

- Install Kiwi Syslog Server on your PC
- Configure logging on R1
- Test output from Kiwi Syslog

Install Kiwi Syslog Server & Configure Logging

Install Kiwi Syslog Server on 192.168.10.2 with default configuration.

Ensure logging is on.
R1(config)# **logging on**

Specify the server that will receive syslog messages from router by issuing the "logging ip_address" command where ip_address is the address of external server.

R1(config)# **logging 192.168.10.2**

To limit severity level of syslog messages sent to syslog server, set the appropriate logging trap level with the logging trap level command. There are 8 severity levels of messages as shown in the table below.

Name	Meaning	Severity Level
alerts	Immediate action needed	(severity=1)
critical	Critical conditions	(severity=2)
debugging	Debugging messages	(severity=7)
emergencies	System is unusable	(severity=0)
errors	Error conditions	(severity=3)
informational	Informational messages	(severity=6)
notifications	Normal but significant conditions	(severity=5)
warnings	Warning conditions	(severity=4)

Tip - When higher number is chosen, messages with lesser severity level are automatically logged. For Example if "logging trap level informational" is applied which is at level 6, it will also include messages from level 0-5

R1(config)# **logging trap debugging**

We will test and verify by running the icmp debugging command and ping the router's own ip address and view what happened in the Syslog Server.

R1#**debug ip icmp**
ICMP packet debugging is on
R1#**ping 192.168.10.1**

Type escape sequence to abort.
Sending 5, 100-byte ICMP Echos to 192.168.10.1, timeout is 2 seconds:
!!!!!
Success rate is 100 percent (5/5), round-trip min/avg/max = 4/6/8 ms
R1#
*Mar 1 00:05:31.451: ICMP: echo reply sent, src 192.168.10.1, dst 192.168.10.1
*Mar 1 00:05:31.455: ICMP: echo reply rcvd, src 192.168.10.1, dst 192.168.10.1
*Mar 1 00:05:31.459: ICMP: echo reply sent, src 192.168.10.1, dst 192.168.10.1
*Mar 1 00:05:31.463: ICMP: echo reply rcvd, src 192.168.10.1, dst 192.168.10.1

*Mar 1 00:05:31.467: ICMP: echo reply sent, src 192.168.10.1, dst 192.168.10.1
*Mar 1 00:05:31.471: ICMP: echo reply rcvd, src 192.168.10.1, dst 192.168.10.1

Result in Kiwi Syslog server

Now let's use the show command to see exactly what is happening from a message perspective.

R1#**show logging**
Syslog logging: enabled (11 messages dropped, 0 messages rate-limited,
        0 flushes, 0 overruns, xml disabled, filtering disabled)
   Console logging: level debugging, 60 messages logged, xml disabled,
            filtering disabled
   Monitor logging: level debugging, 0 messages logged, xml disabled,
            filtering disabled
   Buffer logging: disabled, xml disabled,
            filtering disabled
   Logging Exception size (4096 bytes)
   Count and timestamp logging messages: disabled
No active filter modules.

   Trap logging: level debugging, 58 message lines logged
      Logging to 192.168.10.2(global) (udp port 514, audit disabled, link up)
, 35 message lines logged, xml disabled,
         filtering disabled

Now let's configure the Kiwi Syslog to accept SNMP traps. In Kiwi Syslog Server, go to File-> Setup -> Inputs-> SNMP .Check the **Listen for SNMP Traps** box in Setup of Kiwi Syslog Server. Press **OK.**

Next we will enable the community string on R1. The default values for these strings are public for read only and private for read-write. Using these default community strings are not recommended because they act as password to permit access to the agent on the router. Thus they should be changed to some other string. We will be using router_1 with read only.

R1(config)# **snmp-server community router_1 ro**

Now enable All SNMP traps to be sent and specify the location of SNMP Server where traps will be sent.

R1(config)# **snmp-server enable traps snmp**

R1(config)# **snmp-server host 192.168.10.2 router_1**

Finally, let's test and verify this works by seeing it record in the Syslog Server.

R1(config)#**interface loopback 99**

*Mar 1 00:25:01.9: %LINEPROTO-5-UPDOWN: Line protocol on Interface Loopback99, changed state up

Configure Logging to a Remote Syslog Server Review

1. What is the range of logging severity levels for syslog messages?

_____

2. Which logging level is the most verbose?

_____

3. Which logging level is the least verbose?

_____

4. How can the internal logging buffer be checked?

_____

5. What does the "syslog host 192.168.12.12" command do?

_____

6. What destination port and transport protocol is used to deliver syslog messages?

_____

7. Try the privileged mode command "clear log". What happens to "show log"?

_____

8. Can the internal logging buffer size be modified?

_____

Answers

1. 0 to 7
2. 7 - Debugging
3. 0 - Emergency
4. show log
5. Syslog service on an external server
6. UDP port 512
7. It has been emptied of all entries except for that the logging was cleared.
8. Yes, by the "logging buffered" configuration command.

NetFlow

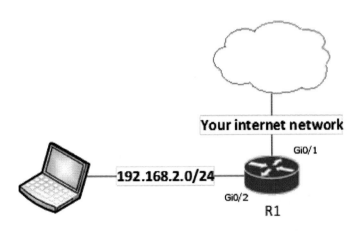

The purpose of this lab is to explore the basic functionality of Cisco NetFlow.

Hardware & Configuration Required for this Lab

- One Cisco ISR Router with two Fast Ethernet interfaces such as an 1841, 2801, or 2811.
- Ideally this lab would work best with an internet connection, but if that is not possible you can always generate traffic with pings and such.
- Two crossover Cat 5 cables
- One PC to connect to the router. You can install the NetFlow server on this computer or a separate computer to make it a little more complicated.
- You will also need to install a NetFlow collector to receive the NetFlow information. We recommend the Solarwinds free NetFlow tool which you can get at solarwinds.com. However any collector will do if you prefer to use another tool.

Commands Used in this Lab

flow exporter – Defines the NetFlow exporter where the NetFlow info is sent.
flow monitor – Defines the NetFlow monitor, what is recorded
destination – Defines where traffic is sent.
transport udp <port> - Defines what port to send the NetFlow traffic.
export-protocol – Defines what version of NetFlow to use
exporter <name> – Defines the Exporter used by the monitor
record NetFlow ipv4 original-input – Defines that all IPv4 traffic will be recorded.
ip flow monitor <name> <direction> – Adds an interface to NetFlow

---

Inital Configs – Since every lab will have a different configuration to get to the Internet, we will cover how our lab is setup. We will have to assume that once you made it this far in the book you are pretty comfortable with your Cisco equipment and you can setup an Internet connection through your router. In our example, we are using NAT from my LAN 192.168.2.0/24 to my outside interface and sends it to my routers default gateway 192.168.1.254. Please note our lab example was done on an ISR Router with Gigabit Interfaces. This will work fine ISR 100mb routers such as an 1841, 2801 or 2811 but you will need to change the port designations. It is shown this way to give you a little more real world experience.

R1
line con 0
logging synch

interface GigabitEthernet1
 ip address 192.168.1.50 255.255.255.0
 ip nat outside

interface GigabitEthernet2
 ip address 192.168.2.1 255.255.255.0
 ip nat inside

ip nat inside source list NAT interface GigabitEthernet1 overload

ip route 0.0.0.0 0.0.0.0 192.168.1.254
ip route vrf Mgmt-intf 0.0.0.0 0.0.0.0 FastEthernet0 dhcp

ip access-list extended NAT
permit ip 192.168.2.0 0.0.0.255 any

So what is NetFlow? NetFlow is a means of reporting on traffic on our network. Previously it would be relevantly difficult to generate a report of how many people are using Skype or browsing Facebook. But with NetFlow it generates dynamic graphs that you can use to better understand the various applications that run in your network.

The configuration of NetFlow on the router is fairly simple for our lab, but it can be very complex depending on the needs the enterprise. The basic steps are to define the Exporter which is the NetFlow server. If you are using a server other than the Solarwinds collector, you may need to adjust the NetFlow version and transport information.

R1(config)#**flow exporter NETFLOW-EXPORTER**
R1(config-flow-exporter)#**destination 192.168.1.13**

R1(config-flow-exporter)#**transport udp 2055**
R1(config-flow-exporter)#**export-protocol NetFlow-v5**

The next step is to define what type of traffic you want NetFlow to record, the options are almost endless so we are just going to capture IPv4 traffic.

R1(config-flow-exporter)#**flow monitor NETFLOW-MONITOR**
R1(config-flow-monitor)# **exporter NETFLOW-EXPORTER**
R1(config-flow-monitor)# **record NetFlow ipv4 original-input**

The Solarwinds tool also requires SNMP to be setup. Thus we will setup a simple community.
R1(config)#**snmp-server community NetFlow RW**

The final step is to assign the NetFlow monitor to the interfaces on your router. We will configure for NetFlow to send traffic in both directions from each interface.

interface GigabitEthernet1

ip flow monitor NETFLOW-MONITOR input
ip flow monitor NETFLOW-MONITOR output

interface GigabitEthernet2

ip flow monitor NETFLOW-MONITOR input
ip flow monitor NETFLOW-MONITOR output

Open up the computer you installed the NetFlow tool and click Add a device. Enter the IP address and SNMP community and click **OK**.

Now select your LAN interface and click **Start Flow Capture.**

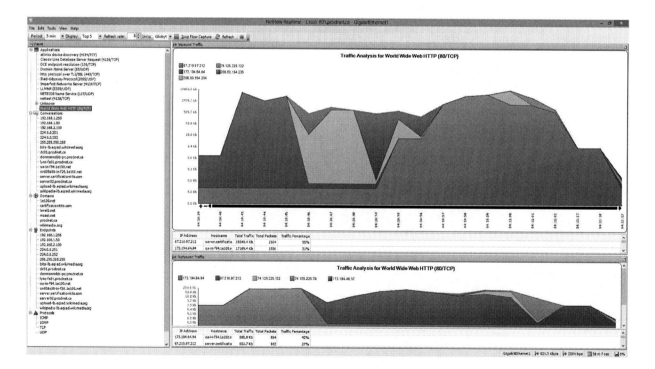

Now on your computer, browse the web for a few minutes and look at the NetFlow tool. After a bit you will see information about your browser traffic. Pretty interesting, huh?

Routing Redundancy with HSRP and VRRP

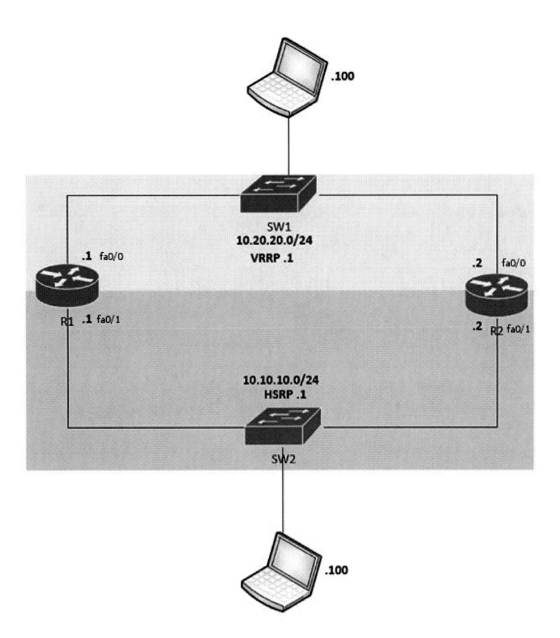

The purpose of this lab is to explore the basic functionality of Cisco's Hot Standby Router Protocol and the industry standard version the Virtual Router Redundancy Protocol.

Hardware & Configuration Required for this Lab

- Two Cisco routers with two Fast Ethernet interfaces
- Six straight through Cat 5 cables
- Two Switches
- Two PCs to connect to the switch to allow testing. If you don't have enough PCs, you can also test by adding a Vlan Switched Virtual Interface to your switches and giving it the proper IP address.

Commands Used in this Lab

Standby <group> ip – Defines the HSRP virtual IP
Standby <group> priority – Defines the HSRP interface priority
Standby <group> preempt – Tells HSRP to take control of the router if it has higher priority
Standby <group> track- Tracks an interface or SLA to find upstream issues
Show standby – Shows HSRP status
vrrp <group> ip – Defines the HSRP virtual IP
vrrp <group> priority – Defines the HSRP interface priority
vrrp <group> track – Tracks an interface or SLA to find upstream issues
show vrrp- Shows VRRP status

Inital Configs - Where you see *Initial Configs,* these are basic configuration steps that by now you should be able to perform on the devices by yourself without us detailing them step by step. Generally you simply go into enable and then configuration mode and start the configuration. **Note:** If your interfaces don't match the configs simply change the interface names to what matches your lab before pasting.

R1
hostname R1
line con 0
logging synch
exit
interface FastEthernet0/0
ip address 10.20.20.11 255.255.255.0
no shut
interface FastEthernet0/1
ip address 10.10.10.11 255.255.255.0
no shut

R2
hostname R2
line con 0
logging synch
exit
interface FastEthernet0/0
ip address 10.20.20.12 255.255.255.0
no shut
interface FastEthernet0/1
ip address 10.10.10.12 255.255.255.0
no shut

PC Configuration

The problem with the classic default gateway in a enterprise environment is since all traffic needs to pass through the router on its way through the network or the internet, the router becomes a single point of failure. That means that if anything happens to the router, all network traffic will come to a crashing stop until that issue is fixed.

This is why Cisco offers four First Hop Redundancy Protocols in most of their layer 3 products. The protocols are:

Hot Standby Redundancy Protocol (HSRP) – This is Cisco's propriety take at offering redundancy and load sharing on routers. The routers behave in a Active/Passive nature meaning that only the Active router is speaking and the passive routers are waiting for a failure.

Virtual Router Redundancy Protocol (VRRP) – This is the industry standard method of providing redundancy and load sharing on routers. The routers behave in a Active/Passive nature meaning that only the Active router is speaking and the passive routers are waiting for a failure.

Gateway Load Balancing Protocol (GLBP) – This protocol provides load balancing between routers. This is different from HSRP and VRRP because it works in a Active/Active nature so traffic is split between all routers that are participating in the GLBP session. **Note:** GLBP is out of scope for these labs and is only mentioned so you are aware of it in the future.

ICMP Router Discovery Protocol (IRDP) – This protocol allows the host to try to discover additional gateways by using Router Soliciation messages. This is pretty obsure these days and is only really interesting because IPv6 relies on this type of method to do its autoconfigation. **Note:** This too is out of scope.

You may have noticed from the above descriptions that VRRP and HSRP are descibed almost exactly the same way. This isn't because I'm being lazy! It is because the two protocols are almost exactly the same except for a few changes. What offen happens in the industry is a vendor like Cisco will develop a protocol like say HSRP to solve a issue (in this case redundancy) and will adopt it for its devices. To stay competitive, other vendors like Juniper will start making their own protocols to solve the issue their own way.

The problem is that propriety protocols don't play nicely with other vendors at all. So you will not have a easy time mixing different vendor devices in your environment. To solve this the IETF will create a industry standard protocol that every vendor needs to follow (for the most part). This means that you could configure VRRP between a Cisco router and a Juniper router if you were so inclined and it would work just fine.

Here is a break down of the two protocols:

HSRP	VRRP
Proprietary protocol	Standards based
RFC 2281	RFC 3768

Hello time is 3 seconds Hold time is 10 seconds	Hello time is 1 second Hold time is 3 seconds
One Active, One Standby, All other routers are listening.	One Master, all other routers are backup
HSRP uses UDP port 1985	VRRP uses IP protocol 112
Can track an interface for failover	Can track an interface for failover
HSRP routers use multicast hello packets to 224.0.0.2 (all routers) for version 1 or 224.0.0.102 for version 2.	Communicates via multicast address 224.0.0.18
All virtual routers use MAC address 0000.0c07.acXX where XX is the group ID.	All virtual routers must use 00-00-5E-00-01-XX as its Media Access Control (MAC) address

Configuring HSRP

To configure HSRP, it is a simple matter putting a couple commands under each interface that is going to connect to a HSRP group. The syntax is: **standby <group #> ip <virtual IP>**

HSRP works under the concept of group. This allows HSRP to offer several virtual IP addresses on a interface. Because most First Hop Redundancy Protocols are Active/Passive , only one router at a time is actively passing the network traffic. The other routers are basically waiting around for the active router to go offline before they do anything. To be more efficient, group numbers allows the administrator to split up the traffic between HSRP routers to achieve load sharing.

This is done in the below picture by making R1 active for the 192.168.1.0/24 network and R2 active for the 192.168.2.0/24 on the interface.

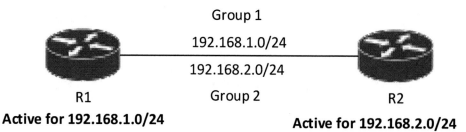

Group 1
192.168.1.0/24
192.168.2.0/24
Group 2

R1   R2
Active for 192.168.1.0/24
                              Active for 192.168.2.0/24

Let's configure HSRP between our 10.10.10.0/24 subnet and we will use group 1.

R1(config)#**int fa0/1**
R1(config-if)#**standby 1 ip 10.10.10.1**
%HSRP-5-STATECHANGE: FastEthernet0/1 Grp 1 state Standby -> Active

R2(config)#**int fa0/1**
R2(config-if)#**standby 1 ip 10.10.10.1**
%HSRP-5-STATECHANGE: FastEthernet0/1 Grp 1 state Speak -> Standby

After about 30 seconds of entering the command, we can see HSRP declare R1 Active and R2 is on Standby.

We can verify HSRP is running happily with the **show standby** command.

R1#**show standby**
FastEthernet0/1 - Group 1
  State is Active
    2 state changes, last state change 00:02:15
  Virtual IP address is 10.10.10.1
  Active virtual MAC address is 0000.0c07.ac01
    Local virtual MAC address is 0000.0c07.ac01 (v1 default)
  Hello time 3 sec, hold time 10 sec
    Next hello sent in 2.240 secs
  Preemption disabled
  Active router is local
  Standby router is 10.10.10.12, priority 100 (expires in 8.784 sec)
  Priority 100 (default 100)
  Group name is "hsrp-Fa0/1-1" (default)

The command shows us most of what we need to know about the HSRP session. It shows the Group number, the virtual IP and mac address for the HSRP group. It also shows the timers, priority, the preemption status and neighbor info.

R2#**show standby**
FastEthernet0/1 - Group 1
  State is Standby

1 state change, last state change 00:09:24

Virtual IP address is 10.10.10.1

Active virtual MAC address is 0000.0c07.ac01

  Local virtual MAC address is 0000.0c07.ac01 (v1 default)

Hello time 3 sec, hold time 10 sec

  Next hello sent in 1.520 secs

Preemption disabled

Active router is 10.10.10.11, priority 100 (expires in 10.960 sec)

  Standby router is local

Priority 100 (default 100)

  Group name is "hsrp-Fa0/1-1" (default)

We can also see from the PC that it can ping its default gateway 10.10.10.1 which is the virtual IP address.

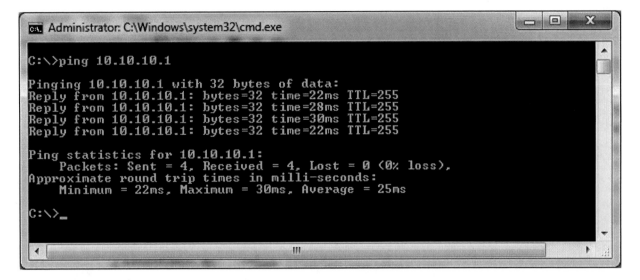

The election process for HSRP is pretty simple because the highest priority wins. By default a router will have a default priority of 100. In the event of a tie, then the HSRP router interface with the highest IP wins the election. At this point, some of you might be wondering why R1 won the election since R2 has a higher IP address. The reason it won is simply because we enabled HSRP on R1 first and much like OSPF, it won't give up its Active status until we make it.

HSRP priority can be adjusted with the **standby 1 priority 200** command. Let's make R2 have a higher priority.

R2(config)#**int f0/1**
R2(config-if)#**standby 1 priority 200**

Now if we check the HSRP status we will see that R2 is still standby even though we have gave it a higher priority.

R2(config-if)#**do show standby**
FastEthernet0/1 - Group 1
  State is Standby
    1 state change, last state change 00:23:29
  Virtual IP address is 10.10.10.1
  Active virtual MAC address is 0000.0c07.ac01
    Local virtual MAC address is 0000.0c07.ac01 (v1 default)
  Hello time 3 sec, hold time 10 sec
    Next hello sent in 1.696 secs
  Preemption disabled
  Active router is 10.10.10.11, priority 100 (expires in 11.024 sec)
  Standby router is local
  Priority 200 (configured 200)
  Group name is "hsrp-Fa0/1-1" (default)

This is because Preemption is disabled. This means that once a router becomes active, it won't switch back to standby unless it goes offline. Preemption allows a HSRP with a higher priority to always take control and become active.

The idea is that if one the routers is the prefered transit for your network, say the active router is a Cisco 7200 and the standby router is a old Cisco 2600 you had lying around, if the Cisco 7200 reboots you wouldn't want the 2600 to be routing traffic for any longer than it needs to.

We can enable preemption with the standby 1 preempt command under the interface. It is a good idea to configure it on all of the HSRP interfaces to keep things consistant.

R1(config)#**int fa0/1**
R1(config-if)#**standby 1 preempt**

Once we enter the command on R2 it immediately becomes active.

R2(config)#**int fa0/1**
R2(config-if)#**standby 1 preempt**
%HSRP-5-STATECHANGE: FastEthernet0/1 Grp 1 state Standby -> Active

To test that HSRP is working properly, lets enable a debug R1 and start a ping on our test PC. Then we'll cause an outage by preemption R2 from the switch and see what happens. Once the hello timers expire, R1 declares R2 dead and makes its virtual IP and mac address active.

R1#**debug standby**

HSRP: Fa0/1 Interface adv out, Passive, active 0 passive 1

HSRP: Fa0/1 Grp 1 Hello out 10.10.10.11 Standby pri 100 vIP 10.10.10.1

HSRP: Fa0/1 Grp 1 Hello out 10.10.10.11 Standby pri 100 vIP 10.10.10.1

HSRP: Fa0/1 Grp 1 Standby: c/Active timer expired (10.10.10.12)

HSRP: Fa0/1 Grp 1 Active router is local, was 10.10.10.12

HSRP: Fa0/1 Nbr 10.10.10.12 no longer active for group 1 (Standby)

HSRP: Fa0/1 Nbr 10.10.10.12 Was active or standby - start passive holddown

HSRP: Fa0/1 Grp 1 Standby router is unknown, was local

HSRP: Fa0/1 Grp 1 Standby -> Active

%HSRP-5-STATECHANGE: FastEthernet0/1 Grp 1 state Standby -> Active

HSRP: Fa0/1 Interface adv out, Active, active 1 passive 0

HSRP: Fa0/1 Grp 1 Redundancy "hsrp-Fa1/0-1" state Standby -> Active

HSRP: Fa0/1 Grp 1 Hello out 10.10.10.11 Active pri 100 vIP 10.10.10.1

HSRP: Fa0/1 Grp 1 Activating MAC 0000.0c07.ac01

HSRP: Fa0/1 Grp 1 Adding 0000.0c07.ac01 to MAC address filter

HSRP: Fa0/1 IP Redundancy "hsrp-Fa1/0-1" standby, local -> unknown

HSRP: Fa0/1 IP Redundancy "hsrp-Fa1/0-1" update, Standby -> Active

HSRP: Fa0/1 Grp 1 Hello out 10.10.10.11 Active pri 100 vIP 10.10.10.1

HSRP: Fa0/1 IP Redundancy "hsrp-Fa1/0-1" update, Active -> Active

On the PC side we can see we only lost 3 packets or so before it recovered. Once R2 comes back up it becomes active again because it has the highest priority.

Of course it is also possible to adjust HSRP's timers to respond to a outage quicker. This is done with the standby <group> timers <hello> <holdtime> command.

R1(config-if)#**standby 1 timers 1 3**
R2(config-if)#**standby 1 timers 1 3**

It is also possible to set the hello in milliseconds for ultra fast detection with the standby <group> timers msec <hello> <holdtime> command
Note: As a rule don't enable debugs to the console if you are using sub second timers as you can overload the console and lock yourself out of the router! Instead log debugs to the buffer and look at it from there.

Because HSRP is a tempting target of man in the middle attacks, it also supports both plain text and MD5 authentication. You can setup plain-text authentication with the following command under the interface **standby <group number> authentication text <password>** and MD5 with **standby 1 authentication md5 key-string <password>**

As a rule of thumb, in the real world you will likely want to use MD5 all your network passwords because plain-text passwords can be sniffed using a tool like Wireshark. Plain-text is really meant for administrative purposes such as making sure a router doesn't join the wrong HSRP group etc.

HSRP also supports keychains as well which allows for periodic changing of the MD5 password. I won't get too much into keychains right now, but you can set one with the **standby <group number> authentication md5 key-chain <keychain name>**

Let's go ahead and set a MD5 password of CISCO on our routers.

R1(config)#**int fa0/1**
R1(config-if)#**standby 1 authentication md5 key-string CISCO**
%HSRP-4-BADAUTH: Bad authentication from 10.10.10.12, group 1, remote state Active
%HSRP-5-STATECHANGE: FastEthernet0/1 Grp 1 state Standby -> Active

As soon as we enter a password on R1 we can see that it drops R2 for having a bad password (that is no password configured). Then R1 becomes active. Once we add the password to R2, it takes over again because of its higher priority.

R2(config)#**int fa0/1**
%HSRP-4-BADAUTH: Bad authentication from 10.10.10.11, group 1, remote state Active
R2(config-if)#standby 1 authentication md5 key-string CISCO

As configured right now, HSRP is great for when it detects a problem between the HSRP interfaces, but what happens if there is a upstream problem? What if R2 stays active even if isn't able to reach the PC in the 10.20.20.0/24 network?

Fortunately HSRP allows for both interface and SLA tracking to solve this problem. Let's look at interface tracking first. It is configured with the **standby <group number> track <interface to track> <optional decrement value>** command. Once configured, HSRP will watch the state of the upstream interface and if it goes down, it will decrement its priority by a default of 10.

R2(config)#**int fa0/1**
R2(config-if)#**standby 1 track fa0/0**

Now to test this we will shutdown the upstream interface on R2

R2(config-if)#**int fa0/0**
R2(config-if)#**shut**

Once the interface goes down we will see a status message saying that Tracking saw the interface go down.

*Jun 1 11:48:29.349: %TRACKING-5-STATE: 1 interface Fa1/0 line-protocol Up->Down

If we check the show standby output again we will that R2 is still active but now its priority is 190. Since R1 is current at the default priority of 100, R2 will stay active.

R2(config-if)#**do sh standby**
FastEthernet0/1 - Group 1
  State is Active
    2 state changes, last state change 10:56:23
  Virtual IP address is 10.10.10.1
  Active virtual MAC address is 0000.0c07.ac01
    Local virtual MAC address is 0000.0c07.ac01 (v1 default)
  Hello time 1 sec, hold time 3 sec
    Next hello sent in 0.640 secs
  Authentication MD5, key-string
  Preemption enabled
  Active router is local
  Standby router is 10.10.10.11, priority 100 (expires in 3.472 sec) Priority 190 (configured 200)
  Track interface FastEthernet0/0 state Down decrement 10
    Group name is "hsrp-Fa0/1-1" (default)

To fix this we need to set the track decrement value to something that will lower R2's priority to be less than R1's priority. We will set it to be 200.

R2(config)#**int fa0/1**
R2(config-if)#**standby 1 track f0/0 200**

Now we'll shut down the upstream interface again and now we can see R2 going into standby.

R2(config-if)#**int fa0/0**
R2(config-if)#**shut**
%TRACKING-5-STATE: 1 interface Fa0/0 line-protocol Up->Down
%HSRP-5-STATECHANGE: FastEthernet0/1 Grp 1 state Active -> Speak

Checking the show standby output we can see that R2's priority is now 0 because the interface Fa0/0 is down.

R2(config-if)#**do sh standby**
FastEthernet0/1 - Group 1
  State is Standby
    4 state changes, last state change 00:00:14
  Virtual IP address is 10.10.10.1
  Active virtual MAC address is 0000.0c07.ac01
   Local virtual MAC address is 0000.0c07.ac01 (v1 default)
  Hello time 1 sec, hold time 3 sec
   Next hello sent in 0.352 secs
  Authentication MD5, key-string
  Preemption enabled
  Active router is 10.10.10.11, priority 100 (expires in 2.016 sec)
  Standby router is local
  Priority 0 (configured 200)
   Track interface FastEthernet0/0 state Down decrement 200
  Group name is "hsrp-Fa0/1-1" (default)

VRRP is for the most part identical to HSRP when it comes to configuration. The biggest differences to keep in mind is that when VRRP preemption is enabled by default, it uses 1 second hellos instead of 3 second hellos by default.

It is configured by using the vrrp commands under a interface instead of the standby commands. To enable it on our other interfaces, use the **vrrp <group number> ip <virtual ip address>** command.

R1(config)#**int fa0/0**
R1(config-if)#**vrrp 1 ip 10.20.20.1**
%VRRP-6-STATECHANGE: Fa0/0 Grp 1 state Init -> Backup
%VRRP-6-STATECHANGE: Fa0/0 Grp 1 state Init -> Backup
%VRRP-6-STATECHANGE: Fa0/0 Grp 1 state Backup -> Master

Because we enabled R1 first it will assume the role of master

R2(config)#**int fa0/0**
R2(config-if)#**vrrp 1 ip 10.20.20.1**
%VRRP-6-STATECHANGE: Fa0/0 Grp 1 state Init -> Backup
%VRRP-6-STATECHANGE: Fa0/0 Grp 1 state Init -> Backup
%VRRP-6-STATECHANGE: Fa0/0 Grp 1 state Backup -> Master

However because preemption is enabled, R2 will win the election and take control because it has the higher IP address.

R1(config)#

%VRRP-6-STATECHANGE: Fa0/0 Grp 1 state Master -> Backup

We can see the status by using the show vrrp command.

R1(config)#**do show vrrp**
FastEthernet0/0 - Group 1
 State is Backup
 Virtual IP address is 10.20.20.1
 Virtual MAC address is 0000.5e00.0101
 Advertisement interval is 1.000 sec
 Preemption enabled
 Priority is 100
 Master Router is 10.20.20.12, priority is 100
 Master Advertisement interval is 1.000 sec
 Master Down interval is 3.609 sec (expires in 3.441 sec)

R2(config-if)#**do sh vrrp**
FastEthernet0/0 - Group 1
 State is Master
 Virtual IP address is 10.20.20.1
 Virtual MAC address is 0000.5e00.0101
 Advertisement interval is 1.000 sec
 Preemption enabled
 Priority is 100
 Master Router is 10.20.20.12 (local), priority is 100
 Master Advertisement interval is 1.000 sec
 Master Down interval is 3.609 se

VRRP supports the same authentication types as HSRP. You can setup plain-text authentication with the following command under the interface **vrrp <group number> authentication text <password>** and MD5 with **vrrp 1 authentication md5 key-string <password>**

Priority is adjusted with the **vrrp <group #> priority <priority>** command.

Timers are a bit different in VRRP. Because the values can optionally be learned from the current master with the **vrrp <group #> timers learn** command. However in most cases you will likely staticly set the timers with the standby <group> timers <hello command. You can also use sub second timers with VRRP as well with the msec keyword.

R1(config-if)#**vrrp 1 timers advertise 1**
R2(config-if)#**standby 1 timers advertise 1**

The last thing we'll talk about regarding HSRP & VRRP is a basic introduction to SLA tracking.

SLA Tracking is quite complex. But in its simplest form it allows you to monitor a particular IP address to determine if there is a upstream problem. SLA can be used to track everything from connectivity to VoIP call quality to application specific testing. Therefore it is quite complex with dozens of configuration options. For the purposes of this lab, we will just configure a basic ping test to our 10.10.10.100 host.

First we define the monitor on each router.

R1(config)#**ip sla 1**
R1(config-ip-sla)# **icmp-echo 10.10.10.100**
R1(config-ip-sla-echo)# **frequency 5**

R2(config)#**ip sla 1**
R2(config-ip-sla)# **icmp-echo 10.10.10.100**
R2(config-ip-sla-echo)# **frequency 5**

Next we need to enable the SLA monitor.

R1(config)#**ip sla schedule 1 start-time now life forever**
R2(config)#**ip sla schedule 1 start-time now life forever**

Now that the monitor is running we need to bind it to VRRP with the **track** command.

R1(config)#**track 1 ip sla 1**
R2(config)#**track 1 ip sla 1**

Finally we can now call the track object in our VRRP interface config.
Note: Depending on your IOS version VRRP may only support SLA tracking.

R1(config-if)#**int fa0/0**
R1(config-if)#**vrrp 1 track 1**

R2(config)#**int fa0/0**
R2(config-if)#**vrrp 1 track 1**

To test this we will simply disconnect the link to the 10.10.10.100 PC from R2 and see if it switches over. Once SLA detects the loss, it decrements R2 and R1 becomes the master!

R2(config)#
%TRACKING-5-STATE: 1 ip sla 1 state Up->Down
%VRRP-6-STATECHANGE: Fa0/0 Grp 1 state Master -> Backup

Static Inside Source Address Translation

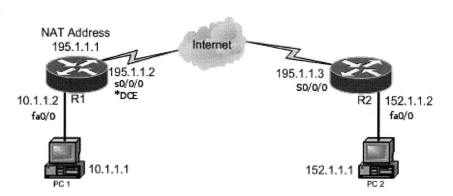

Objective: Configure the routers to support Inside Source Address Translation. This provides a one to one mapping between an inside local address and an inside global address.

Hardware & Configuration Required for this Lab
- Two Cisco routers with one serial port and one Fast Ethernet port
- One back to back DTE/DCE serial cable
- Two PCs
- Two crossover Cat 5 cables
- Configure the cabling as shown in the network diagram
- If the routers have a startup-config, erase it and perform a reload of the routers. Router1 and Router2 are connected via serial0/0/0. Router1 will act as the DCE supplying clock to Router2. The IP addresses are assigned as per the next figure. A PC with an Ethernet NIC is connected to an Ethernet LAN attached to Router1. Router1 is configured for NAT and will translate source IP address 10.1.1.1 to 195.1.1.1.

Ok, so the diagram above is a little intimidating with the Internet cloud, huh? Well, not really. If you think about it, it is nothing more than a WAN connection that can go lots of places versus a point to point WAN connection. So we will simplify the diagram on the following page and you will see it is not so intimidating.

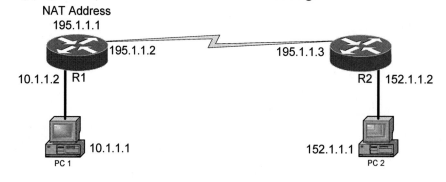

Router Configuration
R1
Router#**config t**
Router(config)#**hostname R1**
R1(config)#**ip nat inside source static 10.1.1.1 195.1.1.1** (*Translates the inside source address 10.1.1.1 to 195.1.1.1*)
R1(config)#**int fa0/0**
R1(config-if)#**ip address 10.1.1.2 255.255.255.0**
R1(config-if)#**no shut**
R1(config-if)#**ip nat inside** (*Marks the interface as connected to the inside*)
R1(config-if)#**int s0/0/0**
R1(config-if)#**ip address 195.1.1.2 255.255.255.0**
R1(config-if)#**ip nat outside** (*Marks the interface as connected to the outside*)
R1(config-if)#**clock rate 500000**
R1(config-if)# **no shut**
R1(config-if)#**ip route 152.1.1.1 255.255.255.255 serial0/0/0**

R2
Router#**config t**
Router(config)#**hostname R1**
R2(config)#**int fa0/0**
R2(config-if)#**ip address 152.1.1.1 255.255.255.0**
R2(config-if)#**no shut**
R2(config-if)#**int s0/0/0**
R2(config-if)#**ip address 195.1.1.3 255.255.255.0**
R2(config-if)#**no shut**

Monitoring and Testing Configuration
From host1 ping host2 (152.1.1.1) and analyze the packets coming from R2 with the **debug ip packet** command. What follows is the output from the command; note that the source address and the ICMP Ping packet is 195.1.1.1.

R2#**debug ip packet**
IP: tableid=0, s=195.1.1.1 (Serial0/0/0), d=152.1.1.1 (FastEthernet0/0), routed via RIB
IP: s=195.1.1.1 (Serial0/0/0), d=152.1.1.1 (FastEthernet0/0), len 128, rcvd 3
IP: tableid=0, s=152.1.1.1 (local), d=195.1.1.1 (Serial0/0/0), routed via RIB
IP: s=152.1.1.1 (local), d=195.1.1.1 (Serial0/0/0), len 128, sending
IP: tableid=0, s=195.1.1.1 (Serial0/0/0), d=152.1.1.1 (FastEthernet0/0), routed via RIB
IP: s=195.1.1.1 (Serial0/0/0), d=152.1.1.1 (FastEthernet0/0), len 128, rcvd 3
IP: tableid=0, s=152.1.1.1 (local), d=195.1.1.1 (Serial0/0/0), routed via RIB
IP: s=152.1.1.1 (local), d=195.1.1.1 (Serial0/0/0), len 128, sending
IP: tableid=0, s=195.1.1.1 (Serial0/0/0), d=152.1.1.1 (FastEthernet0/0), routed via RIB
IP: s=195.1.1.1 (Serial0/0/0), d=152.1.1.1 (FastEthernet0/0), len 128, rcvd 3
IP: tableid=0, s=152.1.1.1 (local), d=195.1.1.1 (Serial0/0/0), routed via RIB
IP: s=152.1.1.1 (local), d=195.1.1.1 (Serial0/0/0), len 128, sending
IP: tableid=0, s=195.1.1.1 (Serial0/0/0), d=152.1.1.1 (FastEthernet0/0), routed via RIB

IP: s=195.1.1.1 (Serial0/0/0), d=152.1.1.1 (FastEthernet0/0), len 128, rcvd 3
IP: tableid=0, s=152.1.1.1 (local), d=195.1.1.1 (Serial0/0/0), routed via RIB
IP: s=152.1.1.1 (local), d=195.1.1.1 (Serial0/0/0), len 128, sending

From the **debug ip nat** output on R1, we can see that the source IP address 10.1.1.1 has been translated to 195.1.1.1. We also see this is a two-way process, the return packet that has the destination IP address 195.1.1.1 is changed back to 10.1.1.1.

R1#**debug ip nat**
NAT: s=10.1.1.1->195.1.1.1, d=152.1.1.1 [17]
NAT*: s=152.1.1.1, d=195.1.1.1->10.1.1.1 [13]
NAT: s=10.1.1.1->195.1.1.1, d=152.1.1.1 [18]
NAT*: s=152.1.1.1, d=195.1.1.1->10.1.1.1 [14]
NAT: s=10.1.1.1->195.1.1.1, d=152.1.1.1 [19]
NAT*: s=152.1.1.1, d=195.1.1.1->10.1.1.1 [15]
NAT: s=10.1.1.1->195.1.1.1, d=152.1.1.1 [20]
NAT*: s=152.1.1.1, d=195.1.1.1->10.1.1.1 [16]

This lab was designed to demonstrate a one-on-one mapping between an inside local address and an inside global address. This method is very inefficient and does not scale well because each registered IP address can only be used by one end station. Static translation is most often used when a host on the inside needs to be accessed by a fixed IP address from the outside world.

Dynamic NAT

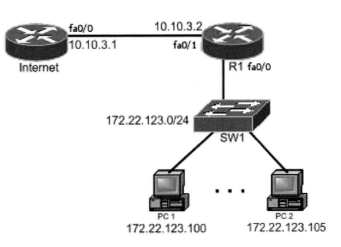

The purpose of this lab is to explore configuring Dynamic NAT on a Cisco router.

Hardware & Configuration Required for this Lab

- One Cisco router
- One Cisco switch (only if your using multiple PCs)
- One or more PCs
- One straight through Cat 5 cable to connect Router (if switch is used)
- One straight through Cat 5 cable per PC (if switch is used)
- One crossover Cat 5 cable to connect PC (if switch if not utilized)

Commands Used in Lab

ip nat pool - Define a NAT pool
ip nat inside source list - Define Dynamic NAT

Initial Configs

R1
 hostname R1
 line console 0
  logging synch

```
int fa0/0
ip add 172.22.123.1 255.255.255.0
no shut
int fa0/1
ip add 10.10.3.2 255.255.255.0
no shut
```

Internet
```
hostname Internet
line console 0
logging synch
int fa0/0
ip add 10.10.3.1 255.255.255.0
no shut
```

PC1

As a refresher, NAT uses the following address types when doing translations:

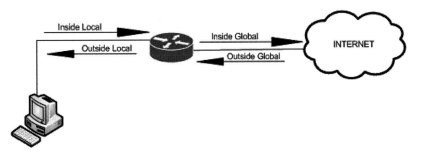

To translate addresses NAT keeps track of several address types as it passes through the router, these are:

Inside Local: This is private IP address a PC is using on your LAN

Inside Global: This is the IP address the PC has been translated to so it can access the internet.

Outside Global: This is the IP address of a host outside of your network

Outside Local This is the IP address that the Outside Global host has been translated to on your network.

For this lab, my "public" WAN IP will be 10.10.3.2 defined on R1 while the Internet is simulated with an ip address of 10.10.3.1. To configure Dynamic NAT you first need to make an access-list that matches what private networks will use NAT.

R1(config)#**ip access-list standard NAT**
R1(config-std-nacl)#**permit 172.22.123.0 0.0.0.255**
R1(config-std-nacl)#**exit**

The next step is to make a NAT Pool that contains global IP addresses that NAT can translate the private IPs to. This is done with the **ip nat pool <name>** command. Then we have to enter the start and end for the global address range.

R1(config)#**ip nat pool WAN-POOL ?**
  A.B.C.D   Start IP address
  netmask   Specify the network mask
  prefix-length Specify the prefix length

In this lab my global IP range is 10.10.3.200 - 10.10.3.201

R1(config)#**ip nat pool WAN-POOL 10.10.3.200 ?**
  A.B.C.D End IP address

R1(config)#**ip nat pool WAN-POOL 10.10.3.200 10.10.3.201 ?**
  netmask   Specify the network mask
  prefix-length Specify the prefix length

At the end of the command we can either specifiy the subnet mask with the **netmask** option or use slash notation with the **prefix-length** option.

R1(config)#**ip nat pool WAN-POOL 10.10.3.200 10.10.3.201 netmask 255.255.255.0**
R1(config)#**ip nat pool WAN-POOL 10.10.3.200 10.10.3.201 prefix-length 24**

Now that we have all the pieces we can configure.
R1(config)#**ip nat inside source list NAT pool WAN-POOL**

Just like with Static NAT we need to define what interfaces are inside or outside.

R1(config)#**int fa0/0**
R1(config-if)#**ip nat inside**
R1(config-if)#**int fa0/1**
R1(config-if)#**ip nat outside**

At this point we can now reach the Internet Router from our PCs. From the PC, initiate three different pings to 10.10.3.1. Use the "**–S**" qualifier to specify different source addresses. Use 172.22.123.100, 172.22.123.105 and 172.22.123.110 as source addresses for the pings. Notice that because our pool only has two IP addreses: 10.10.3.200 and 10.10.3.201 it is only able to translate the first two ping requests the router receives. The 3rd request from 172.22.123.110 is not able to be translated because the pool is empty at the moment.

Checking **show ip nat translations** shows us what IPs in the pool are being used.

R1(config)#**do sh ip nat translation**

Pro	Inside global	Inside local	Outside local	Outside global
icmp	10.10.3.200:10	172.22.123.100:10	10.10.3.1:10	10.10.3.1:10
icmp	10.10.3.200:11	172.22.123.100:11	10.10.3.1:11	10.10.3.1:11
icmp	10.10.3.200:12	172.22.123.100:12	10.10.3.1:12	10.10.3.1:12
icmp	10.10.3.200:13	172.22.123.100:13	10.10.3.1:13	10.10.3.1:13
icmp	10.10.3.200:1	172.22.123.105:1	10.10.3.1:1	10.10.3.1:1
icmp	10.10.3.200:2	172.22.123.105:2	10.10.3.1:2	10.10.3.1:2
icmp	10.10.3.200:3	172.22.123.105:3	10.10.3.1:3	10.10.3.1:3
icmp	10.10.3.200:4	172.22.123.105:4	10.10.3.1:4	10.10.3.1:4

Also checking **show ip nat statistics** will show us how many addresses in the pool have been allocated and how many requests have failed so far.

R1(config)#**do show ip nat statistics**
Total active translations: 2 (0 static, 2 dynamic; 2 extended)
Outside interfaces: FastEthernet0/1
Inside interfaces: FastEthernet0/0
Hits: 12 Misses: 16
Expired translations: 12
Dynamic mappings:

-- Inside Source

access-list NAT pool WAN-POOL refCount 4

 pool WAN-POOL: netmask 255.255.255.0

   start 10.10.3.200 end 10.10.3.201

   type generic, total addresses 2 , allocated 1 (100%), misses 4

If we turn on **debug ip nat** we can see that NAT is dropping packets from
172.22.123.110.

R1(config)#
NAT: translation failed (A), dropping packet s=172.22.123.110 d=10.10.3.1

Turning on **debug ip nat detail** we can see that it is dropping the packets because it's
unable to allocate an IP address from the pool.

R1(config)#**do debug ip nat detail**
IP NAT detailed debugging is on
NAT: Can't create new inside entry - forced_punt_flags: 0
NAT: failed to allocate address for 172.22.123.110, list/map NAT
NAT: translation failed (A), dropping packet s=172.22.123.110 d=10.10.3.1

Obviously in the lab we can simply add more IPs to the pool to solve this problem. But
in the real world IP addresses aren't cheap (at least when your trying to get a few
hundred or thousand to get all of your company's workers online). The solution is to use
NAT with Overloading. Overloading allows a single IP address to be used for NAT about
4096 times which makes it much easier to get everyone online. All we need to do is add
the **overload** keyword to the end of the NAT command.

 R1(config)#**ip nat inside source list NAT pool WAN-POOL overload**

Now all of our hosts can get online. Verify by attempting to ping 10.10.3.1 using three
different sources addresses of 172.22.123.100, 172.22.123.105 and 172.22.123.110.

If we look at the NAT table we can see that all the PCs are using 10.10.3.201 each with
its own socket number (0-2). NAT will load balance between the addresses in the NAT
pool as more traffic comes in.

R1(config)#**do show ip nat translation**
Pro   Inside global   Inside local   Outside local   Outside global
icmp 10.10.3.201:33   172.22.123.100:33 10.10.3.1:33   10.10.3.1:33

```
icmp 10.10.3.201:34      172.22.123.100:34 10.10.3.1:34      10.10.3.1:34
icmp 10.10.3.201:35      172.22.123.100:35 10.10.3.1:35      10.10.3.1:35
icmp 10.10.3.201:36      172.22.123.100:36 10.10.3.1:36      10.10.3.1:36
icmp 10.10.3.201:10      172.22.123.105:10 10.10.3.1:10      10.10.3.1:10
icmp 10.10.3.201:11      172.22.123.105:11 10.10.3.1:11      10.10.3.1:11
icmp 10.10.3.201:12      172.22.123.105:12 10.10.3.1:12      10.10.3.1:12
icmp 10.10.3.201:9       172.22.123.105:9   10.10.3.1:9       10.10.3.1:9
icmp 10.10.3.201:1025 172.22.123.110:10  10.10.3.1:10      10.10.3.1:1025
icmp 10.10.3.201:1026 172.22.123.110:11  10.10.3.1:11      10.10.3.1:1026
icmp 10.10.3.201:1027 172.22.123.110:12  10.10.3.1:12      10.10.3.1:1027
icmp 10.10.3.201:1024 172.22.123.110:9   10.10.3.1:9       10.10.3.1:1024
```

Let's remove our NAT configuration.
R1(config)#**no ip nat inside source list NAT pool WAN-POOL overload**

If we only have a single WAN IP address or we just want more flexiblity then we can skip using pools and just directly configure the interface IP. The syntax for NAT is: **ip nat inside source list <access-list> interface <wan int> <overload>.** Let's setup NAT for our network using this method, we'll use the access-list NAT we made and our WAN interface is Fa0/1.

Note: The overload command is mandatory, if you don't type overload at the end IOS will put it on for you.

R1(config)#**ip nat inside source list NAT interface fa0/1**
R1(config)#**do sh run | in ip nat inside**
ip nat inside source list NAT interface FastEthernet0/1 overload

Notice that the inside global address is now R1's WAN IP. This is also handy for dynamic cable/DSL connections where your WAN IP may change frequently.

R1(config)#**do sh ip nat trans**

Pro	Inside global	Inside local	Outside local	Outside global
icmp	10.10.3.2:37	172.22.123.100:37	10.10.3.1:37	10.10.3.1:37
icmp	10.10.3.2:38	172.22.123.100:38	10.10.3.1:38	10.10.3.1:38
icmp	10.10.3.2:39	172.22.123.100:39	10.10.3.1:39	10.10.3.1:39
icmp	10.10.3.2:40	172.22.123.100:40	10.10.3.1:40	10.10.3.1:40
icmp	10.10.3.2:13	172.22.123.105:13	10.10.3.1:13	10.10.3.1:13
icmp	10.10.3.2:14	172.22.123.105:14	10.10.3.1:14	10.10.3.1:14
icmp	10.10.3.2:15	172.22.123.105:15	10.10.3.1:15	10.10.3.1:15
icmp	10.10.3.2:16	172.22.123.105:16	10.10.3.1:16	10.10.3.1:16
icmp	10.10.3.2:1024	172.22.123.110:13	10.10.3.1:13	10.10.3.1:1024
icmp	10.10.3.2:1025	172.22.123.110:14	10.10.3.1:14	10.10.3.1:1025
icmp	10.10.3.2:1026	172.22.123.110:15	10.10.3.1:15	10.10.3.1:1026
icmp	10.10.3.2:1027	172.22.123.110:16	10.10.3.1:16	10.10.3.1:1027

Overloading an Inside Global Address

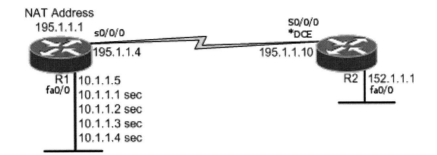

You will configure your routers to support overloading an Inside Global Address. Then you will use commands to view that the port number and address are used as a key to map return packets to the correct inside local IP address.

Hardware & Configuration Required for this Lab
- Two Cisco routers with one serial port and one Ethernet port
- Two back to back DTE/DCE serial cables
- Configure the cabling as shown in the network diagram
- If the routers have a startup-config, erase it and perform a reload of the routers

---

The following steps are taken by R1 when overloading is enabled:

1. HostA (10.1.1.1) opens a connection to Host 152.1.1.1 on the internet.

2. The first packet that R1 receives from HostA causes the router to check its NAT table.

3. If no translation exists, R1 replaces the source address with the global address of 195.1.1.1.

4. HostB(152.1.1.1) receives the packet and responds to HostA by using the inside global IP destination address.

5. When the router receives the packet with the inside global IP address, it performs a NAT table lookup by using the inside global address as a key. It then translates the address to the inside local address of HostA and forwards the packet to HostA.

R1 is configured for Network Address Translation and will dynamically translate any inside source address within the range specified to the unique Internet registered global address 195.1.1.1.

R1
Router>**en**
Router#**config t**
Router(config)#**hostname R1**
R1(config)#**ip nat pool globalpool 195.1.1.1 195.1.1.1 netmask 255.255.255.0** (*Name of the pool and defines range on pool, in this case there is only one address in the pool*)

R1(config)#**ip nat inside source list 1 pool globalpool overload** (*List 1 references access-list 1 and defines which address will be translated. Also defines what global address to use (globalpool) and allows multiple addresses to be translated to one outside global address (overload)*)
R1(config)#**int fa0/0**
R1(config-if)#**ip address 10.1.1.1 255.255.255.0 secondary**
R1(config-if)#**ip address 10.1.1.2 255.255.255.0 secondary**
R1(config-if)#**ip address 10.1.1.3 255.255.255.0 secondary**
R1(config-if)#**ip address 10.1.1.4 255.255.255.0 secondary**

Secondary IP addressees used as test points
R1(config-if)#**ip address 10.1.1.5 255.255.255.0**
R1(config-if)#**no keepalive**
R1(config-if)#**no shut**
R1(config-if)#**ip nat inside** (*Defines the inside interface*)
R1(config)#**int s0/0/0**
R1(config-if)#**ip address 195.1.1.4 255.255.255.0**
R1(config-if)#**no shut**
R1(config-if)#**ip nat outside** (*Defines the outside interface*)
R1(config)#**ip route 152.1.1.1 255.255.255.255 serial 0**
R1(config)#**access-list 1 permit 10.1.1.2** (*Access list 1 defines which inside source addresses that will be translated*)
R1(config)#**access-list 1 permit 10.1.1.1**
R1(config)#**access-list 1 permit 10.1.1.3**
R1(config)#**access-list 1 permit 10.1.1.4**

R2
Router#**config t**
Router(config)#**hostname R2**
R2(config)#**int fa0/0**
R2(config-if)#**ip address 152.1.1.1 255.255.255.0**
R2(config-if)#**no shut**
R2(config-if)#**no keepalive**
R2(config-if)#**int s0/0/0**
R2(config-if)#**ip address 195.1.1.10 255.255.255.0**
R2(config-if)#**clock rate 500000**
R2(config-if)#**no shut**

Monitoring and Testing the Configuration

To test the configuration, ping R2 (195.1.1.10) and using the extended ping command on R1, source the packet from 10.1.1.1 and 10.1.1.2. Monitor the translation using the **debug ip nat** command. The following is the output from that command. Notice that both the inside source addresses 10.1.1.1 and 10.1.1.2 have been translated to 195.1.1.1.

NAT: s=10.1.1.1->195.1.1.1, d=195.1.1.10 [10]
NAT: s=10.1.1.2->195.1.1.1, d=195.1.1.10 [15]

Now show the NAT table using the command **show ip nat translation**. What follows is the output from that command; notice the port number after each IP address. This port number and address are used as a key to map return packets to the correct inside local IP address.

Pro Inside global Inside local Outside local Outside global
icmp 195.1.1.1:**5056** 10.1.1.1:**5056** 195.1.1.10:**5056** 195.1.1.10:**5056**
icmp 195.1.1.1:5057 10.1.1.1:5057 195.1.1.10:5057 195.1.1.10:5057
icmp 195.1.1.1:5058 10.1.1.1:5058 195.1.1.10:5058 195.1.1.10:5058
icmp 195.1.1.1:5059 10.1.1.1:5059 195.1.1.10:5059 195.1.1.10:5059
icmp 195.1.1.1:5060 10.1.1.1:5060 195.1.1.10:5060 195.1.1.10:5060

NAT (Network Address Translation) Review

Questions:

1. The configuration of dynamic NAT requires the use of _____, which is a list of the inside global addresses that the Cisco router uses when translating the inside local addresses.

2. _____ designates the inside interface in a NAT configuration?
3. _____ translates one (and only one) IP address to another.
4. An _____ is a public IP address associated with an inside device.
5. When configuring the 'ip nat inside source' command, which parameter must you specify to perform PAT? _____
6. What forms of NAT incorporates the source IP address (inside local) along with the source port number to make every translation unique? _____
7. You would like to see the active NAT translations that are happening on your router. Your primary interest is in the inside local IPs that are being translated. What command shows you this information? _____

Match the NAT Address Classifications below to the Area Type term underneath.

Classifications

8. _____ An actual address assigned to an inside host
9. _____ An inside address seen from the outside
10. _____ An actual address assigned to an outside host
11. _____ An outside address seen from the inside

Area Types

1. Outside Local
2. Outside Global
3. Inside Global
4. Inside Local

Give the terms below that correspond with the definitions provided.

12. _____ A pool of IP addresses to be used as inside global or outside local addresses in translations.

13. _____ An extension to NAT that translates information at layer four and above, such as TCP and UDP port numbers; dynamic PAT configurations include the overload keyword.

14. _____ The extendable keyword must be appended when multiple overlapping static translations are configured

Answers:

1. Dynamic NAT requires the use of an IP NAT pool that lists the inside global addresses (typically internet-valid) that will be used for the translation.
2. ip nat inside
3. NAT translates only one IP address to another.
4. An inside global IP address is a public IP address assigned to an inside device.
5. Use the overload parameter with the 'ip nat inside source' command to set up PAT.
6. Nat overload uses the source port number to send many unique requests out a single, public IP address.
7. The show ip nat translations command shows you all active translations currently in place on your router. It includes the inside local and global and the outside local and global addresses for each translation.
8. D
9. C
10. B
11. A
12. NAT Pool
13. Port Address Translation (PAT)
14. Extendable Translation

Frame-Relay Switching

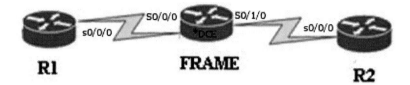

The purpose of this lab is to show you how to setup a basic frame-relay switch.

Hardware & Configuration Required for this Lab

- Two Cisco routers with one serial port
- One Cisco router with at least two serial ports
- Two DCE/DTE back to back cables

Commands Used in this Lab

frame-relay switching – Enables frame-realy switching on a router
encapsulation frame-relay – Enables frame-relay encapsulation on an interface.
frame-relay intf-type dce – Sets the router that will provide clocking
frame-relay <input dlci> interface <output interface> <output dlci – Tells the router how to route the DLCIs

---

Initial Configs - Where you see *Initial Configs,* these are basic configuration steps that by now you should be able to perform on the devices by yourself without us detailing them step by step. Generally you simply go into enable and then configuration mode and start the configuration. We used a 1841 with two WIC-1T cards for serial ports so you can understand any serial numbering modifications you may need to make based on your model router and serial cards.

Frame-Relay Router
line console 0
logging synch
hostname FrameRelay
int s0/0/0
no shut
int s0/1/0
no shut

R1
line console 0
logging synch
hostname R1
int s0/0/0
no shut

R2
line console 0
logging synch
hostname R2
int s0/0/0
no shut

This lab briefly shows you how to setup a router as a frame-relay switch so you can do the frame-relay labs. The first step is to enable frame-relay switching on the router with the **frame-relay switching** command.

FrameRelay(config)#**frame-relay switching**

It's a good idea before to check **show cdp neigbor** to have a reference for what routers are connected to what interfaces. In this very small example, R1 s0/0/0 is connected to FrameRelay s0/0/0 and R2 s0/0/0 is connected to FrameRelay s/0/1/0. This is depicted in the output of the **show cdp neighbors** command below.

FrameRelay#**show cdp neighbors**
Capability Codes: R - Router, T - Trans Bridge, B - Source Route Bridge
          S - Switch, H - Host, I - IGMP, r - Repeater, P - Phone

Device ID	Local Intrfce	Holdtme	Capability	Platform	Port ID
R1	Ser 0/0/0	155	R	C1841	Ser 0/0/0
R2	Ser 0/1/0	120	R	C1841	Ser 0/0/0

Next we'll need to enable frame-relay on all the interfaces on the frame-switch with the **encapsulation frame-relay** command.

FrameRelay (config-if)#**int s0/0/0**
FrameRelay (config-if)#**encapsulation frame-relay**
FrameRelay (config-if)#**int s0/1/0**
FrameRelay (config-if)#**encapsulation frame-relay**

Frame-Relay encapsulation expects to receive the clock rate from the frame-relay switch (in most cases this is your ISP). Since we are configuring a frame-relay switch, we will need to tell the router that it is the DCE end of the connection and needs to provide clock rate. This is done with the **frame-relay intf-type dce** command. We will also need to set a clock rate each interface as well.

FrameRelay (config-if)#**int s0/0/0**
FrameRelay (config-if)#**frame-relay intf-type dce**
FrameRelay (config-if)#**clock rate 64000**
FrameRelay (config-if)#**int s0/0/1**
FrameRelay (config-if)#**frame-relay intf-type dce**
FrameRelay (config-if)#**clock rate 64000**

The final part of the configuration is a bit more complicated. We have to tell the frame-relay switch how to route DLCIs. Remember that DLCIs are layer 2, so the router will route frame-relay traffic on DLCIs alone.

The command we use is the **frame-relay route <input dlci> interface <output interface> <output dlci>** which is an interface command. For example, if we want the frame-switch to route DLCI 102 received on s0/0/0 to s0/0/1 DLCI 201 we would enter the following:

FrameRelay (config-if)# **int s0/0/0**
FrameRelay (config-if)#**frame route 102 interface s0/1/0 201**

You would also have to enter the opposite on s0/0/1 to allow for return traffic.
FrameRelay (config-if)#**int s0/1/0**
FrameRelay (config-if)#**frame route 201 interface s0/0/0 102**

At this point if we configure R1 and R2, we should be able to ping across the frame-relay network.

R1(config)#**int s0/0/0**
R1(config-if)#**encapsulation frame-relay**
R1(config-if)#**ip address 192.168.12.1 255.255.255.0**

R2(config-if)#**int s0/0/0**
R2(config-if)#**encapsulation frame-relay**
R2(config-if)#**ip address 192.168.12.2 255.255.255.0**

Checking **show frame-relay map** we can see that R1 has learned the 102 DLCI. This is a good sign.
R1(config-if)#**do show frame map**
Serial0/0/0 (up): ip 192.168.12.2 dlci 102(0x66,0x1860), dynamic,
         broadcast,, status defined, active

And we can ping just fine.

R1(config-if)#**do ping 192.168.12.2**
Type escape sequence to abort.
Sending 5, 100-byte ICMP Echos to 192.168.12.2, timeout is 2 seconds:
!!!!!
Success rate is 100 percent (5/5), round-trip min/avg/max = 16/35/68 ms

Using the frame-relay route commands on your FrameRelay Switch, you can map traffic throughout your frame-relay network.   While you can choose whatever DLCI values you like. I suggest using a DLCI schema that makes sense to you as it can quickly become confusing, especially with many changes. I generally use a X0Y format where X is the incoming router number and Y is the destination router number. For example, if you had a third router, for R1 to R3 I would use DLCI 103, for R3 to R2 I would use DLCI 302.

Frame-Relay on Physical Interfaces

The purpose of this lab is to get you exposure configuring frame-relay on physical interfaces.

Hardware & Configuration Required for this Lab

- Three Cisco routers with one serial port
- One Cisco router with at least three serial ports
- Three DCE/DTE back to back cables
- **Note:** If you do not have a forth router, simply strip R3 out of your lab and everything else will still work fine.

Commands Used in Lab

show frame-relay pvc – Displays any PVC information learned from the frame-switch.
show frame-relay map - Displays any frame-relay mappings.
frame-relay map ip <neighbor IP> <local dlci> <optional:broadcast> - Statically maps neighbor IPs to DLCIs with the optional broadcast command.

Initial Configs - Where you see *Initial Configs,* these are basic configuration steps that by now you should be able to perform on the devices by yourself without us detailing them step by step. Generally you simply go into enable and then configuration mode and start the configuration. We used an 1841 as the Frame-Relay router with two WIC-2T cards and one WIC-2T card in each branch router.

Frame-Relay Router (signified by the cloud)
Note: Did you know that when you have a config such as the one below, you can do a copy and paste to host under Edit in hyperterminal so you don't have to type this all out manually?

```
frame-relay switching
interface s0/0/0
  no shut
  encapsulation frame-relay
  clock rate 64000
  frame-relay intf-type dce
  frame-relay route 102 interface s0/0/1 201
  frame-relay route 103 interface s0/1/0 301
interface s0/0/1
  no shut
  encapsulation frame-relay
  clock rate 64000
  frame-relay intf-type dce
  frame-relay route 201 interface s0/0/0 102
  frame-relay route 203 interface s0/1/0 302
interface s0/1/0
  no shut
  encapsulation frame-relay
  clock rate 64000
  frame-relay intf-type dce
  frame-relay route 301 interface s0/0/0 103
  frame-relay route 302 interface s0/0/1 203
```

All Routers
```
line console 0
logging synch
int s0/0/0
no shut
```

Note: Configure individual hostnames on each Router (i.e. **R1**, **R2** and **R3**).

Frame-Relay is a popular WAN option because it is cheaper then leased line options and has the "something for nothing" approach. That is where it is possible to get more bandwidth then you are subscribed as long as the Service Provider isn't seeing any congestion. The first step is to enable frame-relay by using the **encapsulation frame-relay** command under the interface.

R1(config)#**int s0/0/0**
R1(config-if)#**encapsulation frame-relay**

R2(config)#**int s0/0/0**
R2(config-if)#**encapsulation frame-relay**

R3(config)#**int s0/0/0**
R3(config-if)#**encapsulation frame-relay**

Checking **show interfaces** afterwards we can see Frame-relay encapsulation is now being used.

```
Serial0/0/0 is up, line protocol is up
  Hardware is GT96K Serial
  MTU 1500 bytes, BW 1544 Kbit/sec, DLY 20000 usec,
    reliability 255/255, txload 1/255, rxload 1/255
  Encapsulation FRAME-RELAY, loopback not set
  Keepalive set (10 sec)
  CRC checking enabled
  LMI enq sent  33, LMI stat recvd 35, LMI upd recvd 0, DTE LMI up
  LMI enq recvd 0, LMI stat sent  0, LMI upd sent  0
  LMI DLCI 1023  LMI type is CISCO  frame relay DTE
  FR SVC disabled, LAPF state down
  Broadcast queue 0/64, broadcasts sent/dropped 0/0, interface broadcasts 0
  Last input 00:00:09, output 00:00:09, output hang never
  Last clearing of "show interface" counters 00:06:38
  Input queue: 0/75/0/0 (size/max/drops/flushes); Total output drops: 0
  Queueing strategy: weighted fair
  Output queue: 0/1000/64/0 (size/max total/threshold/drops)
    Conversations  0/1/256 (active/max active/max total)
    Reserved Conversations 0/0 (allocated/max allocated)
    Available Bandwidth 1158 kilobits/sec
  5 minute input rate 0 bits/sec, 0 packets/sec
  5 minute output rate 0 bits/sec, 0 packets/sec
    35 packets input, 647 bytes, 0 no buffer
    Received 0 broadcasts, 0 runts, 0 giants, 0 throttles
    0 input errors, 0 CRC, 0 frame, 0 overrun, 0 ignored, 0 abort
    41 packets output, 535 bytes, 0 underruns
    0 output errors, 0 collisions, 1 interface resets
    0 unknown protocol drops
    0 output buffer failures, 0 output buffers swapped out
    2 carrier transitions
    DCD=up  DSR=up  DTR=up  RTS=up  CTS=up
```

We can see any PVC information the router has learned from the frame-switch with **show frame-relay pvc**.

There are 3 types of PVC status:
Active - Everything is good

Inactive - The frame-switch knows about the PVC but there is a communication problem.
Deleted - The frame-switch doesn't know about the PVC.

R1#**show frame-relay pvc**
PVC Statistics for interface Serial0/0/0 (Frame Relay DTE)

	Active	Inactive	Deleted	Static
Local	0	0	0	0
Switched	0	0	0	0
Unused	2	0	0	0

DLCI = 102, DLCI USAGE = UNUSED, PVC STATUS = ACTIVE, INTERFACE = Serial0/0/0

input pkts 0   output pkts 0   in bytes 0
out bytes 0   dropped pkts 0   in pkts dropped 0
out pkts dropped 0   out bytes dropped 0
in FECN pkts 0   in BECN pkts 0   out FECN pkts 0
out BECN pkts 0   in DE pkts 0   out DE pkts 0
out bcast pkts 0   out bcast bytes 0
5 minute input rate 0 bits/sec, 0 packets/sec
5 minute output rate 0 bits/sec, 0 packets/sec
pvc create time 00:00:57, last time pvc status changed 00:00:27

DLCI = 103, DLCI USAGE = UNUSED, PVC STATUS = ACTIVE, INTERFACE = Serial0/0/0

input pkts 0   output pkts 0   in bytes 0
out bytes 0   dropped pkts 0   in pkts dropped 0
out pkts dropped 0   out bytes dropped 0
in FECN pkts 0   in BECN pkts 0   out FECN pkts 0
out BECN pkts 0   in DE pkts 0   out DE pkts 0
out bcast pkts 0   out bcast bytes 0
5 minute input rate 0 bits/sec, 0 packets/sec
5 minute output rate 0 bits/sec, 0 packets/sec
pvc create time 00:05:47, last time pvc status changed 00:01:07

Next we'll need to add IP addresses on the router interfaces.

R1(config)#**int s0/0/0**
R1(config-if)#**ip address 123.123.123.1 255.255.255.0**

R2(config)#**int s0/0/0**
R2(config-if)#**ip address 123.123.123.2 255.255.255.0**

R3(config)#**int s0/0/0**
R3(config-if)#**ip address 123.123.123.3 255.255.255.0**

Once we add IP addresses to the interface, frame-relay will try to figure out its DLCIs and what they connect to via Inverse ARP. Inverse ARP does this by simply sending the IP information across the frame-relay link to who ever will listen. If the router receives an inverse arp message back, it creates a dynamic mapping. Frame-Relay mappings can be seen with the **show frame-relay map** command.

We can see that R1 has learned about the 102 and 103 DLCIs and has learned R2's and R3's IP information as well.

R1#**show frame-relay map**
Serial0/0/0 (up): ip 123.123.123.2 dlci 102(0x66,0x1860), dynamic,
         broadcast,, status defined, active
Serial0/0/0 (up): ip 123.123.123.3 dlci 103(0x67,0x1870), dynamic,
         broadcast,, status defined, active

Once the router has learned its DLCIs we can ping the other routers.
R1#**ping 123.123.123.2**
Type escape sequence to abort.
Sending 5, 100-byte ICMP Echos to 123.123.123.2, timeout is 2 seconds:
!!!!!
Success rate is 100 percent (5/5), round-trip min/avg/max = 12/51/96 ms

R1#**ping 123.123.123.3**
Type escape sequence to abort.
Sending 5, 100-byte ICMP Echos to 123.123.123.3, timeout is 2 seconds:
!!!!!
Success rate is 100 percent (5/5), round-trip min/avg/max = 16/42/76 ms

One thing to point about about frame-relay is that a router can't ping its own interface without an explicit mapping. This is because when you ping the router's own interface the router will actually send the ping packet to the frame-switch that will need to send it back.

R1#**ping 123.123.123.1**
Type escape sequence to abort.
Sending 5, 100-byte ICMP Echos to 123.123.123.1, timeout is 2 seconds:
.....
Success rate is 0 percent (0/5)

You can statically map neighbor IPs and what DLCI to use to reach them with the **frame-relay map** command.
The syntax is: **frame-relay map ip <neighbor IP> <local dlci> <optional: broadcast>**

The broadcast keyword is optional since frame-relay is a non-broadcast media. The broadcast keyword simulates broadcast traffic across the link. Let's configure a static mapping on R1 to get to R2's s0/0/0 interface.

R1(config)#**int s0/0/0**
R1(config-if)#**frame-relay map ip 123.123.123.2 102 broadcast**

After we configure the static mapping we can see it in **show frame map**.

R1#**show frame map**
Serial0/0/0 (up): ip 123.123.123.2 dlci 102(0x66,0x1860), **static,**
        broadcast,
        CISCO, status defined, active
Serial0/0/0 (up): ip 123.123.123.3 dlci 103(0x67,0x1870), dynamic,
        broadcast,, status defined, active

Now let's add a static DLCI on R1 so it knows how to reach its own 123.123.123.1
address.

R1(config)#**int s0/0/0**
R1(config-if)#**frame map ip 123.123.123.1 102**

Now R1 can ping its own interface.

R1#**ping 123.123.123.1**
Type escape sequence to abort.
Sending 5, 100-byte ICMP Echos to 123.123.123.1, timeout is 2 seconds:
 !!!!!
Success rate is 100 percent (5/5), round-trip min/avg/max = 28/52/132 ms

Frame-Relay on Point-to-Point Interface

The purpose of this lab to give you exposure to configuring frame-relay on Point to Point subinterfaces.

Hardware & Configuration Required for this Lab

- Two Cisco routers with one serial port
- One Cisco router with at least 2 serial ports
- Two DCE/DTE back to back cables

Commands Used in this Lab

no frame-relay inverse-arp - Used to move prevent Inverse-ARP from mapping DLCIs dynamically.
frame interface-dlci <number> - Binds a DLCI to an interface for point to point interfaces.

Initial Configs - Where you see *Initial Configs,* these are basic configuration steps that by now you should be able to perform on the devices by yourself without us detailing them step by step. Generally you simply go into enable and then configuration mode and start the configuration. We will let you figure out the cabling by reading the configs.

Frame-Relay Router (signified by the cloud)
host FrameRelay
frame-relay switching
interface s0/0/0
   encapsulation frame-relay
   clock rate 64000
   frame-relay intf-type dce
   frame-relay route 102 interface s0/1/0 201

```
  no shut
interface s0/1/0
  encapsulation frame-relay
  clock rate 64000
  frame-relay intf-type dce
  frame-relay route 201 interface s0/0/0 102
  no shut
```

R1
```
hostname R1
line console 0
logging synch
int s0/0/0
no shut
```

R2
```
hostname R2
line console 0
logging synch
int s0/0/0
no shut
```

Just like the other interface modes, the first step is to enable frame-relay by using the **encapsulation frame-relay** command under the physical interface.

R1(config)#**int s0/0/0**
R1(config-if)#**encapsulation frame-relay**

R2(config)#**int s0/0/0**
R2(config-if)#**encapsulation frame-relay**

To prevent Inverse-ARP from mapping the DLCIs, we'll disable the sending Inverse ARPs on the routers with **no frame-relay inverse-arp** on the interface.
Note: You can not prevent the router from receiving inverse-arps.

R1(config-if)#**int s0/0/0**
R1(config-if)#**no frame-relay inverse-arp**

R2(config-if)#**int s0/0/0**
R2(config-if)#**no frame-relay inverse-arp**

To make a point to point interface, we will create a subinterface and select the point to point option.

Note: Like any subinterface, you may choose any interface # you want. It's best to pick a number that makes sense. I typically use part of the subnet.

R1(config)#**int s0/0/0.12 ?**
  multipoint   Treat as a multipoint link
  point-to-point Treat as a point-to-point link

R1(config)#**int s0/0/0.12 point**
R1(config-subif)#

R2(config)#**int s0/0/0.12 point**

Next we'll add the IP addressing on the interfaces.
Note: The router won't attempt Inverse ARP until there is an IP on the interface.

R1(config)#**int s0/0/0.12**
R1(config-subif)#**ip address 12.12.12.13 255.255.255.0**

R2(config)#**int s0/0/0.12**
R2(config-subif)#**ip address 12.12.12.14 255.255.255.0**

At this point there are no frame-relay mappings because we disabled inverse-arp. We will need to manually add them.

R1#**show frame map**

Point to point networks are exactly that and they can't be used networks with multiple points. Because of that, instead of statically mapping the individual DLCIs, you bind the DLCI to the subinterface with the **frame-relay interface-dlci** command. If you try to use the static map command, you will receive an error.

Only the frame-relay interface-dlci command should be used on point-to-point interfaces; not frame-relay map. Let's bind the DLCI to the subinterfaces.

R1(config)#**int s0/0/0.12**
R1(config-subif)#**frame interface-dlci 102**

R2(config)#**int s0/0/0.12**
R2(config-subif)#**frame interface-dlci 201**

At this point R1 & R2 can ping each other.
Note: Point to Point frame-relay networks can ping their own local interfaces without any additional mappings.

R1(config-subif)#**do ping 12.12.12.13**
Type escape sequence to abort.

Sending 5, 100-byte ICMP Echos to 12.12.12.13, timeout is 2 seconds:
!!!!!
Success rate is 100 percent (5/5), round-trip min/avg/max = 16/33/100 ms

R1(config-subif)#**do ping 12.12.12.14**
Type escape sequence to abort.
Sending 5, 100-byte ICMP Echos to 12.12.12.14, timeout is 2 seconds:
!!!!!
Success rate is 100 percent (5/5), round-trip min/avg/max = 8/28/68 ms

Frame-Relay on Multi-Point Interfaces

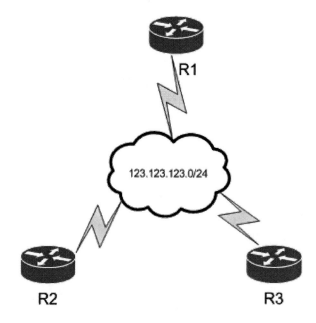

The purpose of this lab is to provide you exposure to configuring frame-relay on multipoint subinterfaces.

Hardware & Configuration Required for this Lab

- Three Cisco routers with one serial port
- One Cisco router with at least three serial ports
- Three DCE/DTE back to back cables
- **Note:** If you do not have a forth router, simply strip R3 out of your lab and everything else will still work fine.

Commands Used in this Lab

frame-relay map ip <ip add> <dlci> - Creates a static mapping

---

Initial Configs - Where you see *Initial Configs,* these are basic configuration steps that by now you should be able to perform on the devices by yourself without us detailing them step by step. Generally you simply go into enable and then configuration mode and start the configuration. This was done with four 1841 routers one with two WIC-2T modules and the rest with one in the branch routers. We will let you figure out the cabling by reading the configs.

Frame-Relay Router (signified by the cloud)
host FrameRelay
frame-relay switching
interface s0/0/0
  no shut
  encapsulation frame-relay
  clock rate 64000
  frame-relay intf-type dce
  frame-relay route 102 interface s0/0/1 201
  frame-relay route 103 interface s0/1/0 301
interface s0/0/1
  no shut
  encapsulation frame-relay
  clock rate 64000
  frame-relay intf-type dce
  frame-relay route 201 interface s0/0/0 102
interface s0/1/0
  no shut
  encapsulation frame-relay
  clock rate 64000
  frame-relay intf-type dce
  frame-relay route 301 interface s0/0/0 103

R1
hostname R1
line console 0
logging synch
exit
int s0/0/0
no shut

R2
hostname R2
line console 0
logging synch
exit
int s0/0/0
no shut

R3
hostname R3
line console 0
logging synch

exit
int s0/0/0
no shut

Just like the other interface modes, the first step is to enable frame-relay by using the **encapsulation frame-relay** command under the physical interface.

R1(config)#**int s0/0/0**
R1(config-if)#**encapsulation frame-relay**

R2(config)#**int s0/0/0**
R2(config-if)#**encapsulation frame-relay**

R3(config)#**int s0/0/0**
R3(config-if)#**encapsulation frame-relay**

To prevent Inverse-ARP from mapping the DLCIs, we'll disable the sending Inverse ARPs on the routers with **no frame-relay inverse-arp** on the interface.
Note: You cannot prevent the router from receiving inverse-arps.

R1(config-if)#**int s0/0/0**
R1(config-if)#**no frame-relay inverse-arp**

R2(config-if)#**int s0/0/0**
R2(config-if)#**no frame-relay inverse-arp**

R3(config)#**int s0/0/0**
R3(config-if)#**no frame-relay inverse-arp**

To make a multipoint interface, we will create a subinterface and select the multipoint option.
Note: Like any subinterface you may choose any interface # you want. It's best to pick a number that makes sense. I typically use part of the subnet.

R1(config)#**int s0/0/0.123 ?**
  multipoint   Treat as a multipoint link
  point-to-point Treat as a point-to-point link

R1(config)#**int s0/0/0.123 multipoint**

R2(config)#**int s0/0/0.123 multipoint**

R3(config)#**int s0/0/0.123 multipoint**

Next we'll add the IP addressing on the interfaces.
Note: The router won't attempt Inverse ARP until there is an IP on the interface.

R1(config)#**int s0/0/0.123**
R1(config-subif)#**ip add 123.123.123.1 255.255.255.0**

R2(config)#**int s0/0/0.123**
R2(config-subif)#**ip add 123.123.123.2 255.255.255.0**

R3(config)#**int s0/0/0.123**
R3(config-subif)#**ip add 123.123.123.3 255.255.255.**0

At this point there are no frame-relay mappings because we disabled inverse-arp. We will need to manually add them.
R1#**show frame map**

This kind of topology is called a Hub and Spoke. We will make R1 the hub that has the full reachability to all the routers. The spokes R2 and R3 only know how to reach the hub.

Static mappings can be done with the **frame-relay map ip <ip add> <dlci> command.** The **broadcast** keyword is optional. It similates broadcast traffic through the frame-relay network. It is handy for trying to get things like routing protocols working.

R1(config)#**int s0/0/0.123**
R1(config-subif)#**frame map ip 123.123.123.2 102 broadcast**
R1(config-subif)#**frame map ip 123.123.123.3 103 broadcast**

R2(config)#**int s0/0/0.123**
R2(config-subif)#**frame map ip 123.123.123.1 201 broadcast**

R3(config)#**int s0/0/0.123**
R3(config-subif)#**frame map ip 123.123.123.1 301 broadcast**

At this point R1 can ping R2 & R3.
R1(config)#**do ping 123.123.123.2**
Type escape sequence to abort.
Sending 5, 100-byte ICMP Echos to 123.123.123.2, timeout is 2 seconds:
!!!!!
Success rate is 100 percent (5/5), round-trip min/avg/max = 8/28/68 ms

R1(config)#**do ping 123.123.123.3**
Type escape sequence to abort.
Sending 5, 100-byte ICMP Echos to 123.123.123.3, timeout is 2 seconds:
!!!!!
Success rate is 100 percent (5/5), round-trip min/avg/max = 8/24/64 ms

R2 & R3 can't ping each other due to the design, but we can fix this in one of two ways. The first is to add additional static mappings and the other is to enable a routing protocol. Let's look at the more mappings option first. Notice that both static mappings use the DLCI to R1 and that there is no **broadcast** keyword. This is because we already have the keyword on the mapping to R1. If you enter it again, the router will send any broadcasts twice which will waste bandwidth and hurt performance.

R2(config)#**int s0/0/0.123**
R2(config-subif)#**frame map ip 123.123.123.3 201**

R3(config)#**int s0/0/0.123**
R3(config-subif)#**frame map ip 123.123.123.2 301**

Now R2 can ping R3.
R2(config)#**do ping 123.123.123.3**
Type escape sequence to abort.
Sending 5, 100-byte ICMP Echos to 123.123.123.3, timeout is 2 seconds:
!!!!!
Success rate is 100 percent (5/5), round-trip min/avg/max = 16/32/92 ms

Let's remove those mappings and enable OSPF on the frame-relay network.
R2(config)#**int s0/0/0.123**
R2(config-subif)#**no frame map ip 123.123.123.3 201**

R3(config)#**int s0/0/0.123**
R3(config-subif)#**no frame map ip 123.123.123.2 301**

After we enable OSPF, we will eventually realize that there is no adjacency coming up. This is because by default OSPF will treat frame-relay links as the NONBROADCAST type. So we will have to either add **neighbor** statements on R1 or change the link type to **point-to-multipoint**.

R1(config)#**router ospf 1**
R1(config-router)#**network 123.123.123.0 0.0.0.255 area 0**

R2(config)#**router ospf 1**
R2(config-router)#**network 123.123.123.0 0.0.0.255 area 0**

R3(config)#**router ospf 1**
R3(config-router)#**network 123.123.123.0 0.0.0.255 area 0**

Let's change the interfaces to **point-to-multipoint** since that will work a bit better then nonbroadcast.

R1(config-router)#**int s0/0/0.123**
R1(config-subif)#**ip ospf network point-to-multipoint**

R2(config-router)#**int s0/0/0.123**
R2(config-subif)#**ip ospf network point-to-multipoint**

R3(config-router)#**int s0/0/0.123**
R3(config-subif)#**ip ospf network point-to-multipoint**

Notice that Point-to-Multipoint OSPF adds /32 routes for the remote frame-relay interfaces.

R2(config-subif)#**do show ip route**

    Codes: C - connected, S - static, R - RIP, M - mobile, B - BGP

    D - EIGRP, EX - EIGRP external, O - OSPF, IA - OSPF inter area

    N1 - OSPF NSSA external type 1, N2 - OSPF NSSA external type 2

    E1 - OSPF external type 1, E2 - OSPF external type 2

    i - IS-IS, su - IS-IS summary, L1 - IS-IS level-1, L2 - IS-IS level-2

    ia - IS-IS inter area, * - candidate default, U - per-user static route

    o - ODR, P - periodic downloaded static route

Gateway of last resort is not set

 123.0.0.0/8 is variably subnetted, 3 subnets, 2 masks

O   **123.123.123.3/32 [110/128] via 123.123.123.1, 00:01:54, Serial0/0/0.123**

O   **123.123.123.1/32 [110/64] via 123.123.123.1, 00:01:54, Serial0/0/0.123**

C   123.123.123.0/24 is directly connected, Serial0/0/0.123

Now we can ping just fine.

R2(config)#**do ping 123.123.123.3**

Type escape sequence to abort.

Sending 5, 100-byte ICMP Echos to 123.123.123.3, timeout is 2 seconds:

!!!!!

Success rate is 100 percent (5/5), round-trip min/avg/max = 16/37/112 ms

Frame Relay Review

Questions:

1. If your router is sending too much information into the Frame Relay cloud, the service provider tags any return traffic with a _____ to notify your router to reduce its transmission rate.
2. You are troubleshooting your Frame Relay connections. After typing in the 'show frame-relay pvc' command, one of your PVCs shows up as DELETED. What causes this? _____

Answers:

1. BECN. The service provider tags any return traffic with a BECN or Backwards Explicit Congestion Notification marking. By default, your router ignores these notifications.
2. Three primary PVC states indicate the status of the line. ACTIVE means there are no problems. INACTIVE means that there is a problem with the remote router. DELETED means that there is a problem with your local router. Typically, this is caused by using the incorrect DLCI information. If the DLCI shows up as DELETED under a multipoint configuration, it shows up as DELETED under a point-to-point configuration. If you were physically disconnected from the service provider, you would not see DLCI information (because LMI is used to send the DLCI status of your router).

PPP Encapsulation

R1 S0/0/0 *DCE 12.12.12.0/30 S0/0/0 R2

The purpose of this lab is to configure a simple serial link using PPP encapsulation.

Hardware & Configuration Required for this Lab

- Two routers with one serial port
- One DCE/DTE back to back serial cable

Commands Used in this Lab

encapsulation ppp - Sets the interface encapsultion to HDLC

Initial Configs - Where you see *Initial Configs,* these are basic configuration steps that by now you should be able to perform on the devices by yourself without us detailing them step by step. Generally you simply go into enable and then configuration mode and start the configuration.

R1
hostname R1
line console 0
logging synch

R2
hostname R2
line console 0
logging synch

PPP is the current standard for serial link encapsulation. It offers many more features then HDLC does such as link authentication (we'll get to that in other labs). Plus it has the benefit of being supported by every vendor, so it's always a safe bet to use.

First let's add the IPs to our serial links.

R1(config)#**int s0/0/0**
R1(config-if)#**ip address 12.12.12.1 255.255.255.252**
R1(config-if)#**no shut**

R2(config)#**int s0/0/0**
R2(config-if)#**ip address 12.12.12.2 255.255.255.252**
R2(config-if)#**no shut**

Just like HDLC, PPP requires clock rate to function.

R1(config)#**int s0/0/0**
R1(config-if)#**clock rate 64000**

To enable PPP encapsulation, we use the **encapsulation ppp** command on the serial interface.

R1(config)#**int s0/0/0**
R1(config-if)#**encapsulation ppp**

R2(config)#**int s0/0/0**
R2(config-if)#**encapsulation ppp**

If we check **show interfaces** we can see the encapsulation is now PPP.

R2#**show interfaces s0/0/0**
Serial0/0/0 is up, line protocol is up (connected)
  Hardware is HD64570
  Internet address is 12.12.12.2/30
  MTU 1500 bytes, BW 1544 Kbit, DLY 20000 usec,
    reliability 255/255, txload 1/255, rxload 1/255
  Encapsulation PPP, loopback not set, keepalive set (10 sec)
  LCP Open
  Open: IPCP, CDPCP
  Last input never, output never, output hang never
  Last clearing of "show interface" counters never
  Input queue: 0/75/0 (size/max/drops); Total output drops: 0
  Queueing strategy: weighted fair
  Output queue: 0/1000/64/0 (size/max total/threshold/drops)
    Conversations 0/0/256 (active/max active/max total)
    Reserved Conversations 0/0 (allocated/max allocated)
    Available Bandwidth 1158 kilobits/sec
  5 minute input rate 0 bits/sec, 0 packets/sec
  5 minute output rate 0 bits/sec, 0 packets/sec

0 packets input, 0 bytes, 0 no buffer
Received 0 broadcasts, 0 runts, 0 giants, 0 throttles
0 input errors, 0 CRC, 0 frame, 0 overrun, 0 ignored, 0 abort
0 packets output, 0 bytes, 0 underruns
0 output errors, 0 collisions, 1 interface resets
0 output buffer failures, 0 output buffers swapped out
0 carrier transitions
DCD=up DSR=up DTR=up RTS=up CTS=up

And we can ping.
R1#**ping 12.12.12.2**
Type escape sequence to abort.
Sending 5, 100-byte ICMP Echos to 12.12.12.2, timeout is 2 seconds:
!!!!!
Success rate is 100 percent (5/5), round-trip min/avg/max = 4/18/44 ms

One thing I want to point out about PPP is that it simply doesn't care about IP information at all. To prove my point, I'm going to change R2's s0/0/0 interface to be in a completely different subnet.

R2(config)#**int s0/0/0**
R2(config-if)#**ip add 222.222.222.222 255.255.255.252**

But even though both ends of the links are in completely different subnets we can still ping R1 from R2!!!!!

R2(config)#**do ping 12.12.12.1**
Type escape sequence to abort.
Sending 5, 100-byte ICMP Echos to 12.12.12.1, timeout is 2 seconds:
!!!!!
Success rate is 100 percent (5/5), round-trip min/avg/max = 4/27/52 ms

Note: This is very important to remember as PPP links are not only static IPs prone to the odd typo, with PPP it won't be immediately obvious what's wrong.

The reason why this works is because PPP automatically adds the /32 route of its neighbor as a connected interface. This is because point-to-point implies there can only be one neighbor thus any traffic is simply sent to the other side.

R1#**show ip route**
Codes: C - connected, S - static, I - IGRP, R - RIP, M - mobile, B - BGP
        D - EIGRP, EX - EIGRP external, O - OSPF, IA - OSPF inter area
        N1 - OSPF NSSA external type 1, N2 - OSPF NSSA external type 2
        E1 - OSPF external type 1, E2 - OSPF external type 2, E - EGP
        i - IS-IS, L1 - IS-IS level-1, L2 - IS-IS level-2, ia - IS-IS inter area

```
          * - candidate default, U - per-user static route, o - ODR
          P - periodic downloaded static route

Gateway of last resort is not set

     12.0.0.0/8 is variably subnetted, 2 subnets, 2 masks
C     12.12.12.0/30 is directly connected, Serial0/0/0
C     12.12.12.2/32 is directly connected, Serial0/0/0
     222.222.222.0/32 is subnetted, 1 subnets
C     222.222.222.222 is directly connected, Serial0/0/0
```

R2#show ip route
```
Codes: C - connected, S - static, I - IGRP, R - RIP, M - mobile, B - BGP
       D - EIGRP, EX - EIGRP external, O - OSPF, IA - OSPF inter area
       N1 - OSPF NSSA external type 1, N2 - OSPF NSSA external type 2
       E1 - OSPF external type 1, E2 - OSPF external type 2, E - EGP
       i - IS-IS, L1 - IS-IS level-1, L2 - IS-IS level-2, ia - IS-IS inter area
       * - candidate default, U - per-user static route, o - ODR
       P - periodic downloaded static route

Gateway of last resort is not set

     12.0.0.0/32 is subnetted, 1 subnets
C     12.12.12.1 is directly connected, Serial0/0/0
     222.222.222.0/30 is subnetted, 1 subnets
C     222.222.222.220 is directly connected, Serial0/0/0
```

PPP PAP Authentication

R1   S0/0/0   *DCE   12.12.12.0/30   S0/0/0   R2

The purpose of this lab is to configure a simple serial link using PPP encapsulation then we will authenticate the link using PAP.

Hardware & Configuration Required for this Lab

- Two routers with one serial port
- One DCE/DTE back to back serial cable

Commands Used in this Lab

encapsulation ppp - Sets the interface encapsultion to HDLC
ppp authentication ppp – Enables PPP authentication on the interface
ppp pap sent –username <user> password <password> - Configures a username and password for ppp on that link

---

Initial Configs - Where you see *Initial Configs,* these are basic configuration steps that by now you should be able to perform on the devices by yourself without us detailing them step by step. Generally you simply go into enable and then configuration mode and start the configuration.

R1
hostname R1
line console 0
logging synch

R2
hostname R2
line console 0
logging synch

PPP supports three methods of authentication:

PAP - A simple clear text authentication protocol. We're going to focus on PAP in this lab.

CHAP - A secure authentication protocol based on MD5 hashs.

EAPS - A complex secure authentication protocol that uses a RADIUS server. This is not in the CCNA curriculum.

First let's add the IPs to our serial links.

R1(config)#**int s0/0/0**
R1(config-if)#**ip address 12.12.12.1 255.255.255.252**
R1(config-if)#**clock rate 64000**
R1(config-if)#**no shut**

R2(config)#**int s0/0/0**
R2(config-if)#**ip address 12.12.12.2 255.255.255.252**
R2(config-if)#**no shut**

To enable PPP encapsulation, we use the **encapsulation ppp** command on the serial interface.

R1(config)#**int s0/0/0**
R1(config-if)#**encap ppp**

R2(config)#**int s0/0/0**
R2(config-if)#**encap ppp**

And we can ping.

R1#**ping 12.12.12.2**
Type escape sequence to abort.
Sending 5, 100-byte ICMP Echos to 12.12.12.2, timeout is 2 seconds:
!!!!!
Success rate is 100 percent (5/5), round-trip min/avg/max = 4/18/44 ms

There are various options with regards to enabling PPP PAP Authentication between R1 and R2. We can have a client/server model where R2 authenticates to R1. The reverse where R1 authenticates to R2; or we can configure bi-directional authentication. Lets start with R2 (the client) authenticating to the R1 (the server).

First we'll enable PAP authentication on R1 by typing: **ppp authentication pap**. As soon as we enter the command, the serial link will go down because R2 is failing authentication.

R1(config)#**int s0/0/0**
R1(config-if)#**ppp authentication pap**
*Mar 1 01:15:53.087: %LINEPROTO-5-UPDOWN: Line protocol on Interface Serial0/0/0, changed state to down

If we enable PPP authentication debugging, we can see that it is requring authorization.

R1#**debug ppp authentication**
PPP authentication debugging is on
*Mar 1 01:17:24.551: Se0/0/0 PPP: Authorization required
*Mar 1 01:17:26.687: Se0/0/0 PPP: Authorization required

Turn off all debugging on R1.
R1#**un all**
All possible debugging has been turned off

To authenticate R2, we will need to add a username and password on R1. This is done with the **username** command. The syntax for the command is: **username <user> password <password>**. In this example, we will use certificationkits for the username and cisco for the password.

R1(config)#**username certificationkits password cisco**

Now on R2 we need to tell it to send that username and password. This is done with the interface command: **ppp pap sent-username <user> password <password>**.

R2(config)#**int s0/0/0**
R2(config-if)#**ppp pap sent-username certificationkits password cisco**
*Mar 1 01:20:47.835: %LINEPROTO-5-UPDOWN: Line protocol on Interface Serial0/0/0, changed state to up

Once we enter the command, we can see the link comes up. Let's look at the debug to see what happens behind the scenes. We will see PAP only authenticates once, so we'll need to flap the link.

R2(config-if)#**do debug ppp auth**
PPP authentication debugging is on
R2(config-if)#**shut**
*Mar 1 01:21:01.707: %LINK-5-CHANGED: Interface Serial0/0/0, changed state to administratively down
*Mar 1 01:21:02.707: %LINEPROTO-5-UPDOWN: Line protocol on Interface Serial0/0/0, changed state to down
R2(config-if)#**no shut**
*Mar 1 01:21:07.271: Se0/0/0 PPP: Using default call direction
*Mar 1 01:21:07.275: Se0/0/0 PPP: Treating connection as a dedicated line
*Mar 1 01:21:07.275: Se0/0/0 PPP: Session handle[87000028] Session id[38]
*Mar 1 01:21:07.275: Se0/0/0 PPP: Authorization required
*Mar 1 01:21:07.279: %LINK-3-UPDOWN: Interface Serial0/0/0, changed state to up
*Mar 1 01:21:07.375: Se0/0/0 PPP: No authorization without authentication

*Mar 1 01:21:07.375: Se0/0/0 PAP: Using hostname from interface PAP
*Mar 1 01:21:07.379: Se0/0/0 PAP: Using password from interface PAP
*Mar 1 01:21:07.379: Se0/0/0 PAP: O AUTH-REQ id 2 len 20 from "certificationkits"
*Mar 1 01:21:07.483: Se0/0/0 PAP: I AUTH-ACK id 2 len 5
*Mar 1 01:21:08.487: %LINEPROTO-5-UPDOWN: Line protocol on Interface Serial0/0/0, changed state to up

The other way to setup PAP is to have both ends of the link configured. Basically you just need to send the username on both ends, you'll get a warning about how we choose a password that can be used for chap and you can just ignore it.

R1(config)#**int s0/0/0**
R1(config-if)#**ppp pap sent-username certificationkits password cisco**
PPP: Warning: You have chosen a username/password combination that
                  is valid for CHAP. This is a potential security hole.

R2(config)#**username certificationkits password cisco**
R2(config)#**int s0/0/0**
R2(config-if)#**ppp authe pap**
*Mar 1 01:50:38.707: %LINEPROTO-5-UPDOWN: Line protocol on Interface Serial0/0/0, changed state to up

PPP CHAP Authentication

S0/0/0   *DCE   12.12.12.0/30   S0/0/0

R1   R2

The purpose of this lab is to configure a simple serial link using PPP encapsulation then we will authenticate the link using CHAP.

Hardware & Configuration Required for this Lab

- Two routers with one serial port
- One DCE/DTE back to back serial cable

Commands Used in this Lab

ppp authentication chap- Enables CHAP server mode on an interface.
ppp chap hostname - Tells the router to send the configured hostname rather then the default hostname
ppp chap password - Tells the router to send the configured password rather then the default password.
debug ppp authentication -Debugs PPP authentication, handy for troubleshooting.

Initial Configs - Where you see *Initial Configs,* these are basic configuration steps that by now you should be able to perform on the devices by yourself without us detailing them step by step. Generally you simply go into enable and then configuration mode and start the configuration.

R1
hostname R1
line console 0
logging synch

R2
hostname R2
line console 0
logging synch

PPP supports three methods of authentication:

PAP - A simple clear text authentication protocol.

CHAP - A secure authentication protocol based on MD5 hashs.

EAPS - A complex secure authentication protocol that uses a RADIUS server.

First let's add the IPs to our serial links.

R1(config)#**int s0/0/0**
R1(config-if)#**ip add 12.12.12.1 255.255.255.252**
R1(config-if)#**clock rate 64000**
R1(config-if)#**no shut**

R2(config)#**int s0/0/0**
R2(config-if)#**ip address 12.12.12.2 255.255.255.252**
R2(config-if)#**no shut**

To enable PPP encapsulation we use the **encapsulation ppp** command on the serial interface.

R1(config)#**int s0/0/0**
R1(config-if)#**encapsulation ppp**

R2(config)#**int s0/0/0**
R2(config-if)#**encapsulation ppp**

And we can ping.

R1#**ping 12.12.12.2**
Type escape sequence to abort.
Sending 5, 100-byte ICMP Echos to 12.12.12.2, timeout is 2 seconds:
!!!!!
Success rate is 100 percent (5/5), round-trip min/avg/max = 4/18/44 ms

CHAP authenticates a peer with the peer's hostname and the configured password for the peer and the authentication is mutual. For example for R2 to authenticate to R1, it needs to have username R1 configured and R1 will need a username R2 configured with a matching password.

R1(config)#**username R2 password 0 cisco**

R2(config)#**username R1 password 0 cisco**

Next we'll make R1 the server by enabling CHAP with the **ppp authentication chap** command under the interface.

R1(config)# **int s0/0/0**
R1(config-if)#**ppp authentication chap**

Looking at the output from a **debug ppp authentication** command, we can see the authentication checking the hostnames.

R1(config)#
*Mar 1 03:59:12.547: Se0/0/0 PPP: Authorization required
*Mar 1 03:59:12.555: Se0/0/0 CHAP: O **CHALLENGE id 68 len 23 from "R1"**
*Mar 1 03:59:12.631: Se0/0/0 CHAP: I **RESPONSE id 68 len 23 from "R2"**
*Mar 1 03:59:12.635: Se0/0/0 PPP: Sent CHAP LOGIN Request
*Mar 1 03:59:12.639: Se0/0/0 PPP: Received LOGIN Response PASS
*Mar 1 03:59:12.643: Se0/0/0 PPP: Sent LCP AUTHOR Request
*Mar 1 03:59:12.647: Se0/0/0 PPP: Sent IPCP AUTHOR Request
*Mar 1 03:59:12.651: Se0/0/0 LCP: Received AAA AUTHOR Response PASS
*Mar 1 03:59:12.651: Se0/0/0 IPCP: Received AAA AUTHOR Response PASS
*Mar 1 03:59:12.655: Se0/0/0 CHAP: O SUCCESS id 68 len 4
*Mar 1 03:59:12.659: Se0/0/0 PPP: Sent CDPCP AUTHOR Request
*Mar 1 03:59:12.663: Se0/0/0 CDPCP: Received AAA AUTHOR Response PASS
*Mar 1 03:59:12.711: Se0/0/0 PPP: Sent IPCP AUTHOR Request

You can also tell CHAP to use/send a different hostname to the server with the **ppp chap hostname** command under the interface. You can also optionally tell CHAP to send a different password as well with **ppp chap password** the router will prefer interface commands over the global defaults. Let's authenticate with the hostname certificationkits and the password cisco.

R2(config)#**int s0/0/0**
R2(config-if)#**ppp chap hostname certificationkits**
R2(config-if)#**ppp chap password cisco**

We'll need to make a user account on R1 so it can authenticate.

R1(config)#**username certificationkits password cisco**

Looking at the output from a **debug ppp authentication** command, we can see it is now authenticating the hostname certificationkits.

R1(config)#
*Mar 1 04:06:26.998: Se0/0/0 PPP: Authorization required
*Mar 1 04:06:27.006: Se0/0/0 CHAP: O CHALLENGE id 69 len 23 from "R1"
*Mar 1 04:06:27.098: Se0/0/0 CHAP: I **RESPONSE id 69 len 30 from "certificationkits"**
*Mar 1 04:06:27.106: Se0/0/0 PPP: Sent CHAP LOGIN Request
*Mar 1 04:06:27.110: Se0/0/0 PPP: Received LOGIN Response PASS
*Mar 1 04:06:27.114: Se0/0/0 PPP: Sent LCP AUTHOR Request
*Mar 1 04:06:27.118: Se0/0/0 PPP: Sent IPCP AUTHOR Request
*Mar 1 04:06:27.122: Se0/0/0 LCP: Received AAA AUTHOR Response PASS
*Mar 1 04:06:27.122: Se0/0/0 IPCP: Received AAA AUTHOR Response PASS
*Mar 1 04:06:27.126: Se0/0/0 CHAP: **O SUCCESS id 69 len 4**

Review Questions:

1. When is CHAP authentication performed? _____
2. What Cisco IOS configuration mode should you be in to enable PPP authentication? _____

Answers:

1. CHAP requires authentication both when the link is initially established and on a periodic basis thereafter. This is awesome because it combats playback attacks and packet sniffing (passwords are not sent).
2. You enable PPP authentication from the interface configuration mode by typing the command 'ppp authentication <chap/pap>'.

HDLC Encapsulation

S0/0/0
*DCE   12.12.12.0/30   S0/0/0
R1   R2

The purpose of this lab is to configure a simple serial link using HDLC encapsulation.

Hardware & Configuration Required for this Lab

- Two routers with one serial port
- One DCE/DTE back to back serial cable

Commands Used in this Lab

clock rate - Used to set the serial clock rate on the DCE end of the connection
show controller - Displays controller level information about interfaces, usually used to determine whether a serial cable is DCE or DTE
encapsulation hdlc - Sets the interface encapsultion to HDLC

Initial Configs - Where you see *Initial Configs,* these are basic configuration steps that by now you should be able to perform on the devices by yourself without us detailing them step by step. Generally you simply go into enable and then configuration mode and start the configuration.

R1
hostname R1
line console 0
logging synch

R2
hostname R2
line console 0
logging synch

HDLC is a very simple open standard serial encapsulation. Unfortunately it was a bit too simple so Cisco (and other vendors) added their own enchancements to the HDLC protocol. The most noteworthy additions is keepalives (yes, the original didn't even support keepalives) and compression options (not really a CCNA topic). Because of the changes, HDLC is now considered a Cisco propriety protocol on Cisco devices, also called Cisco HDLC.

Note: Even though HDLC is considered Cisco proprietry, many vendors such as Juniper support this encapsulation.

HDLC is the default encapsulation for serial links and doesn't have much configuration at all. First let's add the IPs to our serial links.

R1(config)#**int s0/0/0**
R1(config-if)#**ip address 12.12.12.1 255.255.255.252**
R1(config-if)#**no shut**

R2(config)#**int s0/0/0**
R2(config-if)#**ip address 12.12.12.2 255.255.255.252**
R2(config-if)#**no shut**

Next we need to add the **clock rate** command to the DCE end of the serial link. The clock rate command sets the physical clock rate used on the serial links. If you set your clock rate to 128000 bps then it will be impossible for the link to operate above 128 kbs.

The syntax for the command is: **clock rate <bits per second>**

R2(config-if)# **clock rate ?**
With the exception of the following standard values not subject to rounding,
 1200 2400 4800 9600 14400 19200 28800 38400
 56000 64000 128000 2015232
accepted clockrates will be bestfitted (rounded) to the nearest value
supportable by the hardware.
 <246-8064000>   DCE clock rate (bits per second)

Generally speaking in labs you'll use either 64000, 128000, or 2015232 as your clock rate values. We'll use 64000 for this lab. In fact, we can add the **clock rate** on both ends of the link and the DTE router will simply ignore the configuration so it's a good time saver just to enter the value on both routers.

R1(config)#**int s0/0/0**
R1(config-if)#**clock rate 64000**

R2(config)#**int s0/0/0**
R2(config-if)#**clock rate 64000**

Note: On newer IOSs Cisco will automatically default to a 2015232 bps clock rate.

Since Cisco will probably be a bit more picky about clock rate placement you can determine what end of the serial cable is in the router by using the **show controller <interface>** command a ways down it will show the clock rate and the cable type.

R2#**show controllers s0/0/0**
      Interface Serial0/0/0
Hardware is GT96K
DCE V.35, clock rate **64000**
idb at 0x635C7864, driver data structure at 0x635CEF70
wic_info 0x635CF59C
Physical Port 0, SCC Num 0
MPSC Registers:
MMCR_L=0x000304C0, MMCR_H=0x00000000, MPCR=0x00000000
CHR1=0x00FE007E, CHR2=0x00000000, CHR3=0x0000064A, CHR4=0x00000000
CHR5=0x00000000, CHR6=0x00000000, CHR7=0x00000000, CHR8=0x00000000
CHR9=0x00000000, CHR10=0x00003008
SDMA Registers:
SDC=0x00002201, SDCM=0x00000080, SGC=0x0000C000
CRDP=0x074BF140, CTDP=0x074BF390, FTDB=0x074BF390
Main Routing Register=0x00038FC0 BRG Conf Register=0x0005023F
Rx Clk Routing Register=0x76583288 Tx Clk Routing Register=0x76543210
GPP Registers:
(truncated for brevity)

Since that command shows a lot of information that no one really cares about, you can filter the output with **show controller s0/0/0 | in DCE|DTE**. After the pipe, we are including anything that has DCE or DTE on the line, the second pipe is a logical OR.

R1(config)#**do show controller s0/0/0 | in DCE|DTE**
DTE V.35 TX and RX clocks detected.

R2#**show controller serial0/0/0 | in DCE|DTE**
DCE V.35, clock rate **64000**

We should see the interface come up after the clock rates are entered. We can confirm we are using using **HDLC** by looking at **show interfaces**. The output shows the encapsulation is HDLC and the Keepalive (which is Cisco propriety and a great test question is set to 10 seconds).

R1# **show interfaces s0/0/0**
Serial0/0/0 is up, line protocol is up

Hardware is GT96K Serial
Internet address is 12.12.12.1/30
MTU 1500 bytes, BW 1544 Kbit/sec, DLY 20000 usec,
   reliability 255/255, txload 1/255, rxload 1/255
Encapsulation HDLC, loopback not set

Keepalive set (10 sec)
CRC checking enabled
Last input 00:00:06, output 00:00:04, output hang never
Last clearing of "show interface" counters 00:14:00
Input queue: 0/75/0/0 (size/max/drops/flushes); Total output drops: 0
Queueing strategy: weighted fair
Output queue: 0/1000/64/0 (size/max total/threshold/drops)
   Conversations 0/1/256 (active/max active/max total)
   Reserved Conversations 0/0 (allocated/max allocated)
   Available Bandwidth 1158 kilobits/sec
5 minute input rate 0 bits/sec, 0 packets/sec
5 minute output rate 0 bits/sec, 0 packets/sec
   74 packets input, 5330 bytes, 0 no buffer
   Received 74 broadcasts, 0 runts, 0 giants, 0 throttles
   0 input errors, 0 CRC, 0 frame, 0 overrun, 0 ignored, 0 abort
   73 packets output, 5316 bytes, 0 underruns
   0 output errors, 0 collisions, 2 interface resets
   3 unknown protocol drops
   4 unknown protocol drops
   0 output buffer failures, 0 output buffers swapped out
   6 carrier transitions
   DCD=up DSR=up DTR=up RTS=up CTS=up

And we can ping across the interface just fine.
R1#**ping 12.12.12.2**
Type escape sequence to abort.
Sending 5, 100-byte ICMP Echos to 12.12.12.2, timeout is 2 seconds:
!!!!!
Success rate is 100 percent (5/5), round-trip min/avg/max = 4/18/44 ms

If you ever need to change a serial link back to HDLC encapsulation the command
is: **encapsulation hdlc** under the interface.

R1(config)#**int s0/0/0**
R1(config-if)#**encapsulation hdlc**

That is pretty much all you need to know about HDLC.

IPv6 Link Local Addressing

The purpose of this lab is to walk you through how to setup an IPv6 network using Link Local addressing.

Hardware & Configuration Requirements for this Lab

- Two Cisco Routers running an IPv6 capable IOS
- One crossover Cat 5 cable

Commands Used in this Lab

ipv6 enable - Uses IPv6 autoconfiguration to assign a link local address generated with EUI-64
show ipv6 interface brief- Shows a brief summary of configured IPv6 interfaces
show ipv6 route - Shows the IPv6 routing table

Initial Configs - Where you see *Initial Configs,* these are basic configuration steps that by now you should be able to perform on the devices by yourself without us detailing them step by step. Generally you simply go into enable and then configuration mode and start the configuration.

R1
 hostname R1
line console 0
 logging synch

R2
 hostname R2
 line console 0
 logging synch

Link Local addresses is a special type of IPv6 addressing that allows interfaces in your LAN to talk to each other. They are used to provide simple connectivity to hosts and for other IPv6 functions such as provides the host portion to IPv6 autoconfigured addresses. Link Local addresses start with the prefix **FE80** and operates as a point to point link and its addresses aren't kept in the IPv6 routing table. Because of this, there is no need to have unique IPv6 addresses on your router so you could use the same link local address on every interface on your router.

To configure a link local address, you use the **ipv6 address <fe80 prefix> link-local**. Let's configure this on R1 and R2 as well as administratively mark the interface up.

R1(config)#**int fa0/0**
R1(config-if)#**ipv6 address fe80::1 link-local**
R1(config-if)#**no shut**

R2(config)#**int fa0/0**
R2(config-if)#**ipv6 address fe80::2 link-local**
R2(config-if)#**no shut**

We can view the IPv6 address on the interfaces the same way we can check IPv4 addresses except now we use **ipv6** instead of **ip** in the command.

R1(config)#**do show ipv6 interface brief**
FastEthernet0/0   [up/up]

   FE80::1
FastEthernet0/1   [administratively down/down]
Serial0/0/0   [administratively down/down]
Serial0/0/1   [administratively down/down]

R2(config-if)#**do show ipv6 interface brief**
FastEthernet0/0   [up/up]

   FE80::2
FastEthernet0/1   [administratively down/down]
Serial0/0/0   [administratively down/down]
Serial0/0/1   [administratively down/down]

We can ping across the link now, notice that we need to specify the outgoing interface as the link local addresses don't appear in the routing table.

R1(config)#**do ping fe80::2**
Output Interface: **fastethernet0/0**
Type escape sequence to abort.
Sending 5, 100-byte ICMP Echos to FE80::2, timeout is 2 seconds:
Packet sent with a source address of FE80::1

!!!!!
Success rate is 100 percent (5/5), round-trip min/avg/max = 0/1/4 ms

Also it's handy to know that Cisco hasn't made IPv6 entirely friendly yet. For example, when pinging link local addresses, you must type the full interface name you are sending the packet out of.

R1(config)#**do ping fe80::2**
Output Interface: **fa0/0**
% Invalid interface. Use full interface name without spaces (e.g. Serial0/1)

Checking the IPv6 routing table we can see that the prefix **FE80::/10** is being sent to the Null0 interface. The Null0 interface is a special virtual interface that simply discards all traffic silently.

R1(config)#**do show ipv6 route**
IPv6 Routing Table - 1 entries
Codes: C - Connected, L - Local, S - Static, R - RIP, B - BGP
     U - Per-user Static route
     I1 - ISIS L1, I2 - ISIS L2, IA - ISIS interarea, IS - ISIS summary
     O - OSPF intra, OI - OSPF inter, OE1 - OSPF ext 1, OE2 - OSPF ext 2
     ON1 - OSPF NSSA ext 1, ON2 - OSPF NSSA ext 2
L FF00::/8 [0/0]
     via ::, Null0

IPv6 EUI-64 Addressing

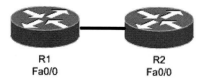

R1
Fa0/0

R2
Fa0/0

The purpose of this lab is to walk you through how to setup an IPv6 network using EUI-64 autoconfiguration.

Hardware & Configuration Required for this Lab

- Two Cisco Routers running an IPv6 capable IOS
- One crossover Cat 5 cable

Commands Used in Lab

ipv6 enable - Uses IPv6 autoconfiguration to assign a link local address generated with EUI-64
show ipv6 interface brief- Shows a brief summary of configured IPv6 interfaces
show ipv6 route - Shows the IPv6 routing table

Initial Configs - Where you see *Initial Configs,* these are basic configuration steps that by now you should be able to perform on the devices by yourself without us detailing them step by step. Generally you simply go into enable and then configuration mode and start the configuration. We will let you figure out the cabling by reading the configs.

R1
hostname R1
line console 0
logging synch

R2
hostname R2
line console 0
logging synch

To configure dynamic link local addresses on an interface you just need to use the **ipv6 enable** command. The command takes a link-local prefix **FE80** and generates a host portion of the address using EUI-64. EUI-64 is created from the interface MAC address or the router's pool of mac-addresses if the interface does not have a mac address such as loopbacks or serial interfaces. Once a mac address is chosen, the router adds **FFFE** in between the vendor-id (3 most significant bytes) and the extension-id (least 3 significant bytes). The next step is to invert the 7th most significant bit (the universal/local bit) and remove any leading zeros.

In the example of R1's Fa0/0 it has a mac address of: 0015.C6E2.7F20 to convert this MAC address to a EUI-64 address it would be through the following steps. First find out the mac-address on your Fa0/0 interface with the **show interface** command, you can filter to include **bia** to reduce the output.

R1(config)#**do show int fa0/0 | in bia**
  Hardware is Lance, address is **0015.c6e2.7f20** (bia 0015.c6e2.7f20)

1. Add **FFFE** between the vendor-id and extension-id 0015.C6**FF.FE**E2.7F20
2. Invert the 7th bit. Each hex number represents a nibble (4 bits) **00** is 00000000 so the 7th bit is currently 0, inverting it it is now a one. 000000**10** = **02** making the address **02**15.C6**FF.FE**E2.7F20
3. Next we will remove any leading zeros and convert the decimals to colons. Making the address **2**15.C6**FF.FE**E2.7F20
4. Finally we need to add the **FE80::** prefix to the address making the final address: FE80::**2**15.C6**FF.FE**E2.7F20

R1(config)#**int fa0/0**
R1(config-if)#**ipv6 enable**

We can view the IPv6 addresses on the router with **show ipv6 interface brief.**
Note: Most of the IPv6 commands simply use the ipv6 keyword instead of the ip keyword in the commands you have been using in other labs.

R1(config)#**do show ipv6 interface brief**
FastEthernet0/0   [up/up]
  FE80::215:C6FF:FEE2:7F20
FastEthernet0/1   [administratively down/down]
Serial0/0/0   [administratively down/down]
Serial0/0/1   [administratively down/down]

Let's work through this again with R2's Fa0/0 interface.

R2(config)#**do show interface fa0/0 | in bia**
  Hardware is AmdFE, address is 0012.80cb.e8e0 (bia 0012.80cb.e8e0)

1. Add **FFFE** between the vendor-id and extension-id 0012.80**FF.FE**CB.E8E0
2. Invert the 7th bit. Each hex number represents a nibble (4 bits) **00** is 0000000**0** so the 7th bit is currently 0, inverting it it is now a one. 0000001**0** = **02** making the address 0212.80**FF.FE**CB.E8E0
3. Next we will remove any leading zeros and convert the decimals to colons. Making the address 212.80**FF.FE**CB.E8E0
4. Finally we need to add the **FE80::** prefix to the address making the final address: FE80::212.80**FF.FE**CB.E8E0

R2(config)#**int fa0/0**
R2(config-if)#**ipv6 enable**

And we'll verify the address we get with the **show ipv6 interface brief** command on R2.

R2(config)#**do sh ipv6 int br**
FastEthernet0/0   [up/up]
  FE80::212:80FF:FECB:E8E0
FastEthernet0/1   [administratively down/down]
Serial0/0/0   [administratively down/down]
Serial0/0/1   [administratively down/down]

We can ping just fine. Notice that we have to specify the output interface this is because link-local addresses are only locally significant to the interface (not globally unique). Thus they don't exist in the routing table so it's effectively a point to point link.

R2#**ping FE80::215:C6FF:FEE2:7F20**
Output Interface: fastethernet0/0
Type escape sequence to abort.
Sending 5, 100-byte ICMP Echos to FE80::215:C6FF:FEE2:7F20, timeout is 2 seconds:
Packet sent with a source address of FE80::212:80FF:FECB:E8E0
!!!!!
Success rate is 100 percent (5/5), round-trip min/avg/max = 0/2/4 ms

Checking the IPv6 routing table with **show ipv6 route** we can see that Fa0/0 doesn't exist in the routing table and by default all link local addresses are discarded (sent to the Null0 interface).

R2#**show ipv6 route**
IPv6 Routing Table - 1 entries
Codes: C - Connected, L - Local, S - Static, R - RIP, B - BGP

```
     U - Per-user Static route
     I1 - ISIS L1, I2 - ISIS L2, IA - ISIS interarea, IS - ISIS summary
     O - OSPF intra, OI - OSPF inter, OE1 - OSPF ext 1, OE2 - OSPF ext 2
     ON1 - OSPF NSSA ext 1, ON2 - OSPF NSSA ext 2
L   FF00::/8 [0/0]
     via ::, Null0
```

IPv6 Site Local Addressing

The purpose of this lab is to walk you through how to setup an IPv6 network using Link Local addressing.

Hardware & Configuration Required for this Lab

- Two Cisco Routers running an IPv6 capable IOS
- One crossover Cat 5 cable

Commands Used in Lab

ipv6 enable - Uses IPv6 autoconfiguration to assign a link local address generated with EUI-64
show ipv6 interface brief- Shows a brief summary of configured IPv6 interfaces
show ipv6 route - Shows the IPv6 routing table

Initial Configs - Where you see *Initial Configs,* these are basic configuration steps that by now you should be able to perform on the devices by yourself without us detailing them step by step. Generally you simply go into enable and then configuration mode and start the configuration.

R1
hostname R1
line console 0
logging synch

R2
hostname R2
line console 0
logging synch

Site-local addresses act similar to IPv4's private addresses in that they are not routed globally. Although, recently, site-local addresses were removed from the IPv6 standard. Consequently, in future versions of IOS, it is possible that the feature may be removed entirely. It is more likely that Cisco and other vendors will keep the functionality as a proprietry feature since the debate about whether or not to include private addressing and NAT into IPv6 still rages on. If you wish to read more about the deprecation of site-local addresses, you can read RFC 3879: Deprecating Site Local Addresses. Site local addresses use the prefix **FEC0::/10**.

To configure a link local address you use the **ipv6 address <FEC0 prefix> <slash notation>.** Let's configure this on R1 and R2.

R1(config)#**int fa0/0**
R1(config-if)#**ipv6 address fec0::1/64**
R1(config-if)#**no shut**

R2(config)#**int fa0/0**
R2(config-if)#**ipv6 address fec0::2/64**
R2(config-if)#**no shut**

Checking **show ipv6 interface brief** we can see our site local addresses. Notice that the router automatically assigns a Link Local address using EUI-64.

R1(config)#**do show ipv6 int br**
FastEthernet0/0   [up/up]
   FE80::215:C6FF:FEE2:7F20
   FEC0::1
FastEthernet0/1   [administratively down/down]
Serial0/0/0   [administratively down/down]
Serial0/0/1   [administratively down/down]
Vlan1   [administratively down/down]

R2(config)#**do show ipv6 int br**
FastEthernet0/0   [up/up]
   FE80::212:80FF:FECB:E8E0
   FEC0::2
FastEthernet0/1   [administratively down/down]
Serial0/0/0   [administratively down/down]
Serial0/0/1   [administratively down/down]
Vlan1   [administratively down/down]

We can ping across the link using the site-local address. These address types are kept in the routing table so we can ping them without specifying an interface.

R1(config)#**do ping fec0::2**

Type escape sequence to abort.
Sending 5, 100-byte ICMP Echos to FEC0::2, timeout is 2 seconds:
!!!!!
Success rate is 100 percent (5/5), round-trip min/avg/max = 0/1/4 ms

Checking the IPv6 routing table this time we can see we have a connected interface for the **FEC0::/64** network and also a Local route that has Fa0/0's IPv6 address.

R1(config)#**do show ipv6 route**
IPv6 Routing Table - 3 entries
Codes: C - Connected, L - Local, S - Static, R - RIP, B - BGP
    U - Per-user Static route
    I1 - ISIS L1, I2 - ISIS L2, IA - ISIS interarea, IS - ISIS summary
    O - OSPF intra, OI - OSPF inter, OE1 - OSPF ext 1, OE2 - OSPF ext 2
    ON1 - OSPF NSSA ext 1, ON2 - OSPF NSSA ext 2
C **FEC0::/64 [0/0]**
   via ::, FastEthernet0/0
L **FEC0::1/128 [0/0]**
   via ::, FastEthernet0/0
L FF00::/8 [0/0]
   via ::, Null0

We can also use EUI-64 to configure the host portion of our site local addresses by adding the **eui-64** keyword at the end of the address.

R1(config)#**int fa0/0**
R1(config-if)#**ipv6 add fec0::/64 eui-64**

Now we have a new FEC0 address that was generated from the link-local address. Also notice that we still have **FEC0::1/64** configured because IPv6 allows many different IPs on the same interface.

Note: The EUI-64 keyword actually uses the link local address for its host portion. If you manually change the link local address, you will generate a different address.

R1(config)#**do show ipv6 int br**
FastEthernet0/0   [up/up]
  FE80::215:C6FF:FEE2:7F20
  FEC0::1
  FEC0::215:C6FF:FEE2:7F20
FastEthernet0/1   [administratively down/down]
Serial0/0/0   [administratively down/down]
Serial0/0/1   [administratively down/down]

Let's clear the configuration on Fa0/0 and try this out.

R1(config)#**default int fa0/0**
Building configuration...
Interface FastEthernet0/0 set to default configuration

We'll change the link-local to be FE80::100 and use the site-local network:
FEC0:555:AAAA/64

R1(config)#**int fa0/0**
R1(config-if)#**ipv6 address fe80::100 link-local**
R1(config-if)#**ipv6 address fec0:555:aaaa::/64 eui-64**

Checking the IPv6 address, we end up with we can see that ::100 is our host portion of the site local address.

R1(config)#**do show ipv6 int br**
FastEthernet0/0   [up/up]
    FE80::100
    FEC0:555:AAAA::100
FastEthernet0/1   [administratively down/down]
Serial0/0/0   [administratively down/down]
Serial0/0/1   [administratively down/down]

IPv6 Global Addressing

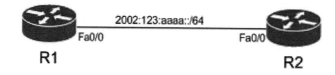

The purpose of this lab is to walk you through how to setup an IPv6 network using Global addressing.

Hardware & Configuration Required for this Lab

- Two Cisco Routers running an IPv6 capable IOS.
- One crossover Cat 5 cable

Commands Used in Lab

ipv6 enable - Uses IPv6 autoconfiguration to assign a link local address generated with EUI-64

show ipv6 interface brief- Shows a brief summary of configured IPv6 interfaces

show ipv6 route - Shows the IPv6 routing table

Initial Configs - Where you see *Initial Configs,* these are basic configuration steps that by now you should be able to perform on the devices by yourself without us detailing them step by step. Generally you simply go into enable and then configuration mode and start the configuration.

R1
hostname R1
line console 0
logging synch

R2
hostname R2
line console 0
logging synch

Global addresses are the same as IPv4's global/public IP addresses in that they are both reachable via the internet. They currently use the prefix **2000::/3**. As an interesting side note, the current global range of **2000::/3** is only 1/8 of the total amount of addresses:**42,535,295,865,117,307,932,921,825,928,971,000,000**

EUI-64 is created from the interface MAC address or the router's pool of mac-addresses if it does not have a mac address (ie: loopbacks and serial interfaces). Once a mac address is chosen, the router adds **FFFE** in between the vendor-id (3 most significant bytes) and the extension-id (least 3 significant bytes). The next step is to invert the 7th most significant bit (the universal/local bit) and remove any leading zeros.

```
R1(config)#int fa0/0
R1(config-if)#ipv6 address 2002:123:aaaa::/64 eui-64
R1(config-if)#no shut

R2(config)#int fa0/0
R2(config-if)#ipv6 address 2002:123:aaaa::/64 eui-64
R2(config-if)#no shut
```

Checking **show ipv6 interface brief** we can see our site local addresses. Notice that the router automatically assigns a Link Local address using EUI-64.

```
R1(config-if)#do show ipv6 int br
FastEthernet0/0        [up/up]
   FE80::215:C6FF:FEE2:7F20
   2002:123:AAAA:0:215:C6FF:FEE2:7F20
FastEthernet0/1        [administratively down/down]
Serial0/0/0            [administratively down/down]
Serial0/0/1            [administratively down/down]


R2(config-if)#do show ipv6 int br
FastEthernet0/0        [up/up]
   FE80::212:80FF:FECB:E8E0
   2002:123:AAAA:0:212:80FF:FECB:E8E0
FastEthernet0/1        [administratively down/down]
Serial0/0/0            [administratively down/down]
Serial0/0/1            [administratively down/down]
```

We can ping across the link using the global address.
```
R1(config)#do ping 2002:123:AAAA:0:212:80FF:FECB:E8E0
Type escape sequence to abort.
Sending 5, 100-byte ICMP Echos to 2002:123:AAAA:0:212:80FF:FECB:E8E0, timeout is 2 seconds:
!!!!!
Success rate is 100 percent (5/5), round-trip min/avg/max = 0/1/4 ms
```
Checking the IPv6 routing table this time we can see we have a connected interface for the **2002:123:AAAA/64** network and also a Local route that has Fa0/0's IPv6 address.

R1(config)#**do show ipv6 route**
IPv6 Routing Table - 3 entries
Codes: C - Connected, L - Local, S - Static, R - RIP, B - BGP
　　　U - Per-user Static route
　　　I1 - ISIS L1, I2 - ISIS L2, IA - ISIS interarea, IS - ISIS summary
　　　O - OSPF intra, OI - OSPF inter, OE1 - OSPF ext 1, OE2 - OSPF ext 2
　　　ON1 - OSPF NSSA ext 1, ON2 - OSPF NSSA ext 2
C　2002:123:AAAA::/64 [0/0]
　via ::, FastEthernet0/0
L　2002:123:AAAA:0:215:C6FF:FEE2:7F20/128 [0/0]
　　via ::, FastEthernet0/0
L　FF00::/8 [0/0]
　　via ::, Null0

Configuring EIGRP IPv6 Routing

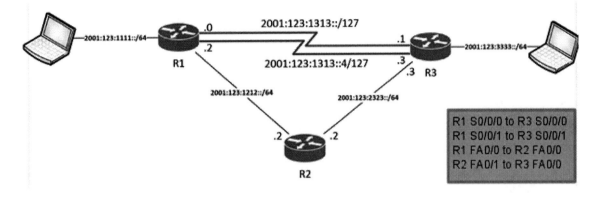

The purpose of this lab is to explore the functionality of routing IPv6 using EIGRP.

Hardware & Configuration Required for this Lab

- Two Cisco routers with two Fast Ethernet interfaces and two serial ports
- One Cisco router with two Fast Ethernet interfaces
- Two crossover Cat 5 cables
- Two DTE/DCE back to back cables
- Two PCs to connect to the routers
- Two straight through Cat 5 cables
- IOS 15.1 Advanced IP Services IOS
- **Special Note:** If you do not have three routers with dual Ethernet ports and two PCs, it's ok. Simply configure the 192.168.11.0 subnet on R1 and the 192.168.33.0 subnet on R3 on loopbacks. Then do your pings from R1 & R3 sourced from the loopback interfaces respectively in place of the PCs and the lab will still work fine.

Commands Used in this Lab

ipv6 unicast-routing – Enables IPv6 routing on the router, by default IPv6 is disabled.
ipv6 router eigrp <as#> – Enables the IPv6 EIGRP routing process under the specified AS#
show ipv6 eigrp neighbor – Displays any EIGRP neighbor information.
show ipv6 eigrp topology - Displays the eigrp topology table and route information
show ipv6 interface brief - Displays IPv6 interface information.
show ipv6 route - Displays the IPv6 routing table.
clock rate – Sets clock speed on a WAN serial link
bandwidth – Logial setting of the bandwidth metric on a link

delay – Logical setting of the delay metric on a link
variance <multiplier> - Used to tell the router what multiple of the feasible distance should be considered for unequal load balancing
ipv6 hello-interval eigrp – sets the hello time on an eigrp interface
ipv6 hold-time eigrp – sets the hold time on an eirgrp interface
debug ipv6 eigrp – Displays route table updates and associated messages

---

Inital Configs - Where you see *Initial Configs,* these are basic configuration steps that by now you should be able to perform on the devices by yourself without us detailing them step by step. Generally you simply go into enable and then configuration mode and start the configuration. **Note:** If your interfaces don't match the configs, simply change the interface names to what matches your lab.

R1

```
hostname R1
line con 0
logging synch
!
interface FastEthernet0/0
 ipv6 address FE80::1 link-local
 ipv6 address 2001:123:1212::/64 eui-64
 no shut
!
interface FastEthernet0/1
 ipv6 address FE80::1 link-local
 ipv6 address 2001:123:1111::/64 eui-64
 no shut
!
interface Serial0/0/0
 ipv6 address FE80::1 link-local
 ipv6 address 2001:123:1313::/127
 clock rate 128000
 no shut
!
interface Serial0/0/1
 ipv6 address FE80::1 link-local
 ipv6 address 2001:123:1313::2/127
 clock rate 128000
 no shut
```

R2

```
hostname R2
line con 0
logging synch
!
interface FastEthernet0/0
ipv6 address FE80::2 link-local
ipv6 address 2001:123:1212::/64 eui-64
no shut
!
interface FastEthernet0/1
ipv6 address FE80::2 link-local
ipv6 address 2001:123:2323::/64 eui-64
no shut
```

R3

```
hostname R3
line con 0
logging synch
!
interface FastEthernet0/0
 ipv6 address FE80::3 link-local
 ipv6 address 2001:123:2323::/64 eui-64
 no shut
!
interface FastEthernet0/1
 ipv6 address FE80::3 link-local
 ipv6 address 2001:123:3333::/64 eui-64
 no shut
!
interface Serial0/0/0
ipv6 address FE80::3 link-local
 ipv6 address 2001:123:1313::1/127
 no shut
!
interface Serial0/0/1
 ipv6 address FE80::3 link-local
 ipv6 address 2001:123:1313::3/127
 no shut
```

IPV6 Addressing and EUI-64

When a router interface is configured with an IPv6 prefix, it will either use the configured fe80 prefix as its link local address or it will use the EUI-64 process to generate the link local address for the interface.

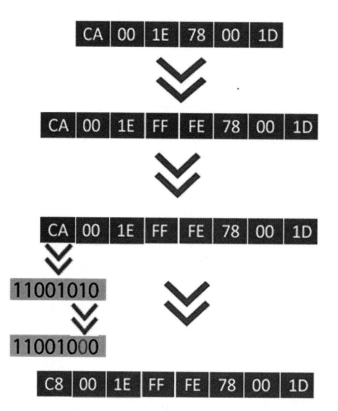

Here is a quick IPv6 review of how IPv6 generates EUI-64 addresses.

1) First we need to determine the configured mac-address on an interface.

Note: Obviously the mac-address will be different on your router compared to ours and therefore you will wind up with a different IPv6 address. If you want to follow along exactly, you can use the mac-address command under the interface to get the same IPv6 ☺

R1#**show int fa0/0 | include address**
  Hardware is i82543 (Livengood), address is **ca00.1e78.001d** (bia ca00.1e78.001d)

2) Then we break the mac address into two 24 bit halves and add the prefix **FFEE** onto the middle portion. Why FFEE? It is simply to identify to the world that it is a EUI-64 address.

3) Take the 7th bit and invert it. In the diagram above, CA becomes C8 in our address. The reason we invert the bit is to help generate addresses on interfaces that don't natively have mac addresses. For example: Serial links, tunnels, and loopbacks.

If everything worked out the way we think it will, the resulting EUI-64 address should match my diagram.

R1(config)#**int fa0/0**
R1(config-if)#**ipv6 address 2001:123:1212::/64 eui-64**

The link local address is now in turn used to generate the prefix end of the EUI-64 address.

R1#**show ipv6 int br f0/0**

FastEthernet0/0   [up/up]
　 FE80::C800:1EFF:FE78:1D
　 2001:123:1212:0:C800:1EFF:FE78:1D

Windows PC Auto-configuration

By default computers running a modern Windows OS (Vista or higher) will attempt to use IPv6 auto configuration or DHCPv6 to assign itself an IPv6 address. DHCPv6 is similar to the same old DHCP configurations except you use the `ipv6 dhcp pool <name>` to configure it. Auto-configuration is new with IPv6 and its goal to allow the device to contact its upstream router and configure itself with an IPv6 address and gateway. This works by using IPv6 Neighbor Discovery to generate an IPv6 address by using Router Advertisements (RA) and Router Solicitation (RS).

When you configure an IPv6 address on an interface and bring it up, it first runs a Duplicate Address Detection (DUD) check on its link local address to make sure it is unique on the network segment. Once DUD gives the all clear, Network Discovery sends a RA out the interface for any downstream devices.

R1(config)#**int fa0/1**
R1(config-if)#**ipv6 address 2001:123:1111::/64 eui-64**
R1(config-if)# **ipv6 address fe80::1 link-local**
R1(config-if)#**no keep**
R1(config-if)#**no shut**

%LINK-3-UPDOWN: Interface FastEthernet0/1, changed state to up
%LINEPROTO-5-UPDOWN: Line protocol on Interface FastEthernet0/1, changed state to up
ICMPv6-ND: L2 came up on FastEthernet0/1
IPv6-Addrmgr-ND: DAD request for FE80::1 on FastEthernet0/1
IPv6-Addrmgr-ND: DAD: FE80::1 is unique.

Then it does the same thing with the full IPv6 prefix.

ICMPv6-ND: Sending NA for FE80::1 on FastEthernet0/1
ICMPv6-ND: L3 came up on FastEthernet0/1
IPv6-Addrmgr-ND: DAD request for 2001:123:1111::1 on FastEthernet0/1
IPv6-Addrmgr-ND: DAD: 2001:123:1111::1 is unique.
ICMPv6-ND: Sending NA for 2001:123:1111::1 on FastEthernet0/1
ICMPv6-ND: Linklocal FE80::1 on FastEthernet0/1, Up
ICMPv6-ND: Received NA for FE80::1 on FastEthernet0/1 from FE80::1
ICMPv6-ND: Received NA for 2001:123:1111::1 on FastEthernet0/1 from 2001:123:1111::1

By default a Cisco router won't do IPV6 auto-configuration unless you tell it to on an interface by interface basis. Also *ipv6 unicast-routing* is required for this to work. See the below commands to enable IPv6 on your interfaces connecting your workstations. If you are using loopbacks instead of real machines, you won't be able to follow along in this section very easily. However this is really out of scope for CCNA and it is just an interesting tidbit.

R1(config)#**ipv6 unicast-routing**
R1(config)#**int fa0/1**
R1(config-if)#**ipv6 nd autoconfig prefix**
R1(config-if)#**ipv6 nd autoconfig default-route** (must be running IOS 15 for this command to work and the lab to fully work and to see all the routes)

The router will then generate an RA and send it out the interface to the FF02::1 address

ICMPv6-ND: Created RA context for FE80::1
ICMPv6-ND: Request to send RA for FE80::1
ICMPv6-ND: Sending RA from FE80::1 to FF02::1 on FastEthernet0/1
ICMPv6-ND: MTU = 1500
ICMPv6-ND: prefix = 2001:123:1111::/64 onlink autoconfig
ICMPv6-ND: 2592000/604800 (valid/preferred)

Once a host requests an IPv6 address, it sends a NS along with its link local and the router sends back the prefix info.

ICMPv6-ND: Received NS for FE80::1 on FastEthernet0/1 from FE80::20C:29FF:FEC8:3E64
ICMPv6-ND: Sending NA for FE80::1 on FastEthernet0/1

On the Windows side of things, the interfaces will automatically request IPv6 addresses so you don't have to configure that portion.

That being said, by default Windows doesn't follow the EUI-64 standard and instead generates a unique identifier that it uses to generate the IPv6 prefix. If you want to have the Windows host follow the address standard that your routers will use, simply start up a command prompt (Run as administrator) and enter the following commands and then reboot your computer.

netsh interface ipv6 set privacy state=disabled store=active
netsh interface ipv6 set privacy state=disabled store=persistent
netsh interface ipv6 set global randomizeidentifiers=disabled store=active
netsh interface ipv6 set global randomizeidentifiers=disabled store=persistent

Once the computer is back up it should get a proper EUI-64 address

EIGRP has been updated to IPv6 along with all the other modern routing protocols. While the basic logic of EIGRP has not been changed in IPv6 EIGRP, it does have a few surprises.

The biggest change is that EIGRP (and all other IPV6 routing protocols) is they are now configured under the interface instead by using a network statement. This may have been an act of mercy for those worried about writing IPv6 network statements for each of their networks ☺.

Before you can do any IPv6 routing, you first need to enable it on the router with the *ipv6 unicast-routing* command. This is because running IPv4 and IPv6 on a router at the same time can be fairly taxing on the processor. So Cisco wants you enable it only when it is needed. If you try to configure EIGRP without enabling routing you will get this helpful message.

R2(config)#**ipv6 router eigrp 123**

% IPv6 routing not enabled

Now that routing has been enabled, you need to define your EIGRP AS number with ipv6 router eigrp <AS>

Note: The same rules apply in IPv6 as it does in IPv4's plain old EIGRP. For peering to happen, the routers in the network need to be in the same locally significant AS number.

Next under each interface you want in EIGRP you need to add the command
ipv6 eigrp <AS>

Let's go ahead and configure EIGRP for our network.

R1

R1(config)#**ipv6 unicast-routing**
R1(config)#**ipv6 router eigrp 123**
R1(config-rtr)#**no shut**
R1(config-rtr)#**int fa0/0**
R1(config-if)#**ipv6 eigrp 123**
R1(config-if)#**int fa0/1**
R1(config-if)#**ipv6 eigrp 123**
R1(config-if)#**int s0/0/0**
R1(config-if)#**ipv6 eigrp 123**
R1(config-if)#**int s0/0/1**
R1(config-if)#**ipv6 eigrp 123**
R1(config-if)#**exit**

R2

R2(config)#**ipv6 unicast-routing**
R2(config)#**ipv6 router eigrp 123**
R2(config-rtr)#**no shut**
R2(config-rtr)#**int fa0/0**
R2(config-if)#**ipv6 eigrp 123**
R2(config-if)#**int fa0/1**
R2(config-if)#**ipv6 eigrp 123**
R2(config-if)#**exit**

R3

R3(config)#**ipv6 unicast-routing**
R3(config)#**ipv6 router eigrp 123**
R3(config-rtr)#**no shut**
R3(config-rtr)#**int fa0/0**
R3(config-if)#**ipv6 eigrp 123**
R3(config-if)#**int fa0/1**
R3(config-if)#**ipv6 eigrp 123**
R3(config-if)#**int s0/0/0**
R3(config-if)#**ipv6 eigrp 123**
R3(config-if)#**int s0/0/1**
R3(config-if)#**ipv6 eigrp 123**

As you saw in the IPv4 lab, EIGRP is a very fast protocol. However you will notice that in this lab peering doesn't appear to be working at all. That's weird. Let's see if we can figure out what is wrong.

R1(config)#**do ping 2001:123:1212::2**

Type escape sequence to abort.
Sending 5, 100-byte ICMP Echos to 2001:123:1212::2, timeout is 2 seconds:
!!!!!
Success rate is 100 percent (5/5), round-trip min/avg/max = 12/20/36 ms

R1(config)#**do ping 2001:123:1313::1**

Type escape sequence to abort.
Sending 5, 100-byte ICMP Echos to 2001:123:1313::1, timeout is 2 seconds:
!!!!!
Success rate is 100 percent (5/5), round-trip min/avg/max = 16/26/40 ms

R1(config)#**do ping 2001:123:1313::3**

Type escape sequence to abort.

Sending 5, 100-byte ICMP Echos to 2001:123:1313::3, timeout is 2 seconds:
!!!!!
Success rate is 100 percent (5/5), round-trip min/avg/max = 12/24/32 ms

Hmm, so we appear to have configured our IPv6 addresses correctly.
Note: The reason why we have manually set the link local to be FE80::x where x is the router number is it makes things easier to follow then having to ping random EUI-64 addresses.

Let's try checking the IPv6 neighbor status with *show ipv6 eigrp neighbor*

R1#show ipv6 eigrp neighbors
IPv6-EIGRP neighbors for process 123
% No router ID for EIGRP 123

No Router-ID is our problem.   Recall that EIGRP's router-id is 32 bit and it automatically utilizes the highest loopback IPv4 or the highest IPv4 address on the router if there is no loopback present.
This is unchanged in the IPv6 version, but that presents a bit of a problem because in our lab we don't have any IP addresses for EIGRP to use. To fix this, we can either define a loopback interface on each router or we can manual define the EIGRP router-id under the routing process. We will define the ID manually with the *eigrp router-id* command.

R1
R1(config)#**ipv6 router eigrp 123**
R1(config-rtr)#**eigrp router-id 1.1.1.1**

R2
R2(config)#**ipv6 router eigrp 123**
R2(config-rtr)#**eigrp router-id 2.2.2.2**

R3
R3(config)#**ipv6 router eigrp 123**
R3(config-rtr)#**eigrp router-id 3.3.3.3**

Pretty much as soon as we finish entering in the router-ids we see adjacency messages.

R1
%DUAL-5-NBRCHANGE: EIGRP-IPv6 123: Neighbor FE80::2 (FastEthernet0/0) is up: new adjacency
R1(config-rtr)#
%DUAL-5-NBRCHANGE: EIGRP-IPv6 123: Neighbor FE80::3 (Serial0/0/0) is up: new adjacency
%DUAL-5-NBRCHANGE: EIGRP-IPv6 123: Neighbor FE80::3 (Serial0/0/1) is up: new adjacency

R2
*May 11 16:37:41.195: %DUAL-5-NBRCHANGE: EIGRP-IPv6 123: Neighbor FE80::1 (FastEthernet0/0) is up: new adjacency
R2(config-rtr)#

*May 11 16:37:54.783: %DUAL-5-NBRCHANGE: EIGRP-IPv6 123: Neighbor FE80::3
(FastEthernet0/1) is up: new adjacency

R3
*May 11 16:37:54.455: %DUAL-5-NBRCHANGE: EIGRP-IPv6 123: Neighbor FE80::1 (Serial0/0/1)
is up: new adjacency
*May 11 16:37:54.499: %DUAL-5-NBRCHANGE: EIGRP-IPv6 123: Neighbor FE80::2
(FastEthernet0/0) is up: new adjacency
*May 11 16:37:54.527: %DUAL-5-NBRCHANGE: EIGRP-IPv6 123: Neighbor FE80::1 (Serial0/0/0)
is up: new adjacency

EIGRP also can use the **show ipv6 protocol** command to show a quick summary of EIGRP
information.

R1#**show ipv6 protocols**
IPv6 Routing Protocol is "connected"
IPv6 Routing Protocol is "static
IPv6 Routing Protocol is "eigrp 123 "
  EIGRP metric weight K1=1, K2=0, K3=1, K4=0, K5=0
  EIGRP maximum hopcount 100
  EIGRP maximum metric variance 1
  Interfaces:
    FastEthernet0/0
    FastEthernet0/1
    Serial0/0/0
    Serial0/0/1
Redistributing: eigrp 123
  Maximum path: 16
  Distance: internal 90 external 170

A handy command to see what adjacencies are up and running is: **show ipv6 eigrp
neighbors**. Just like its IPv4 counterpart, you can use the command to see any EIGRP
adjacencies as well as the queue count which can indicant network issues if the value is
ever above 0. One interesting thing to note is that routing protocols peer with the link
local address of its neighbor. Not the full IPv6 prefix, this is another reason why in labs
it is not a bad idea to manually set the link local address to something that is easy to
figure out for you.

R1# **show ipv6 eigrp neighbors**
IPv6-EIGRP neighbors for process 123

H	Address	Interface	Hold Uptime	SRTT	RTO	Q	Seq
		(sec)	(ms)	Cnt		Num	
2	Link-local address:	Se0/0/1	12 00:00:48	24	200	0	13
	FE80::3						
1	Link-local address:	Se0/0/0	12 00:00:48	24	200	0	14
	FE80::3						

```
0   Link-local address:    Fa0/0        11 00:01:18  6  300  0  9
    FE80::2
```

You can also use **show ipv6 eigrp interfaces** to see a quick summary of what interfaces are running EIGRP and how many peers are learned on each interface.

```
R1#show ipv6 eigrp interfaces
IPv6-EIGRP interfaces for process 123
                Xmit Queue  Mean  Pacing Time  Multicast  Pending
Interface   Peers  Un/Reliable  SRTT  Un/Reliable  Flow Timer  Routes
Fa0/0        1     0/0       6    0/1       50       0
Fa0/1        0     0/0       0    0/1        0       0
Se0/0/0      1     0/0      24    0/15      79       0
Se0/0/1      1     0/0      24    0/15      95       0
```

Another helpful show command is: **show ipv6 eigrp traffic** which shows traffic statistics for EIGRP.

```
R1#show ipv6 eigrp traffic
IPv6-EIGRP Traffic Statistics for process 123
  Hellos sent/received: 527/395
  Updates sent/received: 8/5
  Queries sent/received: 0/0
  Replies sent/received:  0/0
  Acks sent/received:  5/8
  Input queue high water mark 1, 0 drops
  SIA-Queries sent/received: 0/0
  SIA-Replies sent/received: 0/0
```

Now it's time to finally look at the IPv6 routing table. The output is similar to the IPv4 routing table with the notable exception of the next hop field points to a link local IPv6 address instead of the full IPv6 address. Once again this is because routers peer with the link local address instead of the globally routable one. Also because IPv6 EIGRP is a new protocol, it does not have any concept of classful routing and therefore there is no auto-summarization to worry about. However you still can do manual summarization if you have a need to do so in your network or future labs.

```
R1#show ipv6 route
IPv6 Routing Table - default - 12 entries
Codes: C - Connected, L - Local, S - Static, U - Per-user Static route
       B - BGP, M - MIPv6, R - RIP, I1 - ISIS L1
       I2 - ISIS L2, IA - ISIS interarea, IS - ISIS summary, D - EIGRP
       EX - EIGRP external, ND - Neighbor Discovery
       O - OSPF Intra, OI - OSPF Inter, OE1 - OSPF ext 1, OE2 - OSPF ext 2
       ON1 - OSPF NSSA ext 1, ON2 - OSPF NSSA ext 2
S   ::/0 [2/0]
```

```
       via FE80::1, FastEthernet0/1
C   2001:123:1111::/64 [0/0]
       via FastEthernet0/1, directly connected
L   2001:123:1111::1/128 [0/0]
       via FastEthernet0/1, receive
C   2001:123:1212::/64 [0/0]
       via FastEthernet0/0, directly connected
L   2001:123:1212::1/128 [0/0]
       via FastEthernet0/0, receive
C   2001:123:1313::/127 [0/0]
       via Serial0/0/0, directly connected
L   2001:123:1313::/128 [0/0]
       via Serial0/0/0, receive
C   2001:123:1313::2/127 [0/0]
       via Serial0/0/1, directly connected
L   2001:123:1313::2/128 [0/0]
       via Serial0/0/1, receive
D   2001:123:2323::/64 [90/30720]
       via FE80::2, FastEthernet0/0
D   2001:123:3333::/64 [90/33280]
       via FE80::2, FastEthernet0/0
L   FF00::/8 [0/0]
       via Null0, receive
```

Just like in IPv4 you can also filter the routes you want to look at by protocol.

R1#show ipv6 route eigrp
```
IPv6 Routing Table - default - 12 entries
Codes: C - Connected, L - Local, S - Static, U - Per-user Static route
       B - BGP, M - MIPv6, R - RIP, I1 - ISIS L1
       I2 - ISIS L2, IA - ISIS interarea, IS - ISIS summary, D - EIGRP
       EX - EIGRP external, ND - Neighbor Discovery
       O - OSPF Intra, OI - OSPF Inter, OE1 - OSPF ext 1, OE2 - OSPF ext 2
       ON1 - OSPF NSSA ext 1, ON2 - OSPF NSSA ext 2
D   2001:123:2323::/64 [90/30720]
       via FE80::2, FastEthernet0/0
D   2001:123:3333::/64 [90/33280]
       via FE80::2, FastEthernet0/0
```

Here is a ping from the PC connected to R1.

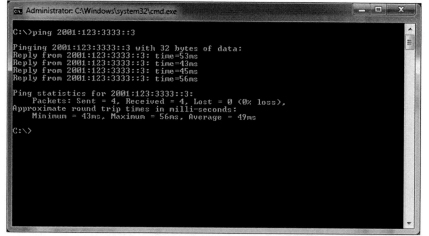

As mentioned above, EIGRP is a very fast protocol that can detect issues very quickly. It does this with the concept of successors and feasible successors. The successor is the route that is chosen for the routing table. This is chosen by the best metric (Bandwidth + Delay by default). Routes also have to pass EIGRPs loop prevention rule which says that the Advertised Distance of a route (R2 -> R3) will be lower than the Feasible Distance (R1 -> R2 -> R3). EIGRP also stores a number of feasible successors so that in case something goes wrong with the successor it can switch routes as soon as it knows there is a problem.

R1#**show ipv6 eigrp topology**
EIGRP-IPv6 Topology Table for AS(123)/ID(1.1.1.1)
Codes: P - Passive, A - Active, U - Update, Q - Query, R - Reply,
    r - reply Status, s - sia Status

P 2001:123:1313::/127, 1 successors, FD is 2169856
    via Connected, Serial0/0/0
P 2001:123:1313::2/127, 1 successors, FD is 2169856
    via Connected, Serial0/0/1
P 2001:123:3333::/64, 1 successors, FD is 33280
    via FE80::2 (33280/30720), FastEthernet0/0
    via FE80::3 (2172416/28160), Serial0/0/1
    via FE80::3 (2172416/28160), Serial0/0/0
P 2001:123:1111::/64, 1 successors, FD is 28160
    via Connected, FastEthernet0/1
P 2001:123:1212::/64, 1 successors, FD is 28160
    via Connected, FastEthernet0/0
P 2001:123:2323::/64, 1 successors, FD is 30720
    via FE80::2 (30720/28160), FastEthernet/0
    via FE80::3 (2172416/28160), Serial0/0/0
    via FE80::3 (2172416/28160), Serial0/0/1

Let's test this out. According to the topology table, R1 is prefering the Fa0/0 interface to reach R3's Fa0/0 interface. After a bit, I disabled R3's Fa0/0 interface by simply unplugging it. Notice now it only takes a few pings from the client's perspective for EIGRP to route around the issue.

To demonstrate how fast the switch over actually is lets debug the routing table with **debug ipv6 routing.** Debug ip routing is not really a CCNA command but it is pretty useful to see any changes to the routing table in real time because it only talks when there is an actual change to the routing table it is not a bad idea to keep it running during labs so you can watch any changes that happens to your network as they happen. Notice that as soon as EIGRP detects the R3 interface is down and removes the route, within the same second it has switched to the serial links to route the traffic.

R1#debug ipv6 routing
IPv6 routing table events debugging is on

R1#
IPv6RT[default]: eigrp 123, Reuse backup for 2001:123:1212::/64, distance 90
IPv6RT[default]: eigrp 123, Reuse backup for 2001:123:1212::/64, distance 90
IPv6RT[default]: eigrp 123, Reuse backup for 2001:123:1212::/64, distance 90

R1#

IPv6RT[default]: eigrp 123, Delete next-hop FE80::2, FastEthernet0/0 for 2001:123:3333::/64

IPv6RT[default]: eigrp 123, Delete 2001:123:3333::/64 from table

IPv6RT[default]: eigrp 123, Route add 2001:123:3333::/64 [new 90/2172416]

IPv6RT[default]: eigrp 123, Added path FE80::3/Serial0/0/1

IPv6RT[default]: eigrp 123, Route add 2001:123:3333::/64 [owner]

IPv6RT[default]: eigrp 123, Added path FE80::3/Serial0/0/0

IPv6RT[default]: Event: 2001:123:3333::/64, Del, owner eigrp, previous None

IPv6RT[default]: Event: 2001:123:3333::/64, Add, owner eigrp, previous None

IPv6RT[default]: eigrp 123, Delete next-hop FE80::2, FastEthernet0/0 for 2001:123:3333::/64

Checking the topology table we can see that the fastethernet route has been removed and R1 is now load balancing between the 2 Serial interfaces because they have the same cost.

R1#show ipv6 eigrp topology

EIGRP-IPv6 Topology Table for AS(123)/ID(1.1.1.1)
Codes: P - Passive, A - Active, U - Update, Q - Query, R - Reply,
    r - reply Status, s - sia Status

P 2001:123:1313::/127, 1 successors, FD is 2169856
    via Connected, Serial2/0
P 2001:123:1313::2/127, 1 successors, FD is 2169856
    via Connected, Serial2/1
P 2001:123:3333::/64, 2 successors, FD is 33280
    via FE80::3 (2172416/28160), Serial0/0/0
    via FE80::3 (2172416/28160), Serial0/0/1
P 2001:123:1111::/64, 1 successors, FD is 28160
    via Connected, FastEthernet0/1
P 2001:123:1212::/64, 1 successors, FD is 28160
    via Connected, FastEthernet0/0
P 2001:123:2323::/64, 1 successors, FD is 30720
    via FE80::2 (30720/28160), FastEthernet0/0
    via FE80::3 (2172416/28160), Serial0/0/0
    via FE80::3 (2172416/28160), Serial0/0/1

Configuring Basic IPv6 OSPFv3

R1   SW1   R2

IPv6 continues to have dynamic routing protocols just like IPv4. OSPF works very similar in theory with IPv6 as it did with IPv4. However, configurations take place more in the interface configuration than in the global configuration. In this lab, we will enable dynamic routing of IPv6 using OSPFv3.

Hardware & Configuration Required for this Lab
- Two Cisco routers which support IPv6 that each have an Ethernet interface and IPv6 capable IOS
- One Cisco switch
- Two straight through Cat 5 cables
- Connect Router #1 FastEthernet0/0 to Switch #1 interface FastEthernet0/1
- Connect Router #2 FastEthernet0/0 to Switch #1 interface FastEthernet0/2

Router Configurations

Begin with the default configuration on both the routers and the switch. If a configuration is in place, erase the startup-configuration and restart the device.

Configure Router #1 with a hostname and IPv6 interfaces.

Router(config)#**hostname R1**
R1(config)#**interface Loopback0**
R1(config-if)#**ipv6 address 2001::1:1/114** (*Note that this uses "ipv6", not "ip".*)
R1(config-if)#**interface FastEthernet0/0**
R1(config-if)#**ipv6 address 2001::A:1/114** (*Note that this is an abbreviated IPv6 address.*)
R1(config-if)#**no shutdown**

Configure Router #2 with a hostname and IPv6 interfaces.

Router(config)#**hostname R2**
R2(config)#**interface Loopback0**
R2(config-if)#**ipv6 address 2001::2:1/114** (*Note that this uses "ipv6", not "ip".*)
R2(config-if)#**interface FastEthernet0/0**

R2(config-if)#**ipv6 address 2001::A:2/114** (*Note that this is an abbreviated IPv6 address.*)
R2(config-if)#**no shutdown**

Lab Exercise

Test IPv6 Routes

Show the IPv6 routing table on Router #1 and verify which routes can be reached.

R1#**show ipv6 route**
IPv6 Routing Table - 5 entries
Codes: C - Connected, L - Local, S - Static, R - RIP, B - BGP
      U - Per-user Static route, M - MIPv6
      I1 - ISIS L1, I2 - ISIS L2, IA - ISIS interarea, IS - ISIS summary
      O - OSPF intra, OI - OSPF inter, OE1 - OSPF ext 1, OE2 - OSPF ext 2
      ON1 - OSPF NSSA ext 1, ON2 - OSPF NSSA ext 2
      D - EIGRP, EX - EIGRP external
C   2001::1:0/114 [0/0]
    via ::, Loopback0
L   2001::1:1/128 [0/0]
    via ::, Loopback0
C   2001::A:0/114 [0/0]
    via ::, FastEthernet0/0
L   2001::A:1/128 [0/0]
    via ::, FastEthernet0/0
L   FF00::/8 [0/0]
    via ::, Null0

R1#**ping ipv6 2001::2:1** (*This is the IPv6 address on Router #2 interface Loopback0.*)

Type escape sequence to abort.
Sending 5, 100-byte ICMP Echos to 2001::2:1, timeout is 2 seconds:
.....
Success rate is 0 percent (0/5)

R1#**ping ipv6 2001::A:1** (*This is the IPv6 address on Router #2 interface FastEthernet0/0.*)

Type escape sequence to abort.
Sending 5, 100-byte ICMP Echos to 2001::A:1, timeout is 2 seconds:
!!!!!
Success rate is 100 percent (5/5), round-trip min/avg/max = 0/1/4 ms

Show the IPv6 routing table on Router #2 and verify which routes can be reached.

R2#**show ipv6 route**
IPv6 Routing Table - 5 entries
Codes: C - Connected, L - Local, S - Static, R - RIP, B - BGP

      U - Per-user Static route, M - MIPv6
      I1 - ISIS L1, I2 - ISIS L2, IA - ISIS interarea, IS - ISIS summary
      O - OSPF intra, OI - OSPF inter, OE1 - OSPF ext 1, OE2 - OSPF ext 2
      ON1 - OSPF NSSA ext 1, ON2 - OSPF NSSA ext 2
      D - EIGRP, EX - EIGRP external
C 2001::2:0/114 [0/0]
   via ::, Loopback0
L 2001::2:1/128 [0/0]
   via ::, Loopback0
C 2001::A:0/114 [0/0]
   via ::, FastEthernet0/0
L 2001::A:2/128 [0/0]
   via ::, FastEthernet0/0
L FF00::/8 [0/0]
   via ::, Null0

R2#ping ipv6 2001::1:2 (*This is the IPv6 address on Router #2 interface Loopback0.*)

Type escape sequence to abort.
Sending 5, 100-byte ICMP Echos to 2001::2:1, timeout is 2 seconds:
.....
Success rate is 0 percent (0/5)

R2#ping ipv6 2001::A:1 (*This is the IPv6 address on Router #1 interface FastEthernet0/0.*)

Type escape sequence to abort.
Sending 5, 100-byte ICMP Echos to 2001::A:1, timeout is 2 seconds:
!!!!!
Success rate is 100 percent (5/5), round-trip min/avg/max = 0/1/4 ms

Configure Dynamic Routing using OSPFv3

Enable routing of IPv6 on each router.

Router #1
R1(config)#**ipv6 unicast-routing**
R1(config)#**ipv6 router ospf 1**
R1(config-rtr)#**router-id 0.0.0.1** (*The router ID does imply the use of IPv4 address.*)

Router #2
R2(config)#**ipv6 unicast-routing**
R2(config)#**ipv6 router ospf 1**
R2(config-rtr)#**router-id 0.0.0.2** (*This needs to be manually configured, different than R1.*)

Add the OSPFv3 configuration command to interface FastEthernet0/0 and Loopback0 on each router. Each interface is participating in OSPF, either to a neighbor or advertising a route, so each needs these commands.

Router #1
R1(config)#**interface Loopback0**
R1(config-if)#**ipv6 ospf 1 area 0**
R1(config-if)#**interface FastEthernet0/0**
R1(configif)#**ipv6 ospf 1 area 0**

Router #2
R2(config)#**interface Loopback0**
R2(config-if)#**ipv6 ospf 1 area 0**
R2(config-if)#**interface FastEthernet0/0**
R2(configif)#**ipv6 ospf 1 area 0**

Re-Test

Attempt to ping the remote IPv6 network from Router #1. **Note** – If you type too quick before OSPF converges this may fail. So type **very** slowly ☺

R1#**ping ipv6 2001::2:1** (*This is the IPv6 address on Router #2 interface Loopback0.*)

Type escape sequence to abort.
Sending 5, 100-byte ICMP Echos to 2001::2:1, timeout is 2 seconds:
!!!!!
Success rate is 100 percent (5/5), round-trip min/avg/max = 0/1/4 ms

Attempt to PING the remote IPv6 network from Router #2.

R2#**ping ipv6 2001::1:1** (*This is the IPv6 address on Router #1 interface Loopback0.*)

Type escape sequence to abort.
Sending 5, 100-byte ICMP Echos to 2001::1:1, timeout is 2 seconds:
!!!!!
Success rate is 100 percent (5/5), round-trip min/avg/max = 0/1/4 ms

Let's look at the routing table on both R1 and R2 with a focus on OSPF learned routes

R1#**show ipv6 route**
IPv6 Routing Table - 6 entries
Codes: C - Connected, L - Local, S - Static, R - RIP, B - BGP
    U - Per-user Static route, M - MIPv6
    I1 - ISIS L1, I2 - ISIS L2, IA - ISIS interarea, IS - ISIS summary
    O - OSPF intra, OI - OSPF inter, OE1 - OSPF ext 1, OE2 - OSPF ext 2
    ON1 - OSPF NSSA ext 1, ON2 - OSPF NSSA ext 2
    D - EIGRP, EX - EIGRP external
C 2001::1:0/114 [0/0]
   via ::, Loopback0
L 2001::1:1/128 [0/0]
   via ::, Loopback0

O 2001::2:1/128 [110/1]
   via FE80::207:ECFF:FEE9:C101, FastEthernet0/0
C 2001::A:0/114 [0/0]
   via ::, FastEthernet0/0
L 2001::A:1/128 [0/0]
   via ::, FastEthernet0/0
L FF00::/8 [0/0]
   via ::, Null0

R2#**show ipv6 route**
IPv6 Routing Table - 6 entries
Codes: C - Connected, L - Local, S - Static, R - RIP, B - BGP
      U - Per-user Static route, M - MIPv6
      I1 - ISIS L1, I2 - ISIS L2, IA - ISIS interarea, IS - ISIS summary
      O - OSPF intra, OI - OSPF inter, OE1 - OSPF ext 1, OE2 - OSPF ext 2
      ON1 - OSPF NSSA ext 1, ON2 - OSPF NSSA ext 2
      D - EIGRP, EX - EIGRP external
O 2001::1:1/128 [110/1]
   via FE80::20C:85FF:FE3C:8D01, FastEthernet0/0
C 2001::2:0/114 [0/0]
   via ::, Loopback0
L 2001::2:1/128 [0/0]
   via ::, Loopback0
C 2001::A:0/114 [0/0]
   via ::, FastEthernet0/0
L 2001::A:2/128 [0/0]
   via ::, FastEthernet0/0
L FF00::/8 [0/0]
   via ::, Null0

Configuring IPv6 over Frame-Relay with OSPFv3

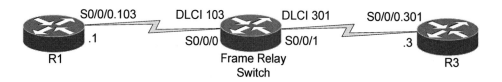

With a depleting IPv4 address stack, there is a compelling need to adopt IPv6 in your network. Thus various protocols are becoming IPv6 compliant and as a result of that we have OSPFv3 enhanced version of the most popular IGP OSPFv2. RFC 2740 details OSPFv3. OSPFv3 shares many key concepts including their basic operations, neighbor relationship, area, interface types, virtual links and many more with its predecessor OSPFv2. Apart from these similarities, the two protocols are different and some of the notable differences are described below.

OSPFv3 configured using interface commands – The network command is removed from OSPFv3. To configure an interface to participate in OSPF process, use the interface subcommand *ipv6 ospf <process_id> area #*. Issue the command *ipv6 router ospf #* in global configuration mode to create an ospf routing instance.

OSPFv3 RID must be set - OSPFv3 can automatically set its 32-bit RID based on the configured IPv4 addresses, using the same rules for OSPFv2. However, if no IPv4 addresses are configured, OSPFv3 cannot automatically choose its router ID. You must manually configure the RID before OSPFv3 will start.

Therefore, let's get to the OSPFv3 basic configuration. Enabling OSPFv3 is very simple once you have identified the desired links participating in ospf process. We will configure IPv6 addressing and verify its reachability.

In the following scenario we have routers R1 & R3 working as OSPF routers. Our central Cisco router R2, will emulate an ISP's Frame Relay network. Use Table-1 for your IP addressing & DLCI requirements. Figure out what interfaces are DCE by reading the config.

Hardware & Configuration Required for this Lab

- Two Cisco Routers with IPv6 support with at least one serial port each running an IPv6 capable IOS
- One dedicated Cisco router acting as Frame Relay switch to emulate ISP cloud. It must have two serial ports and support IPv6.
- Two serial back to back cables

Setup

Connect R1 and R2 routers to the Frame Relay switch:

- Serial 0/0/0 on router R1 to Serial 0/0/0 on Frame-Relay switch R2.
- Serial 0/0/0 on router R3 to Serial 0/0/1 on Frame-Relay switch R2.
- Compare and confirm connections with topology above.

Table -1

Device	Interface	IP Address	DLCI	OSPF Area
R1	S0/0/0.103	2001:ABAD:CAFÉ:123::1/64	103	Area 0
	Loopback 0	2001:ABAD:CAFÉ:1001::1/64		Area 1
R3	S0/0/0.301	2001:ABAD:CAFÉ:123::3/64	301	Area 0
	Loopback 0	2001:ABAD:CAFÉ:3003::3/64		Area 1

Router Configuration

We will first have to configure the central router for Frame Relay switching. Once configured, this router will emulate an ISP Frame Relay network.

FrameRelaySwitch Configuration

Router>**enable** (*entering privileged mode*)
Router# **configure terminal** (*entering global conf. mode*)
Router(config)#**hostname FrameRelaySwitch** (*set host name of router*)
FrameRelaySwitch(config)#**frame-relay switching** (*enable Frame Relay switching*)
FrameRelaySwitch(config)#**interface s0/0/0** (*entering interface conf. mode*)
FrameRelaySwitch(config-if)#**no shutdown**
FrameRelaySwitch(config-if)#**encapsulation frame-relay** (*enabling Frame Relay on an interface*)
FrameRelaySwitch(config-if)#**frame-relay intf-type dce** (*making sure router is in charge of clocking*)
FrameRelaySwitch(config-if)#**frame-relay route 103 interface s0/0/1 301**
    (*configuring Frame Relay routing from DLCI to DLCI – incoming first, outgoing second*)
FrameRelaySwitch(config-if)#**no shutdown** (*starting the interface (off by default)*)
FrameRelaySwitch(config-if)#**interface s0/0/1** (*same procedure for other interface*)
FrameRelaySwitch(config-if)#**encapsulation frame-relay**
FrameRelaySwitch(config-if)#**frame-relay intf-type dce**
FrameRelaySwitch(config-if)#**encapsulation frame-relay**
FrameRelaySwitch(config-if)#**frame-relay route 301 interface s0/0/1 103**
FrameRelaySwitch(config-if)#**no shutdown**
FrameRelaySwitch(config-if)#**exit**
FrameRelaySwitch(config)#**exit**
FrameRelaySwitch#

Now configure the IP Addressing and Frame-Relay setup for R1 and R3 using Table 1.

R1 Configuration

Router>**enable**
Router#**config t**
Router(config)#**hostname R1**
R1(config)#**ipv6 unicast-routing**   (*Enable IPv6 unicast routing*)
R1(config)#**interface Loopback0**   (*Enter loopback 0 interface config*)
R1(config-if)#**description Loopback0**   (*assign a description to interface*)
R1(config-if)#**ipv6 address 2001:ABAD:CAFE:1001::1/64**   (*setting an IPv6 address to the interface*)
R1(config-if)#**interface Serial0/0/0**   (*entering MAIN interface conf. mode*)
R1(config-if)#**no ip address**   (*removing IP address from interface*)
R1(config-if)#**encapsulation frame-relay**   (*enabling Frame Relay on an interface*)
R1(config-if)#**no frame-relay inverse-arp**   (*turn off Inverse-arp*)
R1(config-if)#**no shutdown**   (*starting the interface which is shutdown by default*)
R1(config-if)#**interface Serial0/0/0.103 point-to-point**   (*entering SUBINTERFACE conf. mode*)
R1(config-if)#**ipv6 address 2001:ABAD:CAFE:123::1/64** (*setting an IPv6 address to the interface*)
R1(config-if)#**frame-relay interface-dlci 103**   (*pointing local router to its local DLCI*)
R1(config-fr-dlci)#

R3 Configuration

Router>**enable**
Router#**config t**
Router(config)#**hostname R3**
R3(config)#**no ip domain-lookup**
R3(config)#**ipv6 unicast-routing**
R3(config-if)#**interface Loopback0**
R3(config-if)#**description Loopback0**
R3(config-if)#**ipv6 address 2001:ABAD:CAFE:3003::3/64**
R3(config-if)#**interface Serial0/0/0**
R3(config-if)#**no ip address**
R3(config-if)#**encapsulation frame-relay**
R3(config-if)#**no frame-relay inverse-arp**
R3(config-if)#**no shutdown**
R3(config-if)#**interface Serial0/0/0.301 point-to-point**
R3(config-if)#**ipv6 address 2001:ABAD:CAFE:123::3/64**
R3(config-if)#**frame-relay interface-dlci 301**
R3(config-fr-dlci)#

Before we proceed and configure OSPFv3, we need to test the reachability between R1 & R3 across frame-relay router. To verify, ping the interface on R3 from R1 and vice-versa.

R1#**ping 2001:abad:cafe:123::3**
Sending 5, 100-byte ICMP Echos to 2001:ABAD:CAFE:123::3, timeout is 2 seconds:
!!!!!
Success rate is 100 percent (5/5), round-trip min/avg/max = 24/29/36 ms

R3#**ping 2001:abad:cafe:123::1**
Sending 5, 100-byte ICMP Echos to 2001:ABAD:CAFE:123::1, timeout is 2 seconds:
!!!!!
Success rate is 100 percent (5/5), round-trip min/avg/max = 24/35/48 ms

Now so you are sure of reachability, start configuring OSPFv3 process using following
steps and Table 1.

Step 1 - Identify the desired links connected to each OSPFv3 router. Use Table 1.
Step 2 - Determine the OSPF area to which each router interface should belong.
Step 3 - Configure OSPF on the interfaces.
Step 4 - Configure routing process commands, including a router ID on IPv6-only router.
Step 5 - Verify OSPF configuration, routing tables, and reachability.

OSPFv3 configuration on R1
R1>**enable** (*entering privileged mode*)
R1#**configure terminal** (*entering global conf. mode*)
R1(config)# **ipv6 router ospf 1** (*enable OSPFv3 process*)
R1(config-rtr)# **router-id 1.1.1.1** (*Set router id*)
R1(config-rtr)#**interface s0/0/0.103** (*entering interface conf. mode*)
R1(config-if)# **ipv6 ospf 1 area 0** (*enable OSPFv3 on interface*)
R1(config-if)#**interface loopback0**(*entering interface conf. mode*)
R1(config-if)# **ipv6 ospf 1 area 1**(*enable OSPFv3 on interface*)

OSPFv3 configuration on R3
R3>**enable** (*entering privileged mode*)
R3#**configure terminal** (*entering global conf. mode*)
R3(config)# **ipv6 router ospf 1** (*enable OSPFv3 process*)
R3(config-rtr)# **router-id 3.3.3.3** (*Set router id*)
R3(config-rtr)#**interface s0/0/0.301**(*entering interface conf. mode*)
R3(config-if)# **ipv6 ospf 1 area 0**(*enable OSPFv3 on interface*)
R3(config-if)#**interface loopback0**(*entering interface conf. mode*)
R3(config-if)# **ipv6 ospf 1 area 3**(*enable OSPFv3 on interface*)

Monitoring and Troubleshooting the Configuration

Check the OSPF neighborship and the route learn via OSPF on R1.

R1#**sh ipv6 ospf neighbor** (*Checking OSPF neighbors*)
Neighbor ID   Pri State   Dead Time Interface ID Interface
3.3.3.3   1   FULL/ -   00:00:32   12   Serial0/0/0.103

As expected R1 has neighbor R3 on its serial subinterface. Now look for the routes learned.

R1#**sh ipv6 route ospf**   (*verify the OSPF learned routes*)
IPv6 Routing Table - 7 entries
Codes: C - Connected, L - Local, S - Static, R - RIP, B - BGP

U - Per-user Static route
I1 - ISIS L1, I2 - ISIS L2, IA - ISIS interarea, IS - ISIS summary
O - OSPF intra, OI - OSPF inter, OE1 - OSPF ext 1, OE2 - OSPF ext 2
ON1 - OSPF NSSA ext 1, ON2 - OSPF NSSA ext 2

OI 2001:ABAD:CAFE:3003::3/128 [110/64]
*   via FE80::C802:2EFF:FE30:0, Serial0/0/0.103*

The R3 loopback address is learned at R1 as inter-area ospf route since the R3 loopback is in different area i.e area 3. Now try to ping the R3 loopback learned via OSPF. You should be successful.

R1#ping 2001:abad:cafe:3003::3
Type escape sequence to abort.
Sending 5, 100-byte ICMP Echos to 2001:ABAD:CAFE:3003::3, timeout is 2 seconds:
!!!!!
Success rate is 100 percent (5/5), round-trip min/avg/max = 24/32/40 ms

Other Useful Commands for verification are:
show ipv6 interface brief - *display IPv6 interfaces*
show ipv6 ospf 1 - *display timer and protocol related info*
show ipv6 ospf 1 database - *display prefixes learned and LSA age etc.*
show ipv6 ospf interface - *displays interfaces participating in OSPF*

Questions

1. How can you advertise prefixes in OSPFv3?

   _____

2. How to create OSPFv3 process on a router?

   _____

3. How can you check OSPFv3 timers?

   _____

4. What is the administrative distance for OSPFv3 on Cisco routers?

   _____

Answers

1. Using "ipv6 ospf <process_id> area #" under interface subcommand.
2. Using "IPv6 router ospf 1" global config command.
3. Issue "show ipv6 ospf 1" global config command.
4. It is same as OSPFv2 i.e. 110 in Cisco routers.

Configuring an IPSec Tunnel

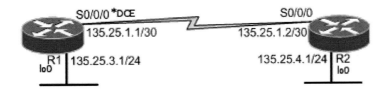

Hardware & Configuration Required for this Lab
• Two Cisco routers each having one Ethernet and one serial port
• One Cisco DTE/DCE back to back cable

Router Configurations
R1
hostname R1
int lo0
  ip address 135.25.3.1 255.255.255.0
int s0/0/0
  ip address 135.25.1.1 255.255.255.252
  clockrate 64000
  no shut
router ospf 64
  network 135.25.0.0 0.0.255.255 area 0

R2
hostname R2
int lo0
  ip address 135.25.4.1 255.255.255.0
int s0/0/0
  ip address 135.25.1.2 255.255.255.252
  no shut
router ospf 64
  network 135.25.0.0 0.0.255.255 area 0

Monitoring and Testing the Configuration
The first step is to create the IKE crypto policy. IKE is used to create the security association (SA) between the routers. Under the IKE policy, the encryption algorithm, hash algorithm, authentication method, Diffe-Hellman group identifier, and SA lifetime are configured. If these parameters do not match, the SA negotiation will fail. The following command turns on the IKE policy 1 on R1 and R2.

R1(config)#**crypto isakmp policy 1**
R2(config)#**crypto isakmp policy 1**

Up to 10,000 policies can be defined. The priority value (the number at the end of the command) is used to determine the priority of each policy. The lower the number the higher the priority. During negotiation, each policy is evaluated in order of priority. The authentication type is defined under the IKE policy. Three types of authentication can be used: RSA-SIG, RSA-ENGR or preshare. For this lab, we will be using preshare keys. If RSA-SIG were used, a CA would be needed to issue certificates. The following commands enable the IKE policy to use preshare keys.

R1(config)#**crypto isakmp policy 1**
R1(config-isakmp)#**authentication pre-share**
R2(config)#**crypto isakmp policy 1**
R2(config-isakmp)#**authentication pre-share**

Since preshared keys are being used. A shared key must be defined along with the peer's identity. The identity can be either the peer's IP address or name. For this lab, the IP address of the serial interface of each router will be the peer address and the shared secret will be cisco. The following command defines the key that will be used and the peer address.

R1(config)#**crypto isakmp key cisco address 135.25.1.2**
R2(config)#**crypto isakmp key cisco address 135.25.1.1**

View the crypto policy on R1 and R2 with the **show crypto isakmp policy** command. Notice that two policies exist; the one we just created and a default policy. The only difference is in the authentication method. The default policy is using RSA-SIG as the authentication method, while the policy we just created is using preshared key.

R1#**show crypto isakmp policy**
Global IKE policy
Protection suite of priority 1
    encryption algorithm: DES - Data Encryption Standard (56 bit keys).
    hash algorithm: Secure Hash Standard
    authentication method: Pre-Shared Key
    Diffie-Hellman group: #1 (768 bit)
    lifetime: 86400 seconds, no volume limit
Default protection suite
    encryption algorithm: DES - Data Encryption Standard (56 bit keys).
    hash algorithm: Secure Hash Standard
    authentication method: Rivest-Shamir-Adleman Signature
    Diffie-Hellman group: #1 (768 bit)
    lifetime: 86400 seconds, no volume limit

The next step is to define the transform set or sets that will be used. A transform is simply the algorithm or algorithms that the router is willing to use for the session. The various transform sets are offered to the receiver during IKE. The receiver selects the one that will be used.

For this lab we will be using encryption only-just one transform needs to be defined. The following command defines the transform set on R1 and R2.

R1(config)#**crypto ipsec transform-set encr-only esp-aes**
R2(config)#**crypto ipsec transform-set encr-only esp-aes**

The current transform set can be viewed with the command show crypto ipsec transform-set.

RouterA#**sh crypto ipsec transform-set**
Transform set encr-only: { esp-aes }
     will negotiate = { Tunnel, },

The next step is to define the traffic that will be given security protection. This is done using an extended access list. For this lab, all traffic from the network 135.25.3.0 to network 135.25.4.0 should be encrypted. Only the traffic that you wish to protect needs to be defined. In access-list terminology, 'permit' means 'protect' and 'deny' means 'don't protect.' All traffic that is denied will pass in the clear.

R1(config)#**access-list 101 permit ip 135.25.3.0 0.0.0.255 135.25.4.0 0.0.0.255**
R2(config)#**access-list 101 permit ip 135.25.4.0 0.0.0.255 135.25.3.0 0.0.0.255**

The next step is to define a crypto map, which combines the policy and traffic information. The crypto map contains the traffic to which security must be applied (defined by the access-list), the actual algorithm to apply, (defined by the transform) and the crypto endpoint (the remote peer). An IPSec crypto map is defined with a tag, a sequence number and the encryption method.

The following commands define a crypto map on R1 and R2.
R1(config)#**crypto map peer-R2 local-address serial 0/0/0**
R1(config)#**crypto map peer-R2 10 ipsec-isakmp**
R1(config-crypto-map)#**set peer 135.25.1.2**
R1(config-crypto-map)#**set transform-set encr-only**
R1(config-crypto-map)#**match address 101**

R2(config)#**crypto map peer-R1 local-address serial 0/0/0**
R2(config)#**crypto map peer-R1 10 ipsec-isakmp**
R2(config-crypto-map)#**set peer 135.25.1.1**
R2(config-crypto-map)#**set transform-set encr-only**
R2(config-crypto-map)#**match address 101**

The last thing to do is apply the crypto map to an interface. You must assign a crypto map set to an interface before that interface can provide IPSec services. The following commands assign the crypto map to the interface connecting R1 and R2.

R1(config)#**int s0/0/0**

R1(config-if)#**crypto map peer-R2**

R2(config)#**int s0/0/0**
R2(config-if)#**crypto map peer-R1**

Display the active IPSec connections on RouterA with the command show crypto engine connections active. Notice that there are no active connections. This is because no traffic matching the crypto map has been sent.

R1#**show crypto engine connections active**
ID Interface IP-Address State Algorithm
Encrypt Decrypt

Turn the following debug commands on RouterA.
R1#**debug crypto ipsec**
R1#**debug crypto isakmp**

Now ping from R1 sourcing the packet from the loopback interface (135.25.3.1) to 135.25.4.1.

R1#**ping** *(Extended ping sourcing the packet from the loopback interface)*
Protocol [ip]:
Target IP address: **135.25.4.1**
Repeat count [5]:
Datagram size [100]:
Timeout in seconds [2]:
Extended commands [n]: **y**
Source address or interface: **135.25.3.1** *(Source address is the loopback interface of R1)*
Type of service [0]:
Set DF bit in IP header? [no]:
Validate reply data? [no]:
Data pattern [0xABCD]:
Loose, Strict, Record, Timestamp, Verbose[none]:
Sweep range of sizes [n]:
Type escape sequence to abort.
Sending 5, 100-byte ICMP Echos to 135.25.4.1, timeout is 2 seconds:
!!!!!
Success rate is 100 percent (5/5), round-trip min/avg/max = 4/4/4 ms

Watch the output from the debug commands and you should see traffic being encrypted over the serial interfaces.

Now display the crypto engine on R1 with the command **show crypto engine connections active**. Notice that R1 now has two security associations; one for outgoing and one for incoming traffic.

IPSEC Review

Match the terms below that correspond with the definitions provided.

HMAC	ESP	Diffie-Hellman Exchange
Data Integrity	AH	Data Origin Authentication
Tunnel Mode	ISAKMP	Data Confidentiality
IKE	Anti-Reply	Transport Mode

1. _____ A framework for the negotiation and management of security associations between peers (traverses UDP/500)
2. _____ Responsible for key agreement using asymmetric cryptography
3. _____ Provides data encryption, data integrity, & peer authentication
4. _____ Provides data integrity and peer authentication, but not data encryption
5. _____ The ESP or AH header is inserted behind the IP header; the IP header can be authenticated but not encrypted
6. _____ A new IP header is created in place of the original; this allows for encryption of the entire original packet
7. _____ Secure hashing (HMAC) is used to ensure data has not been altered in transit
8. _____ Encryption is used to ensure data cannot be intercepted by a third party
9. _____ Authentication of the SA peer
10. _____ Sequence numbers are used to detect and discard duplicate packets
11. _____ A hash of the data and secret key used to provide message authenticity
12. _____ A shared secret key is established over an insecure path using public and private keys

Answers:

1. Internet Security Association and Key Management Protocol (ISAKMP)
2. Internet Key Exchange (IKE)
3. Encapsulating Security Payload (ESP)
4. Authentication Header (AH)
5. Transport Mode
6. Tunnel Mode
7. Data Integrity
8. Data Confidentiality
9. Data Origin Authentication
10. Anti-replay
11. Hash Message Authentication Code (HMAC)
12. Diffie-Hellman Exchange

GRE Over IPSec Virtual Tunnel

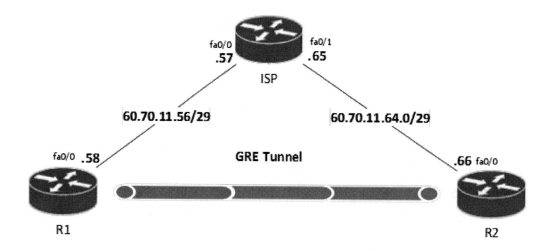

The purpose of this lab is to explore using IPSec Virtual Tunnel Interface to securely tunnel traffic between sites using the Generic Routing Encapsulation protocol.

Hardware & Configuration Required for this Lab

- Three Cisco routers
- Two crossover Cat 5 Ethernet cables
- Routers running Advanced IP Services or better

Commands Used in this Lab

Crypto isakmp policy <#> - Creates a ISKMP policy

crypto isakmp key <preshare> address <peer> - Specify what pre-share key to use with peers.

crypto IPSec transform-set <name> <encryption> <hash>- Specifies what settings to use in Phase 2

crypto IPSec profile <name> - Creates a IPSEC profile for tunnel interfaces.

interface tunnel <#>- Creates a tunnel interface

tunnel source <address> - Specify the source address of the GRE tunnel

tunnel destination <address> - Specify the destination address of the GRE tunnel

tunnel mode IPSec ipv4 - Specifies the GRE tunnel will use IPSEC

tunnel protection IPSec profile <name> - Binds the IPSEC profile to the GRE tunnel

Initial Configs

R1
hostname R1
line console 0
 logging synch
interface FastEthernet0/0
 ip address 60.70.11.58 255.255.255.248
 no shut
ip route 0.0.0.0 0.0.0.0 60.70.11.57

R2
 hostname R2
 line console 0
 logging synch
interface FastEthernet0/0
 ip address 60.70.11.66 255.255.255.248
 no shut
ip route 0.0.0.0 0.0.0.0 60.70.11.65

ISP
hostname ISP
 line console 0
 logging synch
interface FastEthernet0/0
 ip address 60.70.11.57 255.255.255.248
 no shut
interface FastEthernet0/1
ip address 60.70.11.65 255.255.255.248
 no shut

IPSEC over Virtual Tunnel Interfaces is a means of securely tunneling traffic between routers. It is mostly used in the enterprise as a site to site VPN to other sites or branches. Using VTIs instead of traditional Site to Site VPN tunnels have a few advantages. Primarily, traffic does not need to be explicitly defined as to what traffic goes over the tunnels as they can be dynamically created when used with DMVPN and it allows mult-cast packets.

The first step in any IPSEC implementation is to create the ISAKMP policy. An ISAKMP policy has three important pieces of information and must match on the both sides of the tunnel.

The first piece of information defines the encryption used for the VPN tunnel. Available options vary depending on the device and the IOS version/feature set. The main options are DES, 3DES, and AES. **Note**: DES is very old and has been broken quite a while ago! Do not use it in production if you have a choice. Because certain countries forbid strong encryption from being used you may have to get an additional license from Cisco to use 3DES etc.

The second part is what hashing algorithm the tunnel will use. Generally you have a choice between MD5 & SHA.

The third part tells the router what authentication method to use for the tunnel. You have a choice between Pre-share keys or using certificates. Since certificates are out of scope for these labs, we will use pre-share keys.

Another option of interest is the Group. Group controls the level of encryption for the Diffie-Hellman key exchange. I generally use group 2 which is a 1024 bit key.

```
R1(config)#crypto isakmp policy 10
R1(config-isakmp)# encr 3des
R1(config-isakmp)# hash md5
R1(config-isakmp)# authentication pre-share
R1(config-isakmp)# group 2

R2(config)#crypto isakmp policy 10
R2(config-isakmp)# encr 3des
R2(config-isakmp)# hash md5
R2(config-isakmp)# authentication pre-share
R2(config-isakmp)# group 2
```

Next we need to define the pre-share key for the tunnel. We will use CISCO. On Cisco routers we use the `crypto isakmp key <PRESHARE> address <peer IP address>` to define the key.

There is a gotcha with this command. Because it used the address keyword to ask for the key, it is one of those strange Cisco commands that you can't get context sensitive help with.

```
R2(config)#crypto isakmp key CISCO ?
% Unrecognized command
```

For the peer portion, you can either explicitly define the peer address or you can enter 0.0.0.0 to specify to use this pre-share key with anyone who tries to connect. Since I prefer to be explicit when I configure VPNs, I will set the peer addresses

```
R1(config)#crypto isakmp key CISCO address 60.70.11.66
```

R2(config)#**crypto isakmp key CISCO address 60.70.11.58**

Now that ISAKMP is configured the phase 1 portion is completed, we can move on to phase 2 with the IPSEC portion of the setup. First up is the Transform set.
The command is **crypto IPSec transform-set <Name> <transport encryption> <transport hash>**
We will use 3DES and MD5 for this lab.

R1(config)#**crypto ipsec transform-set ESP-3DES-MD5 esp-3des esp-md5-hmac**
R2(config)#**crypto ipsec transform-set ESP-3DES-MD5 esp-3des esp-md5-hmac**

Next we have to make an IPSEC profile that we use to bind the IPSEC configuration to the GRE tunnel we will be making in a minute. All we need to do is drop back a level and create the profile and specify our transform-set.

R1(config)#**crypto IPSec profile IPSEC-PROFILE**
R1(IPSec-profile)#**set transform-set ESP-3DES-MD5**

R2(config)#**crypto IPSec profile IPSEC-PROFILE**
R2(IPSec-profile)#**set transform-set ESP-3DES-MD5**

All that is left now is to make the GRE tunnel between R1 and R2. To make a GRE tunnel we first create a tunnel interface with the **interface tunnel <#>** command. Next we add an IP address like any other interface.

R1(IPSec-profile)#**interface Tunnel1**
R1(config-if)# **ip address 10.99.99.12 255.255.255.0**

Then we define the source and destination of the GRE tunnel. This is the public IPs of each router.
R1(config-if)# **tunnel source fa0/0**
R1(config-if)# **tunnel destination 60.70.11.66**

We enable IPSEC with the **tunnel mode IPSec ipv4** command.
R1(config-if)# **tunnel mode IPSec ipv4**

Finally we bind our IPSEC profile with the GRE interface with the **tunnel protection IPSec profile <name>** command.

R1(config-if)# **tunnel protection IPSec profile IPSEC-PROFILE**
*Mar 1 01:09:37.663: %CRYPTO-6-ISAKMP_ON_OFF: ISAKMP is ON
*Mar 1 01:09:53.323: %LINEPROTO-5-UPDOWN: Line protocol on Interface Tunnel1, changed state to up

Here is R2's configuration.

R2(config)#**interface Tunnel1**
R2(config-if)# **ip address 10.99.99.12 255.255.255.0**
R2(config-if)# **tunnel source fa0/0**
R2(config-if)# **tunnel destination 60.70.11.58**
R2(config-if)# **tunnel mode IPSec ipv4**
R2(config-if)# **tunnel protection IPSec profile IPSEC-PROFILE**
*Mar 1 01:09:37.663: %CRYPTO-6-ISAKMP_ON_OFF: ISAKMP is ON
*Mar 1 01:09:53.323: %LINEPROTO-5-UPDOWN: Line protocol on Interface Tunnel1, changed state to up

We can check if the tunnel is established properly with the **show crypto iskmp sa** command. When things are working properly, we expect to see the state in QM_IDLE. Any other state means that there is likely a problem and you need to start troubleshooting.

R1(config)#**do show crypto isakmp sa**

dst   src   state   conn-id slot status
60.70.11.58   60.70.11.66   **QM_IDLE**   1   0 ACTIVE

Right now we have a VPN tunnel but nothing to test it with. So we will create a Loopback network on R1 and R2. We will use 192.168.1.1/24 on R1 and 192.168.2.1/24 on R2.

R1(config)#**int l0**
R1(config-if)#**ip add 192.168.1.1 255.255.255.0**

R2(config)#**int l0**
R2(config-if)#**ip add 192.168.2.1 255.255.255.0**

Once we have the loopbacks, we will need to drop back a level and setup static routes to establish connectivity across the tunnel.

R1(config)#**ip route 192.168.2.0 255.255.255.0 tun 1**
R2(config)#**ip route 192.168.1.0 255.255.255.0 tun 1**

The last thing to do is to verify we can reach our test networks across the tunnel.

R1(config)#**do ping 192.168.2.1 so l0**
Type escape sequence to abort.
Sending 5, 100-byte ICMP Echos to 192.168.2.1, timeout is 2 seconds:

Packet sent with a source address of 192.168.1.1
!!!!!

Success rate is 100 percent (5/5), round-trip min/avg/max = 20/49/68 ms

R2(config)#**do ping 192.168.1.1 so l0**

Type escape sequence to abort.
Sending 5, 100-byte ICMP Echos to 192.168.1.1, timeout is 2 seconds:
Packet sent with a source address of 192.168.2.1
!!!!!
Success rate is 100 percent (5/5), round-trip min/avg/max = 40/50/60 ms

Cisco Configuration Professional (CCP)

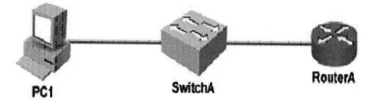

PC1   SwitchA   RouterA

Cisco Configuration Professional (CCP) is the replacement for Security Device Manager(SDM). We will review how to use Cisco Configuration Professional Express (Cisco CP Express) and Cisco Configuration Professional (Cisco CP). It is our guess you are going to see it quite soon in CCNA Security and then it will migrate to the CCNA exam. The cheapest router CCP will run on is the 1841 model. But don't worry, it will more than likely only be a small portion of the exam as the backbone of the CCNA exam will always be administered by the CLI as it was when SDM was on the CCNA exam.

Hardware & Configuration Required for this Lab

- One Cisco 1841 router or above that supports CCP with one Ethernet port
- One crossover Cat 5 cable for a direct PC to router connection or two straight through Cat 5 cables and a switch to put in between them

---

Cisco **Configuration Professional Expres**s is a graphical configuration tool that allows you configure a Cisco device without using the CLI. It is installed in **device's** Flash memory.

Cisco **Configuration Professional** is a full-featured device management tool that allows you to configure, monitor, and troubleshoot LAN and WAN interfaces, firewall, IPSec VPN, dynamic routing, wireless, and other security features. It is installed on a **PC**. This lab shows you how to set up a PC to connect to the router, give the router an initial network configuration using Cisco CP Express, and then begin using Cisco CP.

Configure the Router for Cisco CP

Cisco CP Express and Cisco CP require the following basic configuration in order to connect to the router and manage it.

- An http or https server must be enabled with local authentication.

- A local user account with privilege level 15 and accompanying password must be configured.

- Vty line with protocol ssh/telnet must be enabled with local authentication. This is needed for interactive commands.

- An http timeout policy must be configured with the parameters shown in the following procedure to avoid a known launch issue with Cisco CP.

- The PC on which Cisco CP is to run and the interface through which Cisco CP will be launched must be configured with IP addresses from the same subnet.

We will follow the procedure below to ensure that the router configuration meets these requirements:

Copying the Default Configuration File to Router NVRAM

If you want to start with a factory default configuration that is designed to support Cisco CP, you can use the procedure in this section. The factory default configuration includes all the commands necessary to support Cisco CP and configures an Ethernet interface with the IP address 10.10.10.1.

To copy the default configuration file from router Flash memory to NVRAM, complete the following steps.:

Step 1 Log on to the router through the Console port or through an Ethernet port.

Step 2 If you use the Console port, and no running configuration is present in the router, the Setup command Facility starts automatically, and displays the following text:

--- System Configuration Dialog ---
Continue with configuration dialog? [yes/no]:
Enter **no** so that you can enter Cisco IOS CLI commands directly.

If the Setup Command Facility does not start automatically, a running configuration is present, and you should go to the next step.

Step 3 When the router displays the user EXEC mode prompt, enter the **enable** command, and the enable password, if one is configured, as shown below:

Router> **enable**
password *password*
Router#

Step 4 To identify the default configuration file, enter the **show flash** command. The filename is of the form cpconfig-*modelnumber*.cfg, where *modelnumber* represents the router series. For example the configuration file name for the Cisco 860 and 880 series routers is cpconfig-8xx.cfg.

Router# **show flash**
-#- --length-- -----date/time------ path
1   2903 Apr 15 2008 20:34:48 +00:00 cpconfig-8xx.cfg
2   115712 Apr 15 2008 20:34:50 +00:00 home.tar
3   2279424 Apr 15 2008 20:34:54 +00:00 cpexpress.tar
Router#

Step 5 To copy the default configuration file to router NVRAM, enter the **copy flash: nvram:** command, as shown in the following example:

Router# **copy flash: cpconfig-8xx.cfg nvram:**
When the default configuration file is in NVRAM, it becomes the router startup configuration.

Step 6 To make the new startup configuration the running configuration, so that the router can support Cisco CP, enter the **copy startup-config running-config** command, as shown in the following example:

Router# **copy startup-config running-config**

Entering the Configuration Commands Manually

If you don't want to use the factory default configuration because the router already has a configuration, or for any other reason, you can use the procedure in this section to add each required command to the configuration. To enter the Cisco IOS commands manually, complete the following steps:

Step 1 Log on to the router through the Console port or through an Ethernet port.

Step 2 If you use the Console port, and no running configuration is present in the router, the Setup command Facility starts automatically, and displays the following text:

--- System Configuration Dialog ---
Continue with configuration dialog? [yes/no]:
Enter **no** so that you can enter Cisco IOS CLI commands directly.

If the Setup Command Facility does not start automatically, a running configuration is present, and you should go to the next step.

Step 3 When the router displays the user EXEC mode prompt, enter the **enable** command, and the enable password, if one is configured, as shown below:

Router> **enable**
password *password*

Step 4 Enter config mode by entering the config terminal command, as shown in the following example.

Router> **config terminal**
Router(config)#

Step 5 Using the command syntax shown, create a user account with privilege level 15.

Router(config)# **username** *name* **privilege 15 secret 0** *password*

Step 6 If no router interface is configured with an IP address, configure one so that you can access the router over the network. The following example shows the interface Fast Ethernet 0 configured.

Router(config)# **int FastEthernet0**
Router(config-if)# **ip address 10.10.10.1 255.255.255.248**
Router(config-if)# **no shutdown**
Router(config-if)# **exit**

If you are going to connect the PC directly to the router, the PC must be on the same subnet as this interface.

Step 7 Configure the router as an http server for nonsecure communication, or as an https server for secure communication.

To configure the router as an http server, enter the **ip http server** command shown in the example:

Router(config)# **ip http server**
To configure the router as an https server, enter the **ip http secure-server** command shown in the example:

Router(config)# ip http secure-server
Step 8 Configure the router for local authentication, by entering the **ip http authentication local** command, as shown in the example:

Router(config)# ip http authentication local
Step 9 Configure the http timeout policy as shown in the example:

Router(config)# **ip http timeout-policy idle 60 life 86400 requests 10000**
Step 10 Configure the vty lines for privilege level 15. For nonsecure access, enter the **transport input telnet** command. For secure access, enter the **transport input telnet ssh**command. An example of these commands follows:

Router(config)# **line vty 0 4**
Router(config-line)# **privilege level 15**
Router(config-line)# **login local**
Router(config-line)# **transport input telnet**
Router(config-line)# **transport input telnet ssh**
Router(config-line)# **exit**
Router(config)# **line vty 5 15**
Router(config-line)# **privilege level 15**
Router(config-line)# **login local**
Router(config-line)# **transport input telnet**
Router(config-line)# **transport input telnet ssh**
Router(config-line)# **end**

Configure the IP Address on the PC

This task section explains how to configure an IP address on the PC so that you can connect to Cisco CP Express and begin configuring the router. The default configuration file assigns an IP address to a LAN interface on the router, and you must configure the PC to be on the same subnet as the router LAN interface. If the router is a fixed-interface model, it is configured as a DHCP server, and the PC must be configured to accept an IP address automatically. If the router can accept modular interfaces, it is not configured as a DHCP server, and you must configure the PC with a static IP address on the same subnet as the router. To configure the IP address on the PC, complete the following steps:

Step 1 Find your router model number in Table 3. Note the required IP address configuration for the PC.

Table 2 Required PC IP Address Configurations		
Router Model	DHCP Server	Required PC IP Address Configuration
Cisco 815, Cisco 86x, Cisco 88x, Cisco 180x, Cisco 1805, Cisco 1811 and 1812	Yes	Obtain an IP address automatically.
Cisco 1841, Cisco 1861, Cisco 2801, Cisco 2811	No	Static IP address from 10.10.10.2 to 10.10.10.6 Subnet Mask: 255.255.255.248
Cisco 28xx, Cisco 38xx	No	Static IP address from 10.10.10.2 to 10.10.10.6 Subnet Mask: 255.255.255.248

Step 2 Configure the IP address on the PC.

If the PC runs Microsoft Windows XP, complete the following steps to display the Internet Protocol TCP/IP Properties dialog:

    a. Click **Start > Control Panel > Network Connections > Local Area Connection**.

    b. In the item list, select **Internet Protocol (TCP/IP)**.

    c. Click **Properties**.

    d. Go to Step 3.

If the PC runs Microsoft Windows Vista, complete the following steps to display the Internet Protocol TCP/IP Properties dialog:

    a. Click **Start > Control Panel > Network and Sharing Center**.

    b. In the Tasks column on the left, click **Manage network connections**.

    c. In the Network Connections screen, click **Local Area Connection**.

    d. In the Networking tab of the Local Area Connection Properties dialog, select **Internet Protocol Version 4**, and click **Properties**.

    e. Go to Step 3

Step 3 In the General tab, configure the IP address.

To configure the PC to obtain an IP address from a DHCP server,
click **Obtain an IP address automatically**. See Figure 1.

Figure 1 Configuring the PC to Obtain an IP Address Automatically

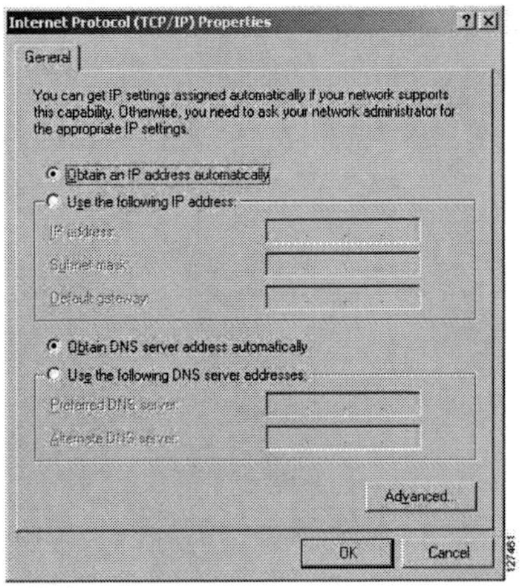

- Click **OK** to close the dialog.

To configure the PC with a static IP address of 10.10.10.2 and a subnet mask of
255.255.255.248, complete the following steps in the General Tab:

- Click **Use the following IP address**. See Figure 2.

Figure 2 Configuring the PC with a Static IP Address

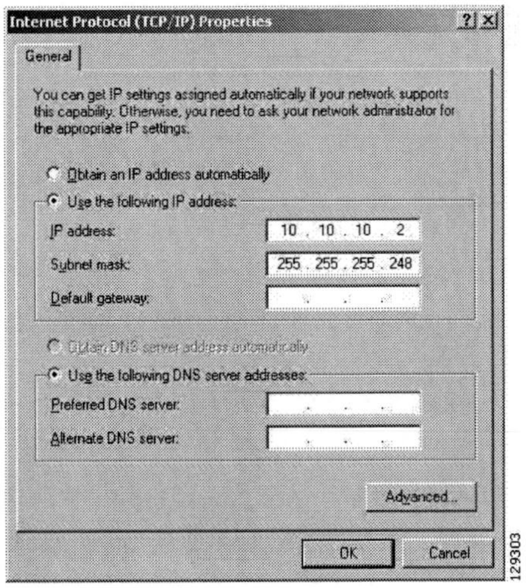

- In the IP address field, enter the following IP address: 10.10.10.2

- In the Subnet mask field, enter the following subnet mask: 255.255.255.248

- Click **OK** to close the dialog.

Connect the PC to the Router and then Run the Cisco CP Express Wizard

This task section explains how to run the Cisco CP Express wizard to give the router a basic configuration.

Cisco CP Express is a Cisco CP program that lets you quickly configure the router LAN and Internet connections. After you use Cisco CP Express to give the router these basic connections, you can use Cisco CP for more complex configurations. Cisco recommends that you use the Cisco CP Express wizard to configure the following features:

- Router name

- Username and passwords

- LAN IP address

- DHCP server, if needed.

Although you can use the wizard to configure a WAN connection, a firewall, and security settings, it is not required that you do so. Cisco CP provides wizards to help you configure these features.

To use the Cisco CP Express wizard, perform the following steps:

Step 1 Open a web browser on the PC, disable any active popup blockers, and enter the following URL:

http://10.10.10.1

Step 2 Enter the username **cisco**, and the password **cisco** in the login window. If other login windows appear during the startup process, enter the same credentials (cisco/cisco). See the Tip section below if the login window does not appear.

Tip If the launch page does not appear when you enter the URL http://10.10.10.1, test the connection between the PC and the router by doing the following:

- Check that the Power LED on the router is on, and that the LED for the port to which you connected the PC is on, indicating an active Ethernet connection between the router and the PC. If this LED is not lit, verify that you are using a crossover cable to connect the PC to the router, or that you are using a straight-through cable between the router and the switch.

- Verify that the web browser "work offline" option is disabled. In Internet Explorer, click the **File** menu, and verify that the "work offline" option is unchecked.

- Verify that the files cpexpress.tar, home.tar, and home.shtml files are loaded into flash memory. Open a Telnet session to 10.10.10.1, entering the username **cisco** and the password**cisco**. Enter the **show flash** command to display the files that are loaded in flash memory.

Note For security reasons, the username cisco and password cisco will expire the first time they are used. Before you log off the router, be sure to enter this Cisco IOS command:

username *username* **privilege 15 secret 0** *password*

Replace *username* and *password* with the username and password that you want to use. This command creates a new user with privilege level 15 and a password for that user. If you do not do this, you will not be able to log into the router after you end the session. Use the new credentials that you create for future sessions, instead of using the username cisco and password cisco.

- Verify that the PC IP address is properly configured. Some routers require that the PC obtain an IP address automatically and some require that it be configured with a static IP address. Find your router in Table 2 to determine how the PC should be configured.

When you connect to the router, the Cisco CP Express Launch page (Figure 3) appears, followed by one or more certificate windows.

Figure 3 Cisco CP Express Launch Page

Step 3 Click **Yes**, or click **Grant** to accept the certificates.

Step 4 The Cisco CP Express Overview page appears and then the Cisco CP Express Wizard page is also displayed (Figure 4). Click **Next** to begin configuring the router.

Figure 4 Cisco CP Express Overview and Wizard Pages

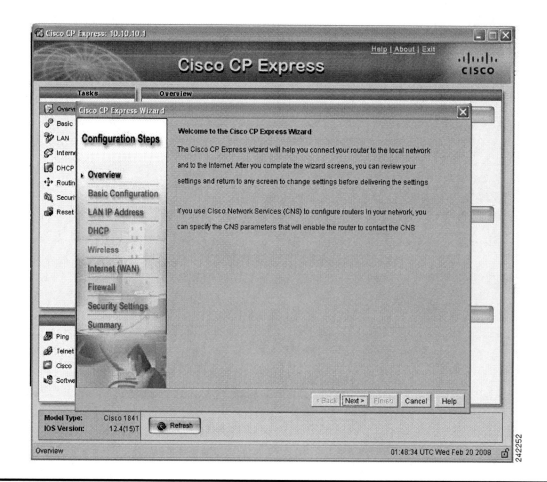

Tip   The Cisco CP Express wizard will ask you to enter an enable secret password to control access to Cisco IOS software. Be sure to write down or remember the enable secret password that you enter. It is not shown in the Enable Password field or in the Summary window, and it cannot be reset without erasing the router configuration. You are also asked to change the router's LAN IP address from its default value.

Step 5   When the Summary window appears, write down the LAN IP address, the username and the user password that you entered, and click **Finish**. You will need this information to reconnect to the router to perform additional configuration.

Step 6   Exit Cisco CP Express and complete "Task 7: Verify the Initial Configuration" to reconfigure the PC and reconnect to your router, using the new IP address that you gave to the LAN interface.

Verify the Initial Configuration

This task section explains how to verify the initial configuration performed with Cisco CP Express.

Step 1 Ensure that the IP address of the PC is on the same subnet as the router LAN interface. The steps to follow depend on whether the PC must be configured to obtain an IP address automatically, or whether it must be configured with a static IP address.

To configure the PC to obtain an IP address automatically, do the following:

    a. Go to the Internet Protocol Properties General Tab by following the instructions in Task 4: Configure the IP Address On the PC.

    b. Click **Obtain an IP address automatically**, as shown in Figure 1. Click **OK** to close the dialog.

    c. Click **Start > Run**.

    d. In the Run field, enter the command **cmd**.

    e. In the displayed command window, enter the **ipconfig /release** command followed by the **ipconfig /renew** command to obtain a new IP address from the router. When you enter these commands you get output similar to the following:

C:\> **ipconfig /release**
Ethernet adapter Local Area Connection:

                Connection-specific DNS Suffix . : somename.com
                IP Address. . . . . : 0.0.0.0
                Subnet Mask . . . . : 0.0.0.0
                Default Gateway . . . . :

C:\> **ipconfig /renew**
Ethernet adapter Local Area Connection:

                Connection-specific DNS Suffix . : somename.com
                IP Address. . . . . : 192.168.1.147
                Subnet Mask . . . . : 255.255.255.0
                Default Gateway . . . . : 192.168.1.1

    Note You must enter the **ipconfig /release** command and the **ipconfig /renew** command even if the PC was originally configured to accept an IP address automatically.

To configure the PC with a new static IP address, do the following:

    a. Go to the Internet Protocol Properties General Tab by following the instructions in Task 4: Configure the IP Address On the PC.

    b. Click **Use the following IP address**. Enter the new IP address and subnet mask. An example is shown in Figure 5.

    c. Click **OK** to close the dialog.

Figure 5 Configuring the PC with a New Static IP address

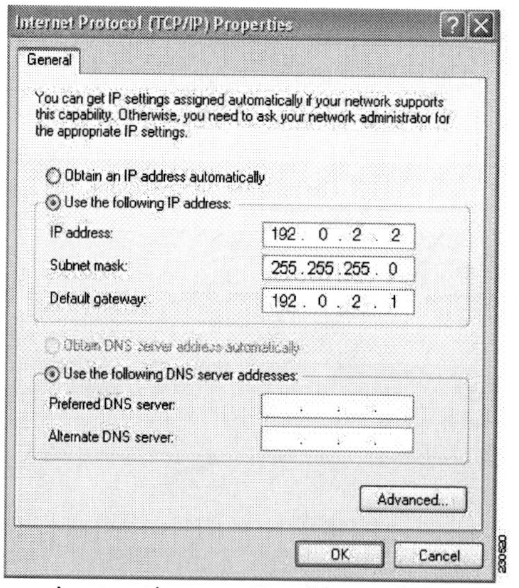

Step 2 Open a web browser and enter the new IP address that you gave the router LAN interface.

http://_new-IP-address_

For example, if you gave the LAN interface the IP address 192.0.2.1, you would enter the command **http://192.0.2.1** in the browser.

Step 3 Enter the username and password that you specified for the router when you completed the Cisco CP Express wizard.

Figure 6 Cisco CP Express Overview Window

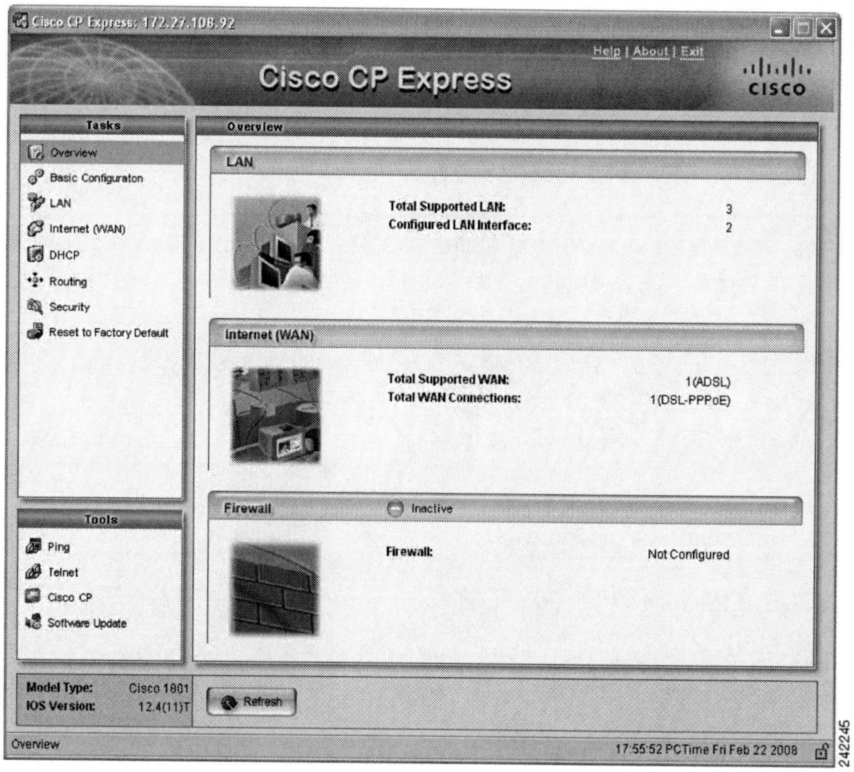

If the Cisco CP Express overview window is displayed, you have validated the LAN interface configuration.

Step 4 Test the Internet (WAN) connection that you configured by opening another web browser window and connecting to a website. If you can connect to a website, such as www.cisco.com, your WAN connection works properly. If you cannot, you can use Cisco CP Express or Cisco CP to correct your WAN settings.

Step 5 Go to "Task 8: Install Cisco CP" to install Cisco CP.

Install Cisco CP

You can install Cisco CP on a PC using the CD, or using the Cisco CP download file from www.cisco.com. The download file has the same contents as the CD. First, locate the installation file, and then start the installation wizard.

Step 1 If you are using the Cisco CP CD place it in the CD drive, and, from the PC desktop, click **My Computer**. If you downloaded Cisco CP from the www.cisco.com, go to the folder in which you unpacked the download file, and then skip to Step 3.

Step 2 CD users double-click the CD drive icon in the My Computer window, for example DVD/CD-RW Drive (D:).

Step 3 All users locate the installation file Cisco-config-pro-k9-*N_N-ln*.exe, where *N_N* is the version number, and *ln* is the language. For example, the installation file for English language Cisco CP 1.0 is Cisco-config-pro-k9-1_0-en.exe.

• If you are installing from the CD, this file is in the root folder.

• If you are installing from the Cisco Configuration Professional package that you downloaded, unzip the archive and locate this file.

Step 4 Double-click the installation file. The Cisco CP Installshield wizard displays the first screen (Figure 7).

Figure 7 Cisco CP Installshield Splash Screen

Step 5 When the Welcome window appears (Figure 8), click **Next** to begin the installation.

Figure 8 Welcome Window

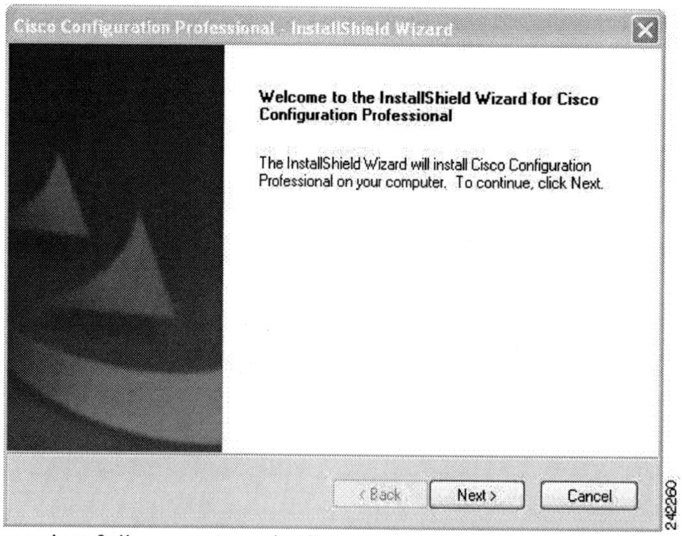

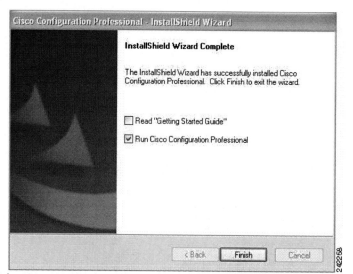

Step 6 In the screens that follow, review the license terms, and choose where you want to install Cisco CP. In the Ready to Install screen, click **Next** to begin copying the files to the PC.

Step 7 In the Install Options screen, choose where you want to create shortcuts for Cisco CP, then click **Next**.

Step 8 In the Install Complete screen (Figure 9), click **Run Cisco Configuration Professional**.

Step 9 To get an overview of Cisco CP, click **Read Getting Started Guide**.

Figure 9 Install Options

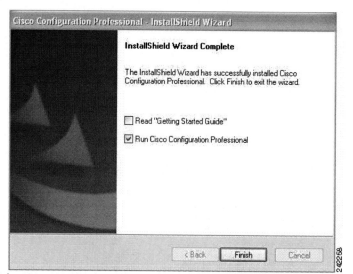

Step 10 Click **Finish**. Cisco CP displays the screen in Figure 10. If you clicked Read Getting Started Guide, the Getting Started Guide PDF launches in another window.

Figure 10 Cisco Configuration Professional Splash Screen

Step 11 Read the section "Task 9: Start Using Cisco CP" to learn how to create a community of devices and how to use Cisco CP to configure them.

Start Using Cisco CP

Cisco CP works with device communities. A community consists of one or more devices that you specify by providing their IP addresses and login credentials. After you create the community, you can begin working with the devices in it.

This section contains the following parts:

- Creating a Community

- Creating an Initial Configuration of a Feature

- Editing a Configuration

Creating a Community

To create a community, complete the following tasks:

Step 1 If Cisco CP is not running, start it by going to **Start > All Programs > CiscoCP**, or by clicking the Cisco Configuration Professional icon on the desktop. The screen in Figure 10 appears. When Cisco CP completes startup, the Select / Create Community screen (Figure 11) is displayed.

Figure 11 Select / Create Community

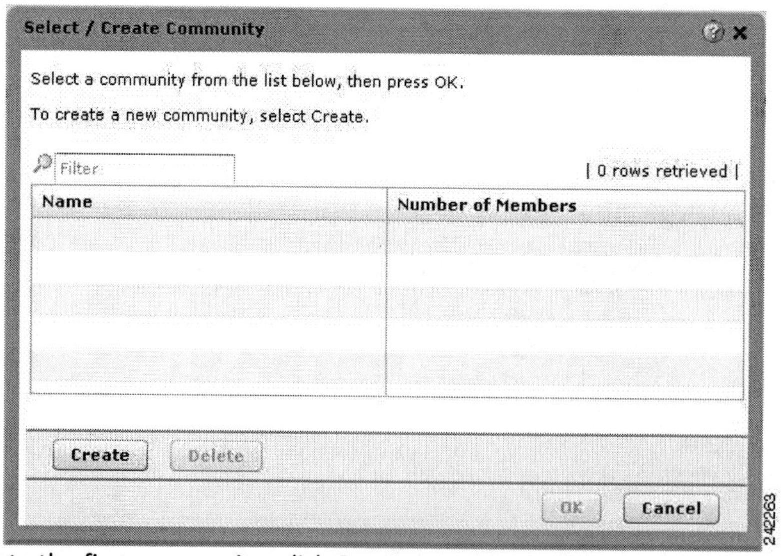

Step 2 To create the first community, click **Create**.

Step 3 When the Enter Community Name screen (Figure 12) appears, enter a name for the community, and click **Next**.

Figure 12 Create Community Wizard Screen: Enter Community Name

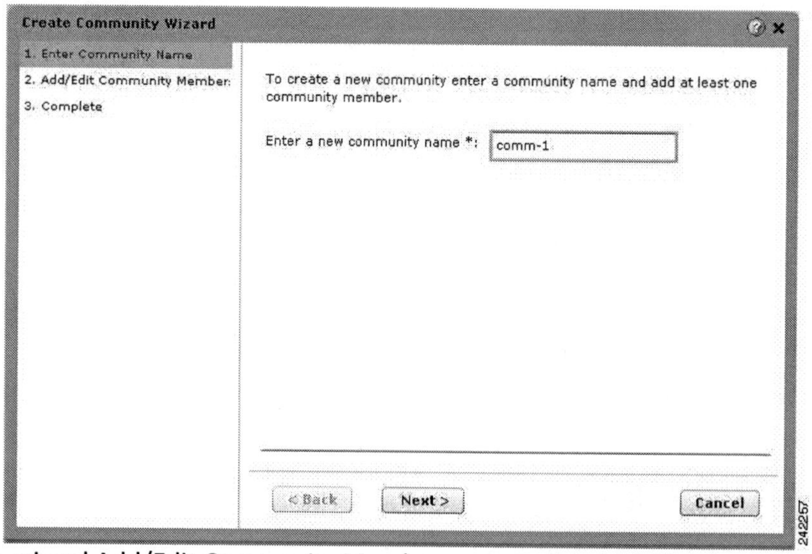

Step 4 In the wizard Add/Edit Community Member screen, click **Add**. The Create Community Entry dialog (Figure 13) is displayed over the Add/Edit Community Member screen.

Figure 13 Create Community Member Dialog

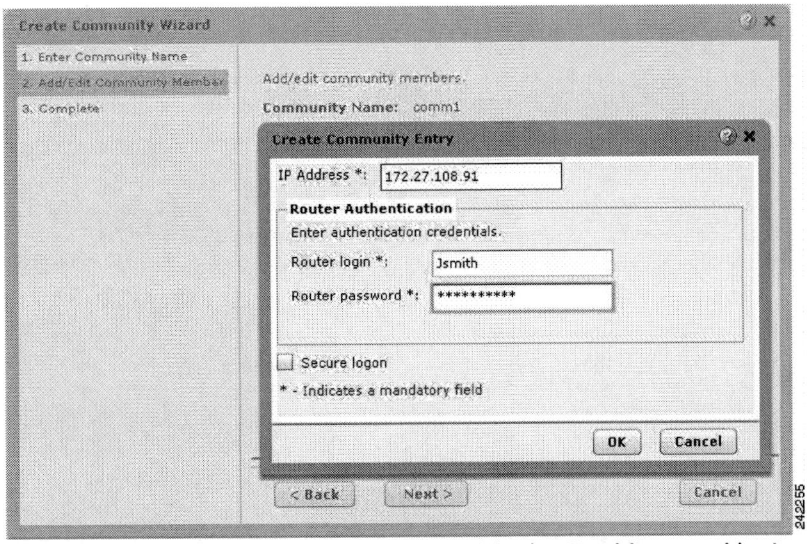

Step 5 To create the community entry, you must provide the IP address and login credentials of a device that you want to add to the community. The username that you specify must have a privilege level of 15.

Step 6 When you have entered the community member information, click **OK**. The Create Community Entry dialog closes and the Add/Edit Community Member screen is updated with the IP address of the device you added (Figure 14).

Figure 14 Add/Edit Community Member Screen

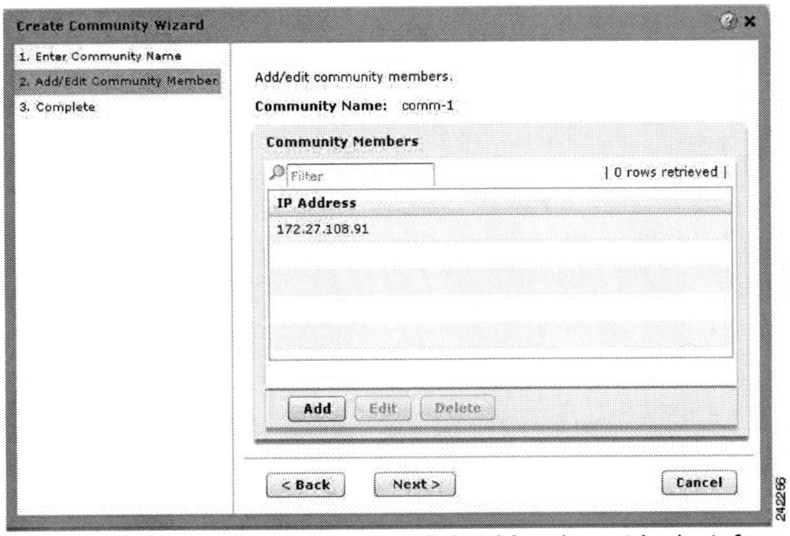

Step 7 To add another device to the community, click **Add** and provide the information in the Create Community Entry dialog.

Step 8 When you are finished adding devices to the community, click **Next**. The Complete screen (Figure 15) is displayed.

Figure 15 Complete Screen

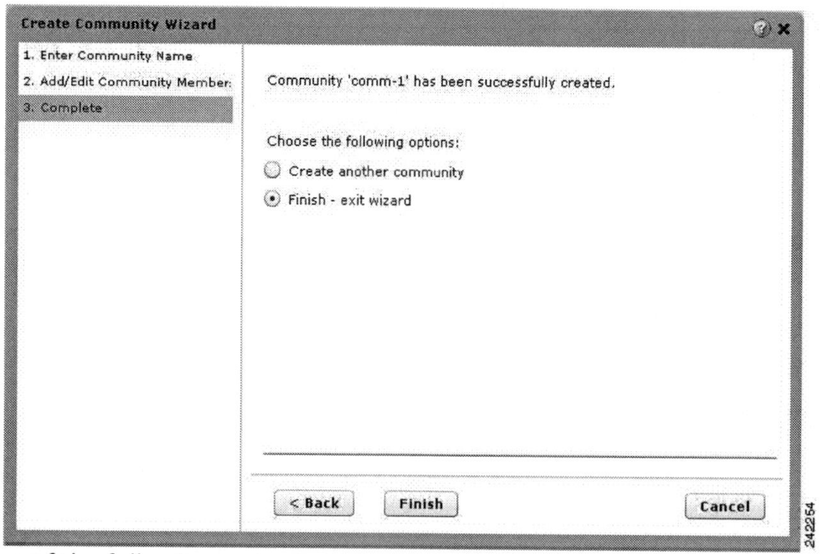

Step 9   Do one of the following:

- To create another community, check **Create another community**, and click **Finish**. Cisco CP returns you to the Enter Community Name screen.

- To exit the wizard, leave **Finish, exit wizard** checked, and click **Finish**. Cisco CP closes the wizard, and redisplays the Select / Create Community screen, updated with information about the communities that you created (Figure 16).

Figure 16 Select / Create Screen

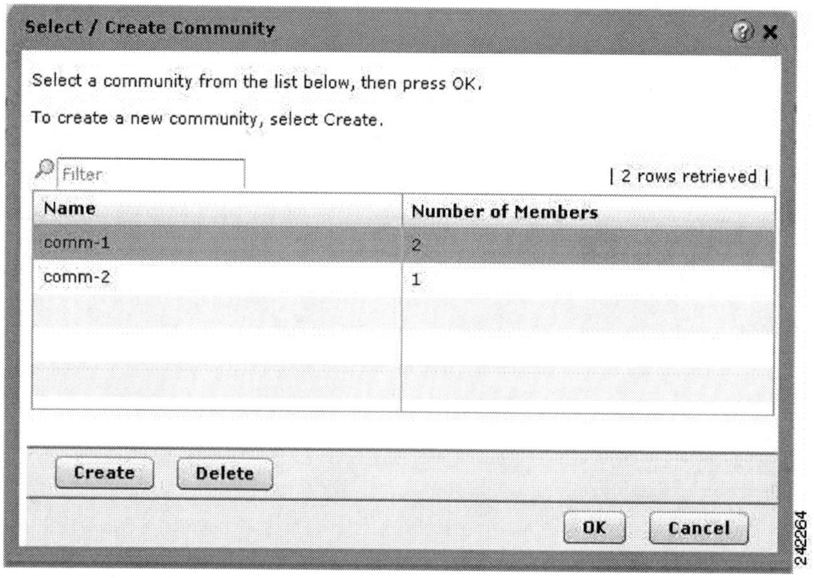

Creating an Initial Configuration of a Feature

This section provides a procedure for configuring a router interface. It is provided as an example of how you create an initial configuration of a feature using Cisco CP.

Step 1 To start, choose the community that the device belongs to, and click **OK**. The Community Information screen (Figure 17) is displayed.

Figure 17 Community Information Screen

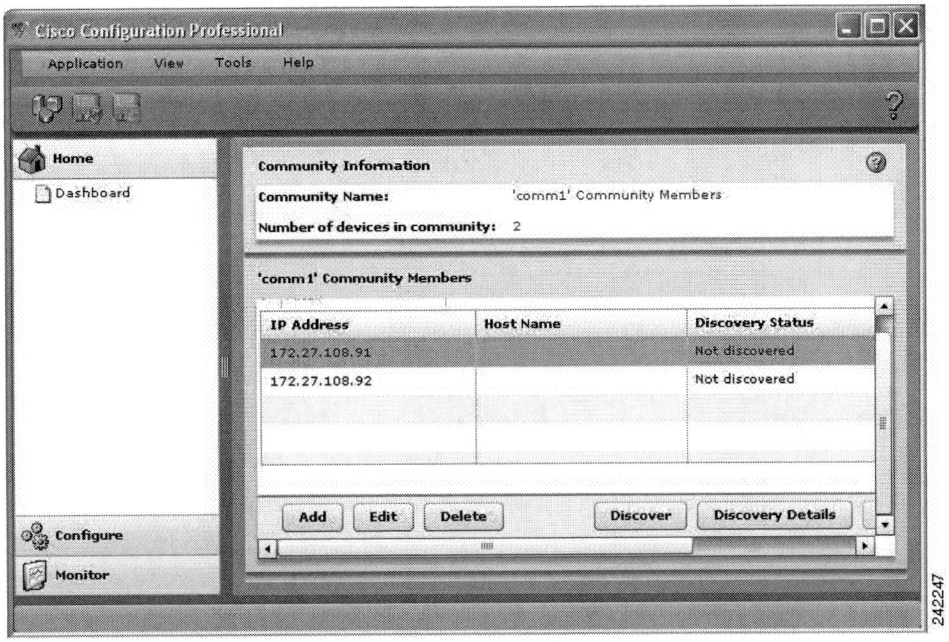

Step 2 In the Community Information screen, choose the device that you want to work with, and click **Discover**. Depending on network conditions, Cisco CP may take several minutes to discover the device. If you want to work with additional devices in the community, choose them and click **Discover**.

Step 3 To begin configuring a discovered device, click on the row for the device, and in the left pane, click **Configure**. Figure 18 shows the Configure tree expanded in the left pane.

Figure 18 Configure Tree

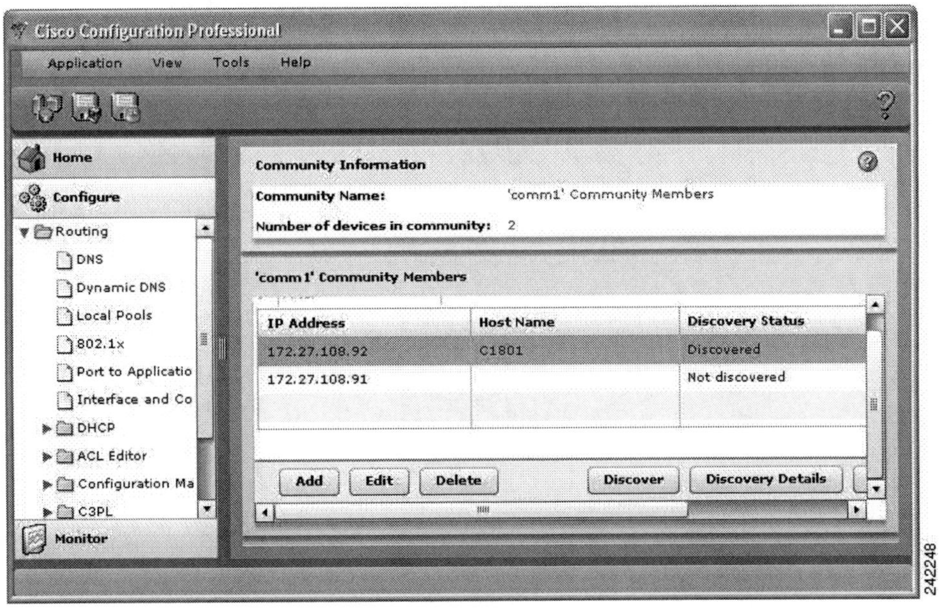

Step 4   In the Configure tree choose the configuration task that you want to perform. The screen for that task appears in the right pane. Figure 19 shows the Interfaces and Connections screen.

Figure 19 Interfaces and Connections

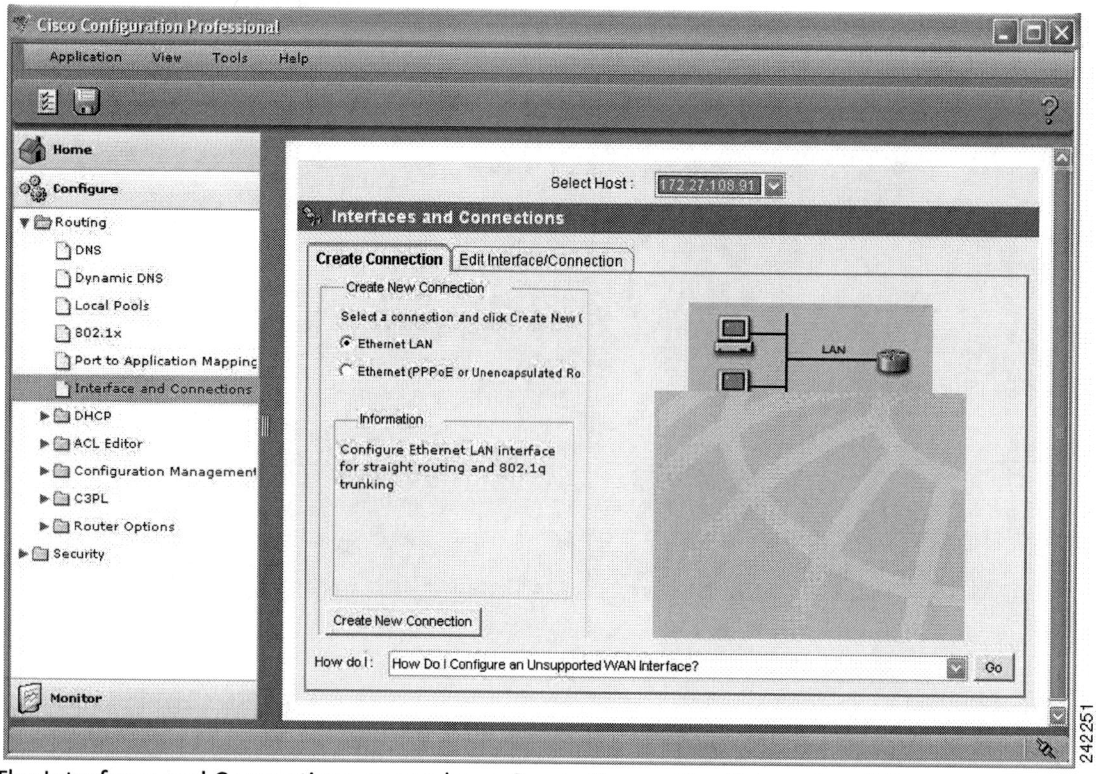

The Interfaces and Connections screen has a Create Connection Tab and an Edit Connection/Interface tab. The Create tabs in Cisco CP screens provide access to smart wizards that guide you through the configuration and that let you know if changes you are making will conflict with the existing configuration. The Edit tabs provide access to screens with additional settings. It is a good practice to create a starting configuration using the wizards, and then to examine the configuration in the screens available from the Edit tab and make any further changes that you need.

Step 5   To begin using a wizard, click the Create or the Launch button provided on the Create tab. The wizard welcome screen is displayed, which describes the tasks you will perform.Figure 20 shows the ADSL connection wizard Welcome screen.

Figure 20 ADSL Connection Wizard Welcome Screen

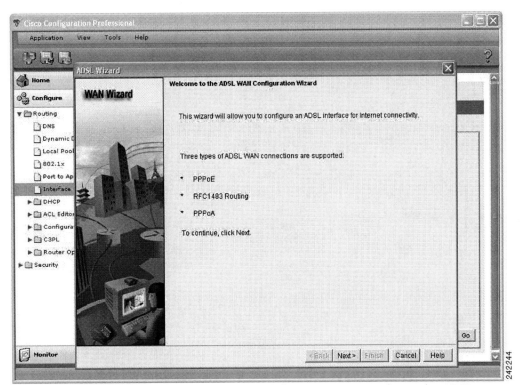

Step 6 To begin configuration using the wizard, click Next. Figure 21 shows the ADSL Encapsulation screen, which allows you to choose the type of encapsulation to use.

Figure 21 ADSL Encapsulation Screen

Step 7 Choose or enter the values that the screen prompts you for.

Step 8 To complete the wizard, use the Next button to move to subsequent screens and complete them. When you have entered all required values, the wizard displays the summary screen. This screen displays the values that you have entered. Figure 22 shows the ADSL Connection Summary screen.

Figure 22 ADSL Connection Summary Screen

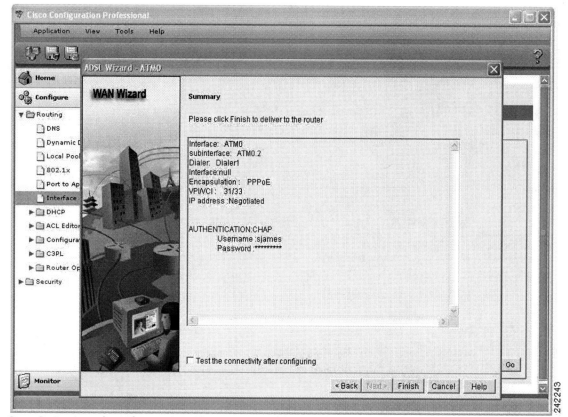

Step 9 Review the information. If you want to change anything, click **Back** to return to the screen in which you need to make changes, make them, and then return to the Summary screen.

Step 10 Click **Finish** to deliver the changes to the router.

Step 11 If you want to save the running configuration to the router startup configuration or to the PC, use the buttons described in Table 4.

Table 4 Save Running Configuration Buttons	
Button	**Function**
	Save running configuration to PC.
	Save running configuration to startup configuration.

Editing a Configuration

Once a configuration has been created using a wizard, you can edit that configuration without returning to the wizard again. Editing the configuration gives you access to additional configuration values that are not available in the wizards. The following example procedure describes editing a Fast Ethernet connection.

To edit a configuration, complete the following tasks:

Step 1 To access the edit screens, click the Edit tab. Figure 23 shows the Edit Interfaces/Connections tab.

Figure 23 Edit Interfaces/Connections

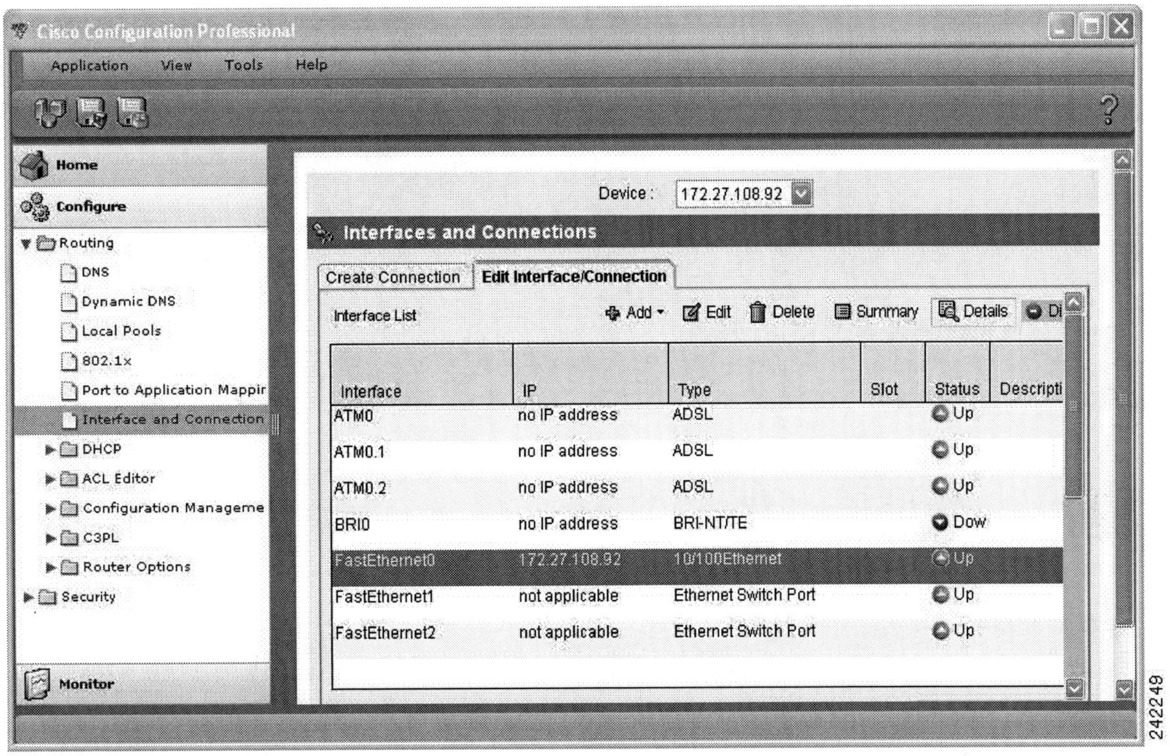

Step 2 To edit a configuration entry, double click the entry. If the screen has an Edit button, choose the entry that you want to change and click **Edit**. A tabbed dialog is displayed.Figure 24 shows Interface and Connections dialogs for a Fast Ethernet connection.

Figure 24 Connection Dialog

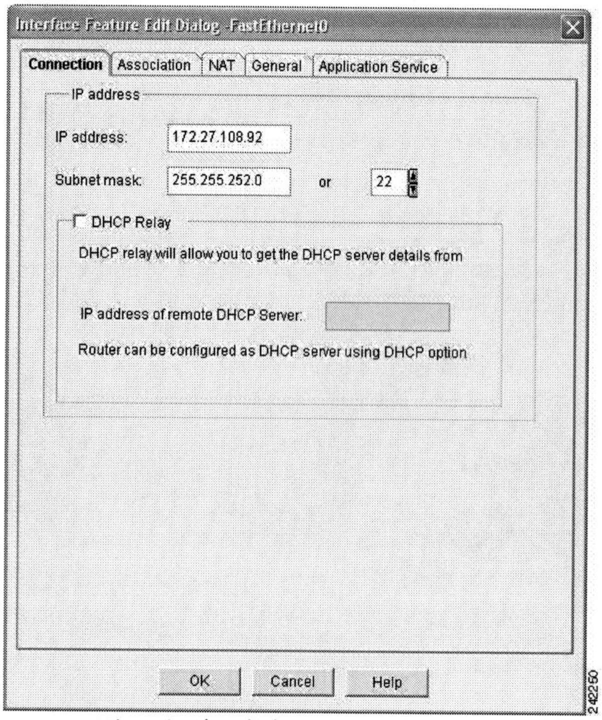

Step 3 Make the necessary settings in the dialog.

Step 4 Click the tab for the next dialog that you need to make changes in, and make those changes.

Step 5 Click **OK** to send the changes to the router, and to close the dialog.

You're Done! Where to Go from Here?

Now that you have used Cisco CP to give your router an initial configuration, you can continue to use Cisco CP to configure additional features or modify existing feature configurations. Hopefully you enjoyed this lab as a peak into the future!

Appendix A
Router Interface Summary

Unless you have all 1841 routers, for a majority of the labs, you will need to examine the following chart to correctly identify what the correct syntax will be for your router and interface. Use the correct syntax in bold below that matches your router.

There is no way to list all of the possible combinations of configurations for each router series. What we have provided are the most common configurations that you will use in your lab. You can further cooberate this by looking closely at the indentifiers on the router that mark the interfaces, slots and ports.

Router Series	Ethernet Interface #1	Ethernet Interface #2	Serial Interface #1	Serial Interface #2
806	Ethernet 0 – **E0**	Etherent 1 – **E1**		
1700	FastEthernet 0 – **FA0**	FastEtherent 1 – **FA1**	Serial 0 – **S0**	Serial 1 – **S1**
1800	FastEthernet 0 - **FA0/0**	FastEthernet 1 – **FA0/1**	Serial 0 – **S0/0/0**	Serial 1 – **S0/0/1**
2500	Ethernet 0 – **E0**	Etherent 1 – **E1**	Serial 0 – **S0**	Serial 1 – **S1**
2600	Ethernet 0/0 – **E0/0** or FastEthernet 0/0 – **FA0/0**	Ethernet 0/1 – **E0/1** or FastEthernet 0/1 - **FA0/1**	Serial 0/0 – **S0/0**	Serial 0/1 – **S0/1**
2800	FastEthernet 0/0 – **FA0/0**	FastEthernet 0/1 - **FA0/1**	Serial 0/0 /0– **S0/0/0**	Serial 0/0/1 – **S0/0/1**

As a special note it can get kind of confusing when you are using an interface card with multiple ports on it such as a WIC-2T.

For instance it is pretty straight forward when you put a WIC-1T serial module in slot 0 of an 1841. That serial port would be referenced by S0/0/0. But then if you put a second WIC-1T serial module in slot 1 of the 1841 it will then be referenced by S0/1/0.

But then if you have a single WIC-2T module which has two serial ports on one module it is in slot 0, it referenced as S0/0/0 and S0/0/1 respectively for the two ports. Then if you add a second WIC-2T into slot 1 it is S0/1/0 and S0/1/1. Does it start to make sense now?

Can you now understand how there is no way to make a book that will 100% match your setup unless you use the exact same topology and cards that we do in each lab?